A PEOPLE'S HERITAGE
Patterns in United States History
Second Edition

CURTIS SOLBERG
Santa Barbara City College
DAVID MORRIS
Laguna Blanca School
ANTHONY KOENINGER
California Polytechnic State University,
San Luis Obispo

KENDALL/HUNT PUBLISHING COMPANY
4050 Westmark Drive   Dubuque, Iowa 52002

Maps by John V. Morris

© 1975 John Wiley & Sons, Inc. Publishers
© 1984, 1994, 2000 by Kendall/Hunt Publishing Company

ISBN 0-7872-6918-2

Printed in the United States of America
10 9 8 7 6 5 4 3 2 1

CONTENTS

PREFACE

American history is not something dead and over.
It is always alive, always growing, always unfinished. . . .

These words, penned by John F. Kennedy more than forty years ago, describe this book's spirit. Despite the illusion of permanence that earlier generations attached to American history, the reader learns that the nation's story is constantly evolving, as each generation makes its own interpretations of events. Even the presidential faces of Washington, Jefferson, Lincoln, and Theodore Roosevelt on Mt. Rushmore provide a current case in point; in the American arena of open debate, even the character and achievements of these icons are subjected to critical scrutiny despite being enshrined in granite.

In the following pages the authors trace certain themes essential to understanding American history; some chapters reflect conventional topics like foreign policy and political reform, while others devote major attention to current relevant concerns such as the environment, the West, minorities, and multiculturalism. These broad themes cannot be discussed in detail in a single volume without burying the contours of the American experience under mounds of historical data. The authors have sought to emphasize the sweep and continuity of American history without sacrificing the intellectual rigor or the pertinent details necessary to a solid understanding of the subject.

A People's Heritage may be used in the short survey course, or in the more traditional full-year course. It may serve as the core text accompanied by supplemental readings, with suggestions at the end of each chapter. The book is designed for college preparatory students or those in the lower division college survey.

"The Residence of David Twining, 1787" by Edward Hicks. (Courtesy Abby Aldrich Rockefeller Folk Art Collection.)

CHAPTER ONE

The Quest for a New Society—
An Emerging American Culture

1000 A.D.
Vikings land at Vinland.

1300
Renaissance begins, marking a new pursuit of science and learning.

1494
Pope Alexander VI divides the unsettled territories of the world between Catholic Spain and Portugal.

1521
Cortés founds the Spanish New World empire with the conquest of the Aztecs in Mexico.

1607
The English empire in North America is established with the first permanent settlement at Jamestown, Virginia.

1608
The French empire is begun at Quebec, Canada.

1629
Massachusetts Bay Colony founded by the Puritans.

1651
First in a series of trade and navigation acts designed by Parliament to regulate English trade with her American colonies.

1740s
The Enlightenment begins with its optimistic view of human progress.

1763
The French and Indian War between Britain and France over control of North America ends in British victory.

THE IDEA OF AMERICA

Western man's quest for a "new" society can be seen centuries before the discovery and settlement of America. The early colonization of Massachusetts Bay was accompanied by the determination of the Puritans to establish a "City Upon a Hill." It was to be a perfect model of true Christian living that, by example, would reform the entire world. The expectation of many Europeans is reflected in their designation of the emerging trans-Atlantic community as the New World. In fact, one scholar refers to the United States as the "first New Nation."

In the post-revolutionary generation many Americans saw their new nation as a model for the world. Thomas Jefferson wrote that other peoples would come to regard America as "a signal for arousing men to burst the chains under which . . . ignorance and superstitions had persuaded them to bind themselves and to assume the blessings and security of self-government." The two centuries that have passed since Jefferson penned this statement have witnessed the slow struggle to realize these ideals and the United States' rise to global leadership. The millions of immigrants who streamed to America's shores during the nineteenth century gave evidence to the economic opportunity and political liberty they sought. In more recent times, especially since the achievements of the Civil Rights movement and the collapse of communism, the United States continues to be a model of success to the rest of the world.

The emergence of this society is particularly interesting because of its unique pattern of development. Never before had a nation been created as the result of the movement of so many people from one part of the world to another. Moreover, its founders gradually realized that their grand blueprints for society were usually not adaptable to New World circumstances. Instead, American culture emerged in ways that were not anticipated and, in the process, forced the numerous traits that are part of the so-called American character. In order to understand the persistent interest in the idea of America, it is necessary to trace the sources of this quest for a new society whose basic contours had emerged by the time of the Revolution.

THE ORIGINS OF THE QUEST

For several thousand years man has dreamed of an Elysium, a more perfect place where he might live in harmony with his fellows and with God. This quest was pursued by the ancient Greeks, whose poet Homer speculated on the nature of a mythical Eden. Others also sang and wrote about this "other world" and, indeed, there is a marked similarity in the description of the place found in the folklore of the Irish, the tales of the Japanese, and the sagas of the Vikings. This literature, in spite of its tendency toward fantasy and the exotic, is important because it helped to stimulate the idea of an earthly paradise in the Western mind. But this other world seemed beyond man's grasp because of the fears and practical uncertainties involved in conquering the great seas and their monstrous inhabitants memorialized by old storytellers.

There are some indications that the Chinese, Phoenicians, Romans, Egyptians, Muslims, or Irish might have been the first "discoverers" of an America already occupied by Asian people who migrated over the Bering Strait as much as 40,000 years ago. But the best evidence shows that as early as the year 1000 A.D. the Norsemen in their finely crafted Viking ships successfully crossed the Atlantic Ocean and became the first white inhabitants of the Western Hemisphere.

Their settlement, called Vinland, located on the northern tip of Newfoundland, lasted for at least three years. The gradual failure of this early experiment in New World living was caused by a number of factors, including the climate, hostile Indians, and the lack of gunpowder.

EUROPE COMES OF AGE

The Norse seafarers who attempted the settlement of North America were casualties of history. Conditions were not yet ripe for the exploration and settlement that they sought to achieve. Indeed, for the next four or five hundred years, there is no written record of further successful efforts by Europeans to conquer the "howling wilderness" of the New World. By the fifteenth and sixteenth centuries, the idea of expansion to the West had assumed a prominent place in European thought. The Renaissance liberated man from the traditional religious and political authorities and encouraged him to exercise his curiosity to learn more about his universe and, therefore, about himself. Guided by observation and reason, this emphasis on individual will and achievement bred a restlessness and self-reliance that provided the necessary dynamism for the explorers, adventurers, and merchants of Europe's early modern period.

Commercial development also paved the way for Europe's widening horizons. After the twelfth century the simple farm economy based on local production and village self-sufficiency began to be replaced by an agricultural system made more sophisticated by the rise of trade and banking. Moreover, during the Christian Crusades of the twelfth and thirteenth centuries, knights from the castles of Europe brought home from the Near East exotic goods rarely enjoyed in the western world before—spices, silk, tapestries, precious stones, and new ideas in art and architecture. Henceforth, merchants began to establish trade links with the markets of the East to buy the luxury goods which the moneyed class in Europe demanded.

At the same time, progress in science and technology helped to facilitate the crossing of the ocean and the search for the fabled garden of Eden. By the fifteenth century a more seaworthy ship called the caravel was built capable of traversing the Atlantic, and more reliable navigational instruments (like the compass) were refined. It had been possible to sail on the Mediterranean guided only by one's experience and the North Star, but venturing into the fearsome Atlantic required a more exact science. These were also the years that witnessed the invention of the printing press and gunpowder, both essential to a people intent on learning the best avenues to expansion and conquest.

By the end of the fifteenth century, the Commercial Revolution had gone beyond European boundaries and the Near East. In an effort to circumvent the long and costly journey overland from the East and through the Mediterranean, Europeans began to talk of an all-water route to the Orient. Merchant-adventurers were interested not only in trade with the Indies, but they also desired to find new sources of gold and silver, as the Oriental trade had drained Europe's store of precious metals. Before the peoples of Europe could embark upon such expeditions involving expansion and trade, it was necessary for them to achieve some semblance of nationality. Only by consolidating their resources and uniting under a single government could a people begin to look outward. And it was in the fifteenth, sixteenth, and seventeenth centuries that this nation-state system of Western Europe developed. The new nation-state was characterized by: (1) a

strong monarch who, by his personal power and prestige, could draw the many diverse parts of his kingdom together, and thereby centralize control; (2) an economy that promoted national self-sufficiency; and (3) a minimum of any energy-consuming religious friction. As the western European nations began to assume their modern shapes on the map, explorers and navigators like Columbus, Cabot, DaGama, Magellan, and Drake were sent around the globe to seek glory and riches for their monarchs.

VARIETIES OF THE MERCANTILE EXPERIENCE

Although Columbus's encounter with America had been preceded by that of other voyagers (he had visited the Norsemen of Iceland and had access to Arab maps prior to his fateful voyage of 1492), the excitement generated by his discovery led to a much broader interest in trans-Atlantic exploration. Until the sixteenth century, the Mediterranean Sea had been the hub of western civilization, the nerve center that connected its various peoples. The state that controlled the Mediterranean usually dominated the political arena. After Columbus returned to the courts of

Intrepid Vikings crossed the Atlantic Ocean in their open boats and made settlements in North America five centuries before Columbus' discovery in 1492. Scholars continue to unearth evidence that other peoples were pre-Columbian, including the ancient Phoenicians, the Japanese, and possibly the Greeks and Romans. (From *The Viking* by Bertil Almgren. Copyright © 1966, Svenska Forlags AB Nordbok; Gothenburg, Sweden.

Spain with the news of the New World's wealth, control of the Atlantic and what lay beyond became a prerequisite for global power.

Meanwhile, other nations were dreaming of new riches. Spain's early adventure into this era of commercial competition was preceded by Portugal which, by the early sixteenth century, had established a trading empire that extended from India through Indonesia. Portuguese explorers, led by Dias and DaGama, had been the first to break the Italian-Turkish monopoly on trade with the Far East by establishing an all-sea route around Africa into India. The fear of overlapping claims between the two Catholic countries was calmed by Pope Alexander VI when Spain and Portugal were allowed to divide the non-Christian world between them. Consequently the discovery of America and the opening of the sea route to the Far East touched off a flurry of activity among the other nation-states, who rejected Spain and Portugal's exclusive claim to these newly discovered lands. For example, France and England sent out sailors and explorers like Cabot and Verrazano during the fifteenth century, and the Netherlands developed a fairly large commercial empire in the East Indies. But in general, it was not until the seventeenth century that the monarchs of these countries had adequately resolved their internal problems and consolidated enough national power to follow up successfully the discoveries made by their adventurers and begin their colonization efforts. Champlain began "New France" at Quebec in what is now Canada at about the same time that the English of the Virginia Company were setting up Jamestown (1607). These efforts signaled the real beginning of competition for empire in the New World.

Those nations participating in this overseas expansion formulated policies to regulate the trade and territories that they acquired. Although nation-states differed in their efforts at colonization, it is important to recognize that all of these nations sought the same objective: to utilize their overseas possessions to increase the wealth and power of the mother country. This aim provided the concept fundamental to the economic theory called mercantilism. Accordingly, colonies were important because they promoted the economic self-sufficiency of the mother country. Not only might they provide raw materials unavailable at home, but they also represented potential markets for the finished goods produced in the mother country. With the fear of overpopulation plaguing seventeenth-century Europe, colonies were also deemed an excellent outlet for the surplus population of the Old World. Finally, mercantilist theory contained the idea of "contingent necessity"—that is, if one nation failed to take advantage of the opportunities of colonial expansion, another nation would, causing a relative decline in power and prestige of the reluctant nation.

Colonies were therefore crucial to a nation's power, and the race for empire in America that began with Pope Alexander VI's partition of the world in 1494 continued for the next three centuries. Conquistadors like Cortés, Pizarro, and Coronado created a huge Spanish empire in South and Central America, reaching up into what is now the southwestern United States. Indeed, it was the Spanish galleons returning to Spain filled with riches from the mines of Mexico and South America that whetted the appetites of the other powers. The rivalry that ensued in seventeenth-century America involved, the Dutch, who colonized the region of the Hudson River Valley; the Swedes, who settled on the Delaware River; the French, whose North American empire grew rapidly after Louis XIV became king in 1658; and finally, the English. England was a latecomer in this race for power through trade. Problems of succession to the throne and Protestant-Catholic conflict prevented the Tudor royal family from following up the discoveries of John Cabot in 1497 and 1498. By the time they had consolidated their power in the reign of Elizabeth I, Spain had a fifty-year headstart. Yet, by 1763, the English dominated North America. What was London's colonial secret of success?

The rise of trading companies, founded yet not controlled by the king, contributed to the eventual success of England's colonial venture. Instead of a completely centralized colonial bureaucracy under the personal direction of the king, as was the case with France's Louis XIV, hundreds of independent trading companies enjoyed considerable freedom in establishing their capitalist enterprises in the Far East, in India, in Russia, and in America. These ventures created great wealth for England and provided attractive opportunities for many Englishmen abroad. An

COLUMBUS

Christopher Columbus (in Italian, Cristoforo Colombo; in Spanish, Cristóbal Colón) was a quintessential Renaissance man. He knew Latin and Spanish and studied history, philosophy, and cosmography. In 1476, at about age sixteen, Columbus left his native Genova to work as a courier for a shipping company. After being shipwrecked on the Portuguese coast, he was taken aboard a Genovese vessel bound for England. The young Columbus landed in the bustling seaport of Bristol. According to Columbus's own accounts, which have never been verified, he journeyed with Bristol fishermen to harvest codfish off the coast of Iceland.

By 1479, Columbus had made his way back to Portugal, taking up residence in Lisbon where he learned navigation and cartography and studied manuscripts on western exploration. He believed that a distance of 2,400 miles separated the western Canary Islands from Japan. His calculations, however, were grossly inaccurate, underestimating the span by eighty percent. The actual distance is more than 12,000 miles. Most European intellectuals believed that the world was spherical but, unlike Columbus, they insisted that the western ocean was much larger and unnavigable by the small ships then in existence.

Since the Portuguese crown had been sponsoring ambitious explorations of the west African coast, Columbus approached Portugal's King João II in 1484 to seek support for his western voyage. The king rejected the proposal after his royal cosmographers informed him that Columbus had badly miscalculated the size of the Atlantic barrier separating Iberia and the Indies. In spring 1486, Columbus presented his plan to Spain's Fernando and Isabela who were skeptical, yet intrigued by the prospects of opening a quicker route to the riches of Asia. The queen was especially eager to spread Catholicism in the Orient. However, the Spanish monarchs, then preoccupied by an internal war against the Moors, who had occupied the Iberian peninsula for seven centuries, postponed a decision regarding state-sponsored exploration. Finally, in spring 1492, after the Moors were defeated, the Spanish crown agreed to sponsor Columbus's western expedition.

Leaving Palos, a port in southern Spain, Columbus commanded three tiny ships setting out toward the west. The morale of the crews eroded as the days passed and no land had been reached and supplies dwindled. Some men became so unnerved that they advocated turning the ships around and returning to Spain. On October 12, seventy days since departing Spain, Columbus and his men reached an island in the Bahamas that Columbus believed lay near the Asian coastline. Sailing southward, the mariners explored Cuba's northeastern coast and an island Columbus named La Española (later renamed Hispaniola).

On Christmas Eve 1492, Columbus's flagship, the *Santa María*, was wrecked on a coral reef on the northern coast of Hispaniola. With the grounding of the *Santa María*, Columbus could not accommodate his entire crew of 120 men aboard the two surviving ships on the homeward voyage. Columbus scuttled the wrecked vessel, using its timbers to construct a fortification named La Navidad, the first European settlement in the New World since the age of Norsemen. At La Navidad, Columbus left forty-two men with orders to search for gold mines and hold the fort until he returned the following year.

Amid cannon volleys and the pealing of cathedral bells, the *Niña* and *Pinta* reentered the port of Palos on March 15, 1493. Two weeks later at nearby Sevilla, Columbus astonished crowds by exhibiting Caribbean natives he had captured, their gold ornaments, beautifully carved masks, pearls, and tropical parrots. A month later at Barcelona, Columbus was welcomed back from his voyage by Fernando and Isabela, who proclaimed him Admiral of the Ocean Sea.

Columbus's second voyage (September 1493–June 1496) comprised an armada of seventeen ships, 1200 men, and a menagerie of sheep, pigs, chickens, horses, and cows, animals that were yet unknown in the western hemisphere. With the assorted livestock, Columbus was expected to begin immediate colonization of the lands he had already discovered along with new lands he might reach. More ominously, the new expedition was provisioned with cannons, crossbows, guns, cavalry, and a pack of attack dogs. Columbus returned to Hispaniola to relieve the crewmembers he had left at La Navidad but found the entire Spanish contingent had been killed by Taíno natives, who had retaliated for oppressive Spanish demands for gold and food.

In 1495, Columbus ordered his soldiers to stamp out native resistance on Hispaniola and confiscate food, gold, and spun cotton. Hundreds of Taínos were killed by gunfire, swords, and dogs, and thousands more were captured, chained, and shipped to Spain where they were sold into slavery. Columbus justified the slave trade by demonizing the natives as "cruel [and] stupid," "a people warlike and numerous, whose customs and religion are very different from our own." Queen Isabela decreed a conditional prohibition against the enslavement of "Indians" in 1500 after a number of theologians condemned the practice and her conscience became distraught. The queen continued to allow the enslavement of natives who attacked Spaniards or continued to practice pagan activities such as cannibalism. With this opening, Spanish colonists had a convenient pretext for enslaving natives.

Columbus's use of natives as forced labor in farming and mining and his initiation of the Caribbean slave trade were the earliest events in the European exploitation of the peoples and resources of the New World. Father Bartolomé de las Casas, conquistador-turned-ecclesiastical advocate of native rights, grieved over Spain's oppression of the indigenous peoples of the Indies that began with Columbus. "What we committed in the Indies," he wrote, "stands out among the most unpardonable offenses ever committed against God and mankind and this trade [in native slaves] as one of the most unjust, evil, and cruel among them." By 1496 the native population of Hispaniola, ravaged by disease, unbearable labor in mines and agricultural fields, and indiscriminate massacres, had been decimated.

Columbus completed two additional voyages across the Atlantic, exploring the coasts of Venezuela and Honduras. In November 1504, he returned to Spain, exhausted and sick. Three weeks later, on November 26, Queen Isabela died. Her death greatly diminished Columbus's influence at court. The widower king, preoccupied with affairs of state and battling illness, had little time for the Admiral of the Ocean Sea, showing no interest in learning details of the fourth voyage from Columbus himself. On May 20, 1506, Columbus died at Valladolid, Spain, still believing he had reached Asia.

---

additional advantage enjoyed by England was her status as an island. Freed of the cost of maintaining a large standing army, the English built a great navy that served both as an element of defense of her worldwide empire and as an important link in her commercial trade. Finally, unlike much of Europe where workers of the lowest class were required to serve their local rulers, there was no serfdom in England. Instead, a class of workers free from bondage to the soil existed, including resourceful and hardworking women. In contrast, the populations of New France and New Spain included few women from the Old World. English women were prepared for the rugged life across the Atlantic and, by serving as the basis of the family unit, they contributed to the rapid growth of society in English America. By the 1760s, the English colonial population outnumbered the French by 15 to 1. And unlike both the French and the Spaniards, the English did not restrict emigration to their colonies.

WHY DID EUROPEANS COME TO AMERICA?

Economic forces at work in England had created insecurity for many of its people. "Overpopulation" was actually the dislocation of thousands of subsistence farmers who had been evicted from the soil by the enclosure acts. This parliamentary legislation allowed public lands to be enclosed in order to raise sheep for the high profits of the expanding textile industry. But the adverse effects of this economic transition were not limited to the poor farmers. Rising inflation during the sixteenth and seventeenth centuries touched the landowning middle class or gentry. Living largely on fixed incomes, they found their economic security slipping. This provided the reason for many to emigrate to America.

     Nor can religion be ignored as a factor leading to emigration. Although the legend that early America was populated by people seeking religious freedom in the New World may be exaggerated, it is nevertheless true that some migrants left their homeland because of the dangers they saw to their faith. In England, for example, some Puritans and other reformers were antagonized by the Crown's hostility towards them, and even suspected that King Charles I was secretly pro-Catholic. Thus, while persecution may not have been as overt as the stories suggest, freedom to worship as they wished figured into the decision of some Englishmen to migrate to the New World. Another impelling motive for English migration to America was the desire for land. The

Early in the seventeenth century Europeans were learning about America's abundance. This imaginary portrait depicts English knights hunting and fishing in Virginia in 1618. Graphic scenes like this one were important in promoting European interest in America. (From T. de Bry, *America* Part X, 1618, Plate XI. Courtesy Rare Book Division, The New York Public Library, Astor, Lenox and Tilden Foundations.)

Old World's large, poor population, coupled with control of its lands by a small but powerful nobility, meant that most European people could never hope to become independent landowners. Yet land was the source of most people's livelihood and therefore personal and family security. It was also the basis of social status and political rights. Landowners had the long-established right to have a say in local political decisions. So although the motives for migration included adventure, religion, and economic unrest, the most important reason seems to have been the desire to become an independent landowner.

European colonists saw this land as a commodity, an attitude based on the beliefs and prejudices they brought with them. Perhaps the strongest element in this Old World attitude was the Judeo-Christian tradition. The Christian church, Catholic or Protestant, played a strong role in molding the European people's attitudes toward life and their relationship to the world around them. One of the primary doctrines placed humanity above the rest of created beings and made nature subservient to man. This was based upon the Biblical account of creation where God commands man to "subdue" the earth and "have dominion" over all living things. Mankind could do what it pleased with the earth. A solitary voice of opposition to this doctrine was that of St. Francis of Assisi, who maintained that all in God's creation were equals and deserving of respect and consideration. St. Francis' view, however, was not widely known and its influence was minimal.

Given this doctrine of superiority, the land itself was judged "good" or "bad" depending upon its domination by and usefulness to people. "Good" land was like the garden of Eden—pastoral, productive, and safe. Wilderness was "bad" land, a desolate, dangerously wild place. In the Old Testament, the garden and the wilderness were also spiritual opposites: the Hebrew people's "promised land" was "a land flowing with milk and honey" like "the garden of the Lord," while the wilderness was "accursed" land ruled by the devil. This combination made wilderness something to be avoided. Old World folklore and mythology reinforced the bias by peopling the wild forests and mountains with assorted ogres, werewolves, semihuman wild men (and women), and other fiendish beasts. Many Germans fervently believed that the "Black Forest" hid witches and other evil creatures, while Rumanian Slavs associated Transylvania country with vampires. It is not hard to understand this supernatural dread. Even today nightfall in wild country plays on the imagination, changing tree limbs into grotesque figures and animal cries into mysterious threats. In the Old World, people shunned the wilderness, keeping to safely cultivated and settled areas where they had "subdued" nature.

Ironically, some persecuted religious sects that righteously hated the wilderness sought it out as a sanctuary from the rest of "sinful" society and as a testing ground to purify one's faith. As justification, they pointed out that the people of Israel escaped from slavery in Egypt and had to journey in the wilderness to become disciplined in faith before they could enter the "promised land." Even more significantly, Jesus Christ "was led up by the Spirit into the wilderness to be tempted by the devil" and emerged ready to speak fearlessly for God. Religious groups like the Puritans and later the Quakers held to the idea of wilderness as a place of refuge and of spiritually purifying trials.

This did not mean that they liked wilderness. When William Bradford stepped off the Mayflower in 1620 he referred to the land as "hideous and desolate." In fact, this primeval environment was a direct threat to the colonist's survival. Necessities like food and shelter had to be wrenched from the wilderness by the backbreaking work of clearing the land, planting crops, and erecting cabins. Dreaded Old World myths seemed to come alive in the New World forests—savage Indians, and "rabid and howling wolves" which, according to one colonist, would "make havoc among you and not leave the bones until morning." There was also the subtle danger of sliding back into barbarism. A traveler in the backwoods in 1749 noted that "a kind of white people are found here, who live like savages. . . ." A nineteenth-century tale out of the West concerns "Big Phil," a mountain man who made it through the hard Sierra winters by eating his Indian wives when the food supply was exhausted.

Generation after generation, Europeans moving into the American frontier lands struggled with primitive conditions. If wilderness was their sworn enemy, then rural civilization with its productive farms and safe, comfortable villages was their friend and the goal of their labor. A Virginia planter in 1630 could not see "how men should make benefit of (wild land) . . . but by habitation and culture." Wilderness was waste or, what was worse, a "dark and dismal Devil's den." By "subduing" it and replacing it with rural civilization, the settlers felt they were doing both themselves and God a service. God had commanded humanity to "have dominion,"and the settlers were having it.

By the early seventeenth century, the reports of the early explorers were coupled with an increasing mass of information about America from the first settlers. They and other propagandists promoted the New World as the perfect spot for European settlement. Poets, ballad writers, pamphleteers, and preachers touched on the same theme, praising the land for its fertility. According to such publicists, the bounty of the American paradise was endless.

THWARTED FIRST PLANTINGS

Early in the seventeenth century, when the first settlements were made in America, the concept of "American" was nonexistent. The settlers saw themselves as Europeans living abroad. Their efforts to duplicate their old way of life are evidenced by the names they chose for their new homes: New Sweden, New Netherland, New England, New Spain, and so forth. These colonials believed that this "New" civilization would be a mirror reflecting its European parent. Their serious, detailed intentions can be seen in the initial efforts to establish many of the colonies, including La Florida, Virginia, and Massachusetts Bay. All of them, however, would have to adapt to American conditions and change their approach to thrive.

La Florida

Beginning early in the sixteenth century, Spanish priests advocated missionary work in La Florida, arguing that a series of missions and pueblos in the province would promote the conversion of numerous souls to the Catholic faith. Beside proselytizing natives, there were other reasons why Spain was attracted to La Florida. In addition to the hope of extracting agricultural and mineral resources, officials envisioned an overland route through La Florida, linking the Spanish silver mines and pueblos in Mexico to the Atlantic coast. This avenue would provide a valuable alternative to the sea lanes around the La Florida peninsula, so often prowled by ruthless foreign buccaneers and battered by hurricanes each autumn.

The Spanish presence in La Florida began in 1513, when Juan Ponce de León commanded three heavily-armed vessels that set out from Puerto Rico in pursuit of an island called Bimini, that, according to native accounts, teemed with gold and other riches. Even more enticing, the natives informed the Spaniards that they would find on Bimini magical rivers or springs whose waters would restore the suppleness of youth to those who drank it. The Spaniards reached a land they believed to be an island which they named La Florida. De León sailed up the Gulf coast of Florida, landing at a natural harbor the Spaniards named Bahía San Carlos, today's Charlotte Harbor. The conquistadors barely had time to drop anchor and sketch a crude map of the bay before Calusa natives, in a small fleet of canoes, attacked the Spanish flotilla. Denied his search for gold or the regenerative waters, de León returned to Puerto Rico.

Although failing in its objectives, the de León expedition had its successes. De León was the first European to explore the southeast corner of North America. And although he never realized that Florida was a peninsula of a vast land mass, his reports about "the island of Florida and others in its district" encouraged the Spanish crown to launch subsequent expeditions to explore and settle the lands lying north of Cuba and Hispaniola during the 1520s and 1530s.

In 1526, Lucas Vásquez de Ayllón led 520 Spanish settlers and African slaves to establish San Miguel de Gualdape, the first European settlement in what is now the United States. The tiny settlement of houses and a church was established just south of the present site of Savannah, Georgia. The colony's name probably derives from *Guale*, the name the Spaniards gave to the native peoples of the South Carolina coast, and whom the English would later call the Creeks.

Ayllón had expected the surrounding territory to be a paradise of almonds, olives, figs, and pearls; instead, he found a desolate land of sand and swamp. The colony was constantly beseiged by native attacks, cold weather, and dwindling provisions. At one point, while natives were attacking the settlement, slaves torched a number of structures and then fled into the woods, taking refuge among the natives. After Ayllón's death from fever only weeks after establishing San Miguel de Gualdape, the survivors abandoned the colony and returned to Hispaniola.

Another expedition of four hundred men to conquer La Florida was launched two years later, led by Pánfilo de Narváez. Upon landing on the Gulf coast of Florida in 1528, the Spaniards encountered hostile natives, who "made many signs and menaces, and appeared to say we must go away from the country." Narváez unflinchingly took possession of the land for the Spanish crown and had his men proclaim to puzzled natives that he was governor. At the native settlement of Tocobaga, today's Tampa Bay, where the Spaniards expected to confiscate native riches, they were disappointed to discover only fields of unripened corn. Their regret was soon lifted, however, when the natives suggested by sign language that a province rich in gold called Apalachee lay to the north.

Narváez and two hundred foot soldiers set out from Tampa Bay with a scant supply of biscuits and bacon. Covering about eight miles a day, the army traversed disease-ridden swamps, bogs, tangled woods, and fallen trees. The men battled heat, humidity, and mosquitoes. After a two month trek, the sick, hungry, and disillusioned Spaniards reached Apalachee, on the site of present-day Tallahassee. Instead of gold, Governor Narváez and his men found a village of clay huts. When he ordered his men to ransack Apalachee maize supplies, the natives responded by releasing a flurry of arrows at the Spaniards, who retreated nearly fifty miles to the Gulf of Mexico. The weakened men constructed crude rafts, hoping to cross the gulf to return to Mexico. Instead, the governor and most of his men drowned in the treacherous waters. Only four conquistadors survived the expedition.

For thirty years La Florida remained dormant in Spain's imperial designs for North America until the early 1560s, when French migrants attempted to settle on the peninsula. In 1562, French Protestants (called Huguenots) established a religious sanctuary near the present site of St. Augustine. After enduring steady misfortune, including a fire that consumed much of the settlers' food supplies, they sailed back to France. Two years later, an expedition of three hundred French soldiers, settlers, and craftsmen established Fort Caroline near the mouth of the St. Johns River in northern Florida. French efforts to convert the natives of La Florida to Protestantism, coupled with the threat to Spanish shipping in the Gulf Stream off La Florida's Atlantic coast, brought the Spaniards back to La Florida. Spanish King Felipe II ordered veteran naval commander Pedro Menéndez de Avilés to annihilate the French garrison, establish Spanish outposts, and carry out mass native conversions. In late 1565, after eliminating the French presence in La Florida, Menéndez and his soldiers established San Agustín, the first *permanent* European settlement in North America. Menéndez was convinced that some rivers cut across La Florida, providing passages between the Atlantic and the Gulf of Mexico. Since he controlled navigational rights over the territory's waterways, Menéndez would have profited handsomely had his interconnected river systems not been a figment of his imagination.

In 1572, Menéndez brought Franciscan missionaries to the colony. In addition to proselytizing natives and recruiting potential enemies as Spanish allies, the mission system also provided soldiers and colonists with an inexpensive, sometimes conscripted, labor force. Tracts of land and native labor, called *encomiendas*, were awarded to Spanish soldiers and colonists who were to provide the natives with protection and instruction in the Catholic faith. However, in the Franciscan missions, natives were often uncompensated for their labor in clearing fields, farming, and construction. While individual Jesuit and Franciscan missionary priests struggled to improve the lives of La Florida's natives, one historian declares that "one cannot forget that the mission system was part of an insidious colonial empire, an empire that ultimately destroyed the very people the Franciscans sought to save."

Under Menéndez, the settlers at San Agustín and other fledgling towns planted wheat, cassava, and corn. The Spanish colonists also experimented with grapevines, pomegranates, orange trees, figs, barley, onions, garlic, and made a brief but failed experiment in silk cultivation. Menéndez's early hopes of planting sugarcane, raising great herds of livestock, and establishing pearl fisheries in the rivers of La Florida were never realized. There were some successes: forest resources were exploited, especially the harvesting of juniper, oak, laurelwood, and sassafras root bark, which was used for the treatment of syphilis. Enterprising settlers began a fur trade with the natives while blacksmiths, carpenters, and merchants helped to build a European economy and society in La Florida.

By 1570, Menéndez founded Cabo Santa Elena, a settlement on the Atlantic coast, north of San Agustín, and Santa Lucia, on the Atlantic coast south of present-day Cape Canaveral. However, constant hostility with the Indians hastened abandonment of both settlements by 1587. Meanwhile, following a clash with native warriors, a Jesuit mission at present-day Biscayne Bay was abandoned in 1571 soon after it was founded. Menéndez had even less success on the west coast of La Florida. Relentless fighting with Indians forced the Spaniards to withdraw from Tocobaga (Tampa Bay) and Bahía de San Carlos (Charlotte Harbor) in 1571. Frustrated by the continued resistance of natives, Menéndez asked Felipe II's permission to sell captured Indian rebels into slavery. The king denied the petition and native belligerence continued, keeping the settlers hemmed in on the coastal regions on the Atlantic and Gulf shores. As a result, Spanish settlers were unable to settle on the richer soils in the interior of the Florida peninsula.

Menéndez died in 1574, leaving behind a mixed legacy in La Florida. He had driven out the French and solidified Spanish hegemony on the peninsula. The pueblo and fort he established at San Agustín became a bulwark in the defense of Spain's claim to La Florida over the next 250 years. However, his efforts to establish thriving missions, pueblos, and presidios failed. Besides chronic native defiance, Menéndez tried to colonize the region with his own money, a task that was far too demanding for limited private resources. Meantime, the crown was unwilling to commit itself to a territory that had yielded no mines, rich agricultural lands, or slaves. Nevertheless, Governor Menéndez had demonstrated the strategic significance of the La Florida peninsula to the homeward route of the Spanish treasure fleet, to Spain's hold on the West Indies, Mexico, and to the largely unknown and untapped lands to the north and west of San Agustín. Largely because of his legacy, Spain was determined to stay in La Florida, though it remained low on Spain's imperial priorities following Menéndez's death.

His successors tried, with little progress, to convert La Florida into a viable commercial center with defensible, well-provisioned and well-manned military positions. The Franciscans continued missionary work among the natives, but they were hampered by inadequate support from the Crown. Civil, military, and spiritual authorities, together with the settlers, found it exceedingly difficult to obtain supplies from Havana, as English privateers frequently plundered supply ships in the Straits of Florida and along the Atlantic shore of the peninsula.

After much of San Agustín was destroyed in a native attack in 1577, the pueblo and presidio were rebuilt only to be sacked and destroyed nine years later by the English buccaneer Francis Drake. The Spaniards rebuilt San Agustín, defending it with heavier artillery and increasing the garrison of soldiers. The settlement's presidio was rebuilt with stone, making it far more formidable than its wooden predecessor. San Agustín remained the only significant Spanish settlement during the centuries-long Spanish occupation of La Florida. During the seventeenth and eighteenth centuries, Spanish settlers in La Florida continued to suffer from native attacks along with raids launched by English settlers from the Carolinas. By 1706, the Franciscan mission system in La Florida had collapsed. Beginning in the 1780s, American settlers periodically entered the Spanish province to trade with the Indians or to attack vulnerable Spanish outposts. Realizing it could not not retain La Florida in the face of American expansion, Spain ceded the territory to the United States in 1819. Unlike later developments in the American Southwest, Hispanic settlers and Spanish architecture disappeared in La Florida soon after the American flag was raised over the peninsula.

Virginia

The English first attempted a colony in North America on tiny Roanoke Island located in North Carolina's Outer Banks, a line of coastal islands, treacherous sandbars, and perpetually shifting underwater shoals. Explorer Arthur Barlowe, who visited the area in 1584, intrigued political leaders and investors with near-lyrical descriptions of the island. He reported that Roanoke was an excellent choice for a permanent and self-sufficient settlement; the climate was temperate and the soil seemed well-suited for agriculture. At Roanoke, Barlowe reported, he and his crews lived at the mouth of a cornucopia of fruits, melons, walnuts, cucumbers, and corn. He described how the English tested the island's soil by planting peas which grew an incredible fourteen inches high in just ten days. "The soil," Barlowe rhapsodized, "is the most plentiful, sweet, fruitful, and wholesome of all the world."

A contingent of 107 men commanded by Ralph Lane as governor formally established an English colony on Roanoke Island in 1585. Lane was instructed to continue exploration of the surrounding area, trade with the natives, establish produce for export, and develop the colony as a base for privateering strikes against Spanish treasure galleons. The Roanoke colony was not

The gentleman-adventureres who comprised the major part of the early labor force of Virginia were reluctant to dirty their hands in manual labor. Not unil the Virginia Company of London began importing indentured servants did the colony enjoy prosperity. (From *Pioneers in America*. Courtesy The National Historical Society, Harrisburg, Pennsylvania.)

Women were scarce in the early history of the colonies. No one realized their value better than the gentleman colonists who paid 120 pounds of tobacco each for their prospective brides. Not only did the arrival of women contribute to the stability of the colonies, but they also made life more amenable. (Harper's Magazine, April 1883).

only the first English settlement in the Americas, but it also produced vital firsthand accounts of aboriginal cultures and natural life as they were prior to massive European migration. Lane's colonists, both soldiers and gentlemen, expected to find gold, silver, and pearls in Virginia, and to return home as rich men. They had no desire to plant, fish, or hunt. As English food reserves became dangerously depleted, skirmishes were fought over native corn and fish. Governor Lane and his exhausted and hungry colonists abandoned Roanoke after only a year.

A second contingent of colonists, including women and children, arrived on Roanoke Island in the summer of 1587. Led by Governor John White, the new settlement was to emphasize agricultural self-sufficiency and the production of goods that could be sold in Europe, rather than gold mining and privateering. During White's early weeks on Roanoke, colonists hunted and fished and constructed houses within a stockaded village. However, realizing that provisions were low and that the planting season had long since passed, the settlers beseeched White to return to England for more supplies and colonists. Only a month after he had arrived, White sailed for England, leaving most of the settlers behind on Roanoke.

White's return to the island colony was delayed three years by the Spanish Armada's invasion of England, which triggered a naval war between England and Spain. When he did finally return in the summer of 1590, White found the houses overgrown with grass, weeds, and pumpkin creepers. He found some of his books torn from the covers, framed pictures and maps rotten and spoiled with rain and mildew, and his suit of armor "almost eaten through with rust." The colonists had all disappeared. Then White found some clues: a tree trunk with the letters CRO carved into it and the word CROATOAN cut into a doorpost. He believed these were messages from the settlers that some or all of them had relocated to Croatoan Island, nearly thirty miles south of Roanoke, near Cape Hatteras. White and his fellow mariners attempted to sail to Croatoan Island but a storm drove their ship off course. The governor returned to England, never returning to Roanoke.

Historians have speculated on a wide array of possible explanations. Perhaps the settlers were massacred by natives at Roanoke and their bodies dragged away. Maybe they died of famine or perished in a terrible hurricane. Or, perhaps, White's hunch was correct: that the colonists had moved, or had attempted to relocate to Croatoan Island, the home of hospitable natives. If so, perhaps the colonists drowned in a boating mishap en route to their new site. If they successfully arrived on the island, their descendants may have migrated into the North Carolina mainland with the Croatoans. Some historians have suggested that the settlers, in search of food, migrated overland nearly fifty miles to Chesapeake Bay, only to be killed by warriors of the Powhatan Confederacy. After more than four hundred years, the fate of the lost colonists of Roanoke remains elusive.

As the sixteenth century closed, the English had reasons both to lament and to celebrate. Roanoke had been an unmitigated disaster. Yet, ironically, at the moment that the Roanoke star had plummeted, the potential future of English colonization in North America never appeared brighter. England's defeat of the Spanish Armada in 1588, and the successful defense of the home island against subsequent Spanish assaults during the long naval war that ensued, had confirmed England's rise as a naval power.

In 1607, King James I issued a charter to a trading company called the Virginia Company of London, whose leaders developed ambitious and wholly unrealistic plans for a North American colony. They instructed settlers in Virginia to find a water passage to Asia, discover and extract precious ore, and produce iron, glass, pitch, silk, and wine. Prospective investors in the colonial enterprise heard lavish accounts of how Virginians would soon be exporting wine, silk, flax for linen, hemp for cordage, pitch, tar, and turpentine. As late as 1619 Michael Drayton, in his poem "The Virginia Voyage," summoned the adventurous among the English to cross the ocean "to get the pearls and gold and ores to hold *Virginia*, earth's only paradise."

The establishment of Jamestown fired the imaginations of stockholders and would-be investors of the Virginia Company. With Roanoke a remote memory, the English had now established a North American colony which promised to furnish raw materials to make the island-nation self-sufficient. There was, foremost, the promise of gold. Covetous of the precious metals the Spaniards had devoured in Mexico and Peru, the gold-starved English were deeply heartened at the prospects of an El Dorado in Virginia. However, the tons of ore the colonists sent back to London were assayed to be worthless.

Like other Europeans who explored and settled the Americas, the English suffered illness and death as they slowly adjusted to a new climate, different soils, and alien environment. Having arrived in May, which might have been the most comfortable season in coastal Virginia, the colonists had no knowledge of the various perils of the Jamestown location. The peninsula was a tidal marshland which in the hot and humid summer became infested with massive swarms of mosquitoes carrying malarial parasites. The marshes and pools of brackish water were almost certainly infested with typhoid bacteria. Many colonists were so desperately ill that few were well enough to stand guard over the tiny settlement. Most were left "groaning in every corner of the fort most pitiful to hear."

The winter of 1609–1610 was an especially bitter season. After their salted meats had been depleted, the settlers were reduced to eating a bland assortment of roots, acorns, and berries. In utter desperation, some colonists even resorted to cannibalizing the dead. By the spring equinox, the population of Jamestown had dwindled from 560 to sixty. "This was the time," John Smith remembered later, "which to this day we call the starving time; it was too vile to say, and scarce to be believed, what [the English] endured." One immigrant damned Virginia, describing it as "a misery, a ruin, a death, a hell."

Soon after the starving time, Jamestown farmer John Rolfe began experimenting with Virginia's indigenous tobacco plants which the natives smoked as part of their diplomatic and religious ceremonies. The local plant, *nicotiana rustica*, was, according to colonist William Strachey, "not of the best kind . . . but poor and weak, and of a biting taste." The English were fond of smoking the more "pleasing" leaf grown by the Spaniards in Trinidad and Caracas. Rolfe knew that the Virginia leaf would not compete effectively with the Spanish product, so, in 1612, he cultivated a more mild tobacco strain, *nicotiana tobacum*, from seeds that he had acquired from the West Indies, demonstrating that it could be adapted to Virginia's soil and climate. Rolfe's experiment was decisive; the colonists found a commodity to ship back to a ready English market.

Smoking and chewing tobacco had been growing in popularity in England, first among the affluent class, then universally, since Sir Walter Raleigh had first popularized the tobacco habit in the 1580s. A few voices were raised warning that tobacco was a poisonous weed. A year after his accession, King James I issued a pamphlet, *A Counterblast to Tobacco* [1604], in which he denigrated tobacco as "that stinking weed" and equated its fumes with the smoke of hell. The king argued that tobacco was "loathsome to the eye, hateful to the nose, harmful to the brain, and dangerous to the lungs." He pleaded with his subjects not to imitate "the barbarous and beastly manners of the wild, godless, and slavish Indians, especially in so vile and stinking a custom." The king's pleas fell largely on deaf ears as Virginia planters lost no time in sending off vast shipments of tobacco. Tobacco exports climbed from 2,300 pounds in 1616 to 19,388 in 1617, 49,528 in 1618, and nearly 60,000 pounds two years later. Subsequent events would prove that the tobacco boom was only beginning. Virginia planters exported a half-million pounds of tobacco in 1627. After the promise of gold had dissipated, and efforts to establish an industrial economy had failed amid the colonists' suffering famine and disease, the emergence of tobacco as a cash crop seemed divinely sent. The settlers immediately planted tobacco in the limited ground within the palisaded settlement. There was such a zeal to reap profit from the crop that colonists were growing tobacco plants in the streets of Jamestown.

Since tobacco was difficult to cultivate in England, combined with the increasing consumer demand for tobacco in the mother country, Virginia planters quickly chalked up hefty profits. The leaf provided planters with a high yield per acre. If cured properly, it could be stored for a long period. English entrepreneurs and Virginia Company officials saw tobacco both as a source of wealth and the economic base that could assure the entire commercial enterprise in Virginia. Further, tobacco cultivated in England's colony in North America would end English dependence on costly imports from Spain's Caribbean possessions.

With fantastic wealth emanating from tobacco cultivation, crop diversification was opposed by Virginia planters at every turn. It is ironic, of course, that such a lethal product guaranteed the survival of the Virginia colony. Tobacco immediately shaped Virginia's society and economy: it thwarted industrial development, created a demand for slave labor, and created a polarized social structure dominated by the planter class who wielded enormous political power. In 1627, James's successor, Charles I, commented that the Virginia colony was "wholly built upon [tobacco] smoke."

The planters' zealous tobacco production created a glut of the commodity in England. With annual surpluses, prices in London soon went into a free fall. Virginia planters had commanded forty shillings a pound for the crops in 1614. In 1619, the price had plummeted to 3.5 shillings. During the 1620s, prices continued to drop as production soared, fluctuating between one and three shillings in 1625.

Because tobacco plants stripped the sparse topsoil in the tidewater region, this reduced the plantations' productivity. As a result, planters were sent scrambling to develop larger estates. Within a decade, serious soil depletion drove planters off farms that they had established only a few years earlier. To nurture the development of seedlings, planters and their servants repeatedly plowed the light, alluvial soil, hastening erosion. Soil exhaustion occurred in areas of the Virginia tidewater not long after the founding of Jamestown as the land was not protected by fertilizer or crop rotation. As the richness of the soil declined and tobacco prices plunged, planters pushed farther westward and north into Powhatan territory in order to establish vast interior plantations.

The Virginia Company saw England's sizeable impoverished population as an ideal source to populate a nearly vacant colony and provide it with a vital labor supply. In an effort to attract workers to the colony, the Virginia Company introduced the system of indentured servitude. Generally, indentured servants were English men and women who wanted to cross the Atlantic but did not have the economic resources to pay shipmasters the exorbitant passenger fees in order to emigrate. Therefore they signed indentures, or contracts, requiring an obligation of two to eight years of labor in Virginia in exchange for passage costs and room and board. Contracts required masters to provide their servants with adequate food, clothing, shelter, sufficient medical care, and some legal protection. Occasionally indentures provided servants with "freedom grants" of clothing, farming implements, and sometimes small tracts of land when their time of service had expired.

Sir Edwyn Sandys, the treasurer of the Virginia Company, initiated sweeping reforms beginning in 1618 to make conditions in Virginia more attractive, thereby encouraging a steady migration of laborers across the ocean. The Company diminished its absolute control over the Virginia government and in 1619 established the House of Burgesses, the first legislative assembly ever convened in North America. The seeds of representative democracy were thus sown in British America as free adult white males elected delegates, called burgesses, to represent them in the newly-established assembly.

In an effort to lure additional laborers across the Atlantic, the Company unveiled a new land policy in 1618 that permitted individuals to acquire property. The *headright* system provided one hundred acres to immigrants who had settled in Virginia before 1616 and who had remained in the colony. Warrants for fifty acres of land were to be awarded to every incoming head of a household and fifty additional acres for every adult family member or servant. Instead of being granted specific parcels of land, the headright system allowed recipients to stake out acreage that had not yet been claimed, wherever it might be found. Although land was abundant, the headright policy fostered rapid but haphazard expansion.

In the wake of a devastating native attack on English settlements in Virginia in 1622, a royal commission investigated the Virginia Company's administration and conditions in the colony. The investigation revealed that under the Company's leadership, Virginia had become a financial sinkhole into which stockholders had invested vast amounts of capital only to see, at best, meager returns. The commission also reported that nearly three thousand immigrants who had migrated to Virginia from 1619 to 1624 had perished, in large measure because the Company had failed to adequately supply the settlers. In 1624, the government formally dissolved the Company and proclaimed Virginia a royal colony.

Massachusetts Bay

The thwarted purpose of La Florida's initial design was echoed by the efforts of the Puritans. Royal resistance to Puritan-inspired reforms of the Anglican Church was increasing, and England faced possible civil war as the 1630s approached. Some Puritans decided to leave the mother country beginning in 1629, but they were not trying to escape a "sinful and unclean world" like their Pilgrim cousins who founded the Plymouth Bay Colony a decade earlier. They wanted to build a New World "City Upon a Hill" that would serve as a model of the true church for all Christendom. It is significant that, unlike the Pilgrims of Plymouth who had landed in "New England" nearly ten years earlier, they retained their membership in the Church of England after migrating to America.

In order to effect the reforms necessary to restore Christ's true church, they secured a charter from the king and set out to make their experiment in holy living a reality. In keeping with their emphasis on an individual's conscience, these Puritans advocated the congregational form of church-government. This doctrine emphasized the power of each individual parish to govern its own affairs and make its own decisions, without interference from the civil authorities. To establish this exemplary society the Puritans looked to the Bible; by a thorough study of the scriptures one might understand God's will. The New England town community permitted the people to come together for the regular worship of God and instruction of their children. It also provided that most community decisions would be made at town meetings.

Very soon the Puritans encountered challenges to their "city on a hill" that threatened its very foundations. Only six years after the initial settlement, the Reverend Roger Williams criticized his fellow Puritans on various grounds, including the interference of the civil authorities with the affairs of his own congregation at Salem, and the illegal expropriation of land from the Indians. A year later a more serious threat appeared when Anne Hutchinson, a member in good standing of the Boston congregation, raised some controversial issues of individual conscience.

She also questioned the authority of the civil magistrates in church matters. Rejecting the sole authority of the clergy to interpret Scripture, she claimed that she had received direct divine revelations. Already the Puritans were learning that the individualism implicit in the congregational ideal was acceptable only to a certain point. The freedom of the individual had its bounds, they concluded, when it conflicted with society's need for order. Both Williams and Hutchinson were banished from the Bay Colony and both helped to establish Rhode Island.

Dissent rose in other quarters as well. By the 1650s Baptists and Quakers began entering Massachusetts from neighboring colonies to spread their "false" doctrines among the Puritans. The authorities of the Bay Colony administered whippings, bodily mutilation, and even the death penalty to adherents of sects that dared to defile Massachusetts with their "ungodly" messages. These actions elicited from exiled Roger Williams of Rhode Island the admonition: "Yourselves [only] pretend liberty of conscience." The Puritans found their "divinely guided" government under increasing attack not only from dissenters in the colonies, but also from England, where religious toleration began to flourish under Charles II. Many Anglican merchants and businessmen, chafing under rules that restricted their profits and excluded them (as non-Puritans) from the ruling class, protested to the king. Under these pressures the Puritans' hold on Massachusetts weakened, and the last dying gasp of their religious dogma was manifested in the fanatical witch-burning hysteria of the late seventeenth century. The excesses of the Salem witch trials during the 1690s seriously discredited the old religious order.

Thus the Puritan dream of a perfect Christian society to serve as a beacon of light to the entire world began to crumble soon after the experiment was launched. Yet certain aspects of the Puritan legacy persisted, influencing the development of American culture to present times. The Puritan stress on a learned clergy led to the founding of Harvard College in 1636 and a public-supported grammar school system that has molded the course of educational excellence throughout American history. The seventeenth-century town meeting provided further impetus to the idea of responsible and democratic government. The strong emphasis the Puritans placed on work and the accumulation of wealth, with the suggestion that a Christian's labor was a part of his offering to God, contributed to the Protestant work ethic; to work hard is to please God. Nor is civil disobedience, which has assumed such prominence in modern life, a new doctrine. Rather, the determination to follow one's conscience at whatever cost is sharply illuminated by Roger Williams, Anne Hutchinson, and the Quaker martyrs. Finally, the Puritans' belief that they were God's Chosen People, destined to establish a "City Upon a Hill" has figured in the modern American mentality. It has been argued, for example, that the United States' involvement around the world in the twentieth century is a modern reflection of the Puritans' sense of mission, and is manifested by the belief in the suitability of democratic institutions for all people.

DISPOSSESSING THE NATIVES

But the European viewpoint ignored the fact that this paradise was already occupied. Native Americans, ranging from hunter-gatherers in California to the sophisticated Iroquois confederacy along the Atlantic Seaboard, called it their home. The colonizing nations, however, were not at all concerned with the legal ethics of possessing Indian lands in the New World. Despite the fact

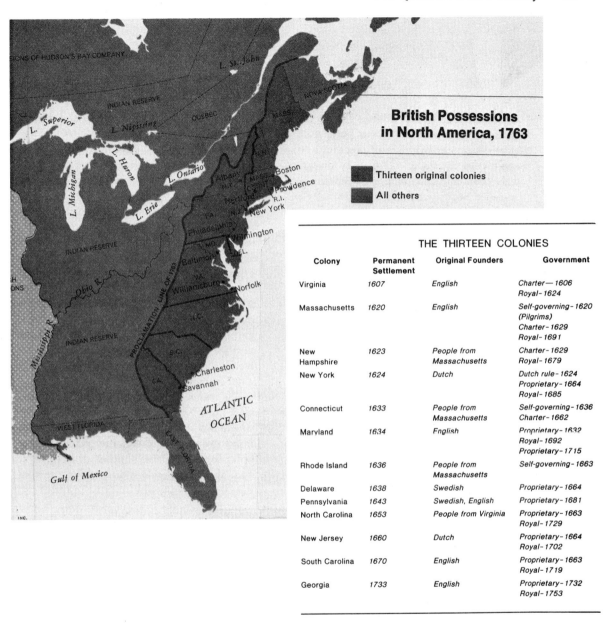

British Possessions in North America, 1763

◼ Thirteen original colonies

◼ All others

THE THIRTEEN COLONIES

Colony	Permanent Settlement	Original Founders	Government
Virginia	1607	English	Charter—1606 Royal-1624
Massachusetts	1620	English	Self-governing-1620 (Pilgrims) Charter-1629 Royal-1691
New Hampshire	1623	People from Massachusetts	Charter-1629 Royal-1679
New York	1624	Dutch	Dutch rule-1624 Proprietary-1664 Royal-1685
Connecticut	1633	People from Massachusetts	Self-governing-1636 Charter-1662
Maryland	1634	English	Proprietary-1632 Royal-1692 Proprietary-1715
Rhode Island	1636	People from Massachusetts	Self-governing-1663
Delaware	1638	Swedish	Proprietary-1664
Pennsylvania	1643	Swedish, English	Proprietary-1681
North Carolina	1653	People from Virginia	Proprietary-1663 Royal-1729
New Jersey	1660	Dutch	Proprietary-1664 Royal-1702
South Carolina	1670	English	Proprietary-1663 Royal-1719
Georgia	1733	English	Proprietary-1732 Royal-1753

Charter colony: a colony governed under a document defining the colony's rights and priveleges (a kind of constitution), issued by the English government.

Royal colony: a colony under the direct authority of the King and his representative, a governor.

Self-governing colony: a colony that had the right of setting up its own government as it wished, so long as it did not violate English law.

Proprietary colony: a colony governed by an individual who had the right to rule as he pleased so long as he did not violate English law.

that early contacts were generally peaceful—the Pilgrims showed their appreciation by sharing a thanksgiving feast with the neighboring Indian tribe—the Indians did not get much credit. A sentence from an early diary—"God caused the Indians to help us with fish . . ."—reveals this attitude. Seventeenth-century Europeans gave thanks to their God, not to their fellow man. Cordial relations between the woodland tribes of the eastern seaboard and the first English colonists were short-lived as issues of conflict began to surface.

Central to the disputes that arose between the European settlers and the natives of North America was the clash of cultural values. The colonists frequently assumed that ulterior motives accompanied Indian "kindness," somehow transmuting that trait to one of "treachery." If Indian customs could not compare with the more "civilized" European way of living, the natives would be subjected to the charge of "barbarism." And because they did not seem to subscribe to the Protestant Ethic of hard work, a century-old belief thoroughly imbued in the Northern European, it was difficult to avoid the conclusion that Indians were a "lazy" people. Europeans traveling in eighteenth-century America constantly referred in their diaries to the "indolence" of the natives. A Frenchman in 1700 observed:

> *I am again struck by the dominant preference of these tribes for indolence. They will go without things that we regard as absolutely necessary merely because it would require a little effort to get them.*

In other words, the belief in the ethnic superiority of European culture permitted white Americans to condemn any values different from those of their own "civilized" world. The primary argument used to remove the Indian from his native soil was the one of "utility," which came to be known as "usufruct" or "use-of-land" argument. The main idea was that man's right to the land depended on the condition that he use the land, cultivating it not only to further his prosperity but also in obedience to the Biblical admonition that man "have dominion" over the land. Since the natives were usually regarded as wandering hunters with no permanent habitation, their title to the land was contested. To live as vagabonds on the land was simply too wasteful in a world in which other nations faced (or thought they faced) problems of overpopulation. This argument provided an extremely popular justification during the eighteenth and nineteenth centuries for dispossessing the Indians of their land. As a result, one late eighteenth-century observer noted: "It is plain as day that they have no right to the land and it is permissible to drive them out at will." The idea that a hunting and gathering society could be forced to submit to a more agricultural economy imposed by force was voiced by many influential spokesmen. Theodore Roosevelt, our first twentieth century president, said "The settler and pioneer have at bottom had justice on their side. This great continent could not have been kept as nothing but a game preserve for squalid savages." It was clear that those who wasted God's land by being nomadic hunters had now lost whatever "natural" title they may have had earlier.

Is it safe to assume, however, that "usofruct" provided a valid rationale for taking Indian lands? Were Native Americans in fact roaming vagabonds? Of course, there was a certain amount of nomadism among the inhabitants of the eastern coast, but agricultural pursuits played a far more prominent role in their economy and society. In general, the usofruct argument conveniently

An anonymous artist's rendering of an Indian town. One expert states that Indians "who had been for generations town-dwelling farmers, as were the majority of North American Indians, came to be characterized as raggle-taggle nomads, interested only in keeping their lands as 'hunting grounds,' which, of course, made it easier to justify seizure of their lands." (Thomas Gilcrease Institute of American Hisory and Art. Tulsa, Oklahoma.)

overlooked the fact that these people were primarily village dwellers. It is ironic that graphic depictions by European visitors of seventeenth-century Indian life often show substantial dwellings, palisaded villages, well-planned streets, and garden plots.

VIRGINIA'S INDIAN WARS

During the summer of 1610, war erupted between the English settlers in Virginia and the local natives led by their chief, Powhatan. The conflict was triggered when Lord Governor Thomas De La Warr arrived at Jamestown with explicit orders to force the natives to provide tributes of maize and animal skins, to become "civil and Christian," and to acknowledge "no other lord but King James." Refusing to submit to English political and cultural domination, Powhatan informed Lord De La Warr that the English were no longer welcome to explore his rivers and that if they did so, his warriors would resist.

To punish Powhatan for his "proud and disdainful answers," the governor in July 1610 dispatched a contingent of heavily-armed colonists to attack a native village at the mouth of the James River. The English killed several natives before the remaining villagers took flight. De La Warr's troops then seized the native cornfields and burned the abandoned homes. A month later, another detachment of armed colonists attacked a native village near Jamestown, where sixteen natives were cut down with swords.

In the sweltering summer of 1611, Sir Thomas Dale led one hundred English soldiers wearing full iron armor to drive the natives from the valuable lands along the James and York Rivers. Realizing that their weapons could do little injury to the English, the natives "did fall into their exorcisms, conjurations, and charms, throwing fire up into the skies, running up and down with rattles and making many diabolical gestures," using "spells and incantations" to call for rain to extinguish the fiery discharges from English muskets. All proved useless to the natives as Dale's troops burned homes and crops, forcing the natives from their lands. Over the next three years, the English prosecuted the war with ferocity, launching sorties against a half-dozen native villages.

Native resistance gradually weakened as thousands of warriors and civilians were slaughtered while their homes and food supplies were destroyed. The Powhatan tribes sued for a truce in the spring of 1614 following another series of devastating English attacks on native communities. The peace was formalized in April after planter John Rolfe married one of Powhatan's daughters, whom the English named Pocahontas. With the establishment of the truce, many colonists assumed that Powhatan's power had been spent. The chief promised that, even if provoked by the English, he would not to make war: "for I am now old and would gladly end my days in peace, so as if the English offer me injury, my country is large enough. I will remove myself farther from you." Such assurances of peace and voluntary evacuation of native lands emboldened the colonists.

As the English became self-sufficient in food production, they no longer needed to conduct trade with the Native Americans. Simply put, the English no longer needed the natives. "There is scarce any man amongst us," a Virginia Company officer said bluntly, "that doth so much as afford them a good thought in his heart." The settlers now seized thousands of acres of native lands, which they acquired by force of arms rather than by barter or compensation. Many planters prayed that the armistice would hold, and established plantations on remote, fertile lands far from the blockhouses, fortifications, and soldiers at Jamestown. Within a decade following the founding of the Virginia colony, white settlements had been established along the James River for nearly one hundred miles. This rapid expansion of English plantations was fueled by the tobacco boom and the Virginia Company's liberal land policy.

In 1617, while on a tour of England with Rolfe, Pocahontas died of tuberculosis at the age of twenty-two. An exhausted, disillusioned, and elderly Powhatan, perhaps in his late eighties, died the following year, leaving the native confederacy in the hands of his half-brother, Opechancanough. The new chief assured the English that he desired that the peace be maintained between the natives and the settlers. Assuring colonial leaders that the sky would collapse before he would do anything to end the peace, Opechancanough sent out his people to the English plantations with turkeys, deer, fish, and fruits. The English were lulled into believing that a new era of tranquillity had dawned. In reality, Opechancanough was plotting a massive strike against the white settlers.

On March 22, 1622, as the English solemnly observed Good Friday religious services, Opechancanough ordered his warriors to exterminate the whites. The natives enjoyed the advantage of surprise and greatly benefited from the wide remoteness of English settlements. Colonists were slaughtered in their fields and homes and in their churches. Warriors killed a reported 347 English men, women, and children. One-third of Virginia's colonists had been massacred in one day.

The colonists sought retribution by pursuing a war of extermination against the Powhatans. The English fanned out from Jamestown, killing all natives on sight, razing native villages, and cutting down or torching native cornfields, to induce famine. By 1626, the Powhatans had lost the war and, in the process, had lost much of the cohesiveness that had bound the various native tidewater communities together.

The decimation of the native communities of the Chesapeake tidelands through disease, famine, and war was apocalyptic. Perhaps as many as 40,000 natives inhabited the region before the founding of Jamestown. By 1626, the population had dwindled to no more than five thousand. Opechancanough and his warriors retreated into the Virginia interior, waiting twenty-two years before launching another assault against the English. In 1644, the ninety-nine-year-old chief Opechancanough, blind, crippled, confined to a litter, led another extensive attack in which three hundred English settlers were killed. By that date, however, the English colonists were far too numerous to be destroyed. Opechancanough was captured and shot in the head. In 1646, the Powhatans were formally banished from their ancestral lands.

New England's Indian Wars

In 1630, when the Puritans began their great migration to New England, they entered the ancestral lands of the Massachusett tribe. The Puritans, armed with muskets and gunpowder, easily dispossessed the natives of their ancient lands. Six years later, Puritan settlers expanded along the Thames River in Southeastern Connecticut, into territory claimed by Pequot natives. Conflict between the two peoples erupted immediately when John Oldham, an English trader, was found hacked to death. The Puritans used the incident as a pretext to launch a military expedition aimed not only at punishing the Pequots for Oldham's murder but, more crucially, to weaken Pequot resistance to English settlements in Connecticut.

In the fall of 1636, the punitive campaign was led by John Endicott, the first governor of Massachusetts Bay. After marching south from Boston, the Puritans reached Pequot land where they hoped to lure the natives into a clearing to ambush them. The Pequots, however, refused the bait. But Endicott, determined to exact a measure of punishment against the tribesmen, ordered his men to burn Pequot crops and, as a parting malicious gesture, to shoot a few of the tribe's pet dogs.

The destruction of the native crops proved disastrous for the Pequots whose food supply was now completely inadequate to sustain them through the winter. By the spring of 1637, the Pequots were determined to retaliate against the English. Pequot warriors sporadically attacked and killed Puritan soldiers and settlers. In April, scores of warriors descended on Wethersfield, Connecticut, killing several white settlers. In the aftermath of that attack, the General Court in Boston ordered Captain John Mason to deliver a devastating blow against the Pequots. Mason led a combined contingent of Puritan soldiers and Narragansett natives, who were the Pequots' longtime adversaries. The Pequots were overwhelmed by the English soldiers, protected in iron armor, and armed with guns and swords.

Under cover of night, Mason's army attacked the main Pequot village nestled on the Mystic River, near Long Island Sound. The Puritans hurled flaming torches at the undefended village composed of straw-thatched huts. Within moments the little hamlet became a raging inferno. As many as five hundred native men, women and children were consumed in the flames. The Narragansetts, who had participated in the raid to humble the Pequots, were horrified at the massive bloodletting. A Puritan soldier later recalled that one Narragansett warrior cried out: "This is evil! This is evil! Too furious, too many killed!"

Those native inhabitants who had escaped the fire to seek refuge in the surrounding woods were hunted down by the Puritans and were shot to death or executed by the sword. The entire predawn engagement at the Mystic River settlement lasted less than an hour. Later that day, Puritan minister Cotton Mather jubilantly proclaimed the slaughter a "divine massacre." William Bradford, who had led the Pilgrims to Cape Cod aboard the *Mayflower* seventeen years earlier, also invoked the grace of God to explain, and glory in, the Puritan victory over the "Pequot heathens." "It was a fearful sight," Bradford wrote, "to see them thus frying in the fire, and the streams of blood quenching the same, and horrible was the stink and scent thereof, but the victory seemed a sweet sacrifice, and [the English] gave the prayers thereof to God, who had wrought so wonderfully for them, thus to enclose their enemies in their hands, and give them so speedy a victory over so proud and insulting an enemy."

Several weeks later, a second group of two hundred Pequots were rounded up by the Puritans. The men were bound and shot, and the boys sold into slavery in the Bermudas. The women and girls were forced into slavery in New England. Within a year of Mason's attack on the Mystic River compound, all the members of the Pequot Nation were either dead or enslaved and Pequot land became the possession of the English.

It didn't matter that Native Americans were not the rootless vagabonds that settlers claimed they were. The Europeans were determined to have the land and convert it into their ideal "home away from home." This Old World vision had to change, however, because ultimately the hopes or theories of Europeans did not fit squarely with the realities of America. In seeking one dream they found another.

THE PHILOSOPHY OF THE UNEXPECTED

In spite of their elaborate plans for colonization in America, those Europeans who tried to dictate the early contours of the colonies were insensitive to what one historian has called "the whisperings of the environment." In simple terms, America's physical abundance made European thinking obsolete. The Old World's large, poor population coupled with control of its lands by a small but powerful nobility meant that many European people could never imagine themselves as independent landowners. Even in seventeenth-century England, inflation and increasing demand created land prices that only the well-to-do could afford.

It was an altogether different story in America. There the immigrant found an abundance of natural riches that was staggering. One European, speaking of the mystery of Virginia early in the eighteenth century, exclaimed: ". . . the length extends into the wilderness, which is not known to any one and the end is impossible to find." Other observers concluded that this abundance was matched by the richness of the soil that they believed would never be exhausted. Livestock flourished in the English colonies, and a visitor from England was surprised by the absence of game laws that for centuries had imposed restrictions on hunting in his native land. Indeed, America's natural bounty was so great that a Polish tourist was shocked to find that in eighteenth century New Jersey the most common method of gathering nuts was to first cut down the tree. It should be no surprise that the European mind, nourished on the principle of scarcity, should find it difficult to grasp the significance of America's abundance.

AMERICA AND THE EUROPEAN ENLIGHTENMENT

During the eighteenth century a philosophical movement arose that provided educated Europeans with a new perspective on America. From the intellectual awakening and the rise of modern science in the fifteenth and sixteenth centuries came the Enlightenment of the eighteenth century. Rejecting the all-powerful God of the Old Testament who glorified Himself and damned sinners, the European intellectuals contributed to a new philosophy called rationalism. Experience had shown these thinkers that through reason and observation the human race could gain a clearer understanding of an orderly universe. This point of view contained a profound confidence in people and their capabilities. It suggested that through careful observation scholars might discern the laws of nature and society, enabling them to construct social and political systems in harmony with these laws. Such systems could end poverty and conflict. Belief in progress became a cornerstone to Enlightenment thought. The French philosopher Condorcet believed that there was no limit to the potential advance of human knowledge; indeed, the application of reason would enable society to achieve perfection.

Enlightenment ideas made the New World once again the focal point of the European mind. For centuries it had been America's physical environment that had made such an impact on the

Old World. But by the late seventeenth century, a new society was rising on the eastern coast of North America that challenged traditional European thought as much as the discovery by Christopher Columbus had 200 years earlier. The full impact of this new society would not be felt until it resulted in the American Revolution itself, but its outlines became increasingly clear to observant western Europeans during the eighteenth century. By the middle of the century the number of social critics and observers who crossed the Atlantic to gain their own firsthand impressions could be counted by the hundreds. The steady progress of American society seemed to confirm Enlightenment principles. In the European mind the image of American abundance was gradually joined by America as the "new social ideal."

One of America's attractions was its social structure. Although most of the colonies had developed some degree of class-stratification by the mid-eighteenth century, society as a whole did not harden into the exact patterns found in England or Europe. The easy availability of land provided the key to the free flow of American society; and the ownership of land was not restricted to people of wealth. A Frenchman noted: "Landed property is so easily acquired that every workman who can use his hands may be looked upon as a person who will soon become a man of property." Social position was determined by land and its very abundance discouraged class rigidity. Indeed, it was not uncommon for indentured servants who sold their labor for a period of from three to seven years in exchange for trans-Atlantic passage to be granted a piece of land upon completion of their term of service. Observers concluded that America's bounty made progress a reality in the English provinces.

Europeans learned that America's abundance also made the social structure more equalitarian than in Europe. The rank and status of European society were largely absent in the colonies. One European observed: "The rich stay in Europe, it is only the middling and poor that emigrate." This "leveling principle" not only created a social structure that was more fluid, but it led to other characteristics that commanded the attention (and sometimes respect) of America's European audience. For example, the scarcity of labor encouraged a relatively high standard of living in America. A French aristocrat-tourist noted: "There is not a family even in the most miserable hut in the midst of the woods, who does not eat meat twice a day at least, and drink tea and coffee; ... the proverbial wish of 'having a chicken in every pot' is more than accomplished in America." Other foreign travelers admitted that there was less poverty in England's colonies than in Old World society. Crime in general seemed far less rampant than in Europe, and because of the opportunities available an Englishman remarked that there were "but few idle drones in the hive."

PHILADELPHIA: LABORATORY OF THE ENLIGHTENMENT

Americans seemed to be a busy people. Nowhere was this more apparent than in the rapid rise of urban communities in the Middle Colonies. Philadelphia, founded in 1682, commanded the special admiration of her European visitors. Not only was the City of Brotherly Love regarded as the loveliest city in America, but even many European cities paled in comparison. The capital of Pennsylvania provided "evidence" that the ideals of eighteenth-century intellectuals could be realized. It boasted wide streets laid out at right angles flanked by sidewalks, street lamps, water pumps at frequent intervals and a sewer system. These were unaccustomed luxuries in most

European cities. The citizenry was offered clean and modern facilities in the hospital (accommodations were even provided for "lunaticks") and free medicine was distributed to the poor. There was an enlightened prison system, a university, two academies, and a library founded by Benjamin Franklin in 1742. Printing became a lucrative business in Philadelphia, and the birth of the American Philosophical Society in 1744 signaled the city's rise to prominence among the intellectuals of the trans-Atlantic community.

What astounded Europeans most of all was the deliberate planning that accompanied Philadelphia's growth. The transition from country to city was occurring at explosive speed, and by the time of the Revolution the most significant social and humanitarian achievements had been made in Pennsylvania. Although the Enlightenment embraced both sides of the Atlantic, it was at Philadelphia more than anywhere else that practice kept pace with theory.

THE BLACK MAN IN A WHITE MAN'S COUNTRY

The great exception to this image of a progressive, enlightened society was, of course, slavery. The first blacks arrived in North America aboard a Dutch slave ship that docked at Jamestown in 1619. Intent upon establishing an agricultural society across this broad expanse of land, the settlers faced an urgent need for labor. In a society with an abundance of land, few would work as hired hands on another's property. This economic necessity dictated the fate of black Africans, who soon became pawns in an international slave trade. Torn from their roots, thrown in among people from all over West Africa who were strangers to each other, ignorant of the language, the customs, or the law, and easy to pick out from the crowd, they were easy to take advantage of. However, blacks in the English colonies seem to have begun as servants, not slaves.

This condition persisted for about 40 years. The most essential feature of slavery appeared as early as the 1640s when court records refer to the sale of some blacks for life. During this strange twilight period, while the terms for black servants were longer and sometimes even indeterminate, there was still reason for hoping that blacks would not find themselves in a state of perpetual slavery. Planters preferred white indentured servants, who were less expensive. But the decade of the 1660s witnessed a decline in the Southern economy that threatened the black man's future. Recovery from a serious drop in tobacco prices did not occur for another 20 years. As the margin of profit narrowed and as costs rose, small-scale tobacco production was seriously hampered. White indentured servants were not coming over in large enough numbers. The planters came to realize that profits could be restored only by expanding production, and they decided to rely on a large work force whose labor could be depended on over the long term.

Therefore, it was argued that lifetime black servitude must be written into law. In 1662 the Royal Company of Adventurers was founded to encourage the importation of black slaves. African Americans would become property that could be used, bought, or sold in any fashion that their owners wished. Planters expected that slave labor would be the wave of the future in the southern colonies.

Few white people during the colonial period were sensitive to the inhumanity of the African slave trade. One company engaging in slave commerce instructed its ship captain to pack his vessel with "negers" and "Cattel" together. These crowded conditions doubtless increased the incidence of disease and epidemics during the voyage to America. The result was a shocking mortality rate, sometimes exceeding 50 percent of the black cargo. (Library of Congress.)

AN AMERICAN CHARACTER EMERGES

Having marginalized the Indians and enslaved the Africans, mainstream colonial society began to take shape in the eighteenth century. Imperceptibly at first, but more clearly over time, that society was becoming less European and more American.

A Challenge to Old Assumptions

During the early years of colonization Old World social patterns were transplanted to the New World—as the initial efforts in La Florida, Virginia, and Massachusetts Bay suggest. The colonies were seen as a projection of Europe across the Atlantic. These settlers who came assumed that they would retain their old habits, manners, and customs indefinitely. Although the rigors of life in the American wilderness demanded some adjustments to New World conditions, it was believed that these adjustments would be temporary. Sooner or later, colonial society would become the mirror image of European culture.

The changes that these transplanted Europeans underwent were usually subtle ones, and sometimes scarcely noticeable. Moreover, the adjustments proved to be less temporary than had been expected. As second and third-generation colonials were born in America without any firsthand experience in traditional English society, the image of the old social patterns became less familiar. Time was blurring the blueprint.

By the eighteenth century, the arrival of thousands of non-English immigrants contributed even more to the breakdown of a plan that was basically English in origin. Migrants from the European continent were made welcome in most of the English colonies and mingled readily with descendants of the first settlers. In the mixed population of New York, the commerce-minded Dutch asked few questions about a settler's religion or ethnic background. As early as 1646 eighteen languages could be heard along the Hudson River. Besides the Dutch, New York's diverse population included Frenchmen, Danes, Norwegians, Swedes, English, Scotch, Irish, Germans, Poles, Bohemians, Portuguese, Italians, and Jews. After 1685 French Protestants called Huguenots appeared in Virginia and the Carolinas, Pennsylvania, New York, and New England (like the Revere family). Large numbers of Germans and Dutch made Pennsylvania a pluralistic colony in language, culture, and religion by the end of the 17th century. In 1700 the population of England's North American possessions numbered 250,000 persons. By the 1760s it had soared to almost two million. By 1770 German migration alone equaled the total colonial population in 1700.

Time, New World conditions, and growing cultural diversity made the original designs of colonization outmoded. Colonists began gradually to realize that they must develop a society that was in tune with the New World environment. Unknowingly, Americans were seeking a new identity.

Equality and Optimism

The sense of identity that emerged was closely related to the American social system. Not only was the socioeconomic structure more fluid, but there was less distance between the classes. In fact, from the beginning the colonial social profile differed from the mother country's. By eliminating the well-born and those of extreme poverty from migration to America, the role of the middle and lower classes who crossed the Atlantic was magnified. From this relatively narrow range of social groups, a distinctly American social structure evolved. America's population was of the "middling sort." This is what a French observer meant when he noted that "the rich and poor are not so far removed from each other as they are in Europe."

If there was an aristocracy in America, it was a working aristocracy whose ranks were more open than its European counterpart. One foreigner visiting in eighteenth-century Virginia was surprised to witness the representatives to the House of Burgesses take their seats coming straight from the tobacco fields still dressed in their work clothes and muddied boots. Another tourist noted: "For here the poor man who is industrious finds opportunities enough for gain, and there is no excuse for the slothful." Whereas in Europe "equality" meant that all men should enjoy roughly the same position or power, in America the emphasis was on "equality of opportunity." Ambition and talent, in other words, were the most important criteria (other than race) for entrance into America's affluent society. Those who were willing to exert themselves and industriously apply their talents would succeed. One European tourist concluded that America was "the best country in the world for poor men." Such opportunities encouraged an optimistic spirit and the belief that by the sweat of his brow, an American might enjoy a better life than had been possible in the Old World.

Mobility

The way to wealth often required that the American not settle down too soon. During the colonial period settlers were constantly on the move westward where land was cheaper and, it was hoped, opportunity more available. Not only did farms change owners frequently, but also a move to a place several hundred miles away did not seem to bother the colonist in the least. The European tradition that fostered strong ties between a person and his land was conspicuously absent in the colonies. Americans seemed to be a people without roots whose vision was focused firmly in the future rather than nostalgically on the past. A French traveler, commenting on this characteristic of mobility, noted: "Americans, indifferent in love and friendship, cling to nothing, attach themselves to nothing. . . . Four times running they will break land for a new home, abandoning without a thought the house in which they were born. . . ." Indeed, the American would "part with his house, his carriage, his horse, his dog—anything at all," if only he was "offered a tempting price."

Practicality

To the extent that colonial American culture had crystallized, it reflected a practical character in the arts and sciences, learning and religion.

The theatre and music were sadly undernourished in the colonies, nor had the other fine arts and literature matured significantly. Colonists still looked to Europe for style and creative art. One critic noted, for example, that there were 30 church buildings in Philadelphia, yet "costly and artistic decoration is not to be found in them." European observers who crossed the Atlantic during the eighteenth century agreed that the Americans were a practical people who had not yet developed a need for the "frills" that adorned Old World societies.

From a European perspective, the education system in England's colonies commanded no more respect than the arts. Institutions of higher learning were particularly vulnerable to criticism. Even Harvard College, founded as early as 1636, was the subject of skepticism by Europeans who saw the school primarily as an institution for clerical studies. Although the elementary schools in New England enjoyed some respectability, in most other provinces they were virtually nonexistent.

Certain factors help to explain the low status of the arts and education in the society of young America. Simply because America was so young, she had not yet had the opportunity to develop her cultural institutions. One could find in the colonies no palaces or castles, nor any painters in the tradition of Leonardo da Vinci or Michelangelo. To establish a cultural tradition required more time than young America had yet experienced. It was also difficult for the arts to flourish because the practical American took advantage of the easy abundance promised by the farming life or the trades. Consequently, little of the artistic genius that existed had yet surfaced. This practical or pragmatic turn of mind was observed by a German visitor: "America has produced as yet no sculptors or engravers. But stone-cutters find a pretty good market." Finally, Americans seemed to stress values other than the traditional aesthetic ones. Profits from commerce consumed the interest of the urban class whose support was essential to the arts, while the vast majority of Americans who lived in rural areas had little inclination and even less opportunity to pursue the accomplishments of highly civilized life.

The role of learning in America was also the result of conditions unique to the New World. Intellect for its own sake was considered irrelevant in the colonies. Some observers noted, for example, that Virginians wished to learn only what was necessary, and in the shortest and best method. If the formal aspects of learning were of minimal importance, perhaps it was because there was merit in America's school of nature. A young British soldier wrote home to his sister in 1756 that there was "as much to be acquired in the Woods of America" as in the English schools. Although "learning" in the European sense was less developed in America, Americans valued common sense and were avid readers. Politics was one topic on the lips of ordinary citizens, encouraged by considerable freedom of the press and the liberty of discussion exercised in the taverns and other public gathering places. This practical approach is understandable because in America politics had a real, practical application. The education of girls also revealed this utilitarian bent. In colonial society sewing was considered one of the more important skills they should learn, far more useful to them than a knowledge of science or literature. Even in the "better" homes of the colonial period the difficulty in engaging house-servants dictated that the young women be trained as housekeepers themselves.

In contrast to the arts and learning, the sciences were in a more advanced and healthier state. Even in this field, however, it was the applied or practical sciences that were most firmly established. A number of eminent American scientists became pioneers in their fields, including the international celebrity from Philadelphia, Benjamin Franklin. Franklin was regarded by the trans-Atlantic intellectuals as the perfect example of the practical scientist, and certainly his stove, bifocals, and shaving cream were designed to be useful to humanity. Similarly, a German scientist called the lightning rod "that beneficent discovery of the great Franklin."

The thread of practicality seen interwoven in the arts, sciences, and learning was also noticeable in American religious life. During the colonial period, most settlers were preoccupied with the task of clearing the land. In addition, except in New England, the distances between places and the subsequent isolation of the people tended to make the regular worship of God difficult for many of the colonials. Despite the many European sects that came as cultural baggage

Benjamin Franklin embodied the American success story. (Courtesy of Historical Society of Pennsylvania.)

to the New World, religious doctrine in colonial society dwindled in importance by the late eighteenth century. And yet, if theological ardor tended to cool in the American environment, the church became quite useful as a social and moral institution. Instead of the frequent violence and bloodshed that had characterized the European religious scene of the previous century, the American church served as a school in Christian morals and ethics, and created occasions for neighbors to meet each other on a fairly regular basis. Americans definitely regarded themselves as a religious people. People who did not attend in order to hear the preaching came to join in the socials. Religion in general was considered a "good thing." Except for the religious fervor of seventeenth-century Puritanism in New England and a spirited religious revival in the 1730s and 1740s called the Great Awakening, churches in the colonies had abandoned their Old World emphasis on theology. Instead of stressing doctrinal matters, colonial religion assumed a more practical role by exhorting moral behavior and providing a social meeting place. This practical character of religion was echoed also by the political roles assumed by many church leaders. Not only was the right to vote and hold office in New England during most of the colonial period restricted to members of the established church, but the people who made the basic decisions regarding local government in colonial Virginia did so from their positions as officers in the church governing boards of each congregation. This arrangement became increasingly less practical as the variety of religious sects in America grew. It became difficult to reconcile democracy with religious restrictions on political participation. Maryland was the first colony to offer religious toleration in 1649, and when Charles II granted a charter to Rhode Island in 1663, he confirmed complete religious freedom in that colony. Practicality contributed to the principle of separation of church and state, an important civil liberty later written into the Bill of Rights.

BENJAMIN FRANKLIN

Benjamin Franklin was born in 1706, the last child in a family of seventeen. Though he had only about four years of schooling, he was a voracious reader and as a teenager he became a talented writer for his brother's Boston newspaper. Clashes with his brother led him to run away from his apprenticeship to Philadelphia where, tired and nearly broke, he got work with another paper. By the time Ben was twenty-four, he owned his own printing business. Three years later he was known throughout the American colonies as the author of *Poor Richard's Almanac.* Here Franklin's own philosophy could be found: "Do not enquire of a stranger 'what is he,' but rather 'what can he do,' 'There are no gains without pains.'" But, pragmatist and self-made man that he was (he made his fortune by forty-two years of age), Franklin was also civic minded. He was involved with plans for the first circulating library in America, the paving of Philadelphia's dusty streets, the founding of the future University of Pennsylvania, and the construction of a city hospital.

After his retirement, Franklin embarked on new careers as a scientist, inventor, statesman and diplomat. He was the first to correctly describe the nature of electricity (and he was lucky with that kite experiment—a Swedish scientist who later tried it was electrocuted). He invented bifocals and the "Franklin stove." As a delegate to an intercolonial meeting on the eve of the French and Indian War, Franklin was the first to propose a plan for colonial unity: the "Albany Plan." He went to England to work for a peaceful resolution to the growing clashes between the British government and the American colonies, only to return home on the eve of Revolution. Shortly after the armed struggle began, Franklin wrote to a British correspondent, "you have begun to burn our towns and murder our people! Your hands . . . are stained with the blood of your relations!"

Franklin worked closely with Thomas Jefferson on the Declaration of Independence, commenting to his fellow signers that "we must all hang together, or most assuredly we shall all hang separately." Sent to France to win aid crucial to the American cause, Franklin succeeded brilliantly. At eighty, he participated in the Constitutional Convention of 1787. During the closing session, he pointed out a painting of a sun on the back of the presiding officer George Washington's chair. "I have often . . . looked at it . . . without being able to tell whether it was rising or setting. But now, at last, I know that it is a rising sun." Benjamin Franklin died three years later, having lived long enough to see the American experiment in republican government put on a sound basis.

THE RISE OF THE BRITISH EMPIRE 1607–1763

During the encounter between European immigrants and the American environment that was developing into a new culture, the British Empire was also taking shape. As late as 1650, however, there was no overall blueprint for the regulation of England's colonies. London's first New World settlements were born a half-century earlier, and were making desperate efforts to survive in the American wilderness against stiff odds. A uniform policy for the colonies was a difficult task because of their considerable diversity in governmental structure, purpose (economic, religious, social), economic development, and ethnic composition.

The year 1651 marked the beginning of a new relationship between the mother country and the colonies. The first Navigation Act was issued by Parliament in that year, defining the colonies' role in the empire as a producer of raw materials and a consumer of England's finished products. New agencies were created to enforce the new imperial decrees. Royal officials were sent to the colonies as a further assurance that the colonials would observe the mercantile restrictions. Central to this imperial design was the mercantilists' belief that the colonies were to remain in a subservient position to the mother country. Their purpose was to enrich England and strengthen the empire. No provision was made for them to grow eventually into a relationship of equality with the government in London. Instead, England would remain at the center and the colonies would continue as dependencies. This basic arrangement had been established and would continue largely unchanged until after 1763.

Was it reasonable to expect this parent-child relationship to endure indefinitely? Actually, for most of the colonial period the effects of the British Acts of Trade and Navigation were minimal because as much as 90 percent of the colonial economy was based not upon commerce and trade directly, but upon local agriculture. Thus, the immediate impact of the trade laws was felt only by a limited (if wealthy and influential) number of the total colonial population. Only the southern planters relied on trade with the mother country from the beginning. Indeed, contemporary scholars would generally agree that the benefits of empire membership—naval protection, a guaranteed market for colonial produce and access to the huge markets of the British empire—were greater than the disadvantages. For most of the colonial period there was little hostility expressed toward government rules and in fact the colonials prospered under the rule of Parliament. Nor was later legislation, like the Hat Act of 1732 and the Iron Act of 1750, oppressive. Although such Parliamentary decrees were designed to protect English producers of these goods from colonial competition, America's negligible industrial development during the eighteenth century minimized the adverse effect of that legislation on the colonies.

Colonial prosperity was reinforced in part by the permissive aspects of British mercantilism. For various reasons, including foreign wars and internal strife, there was never a wholehearted effort by London officials to enforce the mercantile policy in America. British rules that limited profits could be avoided through bribery or smuggling, neither of which was looked down upon in the colonies. The tax and laws against smuggling in the Molasses Act of 1733 failed because Prime Minister Robert Walpole realized that efforts to enforce the law might arouse the ire of the Americans. That could cost London more in their huge profits from the colonial trade than the tax would bring in. Thus, preoccupied with wars and domestic politics and wary of losing commercial income, the British government practiced "salutary neglect." This policy allowed the colonies to follow their own inclinations in their economic and political development.

Finally, relations between London and the colonies seemed healthy because much of the American gentry class emerging by the end of the seventeenth century was beginning to imitate consciously the ways of their English counterparts. The Virginians of Chesapeake society, for example, were active participants in the Church of England, and attempted to pattern their lifestyle after the model provided by the traditional English country gentleman. The desire to imitate the values of the mother country was interpreted as another stabilizing force to preserve the British imperial system.

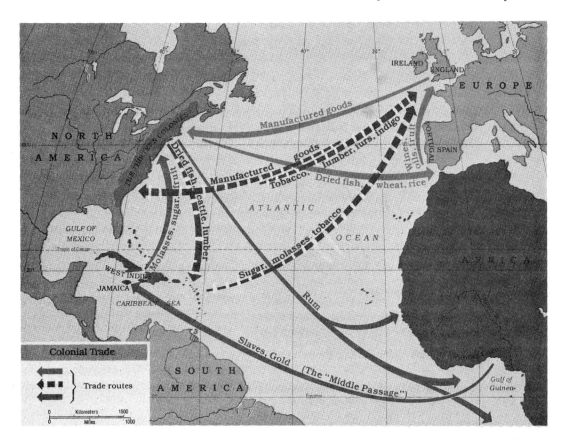

Colonial Trade

Trade routes

Despite that apparent stability, changes were occurring in America. As long as policymakers remained flexible and allowed the colonies their own ways, they had a chance of maintaining their hold over their American domain. Too often, however, the irregular and delayed communications across the Atlantic and the mercantile mentality of superiority prevented a clear understanding of colonial realities. Moreover, the isolation of the provinces from one another during the seventeenth century had allowed strong ties to exist between London and the individual colonies. But as civilization in the New World wilderness matured, that relationship was altered. The eighteenth century witnessed the development of a better colonial road network, more consistent mail and increased intercolonial trade. This increased the colonists' self-sufficiency and self-awareness, causing a corresponding decline in their dependence on London. They were more American than they knew.

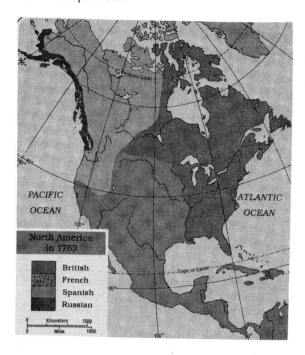

Although the Spanish controlled a large prtion of North America, most of the population and developed resources were in the British area. Spanish power ws declining, and Spain alone was no threat to British dominance in North America.

UNFINISHED BUSINESS

The turning point in the relations between the English colonies and the British government came in 1763. After 80 years of intermittent warfare in America, a defeated France surrendered her American possessions in Canada to the English. Great Britain had won the contest for global supremacy and had resolved her internal strife. After many years of "salutary neglect," the English government now turned her full attention to her colonies, expecting that the Americans would share in the costs as well as the benefits derived from the elimination of the French threat in North America.

Parliament's decision to levy taxes on colonial Englishmen, beginning with the Sugar Act (1764) and the Stamp Act (1765), provoked a resentful response from the Americans. As London insisted on centralizing control of the colonies and enforcing imperial rules, it began to dawn on many Americans that they were not just transplanted Englishmen. For a long time they had been slowly maturing, although neither they nor the authorities in London had perceived this coming of age. Although many of the colonists had tried to imitate English society prior to 1763, they now recognized that a new society had sprung out of their own native soil. That uniqueness was best described by a celebrated French aristocrat who migrated to America in 1765. In a series of essays penned in 1783, Jean de Crevecoeur posed the question, "What then is the American, this new man?":

. . . whence came all these people? They are a mixture of English, Scotch, Irish, French, Dutch, Germans, and Swedes. From this promiscuous breed, that race now called Americans have arisen. . . . In this great American asylum, the poor of Europe have by some means met together, . . . to what purpose should they ask one another what countrymen they are? Alas, two thirds of them had no country. Can a wretch who wanders about, who works and starves, whose life is a continual scene of sore affliction or pinching penury; can that man call England or any other kingdom his country? . . . No! Urged by a variety of motives, here they came. Every thing has tended to regenerate them; new laws, a new mode of living, a new social system; here they are become men. . . . Here the rewards of his industry follow with equal steps the progress of his labour; his labour is founded on the basis of nature, self-interest; can it want a stronger allurement? . . . The American is a new man, who acts upon new principles; he must therefore entertain new ideas, and form new opinions. From involuntary idleness, servile dependence, penury, and useless labour, he has passed to toils of a very different nature, rewarded by ample subsistence. This is an American.

It was clear that a new people had been born in the New World wilderness. It only remained that this new sense of American identity be translated into political terms; and that is the story of the American Revolution. Finally, because of the Revolution, America would continue to occupy an important place in the European mind.

SUGGESTIONS FOR ADDITIONAL READING

Helge Ingstad, *Westward to Vinland; The Discovery of Pre-Columbian Norse House-sites in North America,* (1969). A fascinating narrative of the author's uncovering of the Viking settlement at Newfoundland.

William Cronon, *Changes on the Land,* (1993). A study of the biological impact of the Colombian exchange.

Samuel E. Morrison, *The European Discovery of America: The Northern Voyages and the Southern Voyages* (1971 and 1974 respectively). Engagingly written and superbly illustrated treatments of the early explorations of the New World.

Edmund S. Morgan, *The Puritan Dilemma: The Story of John Winthrop,* (1958). An examination of the founding of Massachusetts Bay and the conflict between freedom and authority.

Daniel Boorstin, *The Americans: The Colonial Experience,* (1959). A study of the evolution of an American civilization from its European beginnings.

Clarence Ver Steeg, *The Formative Years 1607–1763,* (1964). An explanation of the forces that converted transplanted Englishmen into provincial Americans.

Benjamin Franklin, *Autobiography.* A provocative, inside view of colonial America by the most famous American of his era.

"The County Election" by George Caleb Bingham, Collection of the Boatmen's National Bank of St. Louis.

CHAPTER TWO

"WE THE PEOPLE": THE DEVELOPMENT OF AN AMERICAN POLITICAL SYSTEM

1619
House of Burgesses established in Virginia: first representative legislature in North America.

1765
Salutary neglect ends with the passage of the Sugar and Stamp Acts.

1774
Battles of Lexington and Concord: first shots of the American Revolution.

1776
Declaration of Independence.

1777
Articles of Confederation drafted: the first constitution of the United States government.

1789
The Constitution adopted to replace the Articles of Confederation.

1800
Election of Thomas Jefferson, marking the emergence of the two-party system.

1828
Election of Andrew Jackson, signaling the growing spirit of democracy in the American political system, and the birth of the modern Democratic party.

1854
Kansas-Nebraska Act fails to cool North-South tension and leads to the birth of the modern Republican party.

1861
Confederates fire on Fort Sumter, beginning the Civil War.

A VENERABLE EXPERIMENT

When American farmers at Lexington and Concord met British soldiers and began the Revolutionary War, they did indeed fire "the shots heard 'round the world." For the American colonists were the first to wage a successful struggle for independence against an imperial power in modern history. Their example encouraged many of the leaders of the French Revolution and, later, the founders of Latin American independence. The Constitution established by the original 13 states in 1789 was destined to be as influential as the Revolution of 1776. It has been copied, modified, and adopted by more nations than any other governmental form, including the British parliamentary system. And now, the last decade of the twentieth century, it is sweeping the world in the wake of the collapse of Marxism-Leninism.

The reason that the American political system enjoys this honor is not because it is a perfect solution to the problem of government, but simply because it works well. America's brand of democracy has survived wide disagreements among its members, a civil war, several devastating economic depressions, and foreign conflicts, while still managing to guarantee its citizens a relatively high level of civil liberties. Under this system the United States has grown and prospered. But the Founding Fathers only created the framework of government—leaders continued to build on this framework as conditions changed and new issues arose. Institutions like the two-party system developed and new ideas like government-sponsored public works evolved until, by the time of the war with Mexico, the political system appeared to be complete and secure.

Yet this system would be severely strained by the controversy over slavery that finally ended in the Civil War. In Abraham Lincoln's words, the war was a test of whether America "or any nation so conceived and so dedicated, can long endure." In one sense the system itself failed when guns were taken up to settle a political issue. But just as the nation endured the war, so did the American political system.

THE BRITISH HERITAGE

Many of the colonists' ideas about government came from the parliamentary system in England. Even though that island nation was a monarchy, the royal authority wielded by its king was not absolute. He was required to share power with Parliament, a legislative body made up of nobles (House of Lords) and elected commoners (House of Commons). Only Parliament could raise taxes for the Crown, so the king had to pay attention to its views or risk losing money to run his government. As a result of this type of limited government, Englishmen felt secure against tyranny.

They were also accustomed to living in a society that was less rigid than most of those found in continental Europe. Early kings of England had sought support from the landed commoners and merchants against the hostile nobles, making the gentry influential in politics. Compared to the societies of France and Spain, class lines were much more fluid. Middle-class farmers could become wealthy landowners, and prosperous landowners and merchants could aspire to become nobles, frequently through marriage. Englishmen were proud of the fact that England was ruled as much by law as by a king. The Common Law (court and royal decisions that evolved into basic definitions of justice) was supreme in the land. In theory, at least, it guaranteed even poor people recourse to the courts of justice.

Most important, the everyday workings of government at the local level were managed by the gentry [middle class landowners]. Within the Common Law they could handle affairs largely on their own. Though not genuine representatives of the people, who were mostly poor laborers, their interests were similar enough to make them fair legislators. In Parliament they received training in political leadership that enabled them to maintain wide freedom of action in dealing with the king. Struggling to increase their power and influence in government, they realized the importance of political liberty and jealously guarded their rights.

All of these traditions—limited government, the principle of representation, the supremacy of law, local self-government, recourse to the courts, and the political power of landowners and merchants—traveled across the Atlantic to the New World with the colonists as political baggage. These settlers regarded themselves simply as transplanted Englishmen.

TRANSPLANTED ENGLISHMEN

Not long after their arrival in America the colonists realized the necessity for forming some kind of government. Problems occurred as the settlements struggled to cope with unforeseen difficulties that required a formal decision-making process to resolve them. Guidance from England, except in broad generalities, was impossible because of the time required for a ship to cross the Atlantic. Besides, England was too caught up in her own political and religious problems to give her colonies firm instructions or govern them as closely as Spain did her empire.

The Virginia Company, which had been chartered by the king to colonize part of North America for the Crown, was having its own troubles. Regimented and forced to work for seven years as company laborers, the settlers had no personal incentive to make the colony more than a limited success. At the outset, a governor and his council chosen by the Company ruled Virginia. In 1619, however, the governor suggested that they "might have a handle in the governing of themselves." Virginians would be allowed to form a House of Burgesses in free elections, and to act with the governor and his council in making laws. America's first representative legislature was created mostly in the hope that giving the colonists some political participation would, together with offering land grants, stimulate them to raise Virginia's profits. For more than 20 years the House of Burgesses convened in dubious legality until 1639, when the King of England authorized its annual meetings. Americans had taken their first step in securing home rule.

In New England events took a different turn from the beginning. Before the Pilgrims had left Holland in 1619 to form a religious colony in America, they secured a promise from England's king that he would not "molest" them in their new land. They arrived in the New World far to the north of other English settlements. When they realized they were on their own, they drew up the Mayflower Compact, agreeing to "combine ourselves together into a civil Body Politick" to make "just and equal Laws . . . for the general Good of the Colony." After establishing the Plymouth Bay Colony, they created a government with an elected governor and assistants.

The Puritans who established themselves at Massachusetts Bay in 1629 north of Plymouth were not so democratically minded. They had set out to build a model religious community based on the Bible and God's will, a "City Upon a Hill," for their English brethren to emulate. Originally eight Puritan "freemen" or leaders claimed all political power for themselves as "God's elite" and, in consultation with the clergy, ruled the settlement. But soon the other members of the Puritan church's congregation demanded "freeman" status and a voice in their government. They were granted the authority to form a General Court, whose delegates would be elected from every town in the colony, and the power to elect Magistrates (several men who acted as supreme justices in the General Court). But the Magistrates still retained the ultimate power of vetoing General Court measures and deciding matters of law. In Governor John Winthrop's view, the Magistrates were "gods upon earth" and were to act as God's "vice-regents" in keeping the community within His will. Practically speaking, however, each New England village handled most of its own affairs through democratic "town meetings." Puritan government was therefore a mixed democracy.

In fact, both the organizations that arose in New England and Virginia were mixed governments with elements of representative and aristocratic rule combined. Even colonies that were established after these first settlements had this mixed type of government with varying degrees of democracy. First Virginia, then New York and New Jersey became royal colonies and had their governors appointed by the Crown. Brief experiments in feudal systems, where a "lord" would manage huge estates tended by tenant "peasants," failed in Maryland and the Carolinas and these colonies eventually adopted governor-assembly political systems. Some colonies were more democratically minded than others. Rhode Island and Connecticut elected their governors as well as their assemblies.

But whatever the initial system, by 1700 all the American colonies except Georgia were operating under a governor-assembly form of government. By creating this type of political system, the colonists were actually copying in modified form the government they had left behind in England—self rule by gentry at the local level under the Parliament-King system. And like the parent Parliament, colonial assemblies quickly set about acquiring more political influence and power.

GROWTH OF COLONIAL DEMOCRACY

The most important factor that aided the assemblies in their quest for power was the easy availability of land. As in England, land or property was the requirement for voting in the American colonies. But in England land was scarce and voters less than 25 percent of the adult male population. In America land was there for the taking, consequently the number of people directly involved in the political process in the colonies was much greater. Though there were religious qualifications for voting in many of the colonies, few who met the property qualifications were denied suffrage unless they belonged to a particularly "notorious" sect. In colonial Massachusetts of the 1770s, for example, it has been estimated that as many as 80 percent of the province's adult white males were voters. The assemblies spoke for this large constituency, something that colonial governors could hardly ignore.

Originally, the appointed governors possessed broad powers. They could call the assembly to meet or adjourn it at any time, veto any legislation passed by the representative bodies, appoint and dismiss colonial officers, command the militia, and make grants of land. In Crown colonies, the governor was responsible to Parliament and to the King and had to send colonial legislation to England for final approval. Even in the self-governing colonies of Rhode Island and Connecticut where the governors were elected, they had most of the powers of appointed governors.

But governors had to depend upon the assembly for money to operate their colonies. Early in their existence, these representative bodies had demanded the exclusive power to tax, based upon the historic right of Parliament. Virginia's House of Burgesses did not allow the governor to "lay any taxes upon the colony, their land or commodities, otherwise than by the authoritie of the Grand Assembly." Massachusetts' assembly felt that it was not "safe" to pay taxes levied by the governor "for fear of bringing themselves and posterity into bondage." Before 1700 all of the colonial assemblies had won the exclusive power to tax. With this power, they gradually gained further political influence and authority in colonial government. The English Parliament refused to pass laws urged by the colonial governors to make the assemblies more subservient for fear that such laws would be used as precedents to limit Parliament's own authority. In addition, any English governor who wanted to rise to a more important post back in "civilized" London had to win good reports from the influential colonial representatives. Thus, American assemblies gradually grew in power until by the 1750s they could pass laws for their respective colonies, avoiding governors' vetoes and even on occasion direct orders from the King.

Colonial government was slowly transcending its English origins and evolving along independent lines. By undermining the governor's authority, the assemblies were weakening England's hold on her colonies, since it was through the royal governors and their appointed officials that Parliament and the Crown tried to rule. Colonists had taken the English privilege of local rule and made it into a right, overriding in many cases parliamentary "interference" in American affairs as if their assemblies were sovereign little parliaments within colonial territory. With its wider voting base, government in the colonies was far more democratic than its English counterpart, and the representative assembly came to be regarded as the legitimate lawmaking body in the colonies. Complained one Englishman, "The New England Governments are all formed on Republican Principles and those principles are zealously inculcated in the Minds of their Youth in opposition to the Principles of the Constitution of Great Britain." Another royal official wrote back to London arguing that "the authority of the Crown is not sufficiently supported against . . . a republican spirit in the people, whose extreme jealousy of any power not immediately derived from themselves" produced suspicion against royal authority.

THE EMPIRE ENFORCED

The British had encouraged this growing spirit and practice of local rule by their policy of "salutary neglect" toward their American colonies. This policy was born out of necessity. England had allowed private corporations and wealthy families wide latitude in settling North America for the Crown because the English government had neither the money nor the military power to colonize on its own. Even after most of the American colonies had been settled, the King was obliged to let them rule themselves within a general framework of restrictions and obligations

By the time that Patrick Henry gave his famous "Give me liberty or give me death" speech before the Virginia assembly on March 23, 1775, most of the colonial legislatures had wrested power from local crown-appointed officials. The firebrand from Virginia was not alone. As Parliament became more dictatorial, colonial resistance grew. (The Granger Collection.)

that were loosely enforced. England was convulsed by a civil war between 1640 and 1660, and even after the monarchy was restored, a new upheaval, the Glorious Revolution of 1688, occurred before stability returned. Only after England had dealt with its own religious and political problems could Parliament and the Crown turn to organizing the nation's growing empire. Gradually, Great Britain brought eight of the 13 American colonies under its direct control and enacted a series of commercial laws. These Navigation Acts were designed to tie colonies and mother country closer together economically. But divisions of opinion in English politics and the lack of an imperial bureaucracy to oversee the system, combined with a growing colonial tendency to resist controls, prevented it from being implemented.

This salutary neglect came to an end with the French and Indian War of 1754–1763. At the beginning of this war, London was careful not to arouse American hostility by directly taxing and drafting the colonists. Instead, the King called upon the assemblies to provide quotas of supplies and soldiers, even footing the bill for most military expenses the colonies incurred. After the conflict was over the British government was faced with a staggering debt. Since England had fought for her empire, it seemed only fair to government decision makers that the colonies share part of the costs of imperial administration and yield more benefits to the mother country. In this frame of mind, Parliament passed laws to eliminate illegal trade between the colonies and the foreign West Indies, and applied new duties and taxes to the colonies to raise revenue. Troops were to be stationed in the provinces to keep order and prevent Indian troubles, naval vessels would patrol the coasts to catch smugglers, and more efficient tax-collecting methods would be instituted. Admiralty courts would condemn violators without a jury trial, and blanket search warrants called "writs" would permit customs officials to search suspicious premises anywhere, at any time, for anything illegal. Great Britain was determined to centralize control of her empire and run it at a greater profit.

Most of this imperial program was not new—its principles and even some of its specific measures had been embodied in the old series of commercial laws that were issued beginning in 1651. But the difference was that the new laws were being strictly enforced; salutary neglect was over. For the colonists, who had been used to running their own affairs under the old, lax system, the change in policy was jarring. Economically, the new system intensified a recession brought on at the war's end by taking more money out of the colonies. It also struck the profitable smuggling trade (not considered "criminal" in America) of many merchants and imposed new taxes on planters already burdened with debts. Politically, it meant that the colonists' cherished "right" of local rule through representative assemblies was being replaced by centralized control from London. In the decade after 1763, commercial laws including new taxes were enacted by a Parliament in which Americans had no representative and no elected voice to speak for their interests. This was directly contrary to what the colonists regarded as their "rights as Englishmen," and they were determined to resist any encroachments upon those rights.

REVOLUTION

Opposition movements sprang up throughout the colonies against the new imperial system. Even those who did not participate in the general uproar and who felt bound by Parliament's measures resented the British attitude. "It piques my pride," wrote one such colonist on a visit to England, "to hear us called 'our colonies, our plantations,' in such terms and with such airs as if our property and persons were absolutely theirs. . . ." Americans who joined the outcry against the new taxes were more than "piqued." In Virginia, representative Patrick Henry labeled King George III a tyrant, and pamphlets approved by the House of Burgesses declared that anyone supporting Parliament's right to tax Virginians "shall be deemed an Enemy to this his Majesty's Colony." The royal governor of Massachusetts had his home burned to the ground. Delegates from nine colonies sent a letter to the King maintaining that since Americans were not represented in Parliament "no Taxes ever have been, or can be Constitutionally imposed upon them, but by their respective Legislature." New England merchants even organized a group of their fellows in 1765 and convinced them not to import any manufactured goods from England.

Faced with this widespread resistance and pressure from British merchants stifled by the boycott, Parliament repealed most of the tax laws, including the controversial Stamp Act of 1765 which had required colonists to buy special stamps for all newspapers and legal documents. However, it refuted the colonists' "no taxation without representation" argument by affirming its "full power to bind the colonies . . . in all cases whatsoever." Desperate for revenue but hoping to pacify the colonies, the new Townshend administration won passage of a new series of acts in 1767 that taxed colonial imports, an indirect tax hopefully less objectionable to the Americans.

That hope was ill-founded. Once again the colonies exploded in anger and resistance. Mobs assaulted British troops in New York. In Boston, citizen-soldier antagonism exploded into violence and several civilians were shot in a brawl later labeled the "Boston Massacre" by revolutionary propagandists. Britain directed the governors of Massachusetts, Virginia, and New York to dissolve their colonial assemblies that were refusing to cooperate with parliamentary orders. Actually, the meager amount of money collected under the taxes was not worth the trouble. For the second time, in 1770, Parliament repealed its own measures except for a single tax on tea. Since the tax was avoidable, the colonists didn't mind. But another British ministry got into trouble in 1773 when it tried to help the near-bankrupt East India Company by requiring the colonies to buy the company's tea and pay the tax.

The American temper, which had been quiet during the three-year lull between repeal of the old taxes and passage of the Tea Act, flared up almost overnight. "Committees of Correspondence," small groups of American radicals working for revolt, fanned the flames. New York and Philadelphia sent the tea shipments back to Britain as soon as they arrived. Charleston locked it up in a warehouse. In Boston, where the governor appeared determined to force the tax's acceptance, patriots disguised as Indians boarded the ships and dumped the tea into Boston harbor. The "Boston Tea Party" evoked "great Wrath" in Britain and resulted in the passage of the Intolerable Acts in 1774. Boston harbor was closed by naval blockade, army troops were sent and

When Boston radicals, influenced by the rhetoric of Sam Adams, boarded three British ships in the town harbor and dumped more than 300 chests of tea overboard, England's reaction was one of outrage. Parliament responded with the Intolerable Acts, which precipitated the Revolution. It is ironic that these men of principle found it convenient to disguise themselves as Indians in their illegal act. (Courtesy of Brown Brothers.)

housed in private buildings, town meetings were banned, and British General Horatio Gates was given practically unlimited authority.

This move against Boston was seen throughout the colonies as striking at "the liberty of all Americans." Revolutionary tracts written at this time indicate that many colonists felt that there was a conspiracy afoot in London to deprive them of their accustomed liberties and even their rights as Englishmen. The treatment of Boston, a city under martial law, and the act of stripping Massachusetts of her representative institutions seemed to indicate a "plot," though today it is apparent that none existed. Since all the colonies had in some manner defied parliamentary authority, many provincials feared that they might share Boston's fate. Every colony except Georgia sent delegates to a Continental Congress that gathered in Philadelphia on September 5, 1774 to decide on a common position and present a united front to Great Britain. Revolution still seemed too extreme—even George Washington was satisfied that independence was not "desired by any thinking man in all North America." The delegates finally agreed not to import goods from England nor export any materials and called upon local underground committees to expose violators as "enemies of American liberty." An "olive branch" petition professing loyalty and asking George III to overrule his ministers was sent off and the congress adjourned, deciding to meet again in May 1775. But before that letter ever reached London, the King had determined that "Blows must decide." On April 19, 1775, British troops out of Boston on a mission to destroy illegal caches of gunpowder and arms ran into some local "Minutemen" who had been secretly training to fight just such a move. At Lexington someone fired a shot, and after an exchange of gunfire eight Americans were dead. The War for Independence had begun.

The final break between Great Britain and her American colonies came mainly because the Americans were not interested in the British goal of creating a more efficient empire, particularly at the cost of their democratically based representative form of "home rule." Politically, socially, and economically, Americans had outgrown the subordinate position England attempted to force upon them after years of local self-rule. Americans no longer saw their interests as identical with English concerns and, rather than submit to outside measures, they determined to fight to preserve their rights.

FIRST GOVERNMENT

Though the armed clashes at Lexington and Concord meant war, Americans were reluctant to finalize the break with England. Delegates of the Continental Congress met again in May and asked the King for redress of American grievances. They protested that only in "defence of the freedom that is our birthright . . . against violence actually offered" had Americans resorted to arms. But the King labeled the "rebels" as "desperate Traitors" and announced Britain's determination to suppress the American "rebellion." The struggle wore on and the costs in lives and property mounted. It divided Americans themselves into opposing camps of Loyalist and Patriot, the former retaining their allegiance to the Crown. England's use of the Loyalists, Indians, slaves, and German mercenaries against her former countrymen angered the patriots and deepened the split. With no British concessions forthcoming, the Continental Congress took hesitant steps toward independence and sought French aid. Thomas Paine's pamphlet *Common Sense* helped to convince many Americans that a complete separation from the mother country was the only solution. Finally, the Congress decided to make the break and issued a Declaration of Independence on July 4, 1776, resolving that "these United Colonies are, and, of right, ought to be free and independent states." Ironically, much of the rationale for independence came from John Locke, an English political philosopher who wrote to justify England's rebellion against her own King nearly a century earlier. In the Glorious Revolution of 1688, Locke had argued that when government is no longer responsive to the people, they have the right to overthrow it and establish a new one that would be more responsive to their needs. This idea became popular during the eighteenth-century Enlightenment, and offered a convenient justification for Thomas Jefferson when he wrote the Declaration of Independence to explain America's rebellion.

The newly "free and independent states" now had to form governments to take the place of those they had as colonies. Essentially, the states retained the same governmental structure—a two-house legislature and a governor to act as executive. Only now the upper house was elected instead of appointed by the governor, and the governor himself was carefully circumscribed in his powers and either chosen by the legislature or directly elected. Every state drew up a constitution and a bill of rights that confirmed the principles of democratic government and representative institutions. Qualifications for voting and holding office were essentially the same as in the colonial period, with such low property-holding requirements that most white males over 21 could vote and were eligible to hold office. Most important, the constitutions formed a supreme law that no single branch of the government could alter as Parliament continually did in England.

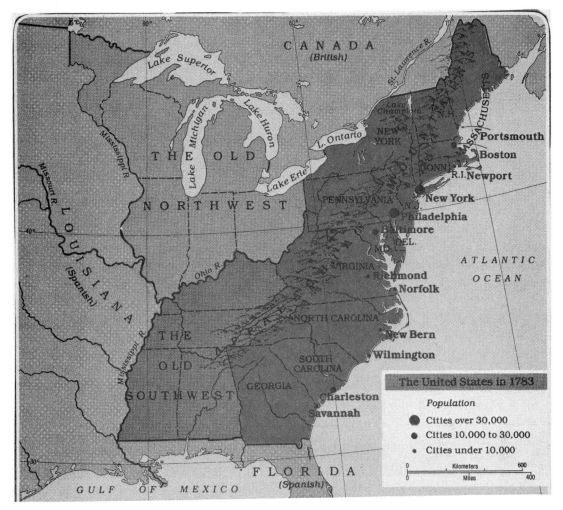

By the Treaty of Paris (1783), the original 13 United States gained vast lands west of the Appalachians to the Mississippi River.

Formation of a loose national government followed along these same lines—close adherence to colonial forms with an eye to preventing any one governmental organ from abusing its power. More than a year after proclaiming American independence in 1776, the Continental Congress finished drafting a plan called the Articles of Confederation. Basically, the Articles legally established the temporary system under which the Americans had been fighting for a year. Congress was empowered to wage war, conduct foreign relations, and raise and borrow money. For troops and taxes it had to depend on the states, which retained the powers of regulating trade and levying taxes. There was no president except the presiding officer of Congress—executive powers were divided between the states and the Congress itself. Under this government the American states won French aid, solved the frustrating problem of financing the war, and fought it to a successful conclusion. Shortly after the struggle ended, Congress managed to convince the states to yield their western lands to the national government, and the Land Ordinances were enacted to promote western settlement and bring the territories into the Union as new states.

A NATIONAL CONSTITUTION

Weaknesses in the Articles of Confederation soon became apparent to many, however. The American states were united only in name; in practice, each preferred to act largely without regard for the consequences to neighboring states or the national government. Without the power to tax or to regulate interstate commerce, Congress had difficulty trying to repay money it had borrowed during the Revolution and difficulty attempting to negotiate new commercial treaties with other nations. The economy had slumped into a post-war depression because of a lack of hard currency and the careless money policies of various states. Congress was also unable to counter Spanish attempts to weaken American settlements in the old Southwest. Neither could the government force the British out of forts along the Great Lakes area that were supposed to have been turned over to the United States after the Revolution. Knowing that Congress could not depend upon the states for support, these foreign nations simply ignored America's diplomatic representatives. One frustrated delegate complained that the national government was "responsible for everything, and able to do nothing."

Two groups of Americans sought to alter this predicament by giving the government more power. One group was composed largely of merchants, businessmen, a few planters, and other large landholders who were discouraged by the economic slump and by the barriers to interstate trade created by conflicting state policies. These men also deplored Congress's inability to negotiate new commercial treaties to offset the loss of trading privileges held when America was part of the British Empire. The other group consisted of Revolutionary leaders in politics and war, men who had worked for the creation of a truly national government during the War for Independence. These nationalists were alarmed at the indecisive way in which Congress had reacted to a rebellion in western Massachusetts by debt-ridden farmers under Daniel Shays in 1786 and at the complete lack of respect America commanded abroad. One of them remarked that there was "something . . . contemptible in the prospect of a number of petty states, with only the appearance of union . . . weak and insignificant in the eyes of other nations." These two groups had many members in common, and late in 1786 they began to work for revision of the Articles to strengthen the national government.

After several false starts, a convention was called to meet in Philadelphia in May of 1787 with the purpose of "revising" the Articles of Confederation. Delegates from all the states but Rhode Island attended. The representatives were nearly all nationalists; a majority had college degrees (uncommon in the eighteenth century), and it is safe to say that no abler or more intelligent body of Americans has ever been gathered together under one roof. It quickly became apparent that the Articles were doomed. No one even submitted a proposal for retaining the current structure of government, the prime consideration being that it would be impossible to gain the unanimous approval of all states required by the Articles for any amendments. The convention then turned to the task of constructing a completely new

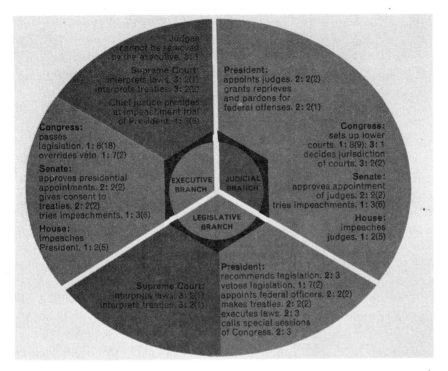

Power in the new national government was distributed in such a way as to prevent any single branch from dominating the whole. Each branch could check the authority of the others.

constitution, one that would embody a more powerful and centralized national government within a representative framework. Though most members were acquainted with political theory, they chose to concentrate on precedent. "Experience must be our only guide," warned one delegate, "Reason may mislead us." Debates, discussions, and arguments followed as the delegates sought to protect the interests of their states and reconcile their ideas on the forms and powers the new government should assume. James Madison played a key role in guiding the convention toward a balanced national government.

The final result was a Constitution that was a "compact of compromises." Northerners reluctantly agreed to allow slaves to count for "three-fifths of a person" to boost southern representation in the new House of Representatives. Small states insisted they have equal representation, so big states agreed to do so in the new Senate. Business interests won a uniform currency and trade rules, while agrarian interests won protection of their exports from taxes. The Constitution's outstanding feature was a balance of powers: between the states and the new federal government, between the three branches of the national government itself, and between democracy and aristocracy. The new federal government would have the power to bind the states in matters of taxation, regulation of commerce, treaties, and war, but the individual states retained significant powers of their own. Within the national government the legislative (Congress), executive (office of President), and judicial (Supreme Court) branches were given different powers and responsibilities that both helped prevent any one from becoming dominant and required cooperation. Delegates who were fearful of "too much democracy" were satisfied with the indirect election of Senators (by state legislatures) and the President (by an electoral college). Others wary of a government too far removed from "the people" contented themselves with the direct election of Representatives and the device of impeachment.

Few of the delegates were entirely happy with their creation, and several refused to endorse the document because it was not exactly what they thought it should be. On many points—the exact powers of the Presidency, the precise line between federal and state authority—the Constitution was vague. This would be the cause of furious constitutional debates in the future, but it would also give the document a flexibility needed to meet changing conditions later generations would face. On one detail the Constitution was crystal clear. It was the "supreme law" of the land and derived its authority directly from "We, the People of the United States." Most of the Philadelphia delegates did sign the completed document. Perhaps their feelings were best summed up by Benjamin Franklin: "Thus I consent . . . because I expect no better, and because I am not sure that it is not the best."

Now the nationalists launched an aggressive campaign to convince the nation to adopt this new Constitution. Widening their support by trying to bring in all Americans who were in some way dissatisfied with government under the Articles, they concentrated on the state conventions that had to ratify the Constitution. They adopted the name "Federalists," since "nationalists" frightened many Americans concerned with states rights. "Anti-federalists" opposed ratifying the Constitution, fearing that it gave too much power to the central government and would threaten individual liberties. The Federalists countered the latter argument by promising to enact a bill of rights that would protect the people's traditional liberties. Three of them (Alexander Hamilton, John Jay, and James Madison) wrote *The Federalist Papers,* arguing in New York's newspapers that the Constitution provided exactly the right balance of authority and freedom that Americans needed. Though frequently in a majority when state conventions met, the antifederalists lost ground through poor organization and the lack of an alternative to the Constitution. The Federalists emerged as the victors. By 1789, all of the states had approved the Constitution except Rhode Island (which joined in 1790). The United States had a new national government.

HAMILTON, JEFFERSON, AND POLITICAL PARTIES

The Federalists had no problem securing the Presidency for their candidate George Washington. He was nearly everyone's choice. Washington was not a brilliant or daringly original man, but as General of the Armies during the Revolution his patience, impeccable character, and patriotic determination to build a strong America had made him the country's most admired and best known figure. He was well aware as he took office that his administration was the "first of everything," and that its actions would "serve to establish a Precedent" for the conduct of future administrations.

Washington also knew that above all else the new government had to establish its authority and stability by dealing firmly with the problems that Congress under the Articles had been unable to solve. Encouragingly, both the House of Representatives and the Senate were firmly in Federalist control, and the President had many men skilled in political affairs within his administration. However, differences soon arose not only with the antifederalists but even within the Federalists' own ranks.

The first clashes came over Alexander Hamilton's economic program for the nation. Hamilton had been Washington's aide during the Revolution and now headed the Treasury Department. He believed that the only way to secure the stability and future development of the country was to build a strong central government. Such a government would build prosperity at home and respect abroad. Hamilton proposed that the central government assume all state and national debts, create a national bank, protect manufactures with higher tariffs, and pass new taxes. Hamilton's proposal would establish American credit (and credibility) abroad by paying off the foreign debt incurred during the Revolution. It would also attract the support of wealthy men for the government by creating conditions favorable to prosperity. Since this program required the use of powers that the Constitution only implied, Hamilton and his following tended to interpret that document broadly.

Secretary of State Thomas Jefferson and Congressman James Madison disagreed. They saw that Hamilton's program was slanted toward merchants and businessmen at the expense of farmers. Madison fought government assumption of debts because it would favor the northern states (which still owed large sums) over the southern states (which had largely paid theirs). Jefferson entered the fray over the bank issue. He observed that the Constitution gave Congress no power to create a national bank, and warned that to "take a single step beyond the boundaries . . . specially drawn around the powers of Congress is to take possession of a boundless field of power, no longer susceptible of any definition." Around Madison and Jefferson gathered a group of antifederalists and former Federalists determined to oppose Hamilton's policies.

Gradually, these interests began to coalesce into two political parties. Hamilton and the Federalists (chiefly northern merchants, businessmen, and wealthier tradesmen) worked to promote their commercial interests and to augment the power of the national government. The followers of Madison and Jefferson, calling themselves "Democratic-Republicans," were generally planters, small farmers, or craftsmen. They felt that the Federalists discriminated against agrarian interests, and feared that the trend toward a more powerful central government with aristocratic overtones threatened individual liberties and the very principle of democratic government.

Neither the Democratic-Republicans nor the Federalists particularly liked the idea of political parties. Federalists in particular feared the growth of "factions" as enemies of national unity, and Washington branded party spirit as the "worst enemy" of popular government. Jefferson once remarked that "If I could not go to Heaven but with a party, I would not go there at all." Increasingly, however, the Federalists regarded themselves as the champions of order and national unity, seeing the Democratic-Republicans as conspirators against the government. The Democratic-Republicans in turn felt obliged to oppose what they considered discrimination against agrarian interests and threats to democratic government and liberty. They regarded themselves as a loyal opposition. By 1792, party spirit was strong and Republicans and Federalists had already begun to organize along national lines.

THE REVOLUTION OF 1800

As a new group just formed, the Democratic-Republicans had a good deal more organizing to do than the already well-established Federalists. Madison began rallying a Congressional opposition and joined Jefferson in creating a pro-Republican press. But Washington's popularity was so great that the Republicans did not oppose his reelection in 1792. Jefferson finally decided to quit Washington's administration as the President's attitudes hardened and became more identified with the Federalists. Party lines continued to stiffen over a new issue—foreign policy.

When the French Revolution began in 1789 it was hailed throughout the United States as a triumph of republicanism over monarchy. But when the revolt in France took a radical and violent turn, denouncing all religion and executing many leading citizens, Federalists were horrified. War broke out between Great Britain and France and threatened to involve the United States as well. Both Hamilton and Jefferson counseled Washington to declare neutrality despite America's treaty of alliance with France dating back to the American Revolution. Jefferson and the Democratic-Republicans, however, generally admired France and wanted American policy to remain friendly to Paris. Hamilton and the Federalists, who feared French radicals and considered the British government a model of strength and order, were determined to stay on good terms with England at any cost. They sent John Jay to London to work out Anglo-American problems that were straining relations between the two nations. Jay returned with a treaty that essentially capitulated to the British position and aroused furious opposition from the Democratic-Republicans and much of the country. Jay's treaty was barely approved.

This was an issue that the Democratic-Republicans could bring before the voters. With Washington retiring, they felt Federalist candidate John Adams was vulnerable. The election of 1796 was close, but Adams just managed to edge out Jefferson for the Presidency. Once in office Adams was faced with a foreign policy crisis. France regarded the Jay Treaty as a violation of America's earlier treaty with her and began seizing United States vessels that traded in the British West Indies. A peace commission sent by Adams to Paris was greeted with demands for bribes and treated with near contempt. When these French actions were made known to the nation, a public uproar followed that catapulted President Adams and the Federalists to new heights of popularity. From 1797 to 1800, an undeclared war raged on the high seas between France and the United States.

Many Federalists took this opportunity to call for legislation that would muzzle their Democratic-Republican critics, whom they considered "a great body of domestic traitors." In 1798, the Federalist-dominated Congress passed the Alien and Sedition Acts that provided for strict control and supervision of "enemy" aliens, and a fine and imprisonment for anyone who published "false, scandalous, and malicious writing" against the federal government. Under this law, four out of five of the editors of leading Democratic-Republican papers were convicted. Alexander Hamilton, still a power in Federalist circles, won authority to head a large army that he hoped to use against republican critics. But the Democratic-Republicans refused to be intimidated. Madison and Jefferson authored the Kentucky and Virginia Resolutions that maintained that the national government had assumed "undelegated powers" and therefore the states had a "duty" to prevent the government from exercising those powers in its territory. This became

THE SUPREME COURT:
DECISIONS THAT STRENGTHENED THE GOVERNMENT

Chief Justice John Marshall, a Federalist and a champion of a strong central government, led the Supreme Court to make a number of decisions that greatly strengthened the authority of the Federal government and the Court itself.

Marbury vs. Madison (1803)

> The court granted itself the authority to decide on the constitutionality of a law passed by Congress, establishing the principle of "judicial review." This made the Supreme Court the final authority on what the Constitution said and what it meant.

Fletcher vs. Peck (1810)

> In this decision, the power of judicial review was extended to acts of state legislatures as well as Congress. This clearly established the authority of the Federal government over the states in questions of constitutionality.

McCulloch vs. Maryland (1819)

> A majority of the court decided that Congress could use its "implied powers" (Article 1, Section 8) to establish institutions and make laws "consistent with the spirit of the Constitution." This allowed the Federal government to deal with circumstances the Constitution did not explicitly speak to.

Cohens vs. Virginia (1821)

> The power of judicial review was extended to decisions of state courts, strengthening the authority of the Supreme Court over the state courts.

Gibbons vs. Ogden (1824)

> The court determined that Congress's power to regulate interstate commerce included the power to prevent states from granting monopolies to private companies. Besides strengthening free enterprise, the court had once again upheld the Federal government's power to intervene in state decisions.

---

the doctrine of "states' rights," maintaining that the Union was a compact of states and that each state had the power to nullify an unconstitutional act of the federal government.

Each party strongly believed that it had to win the election of 1800 to "save the country" from the other. But the Federalists had weakened themselves by dividing over President Adams' decision to end the undeclared war. They were also unpopular because of the Alien and Sedition Acts and the high taxes necessary to support a larger army and navy. Jefferson took advantage of this by promising to repeal the repressive acts, limit the power of the national government, and reduce its operating expenses. Emotions were high—Federalists insisted that a Jefferson victory would lead to a "reign of terror" like that which shook France, while Democratic-Republicans drilled militia to "protect American rights." The Democratic-Republicans swept the election, but

THOMAS JEFFERSON

Thomas Jefferson was born into the Virginia gentry in 1743 and inherited 2,750 acres of land at 14 years of age. While looking after his plantation, he studied law at William and Mary College, poring over his books fifteen hours a day. He later taught himself architecture and built Monticello, filling it with innovations like a dumbwaiter, a calendar-clock and one of the finest libraries in the colonies.

Elected to the House of Burgesses, Jefferson was an early opponent of Parliament's measures. He was appointed a delegate to the Second Continental Congress in 1775, where he drafted the Declaration of Independence as a ringing explanation of American actions.

Returning to Virginia (Jefferson called it "my country"), he wrote and passed the Statue for Religious Freedom and supported free public education. Jefferson was critical of slavery, though a slave-holder himself, and at one point suggested that sons of slaves should be born free. He loved his life at Monticello and was one of the first Americans to practice contour plowing and crop rotation. But the death of his wife Martha caused him to occupy himself with public life once again.

Jefferson spent five years abroad as United States ambassador to France before returning to his homeland to serve President Washington as Secretary of State. He resigned in 1793 in opposition to Washington's increasingly Federalist policies. Running in opposition to John Adams in the election of 1796, he won the Vice Presidency as runner up (the election laws have since been changed). In the next election he beat Adams and became President. After his presidency he founded the University of Virginia before he died on July 4th, 1826.

Presidential candidate Jefferson and Vice-presidential candidate Aaron Burr received the same number of electoral votes. In such cases, election laws required that Congress decide who would be the next President. There the Federalists tried desperately to block Jefferson's victory by throwing their support to Burr. Only when several Federalists abstained for fear that a perpetual deadlock would cripple the country did Jefferson finally win.

The new Democratic-Republican President referred to his party's victory as the "Revolution of 1800." Although the changes it brought about were not quite revolutionary, important ones did occur. Most significantly, political parties and the principle of loyal opposition became established facts of the American political scene. A Democratic-Republican victory through the electoral process in a bitterly fought election had been accepted, and this meant that changes in the nation's course would be decided at the ballot box. The election also marked the beginning of a long decline into oblivion for the Federalist party, whose aristocratic image proved an insurmountable handicap. Political power had shifted from the Northeast to the South and West, where the Democratic-Republicans were strongest. As the Democratic-Republicans were more agrarian and democratically minded, their rise to power meant the ascendancy of expansive agricultural interests and a more democratic course for the national government.

ALEXANDER HAMILTON

Born the illegitimate son of a Scottish merchant in the British West Indies, Alexander Hamilton showed such promise that at 18 he was sent to King's College in New York for an education. A firm patriot, Hamilton wrote articles championing the American cause against Britain and caught the eye of George Washington. He became Washington's aide, and led a bold charge against the British in the Battle of Yorktown.

After the war he married into New York's elite and began a law practice. Soon he became involved in politics and, as a strong nationalist, was one of the first to call for a convention to write a new constitution. At the convention his ideas were so aristocratic that few of his fellow delegates would listen to him. But in the campaign to win approval for the new Constitution Hamilton wrote 50 of the Federalist essays that were critical to New York's ratification.

President Washington made Hamilton the nation's first Secretary of the Treasury, and the young genius used this position to strengthen the power of the federal government by tying the interests of the wealthy merchant class to it. His feud with Thomas Jefferson spilled over into the press and led to the start of political parties in America. Hamilton resigned his post in 1795, but continued to play a strong role in the Federalist party. He and John Adams vied for control of the party during Adams' presidency, splitting the Federalists. In the crucial election of 1800, when Hamilton's arch-enemy Jefferson was tied with his arch-New York rival Burr, Hamilton threw his support to the more principled Jefferson.

This was a fateful decision. Hamilton and Burr met once again in Burr's bid for the governorship of New York, and again Hamilton threw his influence against Burr. The angry Burr challenged him to a duel and, against his better judgment, Hamilton accepted. In the early morning of July II, 1804, the two met. Hamilton apparently fired into the air, but Burr's shot mortally wounded Hamilton and he died the following day.

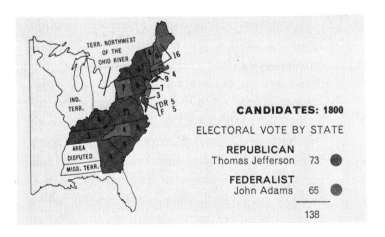

CANDIDATES: 1800

ELECTORAL VOTE BY STATE

REPUBLICAN
Thomas Jefferson 73

FEDERALIST
John Adams 65

138

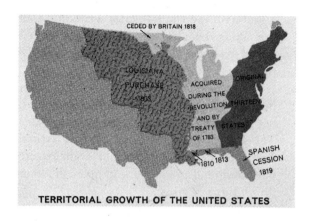

TERRITORIAL GROWTH OF THE UNITED STATES

DEMOCRATIC NATIONALISM

President Thomas Jefferson lost no time in charting such a course. He proposed a "wise and frugal government," and set about lowering taxes and reducing the national debt. Wishing to leave men free to "regulate their own pursuits," his administration generally tried to minimize the regulatory functions of the national government. Yet Jefferson also favored the "encouragement of agriculture and commerce as its handmaid." The Democratic-Republicans aided the westward movement by making it easier for settlers to claim land on the frontier and by sponsoring the explorations of Zebulon Pike and Lewis and Clark. Jefferson's administration also bought the Louisiana Territory from the French in 1803, despite constitutional scruples over its authority to do so. This purchase doubled the national domain and secured for American commerce a Mississippi outlet, the trading port of New Orleans.

The Democratic-Republican government also faced a dangerous dilemma. The factor that contributed most to American prosperity seemed at the same time to threaten the United States with war. After a short peace, Great Britain and France had gone to war again in 1803. At first, the increased demand for neutral vessels to carry goods normally shipped by the belligerents brought a meteoric rise in American commerce on the high seas. As the European conflict intensified, however, both Britain and France began to resent the Americans, who were growing rich by trading with both sides. They began seizing United States ships and cargoes in violation of American neutral rights, and Britain even forced some American seamen to serve in its navy. Jefferson and later Madison used all their power to boycott trade with the belligerents, hoping to get them to respect United States rights. But despite coercive efforts that dwarfed those of the Alien and Sedition acts, the measures failed. America finally went to war with Britain in 1812 when France seemingly offered concessions that London refused to match.

Though the United States came close to losing the War of 1812, Americans were proud of having stood up to the world's greatest power. A new sense of nationalism swept the country, dooming the Federalist party, which had opposed the war. The Democratic-Republicans emerged from the conflict to win an overwhelming victory in the elections of 1816—so overwhelming that for the next eight years they were virtually unopposed. In the new spirit of nationalism, they increased efforts to settle the West, develop natural resources, and become economically independent of Great Britain. The national bank was recreated, tariffs or taxes were imposed on imports in order to protect American industry, and internal improvements (roads, canals) were encouraged by the government. In a few cases, such as the National Highway and harbor improvements, the government even sponsored such efforts. With his victory in 1816, President Monroe conducted a national goodwill tour that helped unite the country and inaugurate what one newspaper called the "era of good feelings."

Although Monroe was reelected in 1820, the "good feelings" were fast disappearing. The Panic of 1819, a financial crisis and economic depression, created voter dissatisfaction. Sectional differences had become more apparent over the issues of slavery and regional power in Congress during the debate over Missouri's entry into the Union in 1820. The Missouri Compromise maintained the balance between free and slave states and drew a line west at $36° 30'$. Territories north of the line would be free; those to the south would be slave. The Republicans were also on the verge of a split. Many party members were tired of the "Virginia Dynasty" that had ruled the nation for more than 20 years, and the party organization could no longer command the allegiance of other ambitious leaders determined to win the Presidency for themselves and their following by appealing directly to the people.

JACKSON AND THE "COMMON MAN"

This Republican splintering surfaced in the election of 1824. Four candidates, all with their own groups of supporters, ran for President. No one was able to win a majority of the electoral votes and the decision went to the House of Representatives. Andrew Jackson, whose victory at the Battle of New Orleans had made him a national hero, expected victory since he had won the most popular and electoral votes. But another candidate, Henry Clay, threw his support to Jackson's rival, John Quincy Adams, and Adams was chosen President. When Adams selected Clay to be his Secretary of State, Jackson and his followers accused the two of making a "corrupt bargain" and withdrew their support from the new President's administration. Adams found every move he made, even his forward-looking program of internal developments, blocked or frustrated. Referring to this program, Adams lamented that "the system of internal improvements by national energies. . . . The great object of my life . . . has failed."

He was also about to lose the presidency to his archenemy, Andrew Jackson. Ever since his defeat in 1824, Jackson had been building support for a new effort in 1828. His standing as an heroic national figure helped him greatly, especially since almost all of the states now allowed adult white males to vote directly for Presidential electors (for an explanation of the electoral system, see Article II Section I of the Constitution). He was identified with the aspirations of the common people, symbolizing the nationalistic, western, democratic mood of the nation. The new Democratic party formed around Jackson, attracting newspaper and political support. The election itself was one of the dirtiest in American history; Adams being accused of gross corruption and Jackson of murder and immorality. More voters than ever

ANDREW JACKSON

Andrew Jackson was born the son of a Scotch-Irish farmer in the backwoods of North Carolina in 1767. He was a bright boy, quick to fight, reckless, profane, interested mostly in fast horses and cockfights. At thirteen he fought in the Revolution and was taken prisoner. A British officer demanded Andy clean his boots, and when Andy refused the officer swung at him with his sword. Jackson never lost the scar or his hatred of the British.

Acquiring his law degree after the war, Jackson moved west to Tennessee and became public prosecutor. He boarded at a widow's house where he met the lady's attractive and unhappily married daughter, Rachael. When Rachael's husband began divorce proceedings, the two ran off and got married. At first the young marrieds lived comfortably on a small plantation and traded in horses, cotton, and slaves. But Jackson nearly went bankrupt because of unwise investments, and they found out that they had been married before Rachael's divorce had been finalized. Jackson fought several duels with those who made snide comments about his wife, in one case defeating the best shot in Tennessee by calmly letting his opponent fire first, taking the bullet inches from his heart, and then aiming carefully and killing him.

In 1802 the Tennessee militia elected him their commander while he was serving as a Superior Judge. Twelve years later he broke the Creek Indians at Horseshoe Bend. In 1815 he thrashed the British in the Battle of New Orleans, a victory made possible by the help of pirates who could handle cannon and a British frontal assault on his entrenched troops. When the war was over, he retired to build an estate, the Hermitage, on 640 acres of prime land. But Indian attacks from Spanish Florida caused President Monroe to give Jackson another military assignment—to take 2,000 men into Florida to punish the Indians. Jackson was overenthusiastic. He captured the Spanish towns of St. Marks and Pensacola, kicked out the Spanish governor, hung two British citizens whom he accused of aiding the Indians and then returned to the United States. Although controversial, his threat convinced the Spanish to yield Florida in the Adams-Onis Treaty of 1819.

By 1824 Jackson's friends had drafted him as a candidate for the White House, and he won a plurality of the electoral votes over his four rivals. But the House of Representatives chose John Quincy Adams as President in a questionable deal between Adams' and Clay's supporters. The nation cried "corrupt bargain," and a fighting mad Jackson began almost immediately to organize for the 1828 election. He and his friends built a new political party, the "Democrats," and opposed all of Adams' policies.

The election of 1828 was an overwhelming victory for Jackson as the "champion of the common man" but it was also one of the dirtiest in American history. He and Rachael were attacked in public as "immoral." Before Jackson was inaugurated, Rachael died—in part, friends said, because she could not stand the strain. At the inaugural celebrations Jackson appeared to have aged ten years and was in poor health. But his administration began the so-called "era of the common man"—the Age of Jackson.

---

before turned out at the polls, their new interest in politics encouraged by the Democratic party's emphasis on making Jackson's election a result of the "will of the People."

Jackson triumphed, and after the inauguration many "common men" followed him all the way to the White House to have a free-spirited party on the lawn. The victory destroyed the Republican party's hold on the country, restoring the nation to a competitive two-party system grounded in popular support. Jackson and his supporters had so successfully charac-

THE EVOLUTION OF POLITICAL PARTIES (1787–1854)

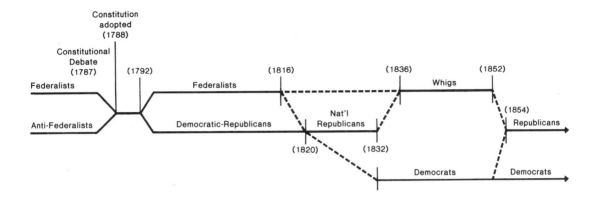

terized the election as a battle between the masses and the special interests that many people saw Jackson's election as *their* victory. The new President immediately set about "reforming" the government. He began the "spoils system," replacing old civil servants with fellow Democrats and insisting that he had a mandate to "kick the rascals out." His administration launched an attack upon the United States Bank, which the Democrats considered an aristocratic institution designed for the benefit of a few wealthy financiers. Throughout his two terms, Jackson attempted to offer "equal protection and equal benefits" to the masses and won the favor of small capitalists by passing a tariff that protected them from foreign competition and gave them a free hand from governmental regulation. But the popular emphasis on opportunity and prosperity excluded the Indians, whom the Jackson administration forced west of the Mississippi.

Parties now went to greater and greater lengths to win popularity through strong state organizations and careful cultivation of the voter. They instituted the national nominating convention and brought a circus-carnival atmosphere to American politics: mass meetings, parades and songs, party badges, and an even stronger emphasis on the candidate being a "man of the people." "Mudslinging" tried to destroy the reputation of the opposition, while the candidate was molded into the proper popular "image" for victory. The Democrats themselves were eventually "out-democrated" by a remnant of the old Republicans now reorganized as the Whigs.

Forces for reform were also building outside of politics. All across the country there were religious crusaders, humanists, militant prohibitionists, educators, and seekers after utopia proclaiming the need to transform American society into a model of perfection for the rest of the world. The drive for tax-supported public education began to gain acceptance in the northern states which embraced the motto "In a republic, ignorance is a crime." Reformer Dorothea Dix won better treatment for the mentally ill. Activists Elizabeth Stanton and Lucretia Mott and other women angry about discrimination against them convened a Women's Rights Convention in New York in 1848. Although they did not win their point at the time,

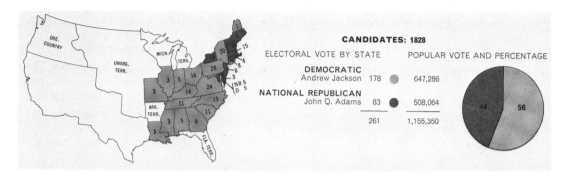

they did achieve the right to enter a few advanced schools on an equal basis, to control their own property in some western states, and to enter formerly closed professions. Counterculturalists like Henry David Thoreau emphasized a person's responsibility to be true to himself and his own conscience.[1] A few tried to establish "pilot" communities—small models carefully designed to be successful examples of the "good life." But most of these experiments failed after a few years.

Even as the reformers and communitarians moved to perfect American society, another force was beginning to tear the country in two. President Jackson's harrowing confrontation with South Carolina in 1832 over a state's right to nullify (declare void) a federal tariff indicated that sectionalism was coming to the fore again in American politics.

SECTIONALISM

This tendency of American politics to arrange itself along geographic lines was present early in the country's history. It arose chiefly out of regional differences in economics. The South, being dominated by the planter class, sought cheap imports to supply its need for manufactured or processed goods and protection for the slave labor system that was the backbone of its economy. The West, consisting mainly of small farmers, desired open markets for its crops and low taxes that would not eat away their meager profits. The North, largely controlled by the merchant classes, wanted a high protective tariff against competitive foreign goods and taxes which would support a national government strong enough to maintain a good climate for investment and growth. These areas had overlapping interests and frequently combined to gain their goals. Southern and Western representatives, with the common agrarian interest in expansion to gain more land, allied to vote for war in 1812 in the hopes of conquering

---

1   In his essay "Civil Disobedience," Thoreau insisted that people refuse to cooperate with official injustice, a principle later championed by the Reverend Martin Luther King, Jr. in the civil rights movements.

To gain the support of voters in the early nineteenth century—sometimes called the Age of the Common Man—the new parties led the way in campaign techniques that identified the candidate as "one of the people." (The New York Public Library Picture Collection.)

Canada and the Floridas. They were also eager supporters of President Jackson's policy of Indian removal.

These sectional alliances came and went, depending upon the issue. The North was frequently able to get Western support for tariffs by promising that some of the funds would go for transportation or communication improvements that would get their crops to market, and by appealing to the West's heady nationalism. Certain combinations proved to be turning points in the nation's political history. When the eastern seaboard states split over Hamiltonian policies

DIFFERENCES BETWEEN NORTH AND SOUTH

North

Becoming urban. Many large cities.
Much manufacturing, iron, textiles, farm machinery, shipbuilding, meat packing, milling flour.
Heavy immigration from Europe, starting with the Irish, settled in cities. Germans and Scandina-
   vians went to farms.
Railroad construction increasing. Connecting lines built over and around Appalachians.
Favored tariffs.
Wanted free land for small farmers.
Wanted a national banking system.
More people voted and took part in government.

South

Mostly rural. Only one large city—New Orleans.
Little manufacturing.
Very little immigration from Europe. Immigrants did not want to go there to compete with slave
   labor.
Little railroad building.
Opposed tariffs.
Wanted public lands sold for good prices
Opposed a national banking system.
Political power and wealth held by a small group.

that favored northeastern merchants and financiers, Southerners were able to elicit the help of Western states to win the election of 1800 and oust the Federalists. Jackson's own triumph in 1828 was due as much to the Democrats' ability to unite both the South and the West behind him as it was to the eastern workers' support.

But southerners quickly became disillusioned with President Jackson when he made it clear that they could not expect reduction of the currently high tariffs. South Carolina decided that its own rights and interests were being ignored, and invoked the doctrine of nullification by attempting to prohibit enforcement of the tariff law within its sovereign boundaries. This "states rights" doctrine, developed by Senator John C. Calhoun, had its roots in the Kentucky and Virginia Resolutions written by Jefferson and Madison to combat the repressive Alien and Sedition Acts. But it went further to insist that, as a last resort, a state might secede from the Union altogether. Jackson's position on this theory was unknown until he rose at a formal dinner and stared Calhoun straight in the eye, offering the toast, "Our Federal Union, it must be preserved!" Finding herself alone and threatened by an invasion of federal troops, South Carolina backed down. Calhoun, once a strong nationalist, now concentrated on building a sense of southern solidarity so that the whole region could act together more effectively against federal power when the next controversy erupted. The Democrats, their unity threatened, determined hereafter to avoid sectional issues, especially slavery. Jackson even put off accepting the prize of

Texas, which had wrested independence from Mexico and asked to join the Union as a slave state, because of the controversy within the party. That trial was coming, and it centered upon the very basis of Southern society and economy—slavery.

SLAVERY & ABOLITIONISM

American colonists justified the Revolution by asserting that "all men have inalienable rights of life, liberty, and the pursuit of happiness" and that "all men are created equal." Yet, in 1776, 539,000 African Americans were held as slaves, chattel property of white planters. Dr. Samuel Johnson, one of England's great writers, was troubled that patriots like George Washington, Thomas Jefferson, and James Madison cried out for American freedom while they themselves owned slaves: "Why is it that we hear the loudest yelps for freedom (in America) from the drivers of Negroes?" In private correspondence, Jefferson argued the impracticality of slavery, since no one whose labor was forced worked as efficiently as those who were paid for their labor. He believed that slavery would eventually be deemed immoral and would die out. Hence, Jefferson argued, there was no need to institute abolitionist reforms to legislate its extinction. That vision of the future would be denied, however, with the rise of King Cotton. Rather than disappear during the four decades prior to the Civil War, slavery would spread rapidly across the American South.

The period of slavery's expected decline witnessed in fact the years of its greatest expansion. The institution's dramatic growth was fueled largely by inventor Eli Whitney's cotton gin. Astronomical profits resulted from his machine which extracted the seeds from the precious lint, a task which formerly was the handwork of slaves. Whereas formerly it took one slave ten hours to produce a single pound of cotton lint, a cotton gin could process a thousand pounds daily. In 1790, one thousand tons of cotton were produced in the South. Seventy years later, annual production had soared to a million tons. During that same period, the slave population exploded from just over 500,000 to four million. The arable South was transformed into a landscape of cotton. The introduction of steamboats also stimulated the spread of slavery. The elaborate network of southern rivers including the Mississippi was now opened to upstream navigation. These river steamers also lowered transportation costs for southern planters. Whites used slave labor to clear and settle the vast cotton kingdom, extending from Georgia to the Mississippi delta, on to Louisiana, Arkansas, and eventually to eastern Texas.

During the 1820s, northern reformers (and a small number of southern planters) began to call for slavery's abolition. These early reformers, like the members of the American Colonization Society (ACS), emphasized gradual emancipation and colonization, arguing that blacks were "notoriously ignorant, degraded and miserable, mentally diseased (and) broken spirited." "Black removal" was the only means for preventing racial war in the North and inducing southern masters to free their slaves. The motto of the ACS was "We must save the Negro, or the Negro will ruin us." Joining the early abolitionist chorus was David Walker, a former slave and secondhand clothing dealer from Boston. His pamphlet *Appeal to the Colored Citizens of the World* (1829) addressed both races. To whites, he argued that any defense of slavery in the United States was shaken in theory by the American Revolution's principles of equality and the rights of man. Walker thundered: "See your Declaration (of Independence), Americans!!! Do you understand your own language?" His *Appeal* justified slave rebellion and warned white Americans that if justice were deferred, blacks would win their liberty "by the crushing arm of power." As Walker's incendiary tract circulated among black slaves in the deep South, special sessions of southern legislatures were convened to discuss this new threat. Southern mayors unsuccessfully petitioned the mayor of Boston to arrest Walker and confiscate and burn his literature. Yet, before he could be thwarted legally, Walker was silenced permanently. In 1830, he was found dead next to his shop.

These early warnings of black power stirred widespread fear of slave revolts. Yet, rebellions were rare during the 250-year history of American slavery. As early as 1800, Gabriel Prosser gathered a thousand fellow slaves armed with crude swords, guns, and knives in a plot to attack Richmond, Virginia. Under cover of night, the rebels would massacre the white inhabitants, seize the city's arsenal, and foment a general slave insurrection. However, two black informers betrayed the plotters and the governor of Virginia—a slave owner himself—called out hundreds of heavily-armed Virginia militiamen. Prosser and scores of his followers were captured and hanged under the governor's order. Another generation passed before the South faced the next attempt at slave insurrection. In 1822, Denmark Vesey, a free black in Charleston, South Carolina, planned a revolt involving 9,000 blacks in and around Charleston. Vesey hoped to burn Charleston, then the sixth-largest city in the United States. But, reminiscent of the Prosser rebellion, he never got the chance to put his uprising into motion. Word of the conspiracy leaked from one of the slaves and Vesey and his co-conspirators were arrested and executed. On the heels of Prosser and Vesey's aborted revolts, the South suffered Nat Turner's rebellion, the most notorious slave insurrection in the annals of American slavery. Turner had taught himself to read as a child. The young man's hatred for slavery intensified as he was forced to endure grueling field work and permanent separation from his wife. The self-styled mystic believed he was anointed to carry on Christ's agony in a war between slave masters and slaves. In August 1831, Turner led seventy slaves on a bloody house-to-house, plantation-to-plantation rampage through Southampton County, Virginia. Fifty-seven whites were slaughtered during the three-day rebellion. The insurrectionist eluded capture for two months before he was apprehended and hanged.

Fear of slave uprisings made discussion of emancipation less likely. Many southerners became increasingly defiant in their support of slave labor. They compared their beloved region to ancient Greece and Rome, proudly noting that those great civilizations had also embraced slavery. Southern writers like George Fitzhugh saw their society as a neo-classical culture. In *Cannibals All!* Fitzhugh contrasted the lives of poor northern whites, often unemployed and nearly starving, with the fate of southern slaves who, he claimed, were benevolently cared for by their owners. The southern apologist attacked the individualistic creed of northern society. He declared that while industrial workers were brutalized in factories and mines and reduced to "wage slavery," southern slavery was a paternalistic institution. As the South became entrenched in its defense of slavery, abolitionists realized that calls for gradual emancipation were futile. In the 1830s, a more uncompromising and radical abolitionist movement emerged, profoundly influenced by evangelical Christianity. This doctrine preached that salvation was not predetermined, but was a matter of personal choice; one can be saved if one repents one's sins and lives a moral life. These zealous abolitionists rejected gradualism and colonization, demanding the *immediate* abolition of slavery. They asserted that slave owners and their supporters were sinning by depriving slaves of their God-given rights of life and liberty. If slave owners did not repent, these Christian abolitionists believed, they faced the prospect of revolution in this world and damnation in the next.

One leader of this new aggressive abolitionism was William Lloyd Garrison, who demanded unconditional and uncompensated abolition. He insisted that every slaveholder, together with all those who condoned or merely acquiesced in slaveholding, was guilty of a personal sin against God and humanity. On January 1, 1831, Garrison published the first issue of his weekly antislavery newspaper *The Liberator* where he made his famous pledge:

> *I am aware that many object to the severity of my language; but is there not cause for severity? I will be as harsh as truth, and as uncompromising as justice. On this subject [slavery], I do not wish to think, to speak, or write, with moderation. No! No! Tell a man whose house is on fire to give a moderate alarm; tell him to moderately rescue his wife from the hands of the ravishers; tell the mother to gradually extricate her babe from the fire into which it has fallen; but urge me not to use moderation in a cause like the present! I am in earnest. I will not equivocate. I will not excuse. I will not retreat a single inch. AND I WILL BE HEARD.*

Disgusted with conservative abolitionists who advocated gradual, compensated emancipation, Garrison favored "immediatism," accepting no delay. He attacked the ACS, charging that it was an organization dedicated not to the principles of equality, but to ridding the nation of blacks. He savaged the United States Constitution for allowing the slave trade to continue for twenty years while the three-fifths proviso counted five slaves as equal to three whites in calculating southern states' congressional representation. Rather than reversing the nation's fabric of government, Garrison labeled the Constitution "a covenant with death and an agreement with Hell" because of its implicit acceptance of slavery.

This radical antislavery mood resulted in violence, including the martyrdom of abolitionist newspaper editor Elijah P. Lovejoy. Born in 1802 in Maine, Lovejoy was far removed from the hotbed of slavery in the South. Ordained as a Presbyterian minister, his Christian theology collided headlong with all defenses and apologies for slavery. In 1833, Lovejoy moved to St. Louis, in the slave state of Missouri, and began publishing an antislavery newspaper. Three years later, after being driven out of Missouri, Lovejoy set up his printing press in Alton, in the free state of Illinois where mobs destroyed his plant several times. But the persistent Lovejoy continued to publish abolitionist propaganda until 1837 when a pro-slavery mob sacked his office, shot him to death, and threw his printing press into the Mississippi River. Lovejoy's murder sent shock waves throughout the North and South with the news that a *white* man had been killed in the cause of abolitionism.

Frederick Douglass was a leading black abolitionist who demanded freedom and full rights for his people following the Civil War. © Bettmann/CORBIS

Antislavery newspapers were also published by African Americans, including Frederick Douglass's *North Star*. His anguish as a former slave caused him to reveal the evils of slavery as no white abolitionist could. His autobiography, *Narrative of Frederick Douglass* (1845), provides a penetrating analysis of ante-bellum American society. Douglass was a master of political and moral language, mixing religious and secular thought, very much like the writings of Abraham Lincoln. Like the Great Emancipator, Douglass also believed in a providential view of history, that the United States was a nation with a special destiny, though tainted by racism. In 1852, Douglass asked white Americans: "What, to the American slave, is your Fourth of July? I answer: A day that reveals to him, more than all other days in the year, the gross injustice and cruelty to which he is the constant victim. To him your celebration is a sham."

The antislavery movement recruited other blacks like Sojourner Truth, Harriet Tubman, and Henry Highland Garnet. Truth toured the North in advocacy of African American and feminist rights. Joining scores of women itinerant preachers, she addressed crowds regarding the Christian faith, the evils of slavery, and women's right to vote. Tubman, known as "the Moses of her people," escaped from slavery in Maryland in 1849 to begin her work on the underground railroad. She made nineteen clandestine trips to the South, helping hundreds of slaves to escape. When she was in the South, she always carried a pistol with her, explaining: "There was one of two things I had a right to, liberty or death. If I could not have one, I would have the other, for no man should take me alive." Tubman's eloquence was matched by that of Henry Garnet, a former slave and ordained Presbyterian minister. Like Garrison, Garnet condemned the Constitution as a pro-slav-

TERRITORIAL GROWTH OF THE UNITED STATES

ery document. In his famous *Address to Slaves* (delivered in Buffalo, New York in 1843), Reverend Garnet called for slaves to resist their oppressors, preferably by passive resistance such as slowing work or carrying out work stoppages, but if necessary by rising up and murdering their masters. In the address, Garnet declared: "Strike for your lives and liberties. Now is the day and hour. Let every slave in the land do this and the days of slavery are numbered. Rather die freemen than live to be slaves."

By the 1840s sectional differences were transcending the sphere of economics and entering the field of morality. The issue of abolitionism now overshadowed other reform crusades until it seemed the only reform issue. Other causes were dwarfed into insignificance and the "evil of bondage" monopolized attention. While it had been difficult enough to compromise and make adjustments for these differences within American politics when the issue was economic, it became even more difficult when the problem was couched in moral terms. Sectionalism, complicated by the slavery question, was threatening to make the American political system unworkable.

CONFRONTATION: THE SYSTEM TESTED

The acquisition of the Southwest in 1848 as a result of the Mexican War brought the issue of slavery to a head. As agrarian areas that needed new lands, the South and West had been the moving forces (aided in part by Northeastern merchants interested in Oregon and California as bases for Pacific commerce) behind the spirit of expansionism and "manifest destiny" that had swept the nation into war. Now the status of these western lands had to be determined. The southern slave interests wanted to extend the institution into the territories and open up vast lands for cotton cultivation. But western farming interests wished to make the area available to small farming settlers, hoping to exclude slaves both for moral reasons and because they feared planters would take most of the land. Southerners opposed this, realizing that if they did not gain at least half of the new states as slave states they would lose their equal voice in the Senate and be at the mercy of interests that were at best indifferent to them.

As the arm of government responsible for the territories, Congress tried various compromises. In 1850 California entered the Union as a free state, and a more stringent law requiring all escaped slaves to be returned to their owners was passed. The Democrats, with most of their support in the South and West, labored to hold their party together by approving the Compromise of 1850. But no one was satisfied. The Whig Party couldn't handle the issue and collapsed in the election of 1852. The Midwest, now closely tied to the Northeast by a system of canals and railroads that allowed a profitable exchange of produce and manufactured goods, increasingly identified its interests as northern. Abolitionists were finding a growing audience, and their cause received a great boost from Harriet Beecher Stowe's novel *Uncle Tom's Cabin,* an emotionally appealing attack on slavery that became immensely popular. In this atmosphere, laws requiring that fugitive slaves be returned to their owners seemed outrageously immoral and were subjected to widespread contempt. Many states even passed "Personal Liberty Laws" directly contrary to the federal ordinance.

An increasingly isolated minority, Southerners saw their society and institutions under continuing attack. They were incensed by the "criminal" resistance of the North against returning slaves they regarded as property rightfully theirs. These slave-holders fearfully recalled black uprisings like the one in Virginia led by Nat Turner in 1831 that slaughtered 60 whites, and they were angry at abolitionist propaganda that seemed to encourage slave unrest.

Growing hate and suspicion between the two sections made settling the question of slavery in the territories more difficult. Trying to get the divisive issue out of Congress and settle it by the time-honored method of majority rule, Democratic Senator Stephen Douglas proposed "popular sovereignty." Residents in new states would decide themselves whether to become "slave" or "free." His proposal was tried in Kansas and Nebraska after 1854. But "freesoilers" and slave-holders rushed into the area trying to gain a majority for themselves and control the decision, resulting in a bloody conflict that killed the compromise. "Bleeding Kansas" dominated the headlines. Even the Supreme Court failed to resolve the issue. When it ruled in the Dred Scott case that black slaves couldn't become citizens and, as property, could be taken anywhere in the Union, the North angrily ignored the decision. Tensions ran so high in Congress itself that one southern congressman, claiming an abolitionist senator had insulted a member of his family, beat the offending senator into unconsciousness.

In the North a new political party appeared in 1854 that based its platform on the principle that slavery should not be allowed to expand into the territories. Calling themselves "Republicans," they picked up many former Whigs and some northern Democrats tired of always deferring to the South. But Kansas had frightened the nation, and the pro-compromise Democrats beat the Republicans in the election of 1856. The Democrats, however, were paralyzed into inaction, and the Republicans gained in the congressional elections of 1858. By catering to northern economic desires for a high tariff, internal improvements, and a homesteading act offering free lands to western settlers, the new party became more popular in the North while being deemed the embodiment of folly and evil in the South.

Missouri Compromise 1820

■ Free States and Territories

■ Slave States and Territories

■ Maine. Admitted as a Free State, 1820

▨ Missouri. Admitted as a Slave State, 1821

Compromise of 1850

■ Free States and Territories

■ Slave States and Territories

■ Decision Left to Territory

Kansas-Nebraska Act 1854

■ Free States and Territories

▨ Slave States and Territories

■ Open to Slavery under Compromise of 1850

■ Open to Slavery under Kansas-Nebraska Act

These three great compromises ultimately failed to prevent civil war.

Emotions ran high in the Senate debates in May 1856 over the extension of slavery into Kansas. Southern Congressman Preston Brooks took abolitionist Senator Charles Sumner's incendiary two-day speech on the subject personally, and responded by beating Sumner into unconsciousness before his colleagues on the Senate floor. The fact that Brooks was made a hero in the South and Sumner a martyr in the North revealed the widening gap between the two sections. (The New York Public Library Picture Collection.)

POLARIZATION: THE SYSTEM FAILS

Differences between the two sections were now so great that it would only take a spark to set off an explosion of anger and resentment that would break the nation in two. John Brown's raid on Harper's Ferry in October of 1859, an attempt by an antislavery fanatic and his followers to establish a republic for blacks in western Virginia, convinced most Southerners that the welfare of their section was not safe in the Union. As the Presidential election of 1860 approached, Democrats convening in Charleston, South Carolina split over formation of a party platform. Southern Democrats broke away from their party to nominate their own candidate. Elated, the Republicans chose Abraham Lincoln as their standard-bearer (chiefly because he came from the Northwest and was not so prominent that he had many enemies) and identified themselves with northern economic interests and the increasingly popular stand of forbidding slavery in the territories. Although he did not win a majority of the popular vote, Lincoln carried all the Northern states and won enough electoral votes to be elected President.

Southerners were positive that the Republican victory meant that they would only meet further hostility and that their interests would be ignored if they remained in the Union. Well-organized, persuasive secessionists called "fire eaters" loudly called on their states to leave the Union—and they convinced most Southerners. South Carolina was the first to sever its ties with the national government, followed by six other southern states. They met and formed a new nation, the Confederate States of America. The Confederates proceeded to take

ABRAHAM LINCOLN

Abraham Lincoln grew up in Kentucky and southern Illinois where people were hard-drinking, hard-fighting Democrats. He stood out in this culture not only physically (he was well over six feet, homely, and ungainly) but socially—he was a staunch Whig, avoided alcohol and refused to shoot animals. Although Lincoln had almost no formal education and often appeared to be a classic "country hick," associates found him deeply intelligent and politically deft. As a young man he clerked and split logs for fences (he was very strong and became a champion wrestler), eventually practicing law and involving himself with politics.

Slavery, one of the major political issues of Lincoln's day, repelled him. He preferred not to take an abolitionist stand, however, but to limit slavery to the areas where it already existed and place it "in the course of ultimate extinction." Lincoln's attitude towards blacks was more complex. In a letter to a friend he wrote that if American leaders wished to rewrite the Declaration of Independence to read "all men are created equal except Negroes, and foreigners and Catholics" he would prefer to go to Russia, "where they make no pretence of loving liberty." But on another occasion he wrote that "there is a natural disgust in the minds of nearly all white people at the idea of an indiscriminate amalgamation (intermarriage) of the white and black men." Apparently, Lincoln felt that blacks should have economic opportunity and some political rights, but that they should remain socially separate.

Lincoln's political career had its ups and downs. He served only one term in the Congress because his strong stand against the Mexican War as a conspiracy to expand slavery was unpopular in Illinois.

He went back to his law practice in Springfield. But the passage of the Kansas-Nebraska Act in 1854 galvanized him back into political action. He was furious at the act's provision that might allow slavery's expansion even into territories in the west where it had previously been excluded. Lincoln was an organizer of the new Republican party and an early leader. In 1858 he ran against the popular Democrat Stephen Douglas for the U.S. Senate seat and met him in a series of debates. Lincoln's famous statement that "a house divided against itself cannot stand," that "this government cannot endure permanently half slave and half free" may have cost him the election. But he also forced Douglas to repudiate the Dred Scott decision, a move that lost the Democrat so much Southern support that his hopes for an 1860 presidential bid were ruined.

The debates gave Lincoln valuable national publicity, and when the Republican convention met to choose a nominee for president in 1860 Lincoln was their choice. After his victory over the divided Democrats, he sank a last minute compromise that might have averted civil war but would have allowed slavery to expand into the West. When he took the oath of office, troops patrolled the streets of Washington and guards watched from the capital building for potential assassins.

---

over all federal offices and military posts in the South. In Washington, congressional compromises floundered on the question of extending slavery into the territories. Determined to uphold federal authority, President Lincoln sent supplies to beleaguered Fort Sumter in Charleston harbor. Rather than allow them through and have the fort remain in control of the harbor, the Confederates forced the fort to surrender after bombarding it for two days. The Civil War had begun.

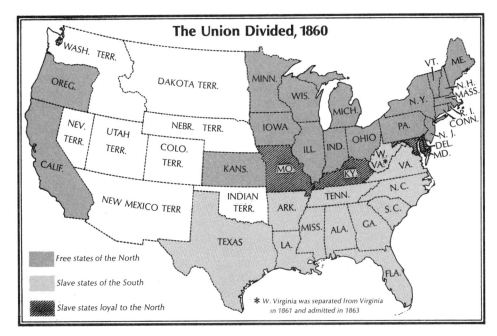

The North's large population and economic strength gave it a decisive edge over the Southern Confederacy in the protracted war that ensued. Because California and Oregon made no significant contribution to the war effort, they are not included in the accompanying graph. (Copyright © 1960, American Heritage Publishing Company, Inc. Reprinted by Permission from *The American Heritage Picture History of the Civil War* by Bruce Catton.)

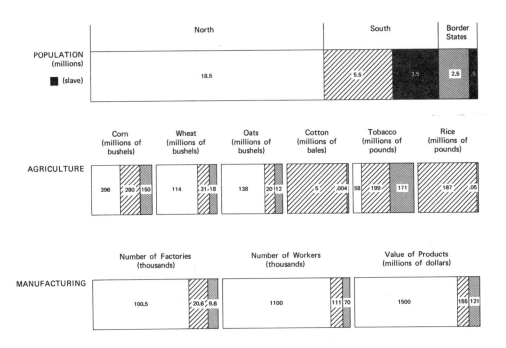

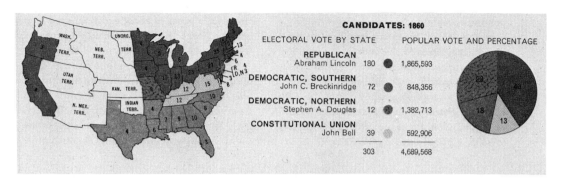

In one sense, the American political system had failed: Congress had not been able to find a formula for compromise, the Supreme Court had been ignored, and the President had not been able to manage the crisis. Even the old Whigs and Democrats had disintegrated instead of finding a way to resolve the issue of slavery's expansion. Finally, the last recourse of democracy, the decision at the ballot box, had been rejected by half the country. It was a costly failure—more Americans would die, and more damage would be done to the country, than in all of the nation's other wars combined.

The resources and will of the North prevailed. The question Lincoln raised at the dedication of a military cemetery at Gettysburg—"whether . . . any nation . . . conceived in liberty . . . can long endure"—was answered. The national government was supreme, and the idea of secession died with the Confederacy. In the government's peril, Lincoln had violated basic First Amendment rights and ordered Americans drafted for the first time in the nation's history. The old union was restored, and with it the political system built up laboriously over four generations.

RECONSTRUCTION

The Civil War ended, but it had left some unresolved issues: how would the former Confederate states be brought back into the Union? How would the millions of dollars in damages be rebuilt? Most importantly, what was to become of the four million new black citizens freed from slavery by the Thirteenth Amendment?

Lincoln had offered only a general principle: "With malice toward none, with charity toward all, let us bind up the nation's wounds." Just five days after General Lee's surrender at Appomattox Courthouse, Virginia, President Lincoln was assassinated by John Wilkes Booth. Although the South had been defeated on the battlefield, it had not given up entirely. Southern States passed "Black codes" that treated freed African Americans very nearly like slaves. Newly chosen representatives that the South sent to Congress were often either former Confederate Army officers or the same men who had led southern states before the war began. Race riots even broke out in some southern cities, and blacks were killed. These events antagonized many in the North, who began to wonder if their husbands and sons had died for nothing. Republican leaders like Thaddeus Stevens in the House and Charles Sumner in the

The Klan terrorized southern blacks in the post-Civil War era, helping conservative southern Democratic governments regain control in the former Confederacy. © Bettmann/CORBIS

Senate took control, winning public support for a program of reconstruction that would remake the South and give African Americans full partnership in the process.

"Radical Reconstruction," as it was called, was tough. All of the former Confederate states were occupied by the U.S. Army. Terrorist organizations like the Ku Klux Klan were suppressed by martial law. Old southern leaders could not vote or hold office unless they asked for a pardon. African Americans were guaranteed equal rights by the Fourteenth Amendment and the vote in the Fifteenth Amendment. Congress declined to break up the old southern plantations and divide the lands among blacks and poor whites, but it did create the Freedman's Bureau. The Bureau became in essence an early "health and human services" agency for both whites and blacks in the South, setting up schools, medical clinics, and aid stations for those left destitute by the war. Some southern whites, tired of the dominance of the old plantation aristocrats, embraced the idea of a "New South" that would develop its urban, industrial, and educational resources as the North had. They believed African Americans were entitled to work and to some services—on a segregated basis. Republican

PRESIDENTS OF THE UNITED STATES

Administration	President	Party	Achievement
1789–1797	George Washington	Federalist	As first President, set many precedents for later administrations. Began foreign policy of neutrality.
1797–1801	John Adams	Federalist	Led an undeclared war with France. Supported politically repressive acts which became unpopular.
1801–1809	Thomas Jefferson	Democratic-Republican	Doubled nation's size with Louisiana Purchase. Tried to keep America out of the Napoleonic Wars.
1809–1817	James Madison	Democratic-Republican	Led America in the War of 1812. Supported the first protective tariff and improved transportation.
1817–1825	James Monroe	Democratic-Republican	President during the "era of good feeling." Warned Europe against power plays in the Monroe Doctrine.
1825–1829	John Q. Adams	National Republican	Won office in the "corrupt bargain." Program of internal improvements died in Congress.
1829–1837	Andrew Jackson	Democrat	First "common man's president." Developed the "spoils system" and resisted nullification.
1837–1841	Martin Van Buren	Democrat	First career politician. His administration suffered through the nation's first major depression.
1841	William H. Harrison	Whig	Famous Indian fighter died after one month in office.
1841–1845	John Tyler	Whig	First Vice President to become president on the death of Harrison. Signed bill annexing Texas.
1845–1849	James K. Polk	Democrat	Led America in War with Mexico which gained the Southwest. Also secured Oregon for the United States.
1849–1850	Zachary Taylor	Whig	Hero of the Mexican War. Died after sixteen months in office.
1850–1853	Millard Fillmore	Whig	Supported Compromise of 1850 which delayed the Civil War.
1853–1857	Franklin Pierce	Democrat	Supported Kansas-Nebraska Act and signed the Gadsden Purchase from Mexico.
1857–1861	James Buchana	Democrat	Tried to keep North-South peace but failed. Opposed secession in principle, but did not act.
1861–1865	Abraham Lincoln	Republican	First Republican president. Led the Union to victory in the Civil War and freed the slaves.

governments in the southern states worked in this direction, replacing in most cases the occupying U.S. Army.

But a combination of factors wrecked the idea of a "New South." The Republican leadership was enfeebled by old age and death. The Panic of 1873 destroyed the just-recovering southern economy, pushing states that had invested in railroads and schools into bankruptcy, killing jobs and forcing more rural blacks into sharecropping poverty. The "New South" enthusiasts were discredited by the Panic and by instances of corruption, reviving the traditional planter elite. Die-hard southerners who had been implacably opposed to black rights joined with the conservative Democratic leaders and regained control of their state governments. African Americans who tried to vote were threatened and sometimes killed. But in the North there was little outrage. The public, focused on industrial and western development, had grown tired of the Reconstruction issue. By 1876, the nation's centennial anniversary, both sides wanted to put aside the wounds of the Civil War and celebrate in unity.

The result was the infamous "Compromise of 1877," negotiated after a disputed presidential election that year. Republicans remained in control of the national government. Southern Democrats were allowed a free hand in their states. African Americans, most of whom worked for white landowners as tenants, had no champions in Washington or local government. They were pressed into an underclass, citizens without the rights of citizenship. Reconstruction had reunited the country, but it had not rebuilt the South or followed though on the promise of equal rights for freedmen. The American experiment in democracy remained a challenge.

SUGGESTIONS FOR ADDITIONAL READING

Clinton Rossiter, *The Seedtime of the Republic,* (1953) Describes the colonial drive for political liberty.

Gordon S. Wood, *The Creation of the American Republic,* (1969). A study of the Confederation-Constitution period, emphasizing a social division over ratification of the Constitution.

George Dangerfield, *The Awakening of American Nationalism,* (1965). An examination of the people, ideas, and forces that contributed to the growth of national unity up to the 1830s.

Morton Borden, *Parties and Politics in the New Republic, 1789–1815,* (1967). A chronicle of the emerging American political system from its birth in 1789 through its first critical tests and the War of 1812.

Edward Pessen, *Jacksonian America,* (1978). A solid survey of Jacksonian democracy.

Clifford S. Griffin, *The Ferment of Reform, 1830–1860,* (1967). An account of the many humanitarian causes and utopian plans that filled this period.

David Donald, *Lincoln Reconsidered,* (1956). A reexamination of some of the myths and misconceptions that surround the people and events of the Civil War.

Bernard Bailyn, *The Origins of American Politics,* (1968). A thorough study of how the principles and practices of American politics evolved.

James McPherson, *Battle Cry of Freedom,* (1988). Considered the finest one-volume history of the Civil War.

(Denver Public Library. Western History Department.)

CHAPTER THREE

THE WEST IN AMERICAN LIFE

1763
Pontiac's Indian rebellion against British domination.

1785–87
Northwest Ordinances encourage American westward expansion.

1803
President Jefferson's Louisiana Purchase doubles the national domain.

1811
Tecumseh's Indian Confederation ruined by loss at Battle of Tippecanoe.

1838
Removal of Indians from the Southeast along the "Trail of Tears."

1848
Treaty of Guadalupe-Hidalgo: Mexico cedes the Southwest to the United States after the Mexican-American War.

1849
California Gold Rush sparks a renewed interest in westward migration.

1862
Homestead Act opens millions of acres of government land to public settlement.

1890
End of the Plains wars; Indians sent to reservations.

1893
Frederick Jackson Turner's "Frontier Hypothesis" explains the impact of the frontier experience upon the development of the American character and institutions.

THE HERITAGE OF THE WEST

The "winning of the West" has commanded Americans' attention for over a century. The tale of the Anglo-American frontier as a 300-year-long "march of Progress and Civilization" ever westward has been reported endlessly in books and popular literature, the cinema, and television. This triumphant viewpoint is reflected by historians who feel that America's western experience has had a profound effect upon the country's institutions and national character. Individualism, a tendency to be always on the move, to identify growth with progress, to lean toward informality and egalitarianism, and to develop democratic government have been partially attributed to the influence of the western frontier. So has the national inclination for violence.

There has also been a "dark side." The westward movement also meant conquest, evidenced by the destruction of the Native American's way of life, and to a lesser degree, the Mexican's. These peoples still have difficulty adapting to life in Anglo-American society, prompting one scholar to observe: "At its core frontier history should be the story of the contact of cultures, their competition, and their continuing relations. It cannot be the story of any one side."

Scholars today are broadening the scope of their inquiry into the West. By focusing on issues of race, gender, class, and the environment, the American West continues to be an arena of lively debate. As a result, the academic trend toward multicultural studies sweeping the nation during the 1990s found fertile ground in the history of the West.

FIRST AMERICANS

For several thousand years before a European set foot in the New World, Indians had lived here long enough to make well-worn paths. By the time Europeans arrived, there were almost 200 major tribes in North America alone, each with its own set of customs and manners. Most of the tribes occupying the Atlantic coast were relatively small. Further inland, close to Lakes Ontario and Erie, was the famous Iroquois Confederacy, the Five Nations whose system of tribal cooperation so impressed Benjamin Franklin that he used it in planning for a federation of the thirteen colonies. Not only was each tribe obliged to come to the aid of the others in time of war, but land controlled by any member tribe was open to all. To the south was a loose Indian confederation led by the Creeks, known as the Five Civilized Tribes because of their agricultural pursuits. Like the Iroquois, their member tribes cooperated in war and commerce. Other single tribes like the Shawnee, Sauk, and Fox also roamed the country west of the Alleghenies.

Across the Mississippi, native life was changed when the Spanish introduced horses. The Sioux, Cheyenne, Pawnee, Comanche, Kiowa, and Arapaho were tribes with mobile cultures. Achievement in war was the measure of a man on the plains. Tepee villages were set up and then moved again with the flow of the seasons and the buffalo. Nearly every necessity used by these Plains Indians was taken from this great shaggy animal that roamed the area in huge herds.

Far older by centuries than their cousins of the Plains, the Pueblo tribes of the Southwest were also vastly different. They lived in a peaceful, town-oriented culture, in apartment-like dwellings of adobe often situated on nearly inaccessible mesas. Developing irrigation methods, the Pueblos lived on subsistence farming and hunting in the arid Southwest. Their neighbors to the northwest, the Californian Indians, pursued a more primitive way of life and were still living

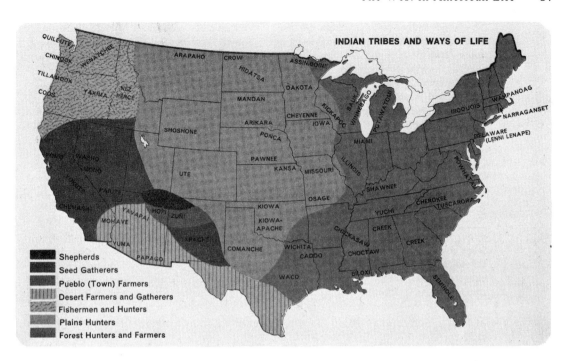

INDIAN TRIBES AND WAYS OF LIFE

Shepherds
Seed Gatherers
Pueblo (Town) Farmers
Desert Farmers and Gatherers
Fishermen and Hunters
Plains Hunters
Forest Hunters and Farmers

in a Stone Age culture as late as the California Gold Rush. Nez Perces and Shoshoni led quiet lives in the valleys of Oregon and Idaho. The Pacific Northwest was home to clans along the coast who developed a sophisticated class society based on fishing and hunting. Finally, there were the Eskimo people in Alaska, whose placid, family-centered culture was sustained mainly by fish and whale blubber.

These first Americans are considered by many historians as the "first ecologists." They usually lived in harmony with their environment. This was partly due to the fact that their low numbers and stone-age technology did not make much of an impact. But they also believed that the land was a living community of thinking, feeling creatures, filled with supernatural power and mystical insight. The totem poles of the Northwest coast Indians were symbols, reflecting the mythical history of clan animals like the raven, bear, or beaver who had accomplished some miracle or feat of heroism. Most Indian groups claimed the earth was their mother, and that their homeland was a uniquely blessed place ("There is no place like Crow country!" exulted one chief.) that they held in trust for future generations. They believed in tribal "turf," but not in private ownership of land. "Sell the country? Why not sell the air, the clouds, the great sea," one incredulous chief replied.

Europeans didn't see it that way. In 1528 a 400-man expedition led by Panfilo de Narvaez landed near present-day Tampa Bay to conquer La Florida for Spain. With the force was Alvar Nunez de Vaca, a conquistador determined to seize wealth and convert the native peoples to Roman Catholicism. Narvaez dispatched his ships, with much of the expedition's food supplies, northward up the Gulf coast to search for a deep-water harbor. His army invaded Apalachee (near

CORONADO

Four years after Cabeza de Vaca's return to Mexico City, conquistador Francisco Vasquez de Coronado assembled a force of hundreds of cavalrymen, foot soldiers, priests, artisans, and native guides and servants to conquer seven rich native cities the Spaniards named Cibola, rumored to be far north of the Spanish settlements in Mexico.

In 1540 Coronado and his men began a two-year quest for these riches through the present-day southwestern United States. Along the way they encountered the Zunis and the Hopis in their austere adobe homes, but no sign of wealth. Then the expedition turned eastward, crossing the Arizona desert, thereby becoming the first Europeans to marvel at the mile-deep chasm of the Grand Canyon. Marching farther east, the Spaniards reached Pecos, New Mexico at the eastern limits of Pueblo territory. There they encountered friendly natives who spoke of a happy kingdom named *Quivira,* located farther east on the Great Plains. Of this Norther American *shangrai-la,* it was said:

> The lord of all that land took his afternoon nap under a great tree hung with golden jingle bells that wafted in the breeze. The tableware was made of silver and the dishes, pitchers and bowls were all made of gold.

Inspired by such glowing reports about Quivira, Coronado became confident that the Spanish flag would soon wave over a North American El Dorado.

Enroute to this land of enchantment, the Spaniards met more tribesmen in the Rio Grande Valley whose winter supplies failed to satisfy Spanish needs. Indian resistance to the intruders resulted in the death of at least 200 natives and the burning to the ground of 12 pueblos. At last, the expedition reached Rio Quivira (south of today's Dodge City). Entering the territory of the Wichita Indians of central Kansas, the Spaniards found no kingdom of lordly rulers, golden eagles, or jingle bell trees. Instead they discovered "nothing but cattle [bison] and sky."

Disappointed by his find, the conquistador then erected a wooden cross, claiming Kansas for Spain, and launched his return to Mexico via the native settlements in the Rio Grande valley. Upon his return to Mexico City his expedition was viewed as a failure. While it is true that Coronado's search for the Seven Cities of Cibola was fruitless, he did bring back to officials in Mexico City and the Spanish court valuable information about the geography of western North America, and the native peoples of the Southwest. The Coronado expedition expanded Spanish horizons, triggering a change in the European perspective of North America, from that of a sizable island to a continental landmass. Despite his failure to find gold, the Coronado *entrada* was a spectacular achievement in North American exploration.

---

modern Tallahassee) following rumors of natives rich in gold. He found only corn and deerskins, and natives with powerful bows whose raids steadily whittled away the little force's manpower. Marching back to the sea to rendezvous with his ships, Narvaez discovered he and his expedition had been abandoned.

Desperate to flee the hostile area, Narvaez and his men hastily constructed five rafts tied together with horse manes and tails for ropes and powered by sails made of shirts stitched together. Nearly 200 Spaniards drowned in the Gulf as the rafts capsized in rough seas. In November the raft with de Vaca and a handful of soldiers washed up on the coast of modern Texas. De Vaca wrote that he and his men were "nearer to death than to life."

Most of the party died over the winter and the rest sought shelter and food with the Indians they had once held in a conqueror's contempt. The Indians of the area shared their meager diet and provided the strangers with animal hides to protect them against the bitter weather. But this initial generosity soured as their visitors did little to earn their keep. Finally, the Spaniards were forced to collect firewood and dig for edible roots. Those that refused or malingered were beaten and verbally abused. De Vaca, however, found that they were free to move between native settlements and began to trade coastal sea snails, conch shells and other items for interior wood, flints and animal skins. He began to appreciate his simple life among the natives, admiring their ingenuity and care for one another.

Years passed. De Vaca reunited with three other expedition survivors, and together they decided to head westward to try to connect with Spanish settlements in northern Mexico. In the summer of 1535, the four began their trek across southern Texas. They found that their basic medical and herbal knowledge, together with prayer and the sign of the cross, enabled them to heal sick or injured natives. They developed a reputation as shamans with powerful magic. Moving from one village to another, the survivors slowly made their way into modern New Mexico accompanied by a retinue of impressed Indians. There, in a village south of the Rio Yaqui, they met a native wearing a Spanish horseshoe nail as a charm to ward off evil spirits. Other villages had been ransacked and burned, and natives told of slave hunters who terrorized the region. They had reached the edge of Spanish civilization.

In the spring of 1536 the bearded, sun-blistered Spaniards stumbled upon a slave-hunting party. The slavers were, de Vaca later wrote, "dumbfounded at the sight of me, strangely undressed and in company with Indians." They were equally shocked at the friendly way the survivors related to their Indian companions. Knowing that the slavers were prepared to capture the natives, de Vaca warned them to flee. The puzzled natives could not believe these shamans were related to the brutal slavers, but they obediently left. The raiders, finding their prey gone, scoffed at de Vaca and his companions and rode off.

De Vaca was profoundly transformed by his eight-year odyssey across a thousand miles of the American Southwest. He had difficulty readjusting to "civilization," and his thinking was permanently altered. Later, writing his memoirs, de Vaca condemned what his country was doing to the native peoples of the New World. But the Indian land and community ethic was not adopted by European colonists who came to the New World. The introduction of their technology, diseases, and numbers was to prove a disastrous event, for it would destroy the Indian's way of life.

THE HISPANIC EXPERIENCE

The North American Indian's first contact with Europeans was with Spanish expeditions into the Gulf Coast and the Southwest. Fighting usually broke out soon after the expeditions arrived. But the land was harsh, the Indians many, and the failure of Coronado's efforts to find the Seven Cities of Gold (1540–41) discouraged further Spanish efforts for a generation.

But the arrival of English seadog Sir Francis Drake on the Pacific coast alarmed the viceroy in Mexico City. A vigorous effort was made to move into the lands north of Mexico to protect Spanish borders. An expedition of over a hundred soldier-settlers with cattle, sheep, goats, and horses under Juan de Onate founded San Juan, New Mexico in 1598. A few years later, his successor founded Santa Fe, which became the center of Hispanic life in the desert Southwest. When the French moved into Texas and set up a small colony, the Mexico viceroy sent another expedition that founded a presidio (garrisoned fort) and mission at San Antonio in 1718. The new lands, however, offered very little to potential settlers and were swept by Navajo, Apache, and Commanche raiders. For years most of the work was done by hardy Jesuit and Fransiscan missionaries like Father Eusebio Kino, who explored, mapped, and founded missions in Franciscan Arizona for twenty-four years.

For a generation these missions and pueblos (towns) barely held on, mostly ignored by Mexico City. Then the threat of Russian fur traders moving down the Pacific coast from Alaska roused the government. An expedition under Don Gaspar de Portolá and Father Serra moved into California, establishing a mission there in 1769 at San Diego. Portolá moved north to found a presidio and mission at Monterey, which was to be the leading California town and center for local government. Father Serra walked the lands between the two settlements, building a series of missions and presidios a day's journey apart for the next fifteen years to solidify Spain's hold on the coast. The Russians stopped just north of San Francisco.

For all the efforts of missionaries, explorers, and settlers, the Hispanic hold on the Southwest was light. As late as 1820, fewer than 50,000 Spanish-speaking people lived in the huge arc from California to Texas. The great distance from central Mexico, the dryness of the area, and the raiding Indians kept Mexicans away from these potentially rich lands. In fact, the Pueblo Revolt of 1660 led by the Tiwa Popé ejected nearly all of the settlers from Arizona and New Mexico for thirty years. The true rulers of this territory were the Indians.

Nevertheless, the Hispanic people of the Southwest had a profound impact on American development. The clustered pueblo village dwellings built around a central plaza shaped southwestern towns and architecture. Catholic missions brought not only Christianity but the Spanish language and Mexican mestizo culture to the area. The missions also introduced citrus groves, metal tools, ranching, and new crops like wheat, cotton, and sugarcane. Irrigation techniques developed by natives were improved and expanded upon, bringing more of the dry lands under cultivation. The coastal Californian Indians found their simple lives revolutionized and regimented, eventually nearly losing their cultures altogether. Even those natives who did not become part of mission life were affected. Horses stolen from Hispanic corrals spread northward to transform the lives of the Plains Indians. Ranchos, especially the estates of thousands of acres in California, pioneered a way of life built on the romantic vaquero (cowboy) and the powerful ranchero (rancher) that would later be adopted by the Anglo-American cowboy. Mexican mining in southern Arizona pioneered construction techniques later used outside countless Anglo-American gold rush boom towns. In short, though they did not control the land, they shaped its culture and development.

ANGLO-AMERICAN COLONIZATION

The poverty of Spain's northern frontier did not detract from the enormous wealth Madrid pulled out of Mexico and Peru. European countries envious of Spain's success turned their eyes toward the New World, seeing it as a source of opportunity for the Old.

Many of the English colonists saw it in the same light. They came to the New World hoping to better their economic and social status, something that was nearly impossible in the rigid societies from which they came. Others made the dangerous journey across the Atlantic fleeing religious persecution, seeking a "promised land" where they would be free to worship and establish a new religious order. So came Puritans, Quakers, French Huguenots, Baptists, and many other sects. With them came soldiers of fortune, mercenaries seeking riches and adventure. Not a few were forced to come over: besides black slaves, debtors and criminals were frequently given the choice of jail or immigration to the New World. For the Anglo-Americans, North America's Atlantic seaboard was the West, a land of opportunity.

And they came laden with "gifts." Besides the wild horses whose ancestors were brought over by the Spaniards, Europeans gave the Indians the gun, liquor, and epidemic disease. Indeed, according to a recent study, North America's population of at least 10 million Indians at the time of the New World's discovery was reduced by millions as a result of contagious diseases brought over by the Europeans. Fields and villages abandoned by plague-struck natives provided Pilgrim settlers with land that had already been cleared. Liquor became practically addictive to many Indians, making them dependent upon unscrupulous white traders at the same time it ruined their health. Still, at least initially, the Indians were generally dealt with in a friendly (if not always honest) manner. For they had control of the land, they knew how to raise New World crops important to the colonists, and they offered a profitable fur trade to the white men. The French, few in numbers and focused on the profitable fur trade, established good relations with neighboring tribes from their St. Lawrence settlements. Even in the English colonies, as long as the settlements were small, peace with the Indians was precariously maintained.

But as the British colonies expanded, game animals were decimated as forests were chopped down for farmland and buildings. Goods offered by seventeenth-century European traders soon resulted in the depletion of many fur-bearing animals. In 1633 alone, the Dutch purchased some 30,000 beaver and otter skins, exhausting Iroquois hunting lands in upper New York. The ecological imbalance provoked by this wholesale slaughter was accompanied by a growing dependence upon the Europeans for such goods as clothing, tools, and weapons to support the Indian's livelihood. Native Americans resisted this encroachment on their tribal territories. As they became more of an obstacle to colonial expansion than a help to the settlements' prosperity, coexistence was thrown aside. Vicious wars erupted. In these conflicts the colonists were frequently aided by other Indians whose tribes were traditional rivals or had become competitors for the fur trade. "Divide and conquer" proved effective—the wars were usually short and brutal. A governor of Plymouth observed during the burning of an Indian town in New England, "It was a fearful sight to see them frying in the fire . . . and horrible was the stink and stench thereof. But the victory seemed a sweet sacrifice and [we] gave praise thereof to God. . . ."

The eastern areas were gradually cleared of Indians and wilderness, both being driven west to the fringes of colonial settlement. British victory in the French and Indian War forced the French out of North America in 1763. The British were now the masters of the continent, but they were also deeply in debt from the war. Trying to economize, they refused to continue the old French policy of gifts of trade goods to the Indians. The result was a well-organized uprising led by Chief Pontiac. Fueled by economic desperation and traditional religious fervor, Pontiac's Rebellion in 1763 became almost a crusade against Anglo-American culture. But that rebellion was futile in the absence of their old French allies. There was no longer any room for the significant political role played by the Indians for more than a century in the contests between England and France in the New World. All Pontiac won was a temporary reprieve. In order to recover from the costly Indian war and to reserve land speculation and fur-trading opportunities for the English crown, the King issued the Proclamation of 1763, forbidding the American colonists from expanding west and creating new conflicts with the Indians.

AN AMERICAN WEST AND THE PIONEER MENTALITY

This law angered the colonists. The French and Indian War had been fought to secure these lands, and now they were off limits. Frontier settlers also believed the proclamation provided security for the Indian at their expense, and speculators and fur traders resented the government monopoly on western lands. Colonists had begun to think of the frontier as their West, just as they were beginning to feel more like Americans with their own interests than like European colonists.

The Revolutionary War between the American rebels and the British, both sides complemented by their Indian allies, made the frontier a battleground once again. U.S. forces under General Wayne broke the remnants of the Iroquois at the Battle of Fallen Timbers. After peace was concluded in 1783, Native Americans watched as settlers poured into the Northwest. Neither the heavy forests, the Appalachian Mountains, a lack of good roads and transport, nor Indian hostility could stop them. They generally came in four waves: hunters and trappers who came west to make money in the fur trade and live off the land; pioneers who squatted on the land and barely made a living, usually moving on after a few years; farmers who cleared the land to settle permanently; and merchants and townsmen who set up services and supplies for the growing settlement, connecting it with more established towns farther east. These migrations were not forced. People were not fleeing from persecution or starvation. They simply saw an opportunity for adventure and for bettering their economic or social conditions by moving west, where everything seemed more wide open.

If this westward movement was vigorous it was also careless. Americans widely assumed that the continent's vast stretches of forest and land were inexhaustible. Coming as they did from Europe, where the land had been occupied for centuries and resources were strictly limited, it is understandable that the abundance they found in the New World seemed infinite by comparison. But people are not likely to take care of land or resources they consider boundless. Virginians eagerly sought new lands west of the Allegheny Mountains because they were destroying their own soil by overplanting it with tobacco, a crop that drew heavily on soil nutrients. George Washington wrote sadly, "Our lands were originally very good, but use and abuse have made them quite otherwise." An Englishman observed in horror while New Jersey farmers, "in order to save themselves the work of shaking or pulling off the nuts . . . find it simpler to cut the tree and gather the nuts from it, as it lies on the ground." Businessmen and settlers often took the cheap and easy way, their eyes fixed on immediate gains and blind to the future price.

Fed by great quantities of natural resources, the United States was experiencing a phenomenal prosperity. Americans rejoiced in their growing development as a nation. "What a people we are! What a country is this of ours," exulted one western newsman, "which but as yesterday was a wilderness." Another summarized the advance of the frontier ever farther westward as the "tramp, tramp, steady and sure, of the advancing hosts of Civilization and Christianity." There was a rampant enthusiasm for the confidence in the nation's progress as every economic indicator gave proof that young America was growing in wealth and power. That the transformation taking place was right and good no sensible man could doubt. A leading minister put it another way—"Progress is God." The continent was in the process of being transformed from "useless" and "ungodly" wilderness into a tamed land of productive farms and villages.

Many of these frontier settlers were not entirely happy with the western policy of their government in Washington. They felt it had moved too slowly against the Indians, that its policy of hard currency and taxes discriminated against them by making it difficult to obtain loans for buying land and maintaining a farm, and that it was simply too far away and preoccupied with "eastern problems" to do them much good. Westerners were developing interests of their own and insisting that the national government pay attention.

Faced with this pressure, the United States government began to develop a western policy. Part of that policy was established in the Land Ordinances of 1785 and 1787, which provided a system of land survey and sale while enabling the new territories to become states in the Union when they reached a certain population level. The West was to be incorporated into the rest of the nation. The Land Ordinances established a fundamental approach that wouldn't change for over a century—to sell the western lands as a source of revenue and to encourage national development. Originally, however, only wealthy speculators could afford the cash only, 640 acre minimum purchase. Another part of that policy dealt with the original inhabitants. Here the frontiersman's unwavering desire to remove the Indians became the aim of the government. By a policy of enforced treaties, frequently agreed to by Indian chiefs without authority from their people to sign anything, the United States began driving the Native American out of the way of white migration and onto land beyond the forseeable reach of settlement beyond the Mississippi.

JEFFERSON AND THE AGRARIAN MYTH

"Some few towns excepted," wrote one American, "we are all tillers of the earth, from Nova Scotia to West Florida." For Thomas Jefferson and other agrarian idealists, this was as much a political statement as a social or economic one. Jefferson saw the farmer as the cornerstone of the American Republic. "The small landholders," he wrote, "are the most precious part of a state." He felt that by producing their own goods and by constant contact with nature and nature's God, they would have the economic self-sufficiency and moral character needed to wisely support a republic. This became known as the "agrarian myth." The large western territory would allow the farmer plenty of room for expansion, preserving America's agricultural society and thereby insuring that the United States would maintain its republican form of government. Jefferson considered it his duty as President to foster agriculture, enlarge the West, and remove any obstacles to agrarian expansion. By 1804 Jefferson had eased federal policy, and a settler could buy 160 acres and take four years to pay.

Following this conviction, Jefferson devoted much of his time to western problems. When the French takeover of New Orleans and the Louisiana territory threatened to close the West's commercial lifeline down the Mississippi, the President negotiated with Napoleon to buy the city. The French emperor, whose European entanglements prevented him from taking proper advantage of the area, decided to sell the whole territory. Jefferson quickly accepted the bargain in 1803, despite personal scruples about his constitutional power to do so. The nation's area had been doubled, and Jefferson congratulated his countrymen on their possession of "a chosen country, with room enough for our descendants to the thousandth and thousandth generation."

To further explore this country the President sent out Zebulon Pike on two expeditions, one up the Mississippi to its source and another into the Southwest. The information gained proved useful to future pioneers and settlers. Jefferson's administration also reduced the price of western land, made it easier to obtain, allotted part of it for schools, and encouraged the building of roads.

A new surge of western settlement resulted. When many of the Indians resisted, some joining with the Spaniards in the south or the British in the north against American expansion, armies were sent against them. Tecumseh, a Shawnee, made an effort to unite all the Indians east of the Mississippi in a common war against the United States. "He is," wrote the territorial governor of Indiana, "one of those uncommon geniuses which spring up occasionally to produce revolutions and overthrow the established order of things. . . ." That same governor led a military force against some of Tecumseh's followers who, instead of waiting for him, launched a premature attack and were defeated at the Battle of Tippecanoe. Tecumseh's aura of invincibility was shattered, and his Indian alliance fell apart. The chance to build an Indian nation in the Midwest and South was gone, but hostilities continued.

Western representatives in Congress insisted that only war would end the Indian menace by allowing the invasion of Canada and Florida to destroy European support for the hostile tribes. This might also bring conquered lands into the United States. Congressman Henry Clay of Kentucky led the "War Hawks" to a declaration of war against the British, who controlled both Canada and Florida, in 1812.

Lewis & Clark

The Lewis and Clark expedition into the uncharted West beyond the Mississippi was nearly the first covert operation authorized by the U.S. government.

President Thomas Jefferson had long been convinced that the future of his young country was in the West, and had talked about an expedition into lands beyond the Mississippi since the 1780s. Determined to lay claim to this territory, Jefferson named his personal secretary, Meriwether Lewis, commander of the proposed Corps of Discovery to explore these potentially rich lands.

An experienced woodsman and soldier, Lewis was sent to Philadelphia for a crash course in botany, medicine, mineralogy, and astronomy. For his second in command, Lewis chose his friend Captain William Clark. Captain Clark's abilities in command, diplomacy and map making complemented Lewis's growing scientific talents. By the time they had established camp across the river from St. Louis and assembled the expedition's men and supplies, Lewis and Clark had become legal. To nearly everyone's surprise, Napoleon had agree to sell all of Louisiana to the United States. The transfer officially concluded at St. Louis in March 1804. On May 21, the forty-five member expedition set off.

The ascent up the Missouri was a nightmare: shifting sandbars, crumbling banks, changing currents, and underwater snags caused the group to get hung up, nearly drowned, and often delayed. Relations with the Indians along the way were generally good, eased by Clark's manner with the natives, gifts, and the size and firepower of the disciplined band. Nearly 1600 miles later, in October, the Corps of Discovery decided to winter with the peaceful, trading Mandan Sioux close to what is now Bismarck, North Dakota. There the party was joined by a French fur trader and his Shoshone wife, Sacajawea, who had been a slave among the Sioux until the trader bought her freedom. The winter got rough—Clark noted in his carefully kept journal that the temperature on December 17 plunged to 74 below zero.

Lewis and Clark broke camp on April 7, 1805, aware of both the excitement and danger of the enterprise. Lewis wrote: "We were now about to penetrate a country at least two thousand miles in width, on which the foot of civilized man had never trodden."

By mid-June the expedition reached the Great Falls of the Missouri, which forced them to go around (portage) and carry the boats for twenty-five days. Lewis encountered a grizzly, which "pitched at [him] open mouthed at full speed." After the bear was frightened off, Lewis decided that he would rather fight two Indians than one bear. But it was not all danger and work. A dram of rum one evening produced a fiddler, and they spent the evening singing and dancing.

Already it was August, and the captains looked in earnest for the Shoshone, whom they hoped could provide them with horses and a way over the looming Rockies before winter sealed off the mountains. With Sacajawea showing the way, they ran into a hunting band. The Indians, at first edgy, then recognized the female guide as the sister of their leader! Welcoming the party with enthusiasm, the Shoshone provided pack horses and news of a hunting trail over the mountains. The grueling ten day trip over the last of the Rocky Mountains finally brought the nearly starved party to the Clearwater River. There the Nez Perce befriended them and provided salmon. Lewis knew they were in reach of the Pacific.

Lewis and Clark ran the rapids of the Snake and Columbia Rivers, taking risks to move quickly and avoid a winter in the Cascade Mountains. As the fog lifted on a rainy November 7th, they finally saw their goal. "Great joy in camp," wrote Clark. "We are in view of the Ocean, this great Pacific Ocean, which we have been so long anxious to see." After wintering near Astoria and the Oregon coast, in March the expedition began the long trek back. They arrived in St. Louis, to a triumphal welcome, on September 23, 1806.

The Corps of Discovery was a huge success. Although there was no easy passage to the Pacific, Lewis and Clark brought back invaluable information on the plants, animals, and geography of the Far West. John Colter, one of the expedition soldiers, requested permission to leave and head back West. Colter became one of the first mountain men and was the discoverer of Yellowstone. The American claim to the Northwest was now secure, and the first move had been made to make the whole West American.

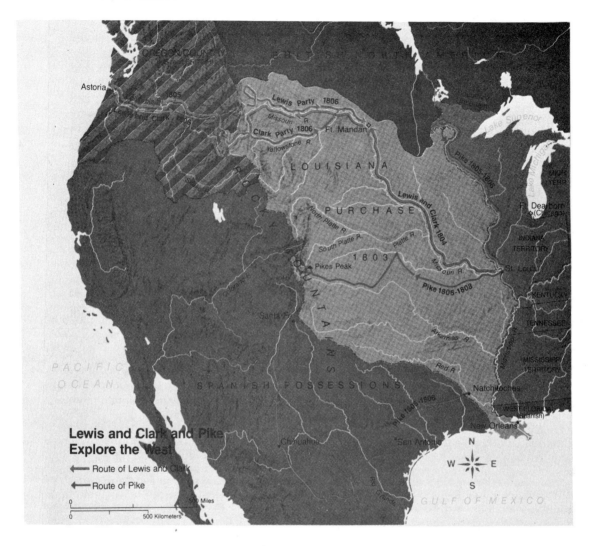

Lewis and Clark and Pike Explore the West

← Route of Lewis and Clark
← Route of Pike

0 — 500 Miles
0 — 500 Kilometers

Many Americans considered victory to be "a mere matter of marching." To such an extent had the agrarian myth grown that the farmer-frontiersman was considered invincible in war as well as the main support of the republic in peace. Early battles did not bear out this confidence, but General Jackson's victory at New Orleans, where his motley force of volunteers defeated British regulars, breathed new life into this belief. The Peace of Ghent removed European support for the Indians, and other U.S. Army victories broke them. The Five Civilized Tribes concluded treaties that allowed them to keep some of their lands in the Southeast. Most of the natives of the Midwest were driven beyond the Mississippi, securing the territory for new waves of settlers.

"TRAIL OF TEARS"

General Andrew Jackson rode to victory in the Presidential elections of 1828 as the "Hero of New Orleans" and the "champion of the common man." His success was indicative of the nation's pride and confidence in the western farmer-frontiersman, of which he was the symbol. On Inauguration Day, mobs followed their hero Jackson to the White House and proceeded to invade that sanctuary, muddy boots and all. Observed one lady spectator, "Ladies and gentlemen only had been expected. . . . But it was the People's day, the People's President, and the People would rule."

"The People" expected certain things from the new president. They had largely ignored former President Adams' program for internal improvements because they were suspicious of the centralized governmental power it would require. Continued waves of western settlers and freewheeling entrepreneurs that made up Jackson's democratic constituency simply wanted a "free hand" and as little interference from Washington as possible. The President could little afford to alienate them.

In 1828 the Five Civilized Tribes of the Creek, Cherokee, Chickasaw, Choctaw, and Seminole had firm treaties with the United States government guaranteeing them possession of the remnants of their traditional lands. But the states of Mississippi, Alabama, and Georgia were increasingly eager to take these lands and open them for white settlement and speculation. Following the discovery of gold in Cherokee territory, Georgia began to pass laws that defied those federal treaties and court orders. This legislation also destroyed the Indians' system of government modeled after that of the United States, and deprived them of their lands. The Cherokees, along with other tribes being subjected to the same sort of illegal actions, sent delegations to Washington to protest. Secretary of War Eaton admitted that the federal government was simply unable to support its own treaties. Enforcement would have required United States troops to side with Indians against whites, an action that would have made Jackson instantly unpopular in the West. The President had already made up his mind to compel the "civilized" tribes to give up their lands and move west of the Mississippi into new reservations, where Jackson promised them they could stay "as long as grass grows or water runs."

Most of the Indians were simply unable to resist combined state and federal pressure to move. Settlers used liquor, fraud, and violence to drive off these Native Americans. First the Creeks, then the Chickasaw and Choctaw, ceded their lands and were moved in mass migrations devastated by hunger, disease, and exposure. A few young army officers did their best to take care of the tribesmen entrusted to them, but they were very few. On two occasions the Cherokees took their case to the Supreme Court. Finally, the Court ruled in the Indians' favor and Chief Justice John Marshall wrote a hot denunciation of state and federal actions in *Worcester vs. Georgia.* But Jackson refused to implement his decision. The President had the last word—"John Marshall has made his decision," he remarked acidly, "now let him enforce it." By 1838 the Army began the removal of the Cherokees from their land in Georgia. Along the "Trail of Tears" that led west, nearly one-fourth of the tribe perished. Even Indians who had cooperated in the removal of their brethren found themselves and their families ousted, victims of broken promises. Florida Seminoles fought the government from the Everglades for 10 years and cost Washington 1500

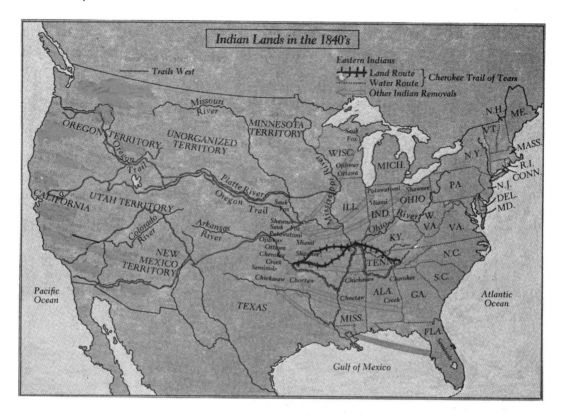

American troops and 20 million dollars to remove. Finally, all but a few were swept aside by the American encroachment on the frontier. In his 1830 Inaugural Address President Andrew Jackson (a former frontiersman himself) asked, "what good man would prefer a country covered with forests and ranged by a few thousand savages to our extensive Republic, studded with cities, towns, and prosperous farms, embellished with all the improvements art can devise or industry execute?" By the 1820s land was sold at the rate of a million acres a year; by the 1840s it was four million. The Department of the Interior had to be created in 1849 to handle this explosion of land sales.

WESTERN EMPIRE

By the late 1830s this westward march of Americans was beginning to be regarded as a natural, inevitable course of action. Even before the Revolution, writers had remarked that the succession of powerful civilizations seemed to move from east to west: "Westward the course of empire takes its way." Benjamin Franklin had seen America as the seat of a new world power, and Thomas Jefferson believed that the entire continent would be peopled from the "original nest" of east coast states. Enough success had occurred since the winning of American independence to bolster the conviction in the 1830s that America's experiment in democracy was the wave of the future. The

"We were drove off like wolves, and our people's feet were bleeding with long marches" wrote one Creek Indian who followed the "Trail of Tears." Another chief commented sadly that white Americans eager to force the tribes off their ancestral lands "cannot appreciate the feelings of a man that loves his country." ("Trails of Tears" by Robert Lindneux. Courtesy Woolaroc Museum, Bartlesville, Oklahoma.)

West was the key to this expanding American empire, for it would provide the raw resources of power and room enough for a growing populace. As conqueror of the West, the farmer-frontiersman was not only the main supporter of democratic government and cherished republican institutions but also the enthusiastic agent of American expansionism. Heady with exuberance at the picture of a nation on the move, convinced that the farmer-frontiersman was invincible, Americans began speaking of a "manifest destiny to occupy and to possess the whole of the Continent which Providence has given us."

"Manifest destiny" was an emotionally charged call to "subdue the continent to establish a new order [democracy and republican institutions] in human affairs to cause a stagnant people to be reborn [referring to the Mexicans] . . . and to shed a new and resplendent glory upon mankind." This combination of agrarian expansionism, missionary idealism, and plain arrogant nationalism fast became a powerful force in national affairs. It also molded the shape of the westward movement, making it a matter of right and an indicator of national progress.

Neither geographical nor national barriers could slow that movement with the force of "manifest destiny" behind it. For years the Great Plains, that wide expanse of grassland stretching from the prairies west of the Mississippi to the foot of the Rocky Mountains, had been regarded as the "Great American Desert." Suffering great extremes of temperature, roamed by warrior tribes like the Sioux and Cheyenne, the area was considered a barrier to further expansion by many Americans. But as early as the 1820s "mountain men," trappers and hunters working for

JEDEDIAH STRONG SMITH

In the spring of 1822, a tall, slim young man twenty-three years of age with a reputation as a crack rifle shot applied for a place on General William Ashley's first fur hunting expedition into the Rocky Mountains. Jedediah Smith was hired. The mountain men Smith would keep company with for most of the rest of his life were rugged, rough individuals, while Smith was a devoted Bible reader who never touched liquor or tobacco. But his courage, skill, and nerve won him wide admiration.

If Smith was looking for adventure when he signed with Ashley, he found it. Ashley's attempt to buy horses from the Arikara Indians led to the loss of a third of his 90 men. A year later, Smith was leading a small band of trappers in Montana when he was attacked by a grizzly. The bear practically scalped him, but it was killed and Smith calmly directed his men how to sew his scalp and ear back up. In 1824 Smith's group reached the Snake Valley ahead of a party from the competing British Hudson Bay Company and had a profitable season. That year he also crossed the South Pass through the Rockies. His report that it could be traversed by wagons later made the pass the gateway to the Far West. Shortly after this trip, Ashley made Smith a partner in his firm. Within a year Ashley left the business and Smith formed a partnership with David Jackson and William Sublette.

Smith's first long trip west took him into southern California and up the central valley, yielding a good harvest of furs. On the way back across Nevada, however, his party nearly died of thirst. His second journey west, beginning in 1827 and lasting two years, was a disaster. The Mojave Indians slaughtered ten of his eighteen men because the Mexicans, suspicious of Smith's arrival a year earlier, had warned them against the Americans. The rest of the band were warned out of California by the Mexican governor. They rendezvoused with another group and headed north into Oregon, exploring and trapping. But Kalawatset Indians allowed into the camp as friends murdered sixteen of the remaining twenty mountain men. The survivors had to trudge 150 miles without supplies or horses to the nearest outpost.

By 1830 Smith was finished with the trapper's life. He knew that most of the West had been denuded of furs and that increasing competition from other fur companies and hostile Indians would cut profits and raise dangers. He went back to St. Louis and appeared ready to settle down, but was talked into scouting for a Santa Fe-bound wagon train. Smith may have been considering a new partnership with Jackson and Sublette in the profitable Santa Fe trade. But while ranging ahead of the wagons and searching for water, Smith was ambushed and murdered by Comanche Indians. He was 31 years old.

---

fur traders in the West, crossed the "desert" to comb the forests of the Pacific Northwest for beaver. Others penetrated the Mexican deserts of the Southwest to tie St. Louis, Missouri and Santa Fe, New Mexico together by trade. In the 1820s trails were blazed through the Rockies and the Sierra Nevada, opening the West Coast to adventurous American pioneers.

When settlers poured into Texas in the 1820s and California in the 1840s they did not find a land occupied only by Indians. This entire area belonged to Mexico, which had revolted against Spain and established its independence in 1821. Mexican people had lived on the land for many years. But the land was rugged, Indian raids made life difficult, and the settlers were few and far from Mexico. At first, Mexican leaders felt that American immigration would help settle the area

In this artist's rendering, the spirit of Manifest Destiny (here garbed in the form of a goddess) guides the American people in their conquest of the continent. Under her protective presence, white settlers boldly take possession of the land unmindful that the Indians regarded this move as an intrusion of their domain. From the artist's perspective, the Indians seem to offer little resistance, simply retreating along with the buffalo. (Collection of Harry T. Peters, Jr.)

and benefit the Mexican economy. Americans like Steve Austin were encouraged to bring settlers into Texas. Soon the new immigrants outnumbered the original Mexican inhabitants. The two groups did not get along well: the Americans, coming from a Protestant culture, disliked the Mexicans' Roman Catholic religion, and could not understand their apparent indifference to the work ethic. Furthermore, they interpreted Mexican hostility toward slavery as a threat to their prosperity. When Mexico tried to curb the settlers' growing dominance of Texas by reasserting its authority, the "Texans" proclaimed their independence in 1836 and defeated a Mexican army sent to put down their rebellion. Nine years later the United States annexed Texas, much to Mexico's anger.

California was a different story, although here too Mexico's control was slipping. Mexican political influence in the province was so weak that an American naval captain observed: "I found a total absence of all government in California." The landed Mexican grandees, with their huge estates, were more concerned with their own affairs than with the area's government. But the American settlers there were neither powerful nor numerous enough to repeat the Texas independence-annexation pattern, nor could Washington buy the province from Mexico, whose government and people were already outraged by United States annexation of Texas in 1845.

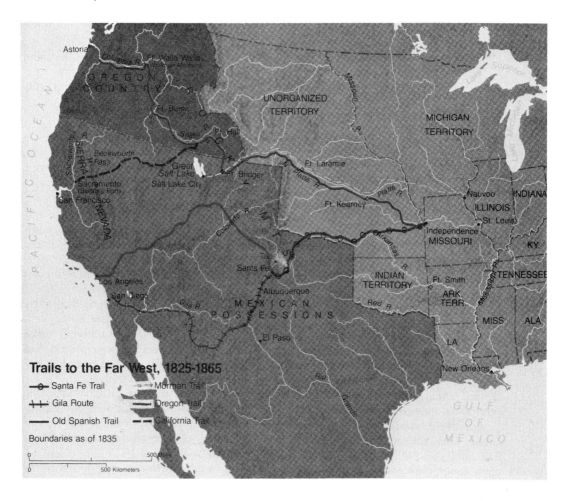

Trails to the Far West, 1825-1865

- Santa Fe Trail
- Gila Route
- Old Spanish Trail
- Morman Trail
- Oregon Trail
- California Trail

Boundaries as of 1835

0 _____ 500 Miles
0 _____ 500 Kilometers

"Manifest destiny," however, would not be denied. Midwesterners had populated the Oregon Territory in the 1840s and President Polk wrung most of it from the British with threats to fight for the "whole of Oregon." A diplomatic compromise was reached and Oregon was divided with Britain at the 49th parallel. Expansion had won another victory. Urged on by settlers' claims of California's richness and merchants' reports of the province's importance to trade, expansionists led by President Polk were finally able to lure the United States into war with hostile Mexico.

The conflict with Mexico was the result of "manifest destiny" sentiment and the expansionist tendencies inherent in the westward movement. It also marked the height of American expansion, as it brought California and the entire Southwest into the Union as new territories with the defeat of Mexico in 1848. "This occupation of territory by the people," proclaimed one newspaper, "is the great movement of the age."

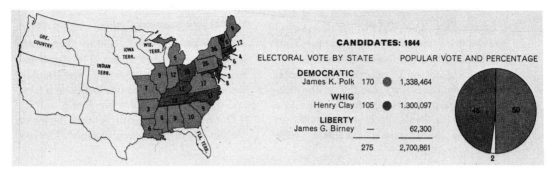

CANDIDATES: 1844

ELECTORAL VOTE BY STATE		POPULAR VOTE AND PERCENTAGE
DEMOCRATIC James K. Polk	170	1,338,464
WHIG Henry Clay	105	1.300,097
LIBERTY James G. Birney	—	62,300
	275	2,700,861

Democratic candidate James K. Polk campaigned on the annexation of Texas and the aquisition of all of Oregon. This "Manifest Destiny" stance, together with the abolitionist Liberty Party vote that caused Clay to lose New York, threw the election to Polk.

Ironically, this opening of the West for settlement was creating as many problems as opportunities. A crisis was approaching over the issue of slavery. The deep South had adopted this "peculiar institution" from Virginia and the Carolinas to produce the high-profit crop of cotton. The Midwest, settled by immigrants from New England, New York, and Pennsylvania, had continued to farm the same diversified crops cultivated in those states. By the 1830s the agrarian myth had split in two. The North still saw the independent frontiersman-farmer as the myth's hero and the Republic's strength. The South, on the other hand, idealized the plantation worked by slaves and preferred to support a new aristocracy. As new territory opened in the West, each section struggled to extend its ideal until finally the nation was plunged into a civil war in 1861.

PROGRESS FOLLOWS THE FRONTIER

Even before the Civil War, changes were taking place in the "Old West" between the Appalachians and the Mississippi. Small farmers whose land barely supported their own families were being replaced by large commercial farmers who grew crops for sale on the national market. To these agriculturalists anxious for open markets, the building of roads and canals to speed their produce to buyers in the cities and the East had become important. This commerce was creating market depots like Cincinnati, Nashville, and Louisville, where banks and small industries gradually began to locate. Development of steam power was quickly followed by the rise of the steamboat in the 1820s and the railroad in the late 1830s, which further aided communication and commerce by increasing transportation's capacity for speed and mass movement of goods. What the Civil War did was to increase the demand for all types of goods and services, fueling an economic boom that was transforming the "Old West" from a rural area to an increasingly urban and industrial one.

When the War for the Union ended, the nation returned to its earlier ambition of conquering the West. Now the keynote was development, as the western lands offered enormous opportunities for private enrichment and national growth. The government encouraged these activities by its

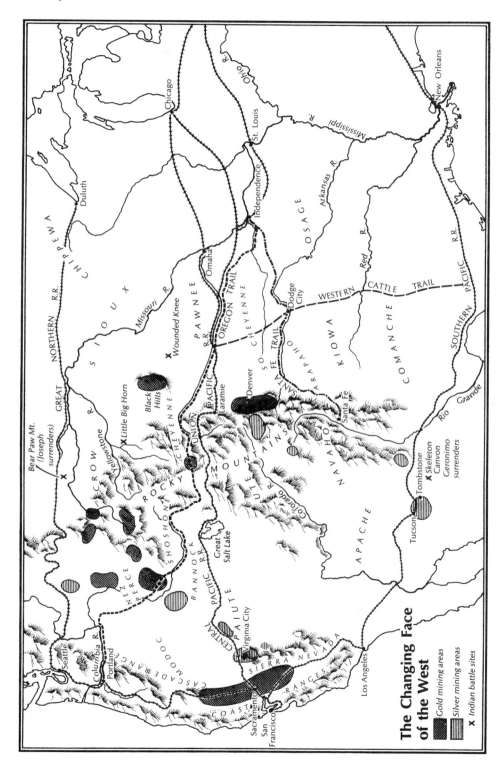

New Orleans

Mississippi R.

Ohio R.

Chicago

St. Louis

Duluth

Independence

OSAGE

Arkansas R.

Omaha

PAWNEE

Red R.

WESTERN   CATTLE   TRAIL

Dodge City

GREAT   NORTHERN   R.R.

CHIPPEWA

SIOUX

Missouri R.

Wounded Knee

OREGON TRAIL

UNION   PACIFIC   R.R.

CHEYENNE

SO.   CHEYENNE

KIOWA

COMANCHE

SOUTHERN   PACIFIC   R.R.

Little Big Horn

Black Hills

Denver

Laramie

SANTA FE TRAIL

ARAPAHO

Santa Fe

Rio Grande

Bear Paw Mt. (Joseph surrenders)

Yellowstone R.

ROCKY   MOUNTAINS

NAVAHO

Skeleton Canyon Geronimo surrenders

Tombstone

CROW

SHOSHONE

UTE

Colorado R.

APACHE

Tucson

NEZ PERCE

BANNOCK

Great Salt Lake

PAIUTE

Virginia City

Seattle

Columbia R.

Portland

CASCADE RANGE

MODOC

CENTRAL   PACIFIC   R.R.

SIERRA NEVADA

COAST   RANGES

Los Angeles

Sacramento

San Francisco

The Changing Face of the West

■ Gold mining areas

▦ Silver mining areas

✕ Indian battle sites

generous land policies and willingness to police the Indians. Recognizing the necessity of connecting California and the West Coast to the rest of the nation, Washington helped the Union Pacific and the Central Pacific build a transcontinental railroad that was finally completed in 1869. Following this first link, other cross-country railroads were constructed to further tie East and West, making western development easier.

Ironically, the people who had done the backbreaking work of carving a rail line through the rugged Sierras and making this connection possible were unwelcome in the West. Chinese labor had first followed the tales of a "gold mountain" in California and later were sent over by contract with Chinese warlords, as railroad labor. Like the other foreign minorities, these Asians were required to pay the foreign miners' tax and to beware of overzealous vigilantes. Anti-Chinese sentiment gained momentum during the 1870s among the laboring classes in California who were suffering from a business depression. The depression coincided with the release of many Chinese immigrant workers upon completion of the Union Pacific line. Soon fear of cheap Asian labor spread to regions in America where the Chinese had never been seen. As early as 1869 a New York newspaper described the perceived threat to traditional America:

> *It is then a flood of this sort of population that is just beginning to sweep over America. Already the Chinese are supplanting Americans and even the Irish in all sorts of manual labor in California. How shall we assimilate this element? How shall we maintain our boasted civilization, how to maintain the reputation of our country, as "the land of the free and the home of the brave?"*

By this time Chinese immigration totaled 100,000 and agitation for exclusion of these foreigners from American shores increased. The debate that ensued focused on arguments that were frankly racist in nature. One aspiring presidential candidate in 1879, speaking in favor of exclusion, concluded that "either the Anglo-Saxon race will possess the Pacific slope or the Mongolians will. . . . We have this day to choose whether we will have . . . the civilization of Christ or the civilization of Confucius." President Rutherford B. Hayes indicated that as a result of our discouraging experience with the Indians and blacks, he would be willing to support "any suitable measures" to prevent further Chinese immigration. By 1882 the clamor against the Chinese reached such proportions that Congress passed an immigration exclusion law.

The railroads that the Chinese helped complete offered a multitude of new opportunities. Ranchers saw the great market for beef in the East and knew that the Great Plains, running from Texas to the Canadian border, offered a huge natural area for raising cattle. The grasslands could be grazed for free, since these government-owned lands were then believed to be too barren to be worth buying. Thus began the range cattle industry in 1866. Stretching from the Rio Grande to the Canadian border, the "Cattle Kingdom" of the western ranchers prospered until the 1880s. Cattlemen drove their herds along the Chisholm Trail and other routes to railheads like Dodge City and Wichita, where the herds would be shipped to meat-packing centers like Chicago. The cowboy became the symbol of this effort, as he was later to become a symbol for the whole West. The legend ignored the fact that the cowboy was originated by Mexican vaqueros, and that many of these hard working young men were black.

The Mining Frontier
🔵 Gold-mining
🔘 Silver-mining

Beyond the prairies and plains of the ranchers were the Rockies. Opened by the mountain men, this area was further developed by miners. Heading anywhere "where gold is found more plenty," prospectors swarmed into any area rumored to hold rich deposits. In their presence towns would spring up, serving whiskey or women or anything else the miners would buy, and then die as the prospectors left for newer, richer fields. When placer or surface mining gave out, companies moved in with the money and engineering skill necessary to bring the gold or silver out of its lode deep in the mountains. Silver City, New Mexico, Deadwood in the Black Hills of Dakota, and Denver, Colorado all grew up around mining areas. Those towns that did not die became magnets for homesteaders and western supply centers, "boosted" by businessmen and speculators determined to make "their" towns successful. Newspaper advertisements and propaganda campaigns to attract capital appeared, and enterprising businesses were launched. Six territories were added to the Union as a result of the mining frontier. "Go West, young man," urged one editor, for a man could make his fortune and be part of a great national movement for progress.

THE WILD, WILD WEST

For nearly four decades, this wide-open, speculative, go-for-broke atmosphere and attitude dominated the Far West. Life was hard, boisterous, risky, and frequently short in the mining towns and cowtowns throughout the frontier. Because there was little law and less government, violence was a part of living. As a young man Mark Twain had traveled west as secretary to his brother and later as a newspaperman. He recorded that to "be a saloon-keeper and to kill a man was to be illustrious," and that during one day in Virginia City, Nevada a "woman was killed by a pistol shot, a man was brained with a sling shot," and another was "disposed of permanently." In towns like Dodge City, Kansas, shootouts over stolen horses, card-cheating, and women were common, not to mention occasional sprees by drunken cowboys to "scare up" the townspeople.

Not all miners were solitary panners for riches like this grizzled prospector. Many used more sophisticated high-yield methods like hydraulic mining that involved crews and expensive machinery. This development gave the growing mining corporations of the West an advantage that spelled the end of the grubstaking forty-niner. (Los Angeles County Museum of Natural History.)

Local law took care of rustlers and horse thieves, and later with U.S. marshals the more "important" crimes like bank holdups and train robberies. But out in open territory justice was swift and usually dealt by the criminal's peers. Claim jumpers were shot by fellow miners and rustlers or horse thieves were hanged by fellow cowboys. Townspeople joined vigilante groups, which served as judge and jury, often holding public hangings for sport and as a "warning to offenders." "Law and Order" was a favorite theme of western towns that were just being established and seeking "respectability." But the most outstanding example of violence in the West was the destruction of the last free American Indians, the Plains tribes.

"I WILL FIGHT NO MORE FOREVER"

The mounted, painted, buffalo-chasing, hard-fighting Plains Indians have become the "typical" American Indian of screen and novel. Ironically, their culture was affected by European influences more than any other group of tribes. Their late-flowering culture was made possible by the introduction of horses from the Spanish Southwest and guns from European and American traders. Even the beads on their colorful garb were imported. But in some ways the stereotype is justified, for the Plains Indian culture was both an amalgamation of many other native societies and an intensification of many of their traits: elaborate codes of combat and an emphasis on war, a strong religion based on rites and sacred objects, and an almost obsessive love of land and the free, roaming life. When this culture clashed with American settlers moving westward, the result was its destruction in the last Indian wars of the West.

When the mountain men penetrated deep into the lands west of the Mississippi bearing weapons, trinkets, and other commodities, they were generally welcomed by the Native Americans. Even when wagon trains of settlers bound for California and Oregon began to enter their

GEORGE ARMSTRONG CUSTER

George Custer had always wanted to be a soldier. At nineteen he won admission to West Point, but he was careless in his studies and earned a record number of demerits. He graduated last in his class in 1861 as the Civil War began. Custer had a flair and vigor about him, however, that impressed people. The commander of the Union Army put Custer on his staff after a chance meeting. A natural athlete and a superb horseman, Custer's daring personal leadership and luck led him from the rank of first lieutenant to that of brigadier general in one year. His cavalry blocked Confederate General Lee's last escape and helped end the Civil War. At the height of his profession, Custer had just turned 25.

When the war ended Custer's rank dropped, but he was given command of the newly formed 7th Cavalry at Fort Riley, Kansas. There he maintained a joyous household with his pretty wife Libbie, and kept a cool distance between himself and his fellow officers. He also earned the dislike of his men for being, according to one, a "hard ass." He drilled them incessantly. He drove them hard, with frequent forced marches, and never seemed to tire himself. On one occasion they pushed 150 miles in 55 hours. On another he left his troops in the field while he had a fling with Libbie for which he was court-martialled and convicted. But friends in high places got him reinstated in less than a year.

The 7th Cavalry had become a crack outfit, and Custer was ordered to implement a new strategy, the winter campaign. The Plains Indians would be hit hard while they were immobile, their villages and supplies destroyed, so that they would be forced to surrender. It worked on the Washita River in November, 1868—fewer than 40 warriors were killed and more than 100 women and children. In the action about nineteen soldiers rode after fleeing Indians, and although Custer was told of shooting in their direction, he refused to investigate. The men were later found dead, though they had clearly lasted long enough to be rescued had Custer gone after them.

The 7th was split up for various duties and then reassembled in 1873 in the Dakota Territory. A year later Custer led an expedition into the Black Hills and confirmed the existence of gold there—gold that lay on Indian holy land, promised to them by treaty. Miners rushed into the area and the Sioux protested. But the government informed the Indians that their treaty lands would have to be changed. The Sioux and other tribes determined not to yield.

Custer, rescued at the last minute from an embarrassing political confrontation in Washington that threatened to end his career, rode with the 7th on a campaign to end Indian resistance. Disobeying orders and apparently determined to win personal glory, Custer drove his troops ahead of their support and ran into a huge Indian encampment on the Little Bighorn. There he divided his forces and attacked. Precisely what happened in the next hour is still controversial, but in the end Custer lay dead along with 264 men of the 7th. He won the glory he sought.

---

lands, the Plains Indians were still more concerned with their own wars of Cheyenne against Comanche, and Sioux against Crow. The wagon trains were sometimes raided for precious horses, but were usually allowed to pass through. These skirmishes were, however, a threat to Yankee commerce and dangerous to the wagonloads of settlers. In 1851 a United States Indian agent held a great council composed of about 12,000 Indians from most of the major tribes and all agreed on a general peace. The Indians were to stay within tribal areas and be considerate of the covered wagons, while the American government promised to keep its people under control.

SITTING BULL

"Slow" was born in 1831 in what is now South Dakota, the only son of a Hunkpapa Sioux warrior. He earned the name because as an infant he was careful and deliberate by nature. But when he had counted his first coup on a Crow enemy, his father gave him a new name given in a vision—"Sitting Bull."

Sitting Bull rose rapidly in tribal esteem. He gained a reputation as a prophet and a man who spoke with spirits. By 25 he had been elected to an elite military society called the Strong Hearts. A few years later he became a chief of the Hunkpapa at the same time that whites first began to move into tribal lands. Asked to sign a treaty that would have ceded some Sioux lands but kept much of their range, Sitting Bull said, "I wish all to know that I do not propose to sell any part of my country."

A new confrontation occurred. The Black Hills, sacred to the Sioux and a part of lands guaranteed them by treaty, were discovered to contain gold in 1874. Within a year, hundreds of miners were trespassing on Sioux land. The government responded by ordering the Indians out of the land and launching an expedition against those Sioux, Cheyenne, and Arapaho who stayed. Sitting Bull forged an alliance, warning that "we must stand together or they will kill us separately." As the warriors gathered, Sitting Bull went through a sacrificial Sun Dance and saw a vision of soldiers falling into the camp. He prophesied a great victory. On June 26, 1876, braves from the main camp overran and slaughtered Lieutenant Colonel Custer's 264 men, the greatest Army defeat in the Indian wars.

Now, however, a determined Army rolled relentlessly over the Indian lands. Most were forced onto the reservation or died, but Sitting Bull's band escaped to Canada. Hunting proved poor and homesickness thinned his ranks in Canada, until after four years Sitting Bull agreed to surrender and live on the reservation. Promised an interview with the President about his people's welfare, Sitting Bull agreed to go on tour with a "wild west show" run by Buffalo Bill Cody. Three years later, in 1888, Sitting Bull returned to the reservation to fight a scheme to cede to Congress 10 million acres of Sioux lands for 50 cents an acre. When Congress raised its offer, the Sioux accepted over Sitting Bull's objections, leading him to observe "there are no Indians left but me."

On the remaining reservation land, crops failed and disease swept the decimated ranks of the Sioux. From the south a new Indian religion arrived called the "Ghost Dance." It promised a resurrection of the Indian dead and a return of the old days before the whites came. Sitting Bull did not believe it, but would not stop it either. Whites became alarmed, and the reservation agent mistakenly saw Sitting Bull as the head of a conspiracy to revive Indian opposition. Indian police were sent to arrest him and, when his followers resisted, they shot the old man in front of his house.

That promise proved impossible to keep. During the late 1860s pioneers began to swarm into Indian territory. Petty arguments over a cow or a horse became small wars that engulfed others who had nothing to do with the original disagreement. Natives who watched prospectors following the scent of precious metals considered them as people gone insane. But where gold strikes were made, communities appeared. Land-hungry settlers and speculators filled the towns, ranchers brought cattle onto the grasslands, and the "Iron Horse" crossed tribal hunting grounds. The buffalo were drastically reduced by all of this, and hunting further depleted the herds. The Plains Indian lifestyle was at risk. The Cheyenne and the Sioux, the Comanche and the Kiowa, would not give up their life without a fight.

There followed a vicious cycle of war and bloodshed. As Indian territory was invaded by white settlers, warriors fought to protect their homeland. It is ironic that the soldiers sent by the Great White Father in Washington to defeat the Indians included large numbers of black Americans. Then treaties were made that established new reservations away from mushrooming white settlements, only to subject the tribesmen to further intrusion by a new wave of immigrants and another war. One of the most experienced U.S. Army Indian fighters wrote, "Greed and avarice on the part of whites . . . is at the bottom of nine-tenths of all our Indian troubles." The wars reached a climax in the 1870s when Lieutenant Colonel Custer's entire detachment of 264 cavalrymen was wiped out by Sioux led by Chiefs Sitting Bull and Crazy Horse. Americans were enraged and humiliated by the defeat, and Washington put forth a concerted effort that by 1880 utterly defeated the remaining Plains Indians. In 1890 an emotional religious revival called the Ghost Dance swept through many reservations. The dancers prayed for the return of the buffalo, the disappearance of the whites, and the resurrection of dead warriors. White hysteria led to the massacre of 200 Ghost Dancers at Wounded Knee in South Dakota, and the movement died with the dancers.

In the Southwest, essentially the same round of events occurred. By 1890 the Kiowa, Comanche, Navaho, and Apache had all been killed or corralled onto reservations. None of the tribes, north or south, was treated properly on these government preserves. The Bureau of Indian Affairs, despite the efforts of some well-meaning agents on the scene, was filled with corruption and hampered by red tape. Profiteers sold rotten beef or thin blankets to the Bureau for distribution to the natives. Forced into barren areas, decimated by whiskey, disease, and hunger, the tribes wasted away. Reformers like Helen Hunt Jackson, in her book *A Century of Dishonor* (1881), protested the Indians' plight. In the 1880s Congress began passing a series of laws designed to eliminate tribal organization and bring Native Americans into white society as individuals, ostensibly for their own benefit. But the individual land allotments carved out of reservation lands were too small or barren to support families. Moreover, the Indian knew nothing of modern, mechanized farming, and while he could sell his parcel of land, only a white man could buy it. In this way Indians were legally dispossessed of nearly 100 million acres of former reservation lands by the 1930s. Finally, this legislation contributed to the destruction of native culture by breaking down tribal customs and responsibilities that had governed the people's lives for centuries. While some reservations have developed and provide a good life, more are still areas of stark poverty and confusion.

Perhaps the plight of the Indians is best represented by Chief Joseph and his Nez Perces. After keeping a precarious peace with Americans for years, white encroachments and treaty violations led to an outburst of angry raids by some of the tribe's young men. This forced Joseph to leave the reservation and try to lead his tribe to Canada. The Indians brilliantly eluded three U.S. army groups sent to force them back, moving northward and fighting when they had to. Settlers were not hurt, and a group of tourists captured as the Nez Perces moved through Yellowstone National Park was released unharmed. Finally, Joseph and his people were brought to bay 30 miles from the Canadian border. Promised they could return to their reservation, he came to the army camp to surrender. "My people ask me for food, and I have none to give. It is cold, and we have no blankets, no wood. I have fought, but from where the sun now stands, I shall fight no more forever." The Army broke its promise to Joseph—he and his people were exiled to a barren

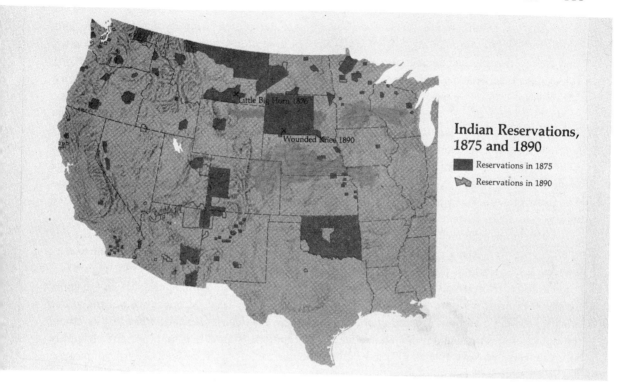

Indian Reservations, 1875 and 1890

Reservations in 1875

Reservations in 1890

Oklahoma base. Remarked the lieutenant who recorded the surrender, "I think that, in his long career, Joseph cannot accuse the Government of the United States of one single act of justice. . . ."

By the end of the century, a young Theodore Roosevelt insisted that Indians were clearly not the equal of white men: "I don't go so far as to think that the only good Indians are the dead Indians, but I believe nine out of every ten are, and I shouldn't inquire too closely into the case of the tenth. The most vicious cowboy has more moral principle than the average Indian." Finally, the Supreme Court in 1902 declared that earlier treaties gave no absolute protection over reservation lands, that reservation lands could be sold in spite of treaty stipulations to the contrary. In effect, this meant that reservation dwellers possessed no property rights.

By the early twentieth century the Native Americans had been subdued. A new image of the Indian as a hapless, hopeless anachronism began to emerge. Increasingly, the real Indians were left to wither away on the reservation. As one writer observed, "in the popular mind the Indian evolved from a troublesome heathen to a mortal enemy to an unfortunate ward of the state to a nonperson."

"OUR BROTHERS WHO WERE SOLD"

Anglo-Americans moving west ran into another culture long established in the Southwest—Mexico's. Technically in control of the huge region since its independence from Spain in 1821, Mexico had done little to develop these lands when the Anglos began to arrive. Mutually profitable trade opened between St. Louis and New Mexico along the Santa Fe Trail by 1822.

Another people found themselves becoming a persecuted minority in their own land. Spanish speaking communities began to dot the Southwest during the 1760s. The half-century that followed witnessed an energetic planting of missions, presidios, and pueblos, before Spain relinquished her northern provinces to the revolutionary government of her former colony, Mexico, in 1821. For more than two decades, the Mexicans ruled the Southwest, a region characterized by the Spanish priests' chain of missions, a system of large ranchos worked by Indian laborers, and a generally sparse population spread across an immense expanse of land.

The earliest confrontation between Mexicans and Americans occurred when the great area of the Southwest was still under the sovereignty of Mexico. First, the Santa Fe Trail opened trading opportunities in New Mexico. Then a desire by the Mexican government to develop Texas led to Anglo-American immigration. By 1836 Americans in Texas had successfully revolted against the Mexican government and established the independent republic of Texas.

To conquer the land and dominate its inhabitants required, of course, a rationale justifying their subjugation. Racial myths about Mexicans appeared as soon as their earliest encounters with the Anglos. As early as the 1830s and 1840s, Mexicans were regarded scornfully as being "lazy," "cowardly," "corrupt," and "cruel." Although the concept of "race" is especially difficult to apply to the Mexicans, who are largely the result of mixture of at least two peoples, yet the above mentioned traits were considered characteristic of the Mexican "race." Distrust of this ethnic group was widespread and reflected in a derogatory statement appearing in the Atlantic Monthly in 1899: "No one can tell what a Greaser thinks; no one can say what masked batteries of passion lie back of his well-mastered eyes. To trust a Greaser is to take a long jump into utter darkness."

As a result of the war with Mexico in 1848, however, the American government obtained the vast territory that later was carved into the states of Nevada, Utah, California, Arizona, New Mexico, and a portion of Colorado. Those Mexicans who chose to become American citizens were guaranteed by the Treaty of Guadalupe-Hidalgo "the enjoyment of their liberty and property." Although the final version of the treaty deleted an earlier explicit safeguard of Mexican land titles (Article X), American officials implied that their government would continue to respect fully the newly enfranchised Mexican Americans' rights of language, religion, and property. Subsequent events were to prove, however, that the spirit of the treaty signators would not be upheld. Because the law itself was imprecise from a strictly legal point of view, opportunists soon learned to circumvent the safeguards designed to protect the Mexicans.

The discovery of gold in California provides an excellent example of the gradual betrayal of the intent of the Treaty of Guadalupe-Hidalgo. After a century of slow population growth, California experienced in 1849 a great influx of people. More newcomers came each day than had come in the previous decade. By 1852 these immigrants numbered almost a quarter-million, most of whom were of non-Hispanic ethnic background. The original Californians, with their Spanish Mexican heritage, now found themselves a submerged fraction of people, surrounded by 10 to 15 times as many strangers. Although these "Californios" pointed proudly to their Spanish heritage, they were considered, according to one western newspaper, "aboriginal Indians, and they must share the destiny of their race." Like Native Americans, the Californios were "in the way" of the Forty-niners, and like their Indian counterparts, they were first defeated in war and then deprived of many of their rights legally and extralegally.

Although many of the native Californians had pioneered in the Gold Rush bonanza of 1848, it did not take long for their Yankee cousins to take steps to restrict their activities. When the first legislature of the new state convened to meet, the state assembly asked Congress to prohibit all persons of foreign birth from the mines, including any naturalized citizens. Such discrimination was echoed in posters that appeared in mining towns, declaring that "foreigners" must leave the mines immediately. At Hangtown, 100 Gringos claimed that the entire riverbed belonged exclusively to Americans who would "tolerate no foreigners." Vigilante groups were organized to deal swiftly with those who refused to comply. Whipping, branding, ear cropping, banishment, and hanging were commonly employed to impress upon the "Greasers" that they were no longer welcome. "To shoot these Greasers ain't the best way," one lyncher asserted. "Give 'em a fair jury trial, and rope 'em up with all the majesty of the law. That's the cure."

The fury of the Forty-niners cut a wide swath, but many of these efforts against Mexican Americans were pursued through legal channels. The Treaty of 1848, for example, contained the implication that the citizens of the newly acquired territory of the Southwest would enjoy bicultural status, including equality in the use of language. Bilingual education was the hope of many Mexican Americans, in order to promote the recognition of Spanish as an official language in addition to English. As early as 1855, however, the state Bureau of Public Instruction declared that the schools must teach solely in the English language. This effort by the nativists was accompanied by another legislative act that suspended the publication of state laws in Spanish.

The rights of the Mexican Americans to their ancient land claims were disregarded just as clearly as the language issue. In 1851, a California state senator proposed that all existing land titles should be carefully examined for any evidence of fraud or legal technicalities. The proposal easily passed the nativist-dominated legislature. To contest this law, the Mexican Americans were forced into costly court litigation, and for those who chose to fight, it was often necessary to divide, sell, or give away parcels of land in order to pay lawyers' fees. The result was that by the mid-1850s land ownership had drastically changed. Through the efforts of the legislature, the legal profession, financial manipulation, and outright force, Yankees had acquired huge tracts of land. Increasingly bitter, many Californios began to complain that they had been betrayed by the vague terms of the Treaty of Guadalupe-Hidalgo, and many people in Mexico berated their own government for "Our brothers who were sold."

The position of Mexicans in the Southwest did not improve in the latter part of the nineteenth century. The completion of the transcontinental railroads brought an even larger number of Yankees westward. A great "land boom" during the 1880s stimulated Anglo migration to California and greatly accelerated the process of "Americanization." In two years or so Los Angeles's census soared 500 percent, making the Anglos an overwhelming majority of the population. The Mexican heritage in mining, irrigation farming, and even ranching was buried. The American cowboy, with his Spanish horned-saddle, *lariat*, "chaps" or *chaparejos,* overshadowed his predecessor, the Mexican *vaquero.*

Ironically, at the same time that Spanish-speaking people were being largely disregarded, the "rediscovery" of the West's "Spanish past" began. The Anglos began to recreate in yearly celebrations or *fiestas* the glories of the "Spanish period," accompanied by a revival of architectural forms and a glorification of the Catholic missions. This vogue was subject to numerous distortions, minimizing the important Mexican influence and giving a romantic luster to the "Old Spanish Days." This cult enjoyed such popularity that the mistreatment of the Californios only a few decades earlier was conveniently forgotten. Nor were these mythmakers aware that there were still thousands of Spanish-speaking people in their midst. As one scholar has pointed out, "For only after they had reduced the real-life Spanish-speaking to the status of a foreign minority did the Yankees feel any deep compassion toward Spanish American culture."

GARDEN OF THE WORLD

As the Indians were being forced onto reservations and Mexican Americans were being made a minority on their own soil, farmers began the trek into the trans-Mississippi West. They followed trails that mountain men and other pioneers had made before them, settling down wherever they could find fertile land. In some areas ranchers and miners had preceded them; in others they were the first white settlers to see the land. Before the Civil War, many had traversed the Oregon Trail and the Old Spanish Trail into Oregon and California, but most of the territory between Omaha and the Pacific Coast had never been touched by the plow.

Several factors changed that, factors that created such a land rush that within a generation after the Civil War most of the western lands were settled. The most important cause of this agrarian westward movement was the appetite for land. Newly arrived immigrants, farmers whose lands had become unproductive or were too small to support their families, men (especially Southerners) uprooted by the war, and others who simply wanted to be more prosperous, all saw the West and its vast stretches of fertile soil as a land of opportunity. The catalyst that made this land accessible and set these people on the roads leading west was the Homestead Act of 1862. Sought by western leaders for years, the Homestead Act made it possible for a settler to own government land on the frontier merely by living on it for five years and making certain improvements. This incentive encouraged many to ignore old reports that described the prairies and the Great Plains as "dry and lifeless deserts," and those who settled there often found prairie soil as fertile as the meadows of Ohio. Western railroads also drew farmers out to the frontier by providing transportation and loudly advertising the West's opportunities, hoping in return to sell some of their own lands and promote business along the tracks. Government policy encouraged western development by making it easy to obtain land. Developers acquired huge quantities through fraud, and most of the grants made under the Homestead and other land acts were acquired by speculators, not farming families.

Within about 20 years nearly all of the good western land was occupied and under cultivation. Many of the farmers were poor, their livestock and crops sufficient to eke out a fair living but little more. Moreover, the harsh conditions of the Plains forced farmers to develop advanced methods of raising crops and livestock. A western agrarian empire began to rise, supported by the more industrialized eastern area of the country that provided a market and a source of advanced farming implements like tractors and threshers. The United States was becoming the world's greatest exporter of farm commodities.

In the years following the Civil War, politicians and newspapermen began referring to the United States as a whole and the American West in particular as the "Garden of the World." This

The Mexican *vaquero* herded large numbers of cattle in the Southwest long before the American cowboy appeared. The above illustration demonstrates that the methods and equipment popularly associated with the cowboy appeared earlier on the Mexican rancheros. (Courtesy of Kennedy Galleries, Inc.)

combination of the old agrarian myth, a belief in progress, and the concept of an American mission to lead the rest of the world, proclaimed that the nation's "boundless resources" would make it the world's benefactor and example. Echoing Jefferson at the beginning of the century, farmers were once again hailed as the country's pride and strength. But even as this utopia was being cheered it was being destroyed by that other arm of progress, the Industrial Revolution. With the help of machines, large-scale commercial agriculture was replacing the farms of the "sturdy yeoman." Wall Street financiers and railroad monopolists were gaining control of the farmers' very life by controlling loans and manipulating freight rates for his crops. Washington was favoring city over country, businessmen over farmers. The farmer became disillusioned with this gap between rhetoric and reality, and many joined the Populists' cries for reform after the depression of the early 1890s.

THE FRONTIER HYPOTHESIS AND ITS NEW WEST CRITICS

The year 1890 also saw a report by the United States Census that the West was so dotted with areas of settlement that there was no longer a continuous frontier line. Three years later, a young historian named Frederick Jackson Turner declared that "The existence of an area of free land, its continuous recession, and the advance of American settlement westward, explain American development." In short, Turner was saying that the nation's democratic institutions and the

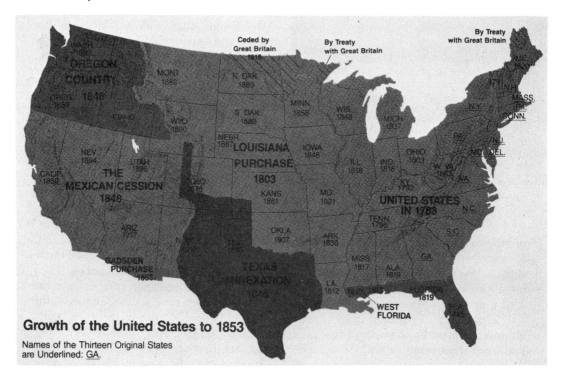

Growth of the United States to 1853

Names of the Thirteen Original States
are Underlined: GA.

American character itself had been molded by the country's constant contact with and conquest of the West since the colonies' earliest seventeenth-century origins along the Atlantic seaboard.

"Not the Constitution," he insisted, "but free land and an abundance of natural resources open to a fit people, made the democratic type of society in America." Because men had to depend upon themselves to succeed and not upon the privileges of class, contact with the frontier promoted individualism and egalitarianism. Given these two characteristics and the need for community cooperation against the hostile wilderness, democracy developed. The necessity of adapting to new ways that could cope with the frontier environment made Europeans into Americans. It also put a premium on material success and practicality. Free western land, Turner believed, also acted as a "safety valve" for the poor and oppressed by offering them a place to escape to. Because there was an abundance of natural resources and land in the West, those who moved there could improve their own situation and rise in society. This reduced class tensions. Settlers' successes affirmed their triumphant march across North America. In short, the influence of the West and the frontier on Americans, Turner concluded, has been deep.

This "frontier hypothesis" has had a great impact on the study of American history. Flexible in his own views, Turner reminded his students that each generation writes the history of the past anew, "with reference to the conditions uppermost in its own time." His offspring have not disappointed him. Today, most historians would say that Turner attributed too much to the influence of the frontier. They would point out that American democracy also had its origins in certain traditional

The cowboy has become a legend of the West. Despite the romance popularly attributed to his life, driving huge herds of cattle over a thousand miles to market was a demanding, dirty job that was not at all glamorous. It is not widely known that of the approximate 40,000 trailhands, 5000 of them were black-skinned. As the railroad took over the cowboy's role of moving cattle over long distances, white and black cowpunchers sought new jobs—whites in rodeos and on dude ranches, and blacks as Pullman porters on the new railroads. (Western History Collections, University of Oklahoma Library.)

forms and laws brought over from England. Moreover, they suggest that the frontier did not really act as a "safety valve" because, statistically, few of the poor and oppressed were able to take advantage of the opportunity; moving west cost money. Mobility, some argue, is more the result of good transportation and communication than a by-product of the westward movement. Others feel that Turner did not put enough emphasis on how much American development was due to cultural baggage brought over by immigrants. They also point out that Turner ignored one of the more negative influences of the frontier, namely violence. Many historians believe that the American penchant for violence (the United States has the highest crime rate in the world) can be attributed to the unruly, brutal climate that dominated the development of the West.

Especially since World War II, "New West" historians have challenged the ethnocentric march suggested by Turner in his milestone treatise of 1893. Rather than an "empty" frontier, settlers flowed into a region already supporting fully-developed societies: Hispanic, Native American, and mixed blood. Hence, the West was *conquered,* not settled. The conventional story of progress must be seen against a backdrop of oppression, greed, and genocide. Modern historians assert that the popular image of the triumphant charge of Anglos across the American landscape ignores a much more complicated interaction among many peoples, men *and* women. Similarly, Turner's promotion of the myth of frontier individualism neglects the persistent and decisive role of the Federal government in promoting almost every area of western growth. Finally, despite Turner's declaration that America's western development culminated a century ago, modern historians are researching the continued dynamic evolution of the West as a region *since* the "closing" of the frontier in 1890. And the passing of the frontier in 1890 did not end

Because both the railroad and the buffalo preferred gentle terrain, a clash between the Iron Horse and the shaggy beasts was inevitable. Roaming herds of buffalo, once estimated at some 15 million, were decimated by the hunters and settlers brought by the railroad. (Library of Congress.)

It has been suggested that the American quest in outer space represents a new frontier to be explored and conquered. Indeed, it was President Kennedy's "New Frontier" program that set the goal of America's landing on the moon before 1970. Exploring this "frontier" requres, however, technological know-how and vast government subsidies that were scarcely necessary on the self-sufficient frontier of Daniel Boone. (NASA.)

pioneer attitudes toward the land. Wilderness, wrote one contributor to the Letters to the Editor column of *The Saturday Evening Post,* "is the dark, the formless, the terrible, the old chaos which our fathers held back . . . when vigilance slackens, it swoops down for a melodramatic revenge." The conquest of nature continued to yield the natural resources necessary for growth and material prosperity. Since Americans judged progress chiefly by these standards, they continued to conclude that conquest equaled progress.

Not only do current writers take issue with the notion that the West expired in 1890, they also question Turner's view of the West as a *process,* rather than as a specific *place.* For them the *real* West began at the 98th meridian with the second tier of states west of the Mississippi River, including the Dakotas, Nebraska, Kansas, Oklahoma, and Texas. The great aridity of the West distinguishes it from the North and the South, the two other large geographical regions within the continental United States. Rejecting Turner's frontier process as the great unifying theme in Western history, "New West" historians suggest that *conquest* provides the key for understanding the West, not just to 1890 but to the present, as controversies rage over such issues as land and water rights, and the struggle for cultural domination. For example, currently the environmental implications of the "conquest mentality" are being scrutinized, an issue of little concern to earlier generations. Similarly, the cultural diversity characteristic of Western development is now receiving vigorous attention. What is emerging is a more complete picture of the dramatic interplay between myth and reality in the life of the West.

SUGGESTIONS FOR ADDITIONAL READING

Henry Nash Smith, *Virgin Land: The American West as Symbol and Myth,* (1957). A study of the social and literary forces that have molded the image of the American West.

William Brandon, *The American Heritage Book of Indians,* (1961). A dramatic, general work on the cultures of the Indians in the Western Hemisphere, and their effect on the conquering European and American peoples.

David J. Weber, *The Spanish Frontier in North America,* (1992). A fascinating narrative of the three centuries of Spain's empire north of Mexico.

John Mack Faragher, *Women and Men on the Overland Trail,* (1979). A provocative study of the journey across the trans-Mississippi West.

Ray A. Billington, *The Far Western Frontier; 1830–1860* (1956). One of the definitive surveys of westward migration.

Bernard de Voto, *The Year of Decision, 1846,* (1943). A colorful account linking American expansion westward, especially the Oregon issue, with far-flung activities along the frontier.

W. S. Greever, *The Bonanza West,* (1963). An excellent account of the western mining frontier.

Lewis Atherton, *The Cattle Kings,* (1961). A study of the dominant years of the cattle barons and the influence of the industry on western development.

Philip Durham and Everett L. Jones, *The Negro Cowboy,* (1965). An examination of the little-known contributions of blacks to the development of the American West.

Richard Slotkin, *Gun Fighter Nation: The Myth of the Frontier in 20th-Century America,* (1992). A provocative study of the frontier's influence on modern Americans' behavior.

WE OWE ALLEGIANCE TO NO CROWN.

CHAPTER FOUR

AMERICA AND THE WORLD: FROM SURVIVAL TO EXPANSION

1775
Battle of Bunker Hill, where the legend of the invincible American "Minuteman" was born.

1796
Washington's Farewell Address promotes a nonaligned U.S. policy.

1801
U.S. Military Academy at West Point is created to give America a professional fighting force.

1803
President Thomas Jefferson doubles the size of the U.S. with the Louisiana Purchase.

1823
The Monroe Doctrine announces a special American interest in the Western Hemisphere.

1848
Treaty of Guadalupe-Hidalgo wrests the Southwest from Mexico: height of Manifest Destiny sentiment.

1866
U.S. pushes French to begin withdrawal from Mexico; first use of the Monroe Doctrine.

1867
U.S. purchases Alaska, but its unpopularity blunts further expansionist plans.

AMERICA ON THE WORLD STAGE

When the United States of America made its debut on the world stage, it had just barely survived an eight year Revolutionary War. Near bankruptcy, with an army of only about a thousand and a navy of fewer than a dozen ships, the young republic was not given good odds for survival, much less for a rise to world influence. Yet within two generations America was firmly established, and in two more the United States was a continental power with a rising role in the Western Hemisphere. During most of that time, Americans saw world affairs as remote and irrelevant to their lives, unless events led to war.

Americans have always been somewhat ambivalent toward war. Thomas Jefferson considered resorting to armed conflict "barbarous," and Benjamin Franklin once commented that "there has never been a good war or a bad peace." The idea that war is merely an extension of diplomacy is traditionally alien to Americans. Instead it is seen as a break with "normalcy," a last resort after diplomacy fails. No President involved in a conflict abroad has ever been free of dissent at home. Yet the United States has launched aggressive wars of expansion against neighboring countries and native Indians, dealt harshly with domestic protest and "dangerous aliens," and glorified their war heroes by making seven of them President. American feelings toward the military have been similarly mixed, a blend of caution and suspicion, pride and support.

On the eve of the 21st century the United States is a major international player, "the world's only superpower." But then, in its early years, the role of the United States was much smaller. Still, then as now, America's impact on the world as an idea—as the home of liberty and opportunity—was profound.

COLONIAL LESSONS

By 1776 Americans already had strong convictions about diplomacy and war developed from their years as the distant colonies of a powerful and influential mother country. This experience had taught colonial leaders some important lessons.

Their first lesson was to rely on themselves. London rarely had the resources to vigorously defend its colonies whenever conflict broke out. Surrounded by foes—the French in Canada, the Spanish on the Florida border, and Indians everywhere—the Americans learned to depend on local volunteers for defense. If Indian skirmishes or raids worsened into serious battles, then all able-bodied men would form a militia to defeat the enemy and retire to their own affairs as soon as the emergency was over, usually serving no more than a season. Americans learned to depend on these volunteers, looking to professional soldiers from Britain only when large-scale, long term fighting with the French or Spanish broke out.

Another lesson was that these imperial wars rarely advanced American interests. Most of these conflicts of the colonial period began in Europe, were fought for European goals and concluded on terms that Europeans negotiated. Colonists tended to call the wars after the current monarch, Queen Anne's War or King William's War, and identify them with Europe's concerns rather than their own. During Queen Anne's War, New England states and ships were raided from the French base in Port Royal. The British urged colonial leaders to try to seize the French capital at Quebec, but the Americans wanted to end the raids. At considerable cost in money and men, the New Englanders seized Port Royal, only to have it returned to France at the bargaining table by British diplomats in return for French concessions in Europe. Americans came to resent being drawn into a seemingly endless series of imperial wars in which their interests had so little weight.

When the French and Indian War began in 1754 and shaped up as a contest for dominance in North America, colonial militia and British regulars campaigned together in large numbers for the first time. It was not a happy alliance. One English commander called his colonial soldiers "the dirtiest, most contemptible cowardly dogs that you can conceive." The British regulars were accustomed to strict discipline, fine uniforms, and fighting in tight lines as though they were on the plains of Europe. Colonial militia were a more independent, motley lot who saw that tactics practiced in Europe simply were not effective in the forests of America. Disasters like the defeat of British troops under General Braddock at the hands of Indians and French rangers in 1755 convinced them they were right.

Americans also learned to mistrust these permanent armies. As soon as France had been defeated and ousted from Canada in 1763, the New England assemblies requested that London withdraw its troops from America. They felt that the regulars were not only a needless financial burden, but were a threat to their local liberties and freedom of action since the troops could be used to strengthen the King's authority. The regulars left, but later returned to Boston under the Quartering Act of 1774, forcing Bostonians to house and supply the very soldiers sent to subdue them.

By that time, feelings over differences with the British had gone from simmer to boil. When the Revolutionary War finally broke out at Lexington and Concord in 1775, it was now British "redcoat" against American militia. In December the Second Continental Congress ordered an American invasion of Quebec to wrest the rich Canadian lands from London's grip. The attack, poorly planned and provisioned, ended in utter disaster as the Americans were forced to retreat. The thwarted attempt to take Quebec nearly ended the Revolution as many in Congress began to suffer nagging doubts about the wisdom of challenging the powerful British empire. Yet most colonists believed that it was too late to turn back. The die had already been cast, John Adams observed. The keys to victory lay in an alliance with a European power who held Britain in contempt. France seemed the most likely ally. Americans who only eleven years earlier had rejoiced in the French defeat, now realized the need for an alliance with France.

Thomas Paine's pamphlet, *Common Sense*, published in January 1776, breathed new fire into the American revolutionary movement. The English propagandist attacked King George III as an imperial ass and assailed the idea of the colonies remaining subject to British rule. "There is something absurd in the idea," he argued, "of a continent being ruled by an island. . . . In no instance has Nature made the satellite more important than the primary planet." Paine's stirring eloquence and rhetorical skills inspired the Americans. He invoked the idea of *mission*, that in America a new republic free of European power and corruption was imminent: "We have it in our power to begin the world over again." Independence was the answer, insisted Paine, for it was only by completely severing ties with England that America could realize that destiny.

THE REVOLUTIONARY WAR

American strategy was simply to defend the states against invading British armies and maintain a government until the British were willing to concede independence. Gaining French aid was considered crucial to a successful defense.

1775

Shooting begins when British forces fire on American militia at Lexington and Concord. Growing numbers of "minutemen" force the British to retreat to Boston with heavy casualties (April).

Bunker Hill outside of Boston lost to the British, but at high cost to their troops. British officers learned not to underestimate the American militia's fighting ability (June).

Assault on Quebec fails and the opportunity for Americans to win support in Canada for the Revolution passes (December).

1776

British forced to evacuate Boston to Washington's army (March).

Washington's army nearly destroyed in battle of Long Island, and the British seize New York (August).

Victory at Trenton raises patriot morale after Washington surprises and captures the British garrison there (December).

1777

British take Philadelphia, the American capital, after defeating Washington at the battles of Brandywine and Germantown (October).

Saratoga victory leads to the capture of Burgoyne's army and the first major American success. When the news reaches France, that nation decides to intervene in the war against the British (October).

1779

Americans recapture Vincennes, securing most of the Ohio Valley for the patriot cause (February).

1780

British capture Charleston after a seige, one of the worst American defeats of the war. They proceed to secure most of North and South Carolina (May).

1781

Battle of Guilford Courthouse ended in British victory, but it was so costly that the British began to withdraw from most of North and South Carolina to the coast in the face of vicious guerrilla war (March).

Yorktown campaign begins with British forces under Cornwallis raiding Virginia. American forces under Washington and French land and sea forces join to trap the British on the coast at Yorktown. The allied victory led to the British decision to give up the war, which by this time included much of Europe and had shaken the whole British Empire (October).

1783

Peace of Paris ends the Revolution. American independence is recognized and the new nation gains a boundary on the Mississippi River (September).

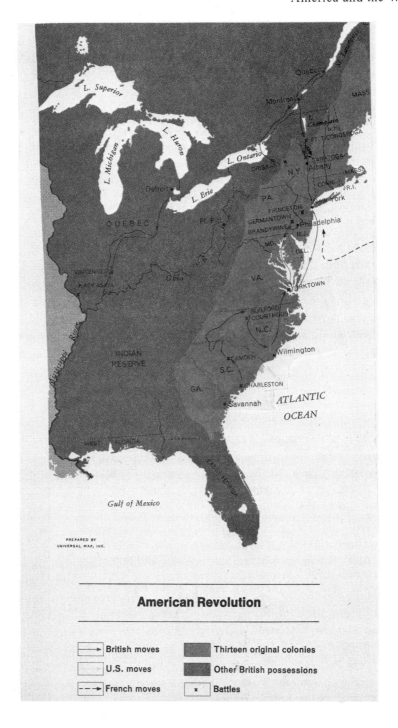

American Revolution

→ British moves	▓ Thirteen original colonies
U.S. moves	▓ Other British possessions
--→ French moves	× Battles

REVOLUTIONARY WAR

But declaring independence in July 1776 did not resolve the crisis for American diplomats, who knew they must have European aid to win their revolutionary war. France, England's habitual enemy, was the first nation America turned to for such assistance. Eager to seek revenge against England following the humilation of 1763, the Paris government began providing covert aid to the United States in early 1776. France, however, was reluctant to openly embrace the American cause for independence; officials were waiting for a substantial American military victory before they would commit their resources publicly to the Americans.

That victory came in October 1777, when the Americans, led by General Horatio Gates, defeated an entire British army at Saratoga, in upstate New York. The outcome of this battle demonstrated that a British victory in America would not be attained as easily as many in London had been assuming. Consequently, the English government dispatched a peace commission under the Earl of Carlisle, to meet with American delegates in Philadelphia; they were to hammer out a negotiated settlement to end the hostilities and keep the American colonies under British rule. The commission proposed to repeal the Tea and Intolerable Acts, to impose no new taxes on the colonies, and to negotiate with the American Congress to suspend all acts passed since 1763. The terms of the Carlisle peace commission might have been acceptable before the Revolutionary War began. However, the Americans were emboldened by their military triumph at Saratoga and could now anticipate substantial aid from France.

The French were profoundly concerned about the Carlisle peace initiative, worrying that the British would retain control of their American colonies. The French and Americans concluded the Treaty of Alliance in February 1778 in which France ensured the liberty, sovereignty, and independence of the United States in exchange for an American pledge to support France if the French should war against Britain in the future.

In 1779, Spain entered the war against Britain on the side of the French, but not as allies of the Americans. Spanish officials did not want to embrace the American revolutionary cause for fear that their colonies in the New World would also seek their independence. The following year, the British declared war on the Dutch. The war had now spread to the Mediterranean, Africa, India, the West Indies, and the high seas. The farmers at Lexington and Concord had fired the "shot heard 'round the world."

By this time the American patriots were deeply committed to the fight, but even with their lives and independence at stake they were suspicious of a professional army. Militia continued to make up most of the American forces, electing their own officers and serving for one to three months. These volunteers were not for the most part sharpshooting frontiersmen but farmers, mechanics, and day laborers. Yet when this "rabble in arms" first met trained British regulars at the Battle of Bunker Hill in 1775 and gave more than they got, the legend of the invincible "Minuteman" was born. So superior were Americans, the myth went, that a farmer could put down his plow, pick up a rifle on a minute's notice, and still beat the best England could send against him. The legend, however, did not hold true in reality—militia generally fought poorly in pitched battles. Had it not been for General Washington's own persistence in creating regular Continental Army units from the few who volunteered for longer service, the American army might have lost

During the outburst of patriotism that followed the American Revolution, one painter offered his version of "the Spirit of '76." This idealized image of the invicible militiaman helped to mold Americans' dependence on a volunteer citizen's army that persisted until the Civil War. (The original painting hangs in the Selectmen's Room, Marblehead, Massachusetts.)

the Revolution. Despite the fact that these Continental regiments aided by the French bore the brunt of fighting during the war, the myth persisted that it was the Minutemen who brought the United States into being by their victories.

Those victories were not attained by any "war machine." The American war effort was disorganized, halting, and plagued by a lack of cooperation between the states. Congress in Philadelphia had to beg, borrow, and steal supplies and soldiers necessary to sustain the American armies. Wrote one organizer, "it is a melancholy fact that near half our men, cannon, muskets, powder, clothes, etc., is to be found nowhere but on paper." Without French munitions and money the war might well have been lost. Many states, cautious about giving Congress too much power and suspicious of standing armies, kept their money and militia for their own local defense. Lack of money to pay the Continentals nearly resulted in a rebellion in 1783 when Congress had to refuse army officers the barest relief from wartime inflation. The angry officers published the Newburgh Address and ominously hinted that "in any political event, the army has its alternative." Washington calmed the men in an emotional and patriotic appeal and eventually got them pensions. Later, perhaps remembering this affair, Congress declared that "standing armies in time of peace are inconsistent with the principles of Republican Governments, dangerous to the liberties of a free people, and generally converted into destructive engines for establishing despotism." Nevertheless, many of those who had served in the Continental Army regarded it as a symbol of national unity and later were among the nationalists who served in the central government.

Nationalism itself was at a high point during and immediately after the Revolution. Those who remained loyal to England, estimated at about one-third of the population, suffered harsh persecution. Called Tories or Loyalists, they lost their civil rights, frequently their property, and even the right to work in some states. Nearly 80,000 were forced to leave America to find new homes in England, Canada, or the West Indies. Nor were Americans ready in most cases to honor the terms of the Peace of Paris, which called upon them to return confiscated Loyalist property. Anti-Tory feelings were especially high in the South, where Loyalist volunteers fighting with the British had nearly turned the tide of war against the patriots. Faith in the revolution was the one creed rebel Americans insisted upon.

That faith was wavering badly by 1781. Six years of fighting had not yielded a clear advantage. But the arrival of a French army and a naval force made it possible to force a conclusion. Franco-American military cooperation under Washington trapped Lord Cornwallis's British army at Yorktown in 1781 and forced his surrender, bringing an end to the Revolutionary War and guaranteeing American independence. The American negotiating team barely hesitated before they decided, in violation of the treaty with France, to conclude a separate agreement with Great Britain containing three important provisions for the Americans: the British formally recognized the independence of the United States, the new American nation was granted all territory from the Atlantic to the Mississippi River and from the St. Lawrence River south to lands just above Spanish Florida, and Britain agreed to evacuate its land forces from American territory "with all convenient speed." The final Treaty of Paris was signed in 1783.

The War for Independence made its impact chiefly in the social and political spheres of American life. Since many Tories were of the upper class or "aristocracy," their exile removed a source of conservatism and tradition. Often their lands were broken up and distributed to returning soldier-patriots, increasing the numbers of the small landowners. Slavery appeared on the path of extinction, as most states forbade the slave trade and all Northern states provided for the eventual end of slavery itself. Politically, states reduced property qualification for voting and drew up bills of rights to protect their citizens' civil liberties. Nationally, America would now be served and led mostly by the men who had made their marks as war statesmen or soldiers.

A NEW NATION'S DIPLOMACY

These nationalist leaders saw in their success the beginning of a "new order in the world" as the freshly minted Great Seal of the United States expressed it. The *New American Magazine* (note the name) trumpeted, "A new world has arisen and will exceed the old!"

But the United States was regarded with more contempt than wonder or awe in Europe. "As to the future grandeur of America," wrote one leading Englishman, "it is one of the idlest and most visionary notions that ever was conceived even by writers of romance." The United States was a republic in a world of monarchies, and a weak republic at that. American statesmen had yet to prove that they could maintain their nation in a hostile world climate.

With this purpose in mind, the first United States government sought to devise a strong foreign policy centering around two principles. The first had been expressed by Congress even before the end of the war. "The true interest of these states," Congress resolved, "requires that they should be as little as possible entangled in the politics and controversies of European nations." America's treaty with France had been a matter of necessity, but government leaders were determined not to extend any further commitments. This decision was an eminently practical one since the United States did not have the power to become involved in the twists and turns of

European diplomacy without risking a war that could mean destruction. Yet it also had strong elements of idealism. Americans felt that their high sense of morality should be reflected in their nation's foreign policy. Thomas Jefferson wrote that power and force may have been legitimate principles in the "dark ages" but he knew of only "one code of morality for men whether acting singly or collectively." This did not prevent Jefferson from later fighting the Barbary pirates in the Tripolitan War, but that involved little risk of a costly conflict. American governments sought to protect the country's interests as any other nation's government would. European power politics, however, threatened to enmesh the United States in more risky fights. In fact, according to Jefferson, European realpolitik was "the pest of the peace of the world."

If this principle of nonalignment had stood alone, then it might have led to an American policy of isolationism similar to that exercised by Japan during the same period. But it was modified by the second principle, accurately summed up by John Adams: "The business of America with Europe was commerce." The United States government avidly sought markets and trade wherever the opportunity for profit appeared. Such a policy was doubly legitimate—it was in the interest of merchants and farmers who depended upon trade for their livelihood, and it benefited the state by building a strong economy essential to the nation's stability and strength. Nor were commercial expansion and an aggressive trading policy beyond the strength of America, despite her weaknesses in the international political scene. Before the Revolution the colonies had been Great Britain's chief market and a vital link in her system of trade. American merchants had also carved out (somewhat illegally in many cases) a large part of the market in the Caribbean among Europe's colonies. These positions of strength could be used as levers to pry open other opportunities for profit.

Ideally, then, the new United States government hoped to steer clear of any political ties with Europe that could draw America into dangerous conflicts, and at the same time expand the country's commercial connections with that continent in the interests of its own citizens and in the interests of national strength. This two-pronged American version of nonalignment immediately ran into difficulty. The United States could not hope to remain unentangled in European controversies as long as Europe retained strongholds in the New World. For example, Spain still had a stranglehold on America's commercial "back door," the Mississippi River. The main obstacle to commercial expansion was that the United States was outside the closed mercantilist trading systems of European nations that monopolized profitable avenues of trade.

As he entered the presidency in 1789, George Washington's biggest concern dealt with the former mother country, Britain. In spite of the provisions of the Treaty of Paris of 1783, which ended the American War for Independence, the British continued to occupy forts in the American northwest. The British presence obstructed the westward movement of American settlers and allowed British trappers to dominate the lucrative fur trade in the Ohio River Valley. American pioneers also charged that native attacks upon them were being instigated by the British, who were supplying the Indians with guns. Americans were further outraged by the issuance of the British Orders-in-Council in 1793, which circumscribed American shipping rights and led to Britain's confiscation of American vessels and their cargo. In addition, scores of American seamen were taken from their ships and forced, or impressed, into the British navy.

Congressman James Madison was incensed. He argued that the American government should comercially retaliate against the British by extending preference to American ships in American ports, imposing taxes on British imports entering the United States, and favoring French trade. Secretary of State Thomas Jefferson supported Madison's pro-French policy. However, Secretary of the Treasury Alexander Hamilton vehemently opposed Madison's proposed discriminatory measures against the British. Hamilton maintained that the only rational foreign policy for the fledgling American nation was friendship and close economic ties to Britain. He argued that any policy to intimidate or oppose Britain was doomed to fail since British economic and military power was preeminent.

President Washington sent United States Chief Justice John Jay as a special envoy to London in an effort to negotiate a peaceful settlement. In Jay's Treaty, the British agreed to leave northern forts and allowed Americans to trade in the British East Indies. However, Britain made no concessions regarding American neutral rights on the high seas. The treaty was also silent on impressment. When the terms of the treaty were made public in March 1795, riots erupted in a number of American cities. Mobs stoned the British embassy in Philadelphia and burned Jay in effigy. Northern manufacturers and shippers, western settlers, and southern planters denounced the treaty which they saw as a shameful capitulation to the former mother country.

In both houses of Congress, representatives criticized the weak treaty. In the House of Representatives, Madison, who had sought to favor American-French trade while discriminating against Britain, savaged the treaty. He threatened to investigate why Jay had returned with such an unsatisfactory accord. President Washington, invoking executive privilege, refused to release documents to the House concerning Jay's mission to London. With Washington throwing his immense prestige behind Jay's Treaty, the Senate ratified it in a vote of 20 to 10.

In his Farewell Address, delivered in 1796, President Washington warned Americans against permanent alliances with foreign nations. "The nation which indulges toward another nation an habitual hatred or an habitual fondness," Washington declared, "is in some degrees a slave." But he also foresaw a danger of war, and warned his countrymen that they should not entangle their "peace and prosperity—in the toils of European ambition, rivalship, interest, humor or caprice." He briefly reminded Americans that the "great rule of conduct" for the United States in foreign relations was that "in extending our commercial relations" to other countries America ought to "have with them as little political connections as possible."

Learning that America and Britain had reached an agreement, France exploded in anger and claimed the United States had violated the Treaty of 1778. The French navy began attacking American ships. United States diplomats trying to solve the problem were met by humiliating demands for a bribe by Paris officials later anonymously called "X, Y and Z." This "X Y Z Affair" in turn made Americans angry and from 1797 to 1800 an undeclared war raged on the high seas between the two nations. President John Adams revived the navy and sent it out to conduct an undeclared war with France. As the ocean battles revived the navy, harsh repression of dissent was also revived at home. Adams' Federalists enacted the Alien and Sedition Acts, which clamped down on Republican political opposition and protests against the war. An army was raised both to prepare for operations against French Louisiana, and, as one Federalist senator put it, "to enable us to lay hands upon traitors" who opposed Adams. However, the army never marched. Adams, fearing national polarization, settled the disagreements with France and cancelled the Treaty of 1778. The Alien and Sedition Acts so angered the nation that they backfired and helped Republican Thomas Jefferson to win the election of 1800. By the time Jefferson took office in 1801, international affairs appeared to have quieted down somewhat.

NONALIGNMENT FALTERS

President Jefferson was confident that he could make nonalignment work. He observed that in times of peace American commerce thrived, and in times of war it could prosper as a "neutral carrier" of goods to the belligerents. Either way, Jefferson wrote, "the New World will fatten on the follies of the Old." None of the warring nations, he reasoned, would attack America's rights to the carrying trade under international law for fear of antagonizing the United States' growing commercial power. The President also felt that since the border with Canada was quiet and Spain had given Americans the right to use New Orleans to ship out western produce, there was no reason to become embroiled in European rivalries. The United States could remain aloof from the "follies" and "corruption" of the Old World.

Jefferson immediately set out to scrap the navy and disband the army, both of which he considered expensive and unnecessary. He felt that America's opportunity lay in commerce, not only with England but with all of the foreign ports that had been closed when the United States had been part of the British Empire. Beginning in the early 1800s American merchants entered a period of unparalleled prosperity. In the Mediterranean this commerce was threatened by the Barbary pirates operating from several North African states. To nearly everyone's surprise, the pacifist-inclined Jefferson ordered the navy to be rebuilt and sent against the pirates rather than increase the tribute demanded by the Barbary states. Like Adams before him, President Jefferson conducted the Tripolitan War without a congressional declaration. In this brief encounter the American navy was born, and before it was recalled from North Africa the new warships had forced the pirates to moderate their demands.

Louisiana Purchase

In the Treaty of Fountainebleau of 1762, France ceded the vast Louisiana territory and the vital Mississippi River to Spain. Under Spanish rule, Americans were permitted to ship cargo down the Mississippi and to store goods in New Orleans warehouses. In 1800, Spain and France had reached a second accord, the Treaty of San Ildefonso, which returned control of the Mississippi River and the Louisiana territory to France.

Americans had several fears. Because the United States had no agreement with France concerning navigation on the Mississippi, the treaty between Madrid and Paris threatened to scuttle American commerce on the river. Americans also worried that French Emperor Napoleon was seeking to reconstruct a powerful French empire in the New World. In October 1802, Americans were informed that they would no longer be permitted to ship goods on the Mississippi River. The announcement enraged American pioneer settlers, whose livelihood depended on river traffic on the Mississippi. They demanded war to free the crucial water artery.

President Thomas Jefferson pursued a diplomatic settlement to cool the tempers of Westerner frontiersmen while staying clear of a war with Napoleon's forces which the United States could not possibly win. Jefferson instructed James Monroe, United States special envoy, and Robert Livingston, United States minister to France, to offer Napoleon's government as much as $10 million for New Orleans and the right to use the Mississippi River. The American diplomats were instructed to inform the French government that if it refused the American offer, Franco-American relations would be severed and a military pact with Britain would be signed. This was an incredible threat considering Jefferson's pre-presidential admiration for France and pronounced antipathy toward Britain.

By the time Monroe and Livingston were set to negotiate, Napoleon had decided to sell all of Louisiana. The heart of the new French empire in North America was to be the island of Hispaniola, rich with sugar and vitally strategic in the Caribbean Sea. However, in 1802, a violent slave rebellion erupted on the island. The insurrection was led by former slave François Dominique Toussaint L'Ouverture, who commanded Haitian blacks in guerrilla strikes against French plantation owners and troops. The French army suppressed the uprising, but only after an enormous cost; the French lost between 30,000 and 50,000 troops killed either in fighting the Haitian rebels or dying from yellow fever, malaria, and other tropical diseases. Napoleon realized that defending the entire Louisiana territory would be an extremely arduous and costly endeavor.

Although Napoleon sought to reestablish French presence in North America, his paramount desire was expanding the French empire in Europe, which he could only accomplish by military force requiring vast amounts of capital. Therefore, Napoleon instructed French Foreign Minister Charles de Talleyrand to offer to sell the entire Louisiana territory, including the Mississippi River, to the Americans for $15 million. Although Livingston and Monroe had been authorized to spend no more than $10 million, they tentatively accepted the French proposal, hoping that President Jefferson would approve. The deal offered Jefferson and the nation three important benefits: it saved Jefferson from having to ally the United States with Britain; it secured the Mississippi River; and it doubled the size of the United States, opening up new expanses of land for farming and settlement.

However, two problems faced Jefferson and the Louisiana purchase. New England Federalists, fearing that their northeastern commercial corner of the country would become less influential if the agricultural sector were extended westward, opposed the Louisiana acquisition by arguing that the Constitution makes no provision for the purchase and assimilation of foreign territory. The second obstacle was Jefferson's concern that he would be viewed as a hypocrite in the United States by violating his professed belief in strict interpretation of the Constitution.

Secretary of State James Madison suggested that in order to be effective, a president must be flexible, bending as times and circumstances dictate. Madison urged the president to champion the Louisiana acquisition while Alexander Hamilton, the staunch Federalist, believed that the Louisiana purchase was judicious. President Jefferson ignored the constitutional issue and submitted the purchase of Louisiana to the Senate for ratification in October 1803. The Senate approved it overwhelmingly, in a vote of 24 to 7.

Closer to home, Jefferson's plans gained major ground with the purchase of the Louisiana Territory in 1803. At one stroke, western commerce secured vital New Orleans, the American domain doubled in size, and a potentially dangerous European power was removed from the continent. Neutrality had been preserved and peaceful prosperity could continue.

Even when war broke out between Great Britain and France shortly thereafter, America continued to thrive under the policy of neutrality. From 1803 to 1805, American commerce experienced a remarkable boom, and the United States became the world's greatest neutral carrier. British shippers resented this trade because they were losing business profits and because the trade was with England's enemies, France and Spain. After the battle of Trafalgar, in which Admiral Nelson smashed the Franco-Spanish fleet and established British naval supremacy, the Royal Navy began to crack down on American commerce. Then Napoleon won the battle of Austerlitz and gained virtual control over the entire European continent. With control of the seas, the British "shark" declared a blockade of Europe. Stalking the continent, the French "tiger" decreed that any ship that traded with England would be seized upon landing in Europe.

American commerce was entangled in this life and death struggle. It could trade with Britain only on stiff British terms and it could not safely trade with Europe at all. Both belligerents were breaking international law and violating America's neutral rights, and England was even forcibly taking seamen from American ships for service in their own navy. Each nation was committed to victory over the other, and was ready to do anything in its power to win the war. United States protests were ignored, but President Jefferson was as opposed in principle to war as he was to yielding any American rights. From a pragmatic point of view, he also recognized the hazards of war. He felt that economic coercion in the form of a boycott of foreign trade (or an embargo) would force the belligerents to respect those rights and bring a return to peaceful prosperity.

When a British frigate fired upon the U.S.S. *Chesapeake* and took off three alleged deserters to serve in England's own navy, war fever swept the country. Rather than give in to this sentiment, Jefferson won congressional support for a halt on all American commerce with Europe. This embargo gave port authorities practically dictatorial powers of enforcement in the hope that a military struggle with England could be avoided. From 1807 to 1809 all trade with the warring nations was shut off as the embargo was strictly enforced throughout the nation. One New Yorker noted that "the coffee-houses were almost empty; the streets near the waterside were almost deserted; the grass had begun to grow upon the wharves." The measure prostrated the commercially-oriented Northeast and sent a wave of protest throughout New England. Yet Britain and France stubbornly held to their war policies and the embargo failed. Jefferson left office knowing that the only alternatives were war or a meek surrender of the nation's rights. Jefferson passed the problem over to James Madison, leaving office in 1809.

For two more years the government tried halfhearted variations of the embargo, hoping the European war would end. The policy of nonalignment seemed impotent, unable either to prevent British naval vessels from seizing American sailors and cargoes just outside their home ports or to stop England from encouraging Indian uprisings on the western frontier. Congressional "War Hawks" like westerner Henry Clay and southerner John Calhoun demanded action. "Gentlemen," cried one, "we must fight. We are forever disgraced if we do not." They presented the question as a matter of national honor, as a choice between the humiliation of giving up American rights under international law or boldly going to war to defend those rights. At the same time, the "War Hawks" blatantly suggested that America could take Canada and the Spanish Floridas and thereby

---

WAR OF 1812

American strategy was to seize Canada from the British and Florida from Spain, Britain's ally. The small American Navy and hundreds of privateers would harry British commerce on the high seas.

1812

Detroit was surrendered by a timid American commander, which set back American plans for the invasion of Canada (August).

1813

British blockade gradually extended all along the east coast of the United States, strangling American commerce and eventually trapping most of the American Navy in port.

Battle of Lake Erie brings that strategic body of water under American control and forces the British to evacuate Detroit (September).

Indian Confederacy broken in the Battle of the Thames River with the defeat of the British and the death of Tecumseh. The American midwest was secured (October).

1814

Southeastern Indians broken by American General Jackson at the Battle of Horseshoe Bend (March).

British burn Washington, D.C., the most humiliating American defeat (August).

British invasion of the north stopped by naval victory at the Battle of Lake Champlain (September).

Americans defend Baltimore successfully against a British attack. Watching the bombardment of Fort McHenry, Francis Scott Key wrote "The Star Spangled Banner" (September).

Peace of Ghent ends the war without any settlement of the issues that began it (December).

1815

British defeated at New Orleans by Jackson's militia (neither side on the battlefield had received news of Ghent). Americans viewed this victory as evidence we had beaten the British soundly in the war (January).

---

gain more valuable territory. Finally, when France appeared to change its anti-American policies in 1812, Congress declared war against England. Ironically, days earlier the British had finally decided to stop their attacks on American commerce.

Early in the war, good news came from the high seas where the American navy won several ship-to-ship battles against the "mistress of the seas." But this was overshadowed by the British blockade of American ports. New England's commercial economy was hard hit, and northeastern Federalists angrily opposed the war. They withheld support from the government and even traded with the British in Canada. Federalists were strong in New England, but outside that area they were harshly persecuted. Pro-administration mobs in Baltimore killed and mutilated several outspoken dissenters in the summer of 1812. As the war dragged on, northeastern Federalists

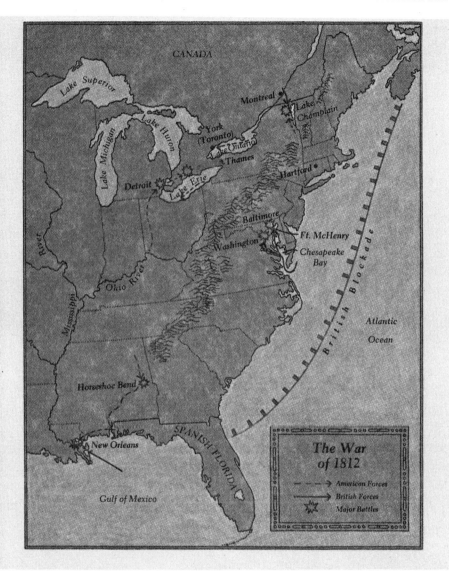

The War
of 1812

convened a protest convention in Hartford, Connecticut and sent delegates to President Madison
with demands that included a veiled threat of secession. By the time they reached Washington,
however, news of General Jackson's victory at New Orleans and the signing of a peace treaty at
Ghent made their mission look ridiculous. The Federalist party was branded as unpatriotic and
defeatist, and it never recovered from the blow.

A nationwide thrill of pride at having stood up to the world's greatest power ran up and
down the United States. Jackson's victory with a ragtag army against regular British soldiers
wiped away the shame of earlier defeats and renewed confidence in the invincible American
fighting man. The government learned some lessons from its early unpreparedness. The develop-

ment of manufacturing, ignored by the Jeffersonians, now grew in importance as it became clear how vital this development was to national strength. The government also beefed up the navy and expanded the army to a peacetime force of 10,000 men. This included training more officers at the United States Military Academy at West Point, which had been established in 1801. The United States now had a small but professional fighting force.

Most importantly, when Britain and the United States agreed to end the war in 1815, Europe grudgingly realized that America was not going to conform to its expectations and disintegrate. The United States had won a secure place in international affairs.

AN AMERICAN MISSION

This sense of security was joined by a new national pride. A perceptive government official observed that "the war has reinstated the national feelings. The people have now more general objects of attachment with which their pride and political opinions are connected. They are more American; they feel and act more like a nation. . . ." The feeling that the United States was leading the way into a "new world order" of democracy, liberty, and entrepreneurial opportunity that had been under siege since the troubles following the Revolution revived.

Spain was the first to feel the impact of America's new assertiveness. During the War of 1812 her province of West Florida had been torn away by a "popular revolution" orchestrated in Washington. President Monroe now demanded that Madrid yield East Florida since the Spanish government could not keep the area's Indians from raiding American settlements. Spain was already in a weak position, and when General Andrew Jackson moved into Florida with an army to "subdue the Indians," Madrid decided it had better compromise before it lost the province altogether. In the Adams-Oñis Treaty of 1819, Spain gave America East Florida and ceded her claim to the Oregon territory in return for a favorable Texas boundary. The United States was now a continental power, and Secretary of State John Quincy Adams exulted that "The acknowledgement of a definite line of boundary to the South Sea forms a great epoch in our history."

American attention then shifted to South America, where the Latin American patriots had all but eliminated Spanish rule by 1815. One congressman reflected public enthusiasm for the movement, hailing "the glorious spectacle of eighteen millions of people, struggling to burst their chains and to be free." Soon after the United States recognized the new Latin American republics in 1822, rumors reached Washington that the Holy Alliance (reactionary European countries that were trying to suppress liberal dissent on the continent) was considering invading South America to restore the area to Spain. To compound this threat the Russians were threatening to move into the Pacific Northwest. Great Britain, knowing that the United States would be alarmed and wanting to keep its profitable trade with the new republics, offered to join with America in opposition to these moves.

But Secretary of State Adams argued that it was time the United States announced its foreign policy principles and claimed a special interest in keeping the Western Hemisphere free of European influences. He convinced President Monroe that it would be more "candid" and "dignified" to act alone rather than to "come in as a cock-boat in the wake of a British man-of-war." Besides, he insisted, England would side with America in any case for reasons of her own.

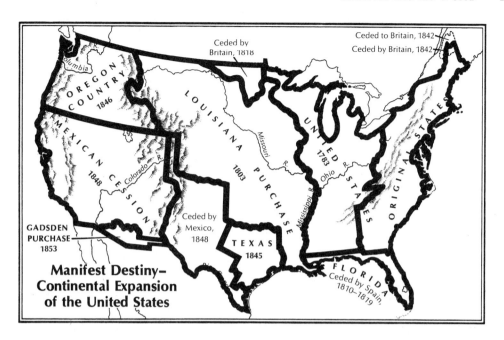

**Manifest Destiny–
Continental Expansion
of the United States**

On December 2, 1823, the President's annual message to Congress presented what became known as the Monroe Doctrine. It held that the "systems" of government of Europe and America were incompatible, and that the United States would regard as "unfriendly" any effort by a European state to extend its "system" to the Western Hemisphere. In return, America would adhere to its traditional policy and stay out of purely European affairs. European statesmen condemned the document as "blustering" and "arrogant," realizing that it was England's navy and not Monroe's Doctrine that discouraged the Holy Alliance's purposes. Initial Latin American enthusiasm waned when the United States did not follow up the President's statement with aid and declined to attend the Panama Congress called by the new republics to discuss inter-American interests in 1826. Washington still hesitated to involve itself directly in the chaotic politics of Latin America, but the Monroe Doctrine boosted the American sense of mission abroad.

MANIFEST DESTINY

At home, a constantly growing agrarian populace demanded more land and sought it in every corner of the continent. The conviction that small farmers were the backbone of the nation created strong government support for this expansionist sentiment. The American merchant marine was now second in size only to Great Britain's, and commercial interests had their eyes on the natural harbors of Puget Sound and San Francisco on the west coast as keys that would command "the trade of the isles of the Pacific, of the East, and of China." The growing nationalism and sense of mission, which held that America should take its democratic system to "less blessed" people on the continent, encouraged these impulses for agrarian and commercial expansion. The devel-

THE MEXICAN WAR

American strategy was initially to seize California and New Mexico and stop Mexican advances into Texas. The Mexican government was then expected to make peace. When Mexico held out, the decision was made to capture its capital and force a surrender.

1846

War begins when Mexican forces attacked American troops under General Taylor in the disputed land between the Nueces and Rio Grande Rivers (April).

Californian capital at Monterey seized by U.S. Naval squadron (July).

Santa Fe falls to Colonel Kearney's American forces (August).

Monterrey, Mexico conquered by Taylor's army, bringing northern Mexico under American control (September).

1847

California secured by U.S. forces under Kearney and Captain Fremont after a battle near Los Angeles (January).

Battle of Buena Vista nearly results in Taylor's defeat, but Mexican troops under the dictator Santa Anna fail to break the American line and are forced to retreat (February).

U.S. Army lands at Vera Cruz under General Scott, opening a new campaign to seize the capital at Mexico City (March).

Mexico City falls to Scott's army after heavy fighting (September).

1848

Treaty of Guadalupe Hidalgo ends the war. It cedes the Southwest to the United States in return for $15 million and promises full citizenship and rights to Mexicans living there who choose to remain under the new government (February).

opment of the railroad, the telegraph and the fast clipper sailing ship had made it possible to connect the east and west coasts of the continent. The press increased public fervor for expansion, proclaiming that it was America's "manifest destiny to overspread and to possess the whole of the continent which Providence has given us."

The United States government was not slow in responding to this cry. The Army Corps of Engineers assisted in river and harbor improvements and the construction of canals and roads, while topographical engineers like John C. Frémont explored western lands.

The regular army, augmented by state militia units, defeated Indians who resisted the tide of settlers moving onto their ancestral hunting grounds and also policed reservations created for the defeated tribes. The government had always considered commercial expansion one of its prime goals and, as an arm of the government, it was only natural for the military to take a similar attitude. Traders dealing with Santa Fe demanded and won army protection of their wagon trains. Naval vessels visiting the port of San Francisco reported that it had "the best harbor in the world"

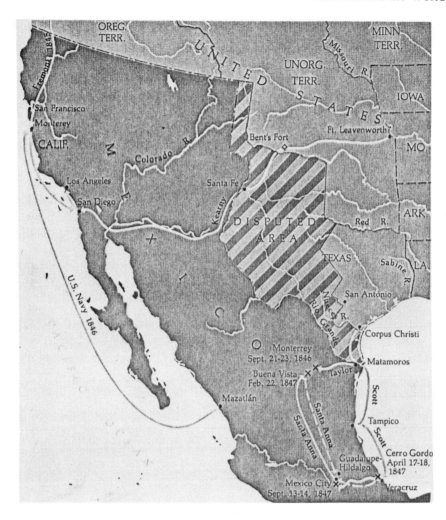

and that it was "the key to the Pacific." When American settlers swarmed into the Northwest and merchants eyed the harbor of Puget Sound, Washington contested Great Britain's right to the Oregon territory. The two governments eventually agreed to compromise and divide it between them.

Disputes with Mexico proved more difficult. When Americans who had emigrated to the Mexican province of Texas revolted against their government, Washington allowed private companies to extend them financial aid that made possible the revolt's success. Later, in 1845, the United States annexed Texas over the angry protests of Mexico. President Polk then concocted a sophisticated plan to win California, prized for its immense resources and the fine harbor at San Francisco. Residents were quietly urged to revolt against Mexico, and a small armed force was sent over the Sierras to support such a move. At the same time, Polk renewed earlier American efforts to buy California. But Mexico felt it had been robbed of Texas and was in no mood to sell. The anticipated revolt never materialized. Unable to gain the province by any other means, Polk precipitated war by sending an army to the disputed Texas-Mexico border. Mexico, anticipating an easy victory, enthusiastically fired the first shots of the war near the Rio Grande in 1846.

The military was called upon to bring this latest expansionist crusade to a successful conclusion. It was a drastically different force from the one that had nearly bungled the War of 1812. The navy had been enlarged and modernized and was led by younger officers who had gained experience in the Barbary affair. By 1847 the new Naval Academy at Annapolis was training midshipmen. The army was built around a strong core of regulars led by young officers who had been trained at West Point and had experience in the Indian wars. It too was modernized and well-equipped and augmented by the ever-present state volunteers. Once the shooting started the Americans piled up a string of victories. The Mexican forces, poorly trained and led, were defeated in a long series of engagements that ended with General Winfield Scott's capture of Mexico City on September 13, 1847. Just as the War of 1812 had seen the birth of an American Navy, so the Mexican War saw the maturing of an American Army. Commanders like Robert E. Lee and Ulysses S. Grant won experience and distinction in the war which were put to grim use in the Civil War fourteen years later.

But this war also had its dissenters. Captain Ulysses Grant called the whole conflict "unholy" and regarded the American march to the Rio Grande as "an act of hostility." Many Northerners saw it as a southern plot to extend slavery into the Southwest. Congressman Abraham Lincoln embarrassed the administration by implying that the Americans had begun the war by invading Mexican soil. Henry David Thoreau went to jail rather than pay taxes that supported the war. Shortly thereafter he wrote *Civil Disobedience,* insisting that in this unjust war "the true place for a just man is prison." One minister even said that if he had to fight in the "damnable war" he would fight on the side of Mexico. Because dissent was centered in the opposition party, it could not be easily suppressed and it even hurried Polk's efforts to end the war.

Expansionists won all they had hoped for with the signing of the Treaty of Guadalupe Hidalgo in 1848—California and the Southwest.

Mexico received 15 million dollars in consolation for losing half her national territory. This settlement essentially completed the boundaries of the continental United States, filled the popular desire for land, gave American merchants the Pacific ports they wanted for trading with the Orient, and marked the height of "manifest destiny" sentiment. But it also ruined relations with Mexico and Latin America for years, and opened the question of whether or not to extend slavery into the newly won territories. North and South, political battle lines were then drawn up over this issue that resisted compromise. Those political fronts eventually became real battle-grounds in a civil war across the nation.

CIVIL WAR SOLDIERS & DIPLOMATS

"The war," wrote one combatant, "was a very extraordinary affair. Nothing like it ever occurred before, and I doubt that anything like it will ever happen again." At the outset all was chivalry and proud patriotism. Several hundred army officers were allowed to resign their commissions and join the Confederacy, men like Robert E. Lee who were to prove brilliant commanders. When both governments called for volunteers they were swamped by more men than they could immediately arm or equip. Northerners fought for "our sacred Union and the Constitution of our Fathers," while Southerners did battle for "our homes, our families, and our rights." Some soldiers wore brilliant uniforms and cavalry charged with trumpets blaring and swords drawn.

The conflict immediately created reactions abroad. In Britain, which had the potential of playing a crucial role in the outcome, opinion was divided. Manufacturers and shippers in Britain, angered by high tariffs imposed by the Union, hoped for a Confederate victory that would secure a flourishing trade with the free-market South. The British working class tended to support the Union. Others in the government worried that the United States was becoming a powerful empire; they hoped that the War between the States would break the emerging American colossus into two nations, thus posing a diminished threat to British commerce in Latin America.

Shortly after the war began at Fort Sumter in April 1861, the British government issued a declaration of neutrality, angering the Lincoln administration fearful that London's diplomatic recognition of the southern confederacy would follow. The American Secretary of State William Henry Seward drafted a caustic note to the British government, threatening war if Britain recognized Confederate independence. However, with continued setbacks on the front suffered by Union forces, any threats from Washington did little to intimidate officials in London.

Diplomatic feathers were further ruffled in late 1861 when a Union warship stopped the British *Trent* as it left Cuban waters, removing two southern emissaries en route to England. Crowds in northern cities cheered the incident and Congress voted the ship captain a gold medal. War fever also gripped England as many saw the seizure of the two men as an act of kidnapping; the Americans were described as "bullies—brash, boorish, crafty, pushy, cowardly, and entirely unamenable to logical argument or conciliatory persuasion." The prime minister considered dispatching warships across the Atlantic and sending troop reinforcements to Canada. That urge was tempered by his realization that war with the North would unleash Yankee privateers to assail British shipping, causing considerable damage to Britain's economy. A conflict with the North might also imperil British Canada. Consequently, London sought a peaceful resolution to the crisis. Seeking a middle ground, the British decided against issuing an ultimatum and a demand for an apology; instead, a strongly-worded protest *implied* that Anglo-American relations would suffer if the two Confederate agents were not released. Despite the President's fear of angry reactions in the North if the two men were freed, his order for their release had the desired result of abating war fever in Britain.

Other issues brought the British government to the brink of war with the Union in 1862. Confederate contracts with Liverpool shipbuilding firms had resulted in the construction of commerce raiders disguised as cargo ships. Over the protests of Washington, new warships like the *Florida* and the *Alabama* left the dry docks and became part of the southern flotilla.

The threat of an open break between the Union government and Britain surfaced as the war entered its second year. Dreading a prolonged conflict due to severe cotton shortages and rioting Lancashire textile workers, London officials proposed an Anglo-French mediation commission which, frankly, would have led to the independence of the Confederacy. Fortunately for the North, General George McClelland's decisive victory over Confederate troops led by General Robert E. Lee at Antietam Creek, Virginia in September 1862 convinced the prime minister that the British must "continue to be lookers-on till the war shall have taken a more decided turn."

The turning point in the crucial battle to resist recognition of the Confederacy by England and France came in September 1862. To defuse English and French criticism of slavery, the President issued the Preliminary Emancipation Proclamation which set January 1, 1863 as the date for freedom of slaves *in states still in rebellion*. Lincoln's announcement did little to bring the British government closer to the Union cause. They denounced the Proclamation as "trash," noting that "the right of slavery is made the reward of loyalty." In other words, if a rebel state returned to the Union, slavery would not be tampered with. Nevertheless, Lincoln's skillful, if disingenuous, use of emancipation gave European capitals further cause to maintain their neutrality.

Anglo-American friction recurred in 1863 when the Lincoln administration learned that warships again were being constructed and outfitted in England, this time in the Laird shipyards of Liverpool. Two ironclad steamships were mounted with seven-foot iron rams designed to pierce wooden-hull ships enforcing the Union blockade. In September Lincoln's government warned the British that if the Laird rams were not discontinued, "it would be superfluous to point out . . . that this is war!" Actually, the mood changed; with the retreat of Confederate troops following the battle at Gettysburg, and securing control of the Mississippi River at Vicksburg, the Union enjoyed a new position of strength. Aware of these changes in the war, the British forbade delivery of the ironclads to the Confederacy and then announced that the ships had been detained, claiming they were needed for England's *own* national defense.

America's First Total War

But after several years and tens of thousands of casualties, the nature of the conflict changed. Civil war became total war. Invading Union armies ravaged the Southern countryside, burning homes and farms and pillaging cities. General Sherman's "March to the Sea" from Atlanta to Savannah cut a swath of destruction nearly 60 miles wide. Confederate troops leveled the town of Chambersburg, Pennsylvania when it could not raise a ransom of $500,000. Sieges like the one at Vicksburg, Mississippi caught civilians in the horrors of war. Trench warfare foreshadowing World War I dominated the 1864 campaign in Virginia. New weapons like ironclad ships, repeating rifles, "Machine guns," mines, and submarines were developed. The conflict also touched the home front as no other war had. A need for mass armies forced both governments to institute the draft. In New York City, poor people angry at the rich who were buying draft substitutes took to the streets for four days, destroying an immense amount of property. The riots ended when troops fired on the crowds, causing more than a thousand civilian casualties. Just behind the battlelines, hospitals were swamped with wounded from the battlefront. Prisoner of war camps were death traps on both sides, and the exchange system broke down in 1864. All of this may not have lessened patriotism, but it did produce a war weariness that almost defeated Lincoln's bid for reelection in 1864 and increased Southern criticism of Confederate President Jefferson Davis.

In the massive effort to win, both sides mobilized all of their material as well as human resources. The South's effort to build a war industry necessary to support its armies eventually failed for simple lack of skilled workers and material. By 1865 the Southern economy was a total

THE CIVIL WAR

Confederate strategy was simply to defend itself from Northern "aggression" and so earn its independence by surviving. The new nation also hoped for aid from Britain and France, or at least recognition.

Union strategy was embodied in the "Anaconda Plan:" 1) to blockade the Confederacy and cut off its supply of essential imports; 2) to cut the South in two by seizing the Mississippi River; and 3) to take its capital, Richmond.

1861
Shooting begins at Fort Sumter, South Carolina when Confederates open fire to remove the Union fortification from Charleston harbor (April).

The first battle at Bull Run ends in Confederate victory, but convinces the North that the struggle will not be short. Union preparations for war begin in earnest (July).

1862
Confederate defenses in the West broken by the fall of Forts Henry and Donelson to Union General Grant (February).

Southern attempt to regain Tennessee fails at the Battle of Shiloh. The initiative in the West now belongs to the Union (April).

Union blocks Confederate offensive in the East at the Battle of Antietam. Britain reconsiders its intent to recognize the Confederacy and Lincoln uses the opportunity to issue his Emancipation Proclamation. The turning point of the war (September).

1863
Battle of Gettysburg marks Confederate General Lee's last attempt to invade the North. Failure here severely cripples Lee's army (July).

Fall of Vicksburg effectively gives the Union control of the Mississippi River and splits the South. Together with Gettysburg, Vicksburg marked the beginning of the end for the Confederacy (July).

1864
Fall of Atlanta opens the Confederate heartland to Union armies and helps insure Lincoln's reelection in November (September).

The March to the Sea by Union General Sherman destroyed Southern resources and morale—the Confederacy could not defend its people (November through December).

1865
Lee's surrender at Appomattox came after Grant broke the Confederate lines at Petersburg, completing a nine-month siege. Lee attempted to escape but was trapped and decided to yield rather than allow his troops to scatter and open guerrilla warfare (April).

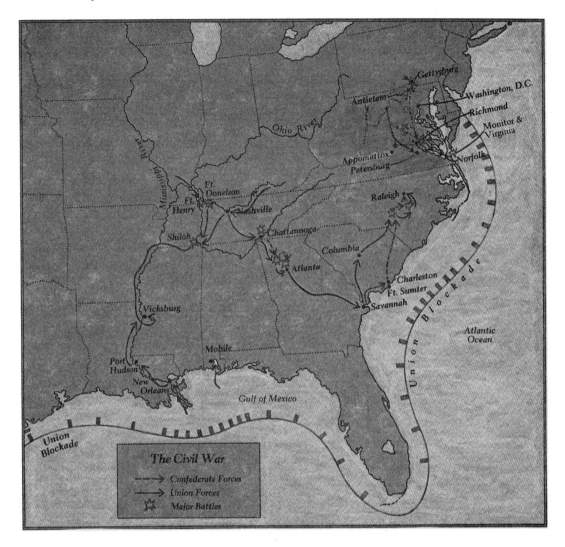

wreck, having lost at least three billion dollars in capital. Complete recovery was slow; even as late as 1932 the South was referred to as the nation's "economic problem number one." But in the North, where business and industry had been strong before the war, the economy thrived. Lincoln's administration favored business by passing protective tariffs, reforming the nation's monetary system, and by encouraging the immigration of skilled labor. Pressed by the necessity of supporting a tremendously increased military force, the government spent huge sums buying everything from shoes to warships. Many business fortunes were founded upon war contracts: Armour in meat packing, Carnegie in iron and steel, and Rockefeller in oil were a few. These ties of contracts and cooperation between government and business continued to grow until, even after the war had ended. critics would call the national administration a "businessman's government."

Many young men who marched off to war anticipated exciting adventures and quick victory. Too often, however, the romance of the war was replaced by the drudgery of camp life, or death on the battlefield. As a witness to many stirring, bloody battles, General Robert E. Lee said: "It is well that war is so terrible—(else) we should grow too fond of it." (Top: "First Virginia Regiment" by Richard Grays. Courtesy Valentine Museum, Richmond, Virginia.) (Bottom: Library of Congress.)

ROBERT E. LEE

Robert Lee was born into a Virginia family in 1807 that was already famous for its military exploits in the Revolutionary War. Young Lee graduated second in his class at West Point and became a captain in the engineers. During the Mexican War he scouted an enemy position at Cerro Gordo that blocked the road to Mexico City. He found a way around the Mexican left flank that allowed the Americans to win the battle and open the road.

After the war Lee became superintendent at West Point for three years. He then accepted a cavalry command in the West, but the patrol work bored him. Lee was home at Arlington, Virginia on leave when John Brown made his desperate raid on Harper's Ferry. He led the company of Marines that stormed the arsenal and captured Brown. Two years later, as civil war loomed, Lee was offered command of the Union armies by President Lincoln. Colonel Lee opposed secession, and the family slaves had been freed long ago. But he anticipated Virginia would leave the Union and he replied that "I could not raise my hand against my birth-place, my home, my children." He resigned from the United States Army and offered his services to his native state.

For the first year of the war, Lee did not live up to his reputation. While under his command, West Virginia was lost to Union forces. It was not until a huge Federal army approached the Confederate capital, Richmond, and the Southern commander was wounded in action that Lee assumed a major role in the conflict. In a brilliant series of moves coordinated with Thomas J. ("Stonewall") Jackson, Lee pushed the larger army back to its base. He then turned north, beat another of Lincoln's armies, and invaded Maryland. Unfortunately for Lee, a copy of his orders was intercepted and he was forced to battle at Antietam in September, 1862. Shifting his weaker army from one threatened point to another, he staved off destruction and managed to retreat to Virginia.

By this time Lee had become a legend. His men followed him unquestioningly. On one occasion, when Lee tried to lead a counterattack to prevent a Union force from splitting his army, his men cried "Lee to the rear!" and would not go forward until he moved back. They then smashed into the Yankees and restored the line. The general was ambivalent about war itself. As he watched massed Union men march in line up a hill to an invulnerable Confederate position, he sighed. "It is well war is so terrible, else we should grow too fond of it." Lee was a brilliant tactician, a master of surprise and attack. His only real weaknesses were a lack of strategic ability and an unwillingness to be blunt with disgruntled or overly cautious subordinates.

After two more victories against the odds at Fredericksburg and Chancellorsville in 1863, Lee once again invaded the North. In the decisive three-day battle of Gettysburg the Southern forces nearly broke the Federal line during the first two days. On the last day, Lee ordered an assault on the center of the Union force. It was disastrous, and as the survivors returned to friendly lines Lee moaned, "It's my fault. All my fault."

This proved to be the military turning point of the war. The following year was a long series of attempts to parry the thrusts of General Grant towards Richmond. Lee's army of northern Virginia successfully blocked the path, inflicting as many deaths on the Yankees as the Confederates had men in their army. But Grant got replacements and kept coming, pinning Lee down to a seige at Petersburg. The North's overwhelming resources finally broke the seige, and Lee's dwindling force was surrounded in retreat. "I must go to General Grant, and I would rather die a thousand deaths," Lee said.

After the surrender at Appomattox Court House, Lee and his family went to Richmond. His home at Arlington had been seized by Union forces. But Lee refused to become bitter, counseling the defeated South to reconcile with the North and becoming a symbol of nobility in defeat. He died as President of Washington College (now Washington and Lee College) five years after the end of the Civil War.

Poor New Yorkers were outraged at the rich man's draft exemption and bitter over social injustices aggravated by the war. Over 50,000 dissenters took to the streets in July, 1863 in four days of rioting against the draft law. (Courtesy of the New York Historical Society, New York City.)

The war also had its political and social effects. Most of the social reform movements active in the 1830s and '40s were swallowed up by the conflict, not to emerge again for nearly a half century. The infant American Peace Society was fragmented by the choice of war or disunion. Many church denominations were split by the passions of war. Both Lincoln and Davis were faced with opposition to the conflict. The Confederate President was handicapped by the states' rights philosophy that was at the heart of the Confederate government, and was mostly helpless to counteract it. Lincoln used his emergency powers (like jailing persons in Maryland without charging them in court for a crime) only when he deemed it absolutely necessary. Politically, with the exception of Grover Cleveland, the war kept the Democratic party out of the White House for nearly 50 years. In each election following the war Republicans would "wave the bloody shirt," reminding the electorate how "traitorous" Democrats had tried to break up the Union. The theory of state sovereignty and secession went down to defeat with the Confederacy in 1865. But as late as the 1990s, states continued to defy the federal government over civil rights, welfare, and environmental questions. Although slavery was abolished and blacks were nominally given equal rights with whites, the attitudes of racial hatred and the reality of discrimination—North and South—were not much altered by the war or by Reconstruction.

Yet something else had changed. The fact that America's process of peaceful political change had been broken, the long years of conflict that killed more men than all of America's other wars combined, the destruction of the Southern culture, and the accelerated industrialization that was altering Northern society brought "the end of American innocence." Wrote one famous historian, "The Civil War . . . introduced into the national consciousness a certain sense of proportion and relation. The world seemed a more complicated place, the future more treacherous, success more difficult."

ENTERING INTO A NEW ERA

American experience during the next quarter of a century seemed to belie that conclusion. During this period the remaining Western lands were settled and Civil War veterans drove the last Indian tribes into extinction or onto reservations. At the same time, American engineers and immigrant labor crisscrossed the continent with railroads, and a rapidly industrializing economy thrust the United States into a new era of problems, prosperity, and potential world power. American businessmen had already entered the race for world markets, and Europeans accustomed to American strength in agricultural produce now found they were faced with stiff competition in manufactured goods as well.

But the American public was more concerned with national recovery and the development and settlement of the West than with further adventures abroad. The American effort to force withdrawal of French forces propping up an unpopular European "emperor" of Mexico drew little notice in the press, though it was the first U.S. effort to enforce the old Monroe Doctrine. While Washington was able to continue promoting commercial expansion in China in the 1870s and to maintain its influence in Latin America, the public would not support efforts to gain new naval bases in the Caribbean. "We cannot have colonies, dependencies, subjects," explained one newspaper, "without renouncing the essential conception of democratic institutions." Even Secretary of State Seward's purchase of Alaska in 1867 from Russia was ridiculed as "Seward's folly" and barely passed Congress. Preoccupied with domestic affairs, Americans seemed to have lost interest in "mission" and expansion.

SUGGESTIONS FOR ADDITIONAL READING

D. M. Fletcher, *The Diplomacy of Annexation,* 1973. How the U.S. realized its "Manifest Destiny" through the end of the Mexican War.

Norman Graebner, *The Foundations of American Foreign Policy,* 1985. A good overview of "realism" in U.S. diplomacy before 1900.

Reginald Horseman, *Causes of the War of 1812,* 1962. The "whys" for the conflict that could have crippled American independence.

Lawrence Kaplan, *Colonies into Nation,* 1973. Follows the course of U.S. diplomacy through the end of John Adam's presidency.

Henry F. May, *The Making of the Monroe Doctrine,* 1975. The development of America's first "mission statement" to the world.

James McPherson, *Battle Cry of Freedom,* 1988. A masterful overview of the Civil War.

Richard Morris, *The Peacemakers,* 1965. How American diplomats "won the peace" and secured U.S. independence.

"The Gun Foundry, Cold Spring, N.Y." by John Ferguson Weir. (Courtesy Putnam County Historical Society, Cold Spring, N.Y.)

CHAPTER FIVE

A CHANGING SCENE: SOCIAL AND CULTURAL RESPONSE TO THE INDUSTRIAL REVOLUTION

1874
The Grange organized by farmers concerned with their low standard of living.

1879
The Standard Oil Trust is formed, controlling 90 percent of American oil refineries.

1883
The Pendleton Act begins the government civil service system.

1885
United States becomes the world's leading industrial power.

1886
American Federation of Labor formed; the first successful national labor union.

1887
The Interstate Commerce Commission is created to regulate the railroads.

1890
Sherman Anti-Trust Act passes to make big business more socially responsible.

1894
Pullman Strike threatens nationwide railroad paralysis before federal troops intervene to restore order.

THE PRICE OF POWER

The industrial revolution that swept the United States in the last three decades of the nineteenth century made America the wealthiest nation and the prime industrial power in the world. It literally changed the face of the nation as well. Urban life began to supplant rural life with the growth of new and larger cities around centers of production and transportation. Attracted by job opportunities and an "exciting life," millions of Europeans left the Old World to come to America while thousands of farmers seeking the same things abandoned their country homes for the bustling city. The force that dominated these decades was change—constant change that brought new ideas, products, issues, conflicts, and new faces to life in America. Things seemed in perpetual motion.

This process put an enormous strain on American society. One observer of the scene felt that "new power"—power of machines, money, and man's own organizations, but especially the power of change itself—was causing society to "disintegrate." The pace of industrialization and urbanization, though cheered and considered by many Americans as an indication of "progress" created at the same time much confusion, anxiety, and frustration. Old and cherished values, customs, and beliefs were being challenged, if not overwhelmed. During this period of American development problems surfaced that still face the country today: inner-city ghettos, crime in the streets, corruption on all levels of government, and especially the conflict between business's freedom of development and the public welfare. To understand the scope of these changes and issues, it is necessary to acquire a feel for "village America."

VILLAGE AMERICA

America before the industrial revolution was a nation of village communities in a rural setting. Even in the country's few large towns life had a village flavor, with neighborhoods forming units that acted as though they were separate unto themselves. The expense and time required for travel combined with the poor state of roads made communication between communities difficult. This restricted interaction and dispersed political power over public policy. In fact, democracy was practically equated with local self-government. The people who lived in these communities shared common values and ethnic backgrounds, and they firmly believed that they could regulate their own lives as they chose. Although these villages and even the farming countryside around them did rely on the outside world, they retained a sense of self-sufficiency.

Being uniform and somewhat self-contained, society in these communities was personal. Business transactions were made between people who knew each other as neighbors. A farmer temporarily in trouble because of a bad crop could go to the local bank and count on his reputation as a dependable and honest man to aid him in getting credit or a loan extension. Buying and selling may have been inefficient and even expensive, but it was on a personal level that gave people a sense of belonging. Politics reflected this same tendency. Whether a person was a Republican or a Democrat often determined his circle of friends and his enemies. Politics was in fact a national avocation, the justification for picnics, rallies, and social busy work. Yet national and state affairs were of only slight interest in themselves. Partisanship was local, identified with local interests and local problems.

The lad in the foreground may not have grasped the significance of the railroad winding
through his village community. As early as the 1850s the revolution in transportation
wrought by the railroads was altering the face of rural America. "The Lackawanna Valley"
by George Inness. Courtesy National Gallery of Art, Washington, D.C. Gift of Mrs.
Huttleston Rogers.

"Local" might be the best description of village America. Believing themselves self-
contained, secure in their homogeneous character, and insulated by the slow pace of life, these
communities faced the future confident that it would not bring anything they could not handle.
But the very progress that they sought to achieve was already beginning to change the nature of
American society and to undermine their control over it.

THE FIRST SURGE

The first indications of change were the developments in transportation during the early 1800s.
To make westward travel and communication easier several turnpike roads were constructed
connecting eastern centers with growing frontier communities. A boom in canal building began
after the Erie Canal, connecting the Hudson River and Lake Erie, proved to be a great financial
success. Along with the canal craze came the development of the steamboat. Soon these coal- and
wood-burning craft were making regular runs up and down the Mississippi and Ohio Rivers,
navigating the Great Lakes, and becoming larger carriers of goods and passengers than the canals.
At the same time the American merchant marine was expanding the nation's markets abroad with
the aid of the graceful clipper ship, and by the 1850s America could boast of the world's largest
commercial fleet.

Transportation
in 1860
——— Principal Roads
– – – – Canals
Railroads

Last and most significant of the developments in transportation was the railroad. An invention imported from England, the steam-driven locomotive pulling a string of cars along steel rails quickly became a common sight in the United States. By 1840, only 13 years after the first railroad was built in Massachusetts, railroad mileage nearly equaled canal mileage. When Congress began to give grants of land to states to encourage construction, a boom occurred that made 30,626 miles operational by 1860. The railroad was the last link in the nationwide system of transportation that bound the country closer together. In 1816 it took 103 hours to make the journey from Philadelphia to Quebec by steamboat and stage; by 1860 the same trip took only 31 hours by railroad. The "iron horse" also expanded the horizons of businesses looking for new markets and encouraged foreign investment in American economic development.

This development continued despite the cycles of prosperous boom and depression that plagued businesses in the United States from the 1820s to the 1850s. Westward expansion increased the material resources of the nation and provided new opportunities for growth. The discovery of gold in California added to the country's financial resources. An even more important financial factor was foreign investments, chiefly in railroads, which by the 1850s had grown to $381 million. Attracted by what seemed to be dazzling opportunities, Germans fleeing the Revolution of 1848 flooded into America as did Irish escaping a potato famine in their country. Joined by numerous Scandinavians, these groups swelled the tide of immigration into the United States. Growing manufacturing and industrial concerns benefited from this influx of labor.

Production increases from the textile factories and from iron industries strengthened the economy. By 1860 America ranked second behind Great Britain in world value of manufactures. Nor did agriculture lag behind; production of cotton and foodstuffs increased even more dramatically than manufactured goods.

The idea spread that industrial progress was good for the nation. Enterprising men who had made their fortunes in commerce were willing to risk investing in new industries and businesses, with the encouragement of government. As a result, the American economy began to experience an accelerated growth or "takeoff" in the 1850s that prepared the way for an industrial revolution of awesome proportions.

INDUSTRIAL TRANSFORMATION

That industrial revolution made the United States the world's leading manufacturing nation by 1885. The takeoff begun before the Civil War slowed overall during the war years, but huge expenditures aided many specific businesses whose products were needed for the armies. The Republican administration in Washington also passed legislation favorable to northern industrial and manufacturing interests, especially a protective tariff. Inventions like the Bessemer process for refining steel became of fundamental importance to emerging industry, so much so that one English observer remarked that "the number of labour-saving appliances in use for almost everything is perfectly astounding." European investment continued to be important and the sale of agricultural products abroad provided even more foreign capital for development. As the immense resources of the West were discovered, they too spurred the accelerating growth of industry. Railroads connecting the east and west coasts and spreading into every corner of the land opened new markets and new sources of raw material at the same time. Immigrants became both workers and customers to serve the expanding economy. Most Americans proudly hailed this industrial transformation, and great emphasis was put on the statistics of growth.

These statistics were impressive, if not staggering. Even though the value of agricultural produce tripled between 1860 and 1900, the value of industrial goods surpassed it by 1890, growing to eight times the 1860 figure. Between 1880 and 1900 the gross national product doubled to more than $37 billion. During the same period steel production multiplied over 100 times. The nation's railroad network made transportation so cheap that one businessman maintained that "a ton of goods can now be carried on the best-managed railroad for a distance of a mile, for a sum so small that outside of China it would be difficult to find a coin of equivalent value to give a boy as a reward for carrying an ounce package across a street."

The giant corporations that produced this huge jump in output were built by entrepreneurs. Businessmen such as Andrew Carnegie, John D. Rockefeller, and J. P. Morgon with millions of laborers and machines transformed the American economy. These men were generally native born of middle-class parents, bred in an atmosphere where business and relatively high social standing were closely associated with family life, and the recipients of a college education. Protestants by faith, they were highly competitive and self-confident, with a passion for their work. Rockefeller was so attentive to detail that, long after becoming rich, he reduced the number of drops of solder used to seal oil drums to save money. J. J. Hill, the railroad magnate, left his private train one

JOHN D. ROCKEFELLER

John D. Rockefeller was born to a middle class family in Richford, New York in 1839. When he was fourteen the family moved to Cleveland, where he began his business career as a clerk while attending high school. He was a smart bookkeeper who saved his pennies and became a junior partner in a produce firm. The year after the first American oil strike, a group of money men in Cleveland sent Rockefeller off to Oil Creek, Pennsylvania to look the situation over and report on the long-range possibilities of the gushers. He was not well received by the wildcats, one of whom called the prim, methodical Rockefeller "that bloodless Baptist preacher." After his survey he went home and blandly reported to his employer that oil had no commercial value.

This was an early sign of what one contemporary called Rockefeller's ability to "see around the corner." He had figured or been told that the black goo was not necessarily an end in itself. It was then oil for lighting, but he guessed that it might become oil for heating, for steamships, for lubrication, and for energy. Rockefeller and a partner pooled their savings and invested every penny they had in a new refinery run by a candle maker. They soon became the largest refiner in the area by gathering up many of the small firms. Rockefeller eliminated waste, made production more efficient, and found other ways to cut costs. Soon, because of his volume of business, he forced the local railroad to give him rebates on freight charges. This in turn allowed him to undersell his Ohio competitors. In the 1870s he pushed into New York and Pennsylvania and gained spectacularly during the long slump after the Panic of 1873. As his Standard Oil Company grew and prospered, he forced railroads to give him drawbacks on the freight rates paid by other refiners! In the 1880s he crushed the last of his competitors by building his own pipelines. By the end of the decade, Standard Oil controlled 90 percent of the country's refining industry.

The Standard Oil Company was the model for all who aspired to "vertical integration" of an entire industry (where one firm owns or controls a complete operation, from the raw materials to the finished product). The company owned its own forests for lumber, made its own drums, manufactured its refinery chemicals, bought up oil terminal facilities, possessed fleets of ships and oil cars on trains, and carried on its own retail marketing. Soon Standard Oil agents were competing actively with Russian oil producers in the markets of Central Europe and teaching Orientals the value of the kerosene lamp. The five-gallon kerosene tin from Standard became a worldwide institution.

Rockefeller accomplished all of this by the age of thirty-three. He became the first billionaire in modern history. But he lived most of his life frugally, not in luxury. At sixty, with the coming of arthritis, he developed a strong conviction that God had allowed him to make all of his money so that he might benefit society. So, with complete sincerity, he began to give it away. Through a foundation created in his own name, he gave $350 million for medical research alone. He was photographed everywhere doing common things "for the people." By the time he had reached ninety, his wealth and position the envy of the country, his health had reduced him to a gruel and graham cracker diet. He died at the age of ninety-eight.

---

bitterly cold Minnesota evening to help his men shovel snow off the tracks. These men were in business for more than profits; they also sought challenge and adventure in what one of them called "The Great Game." They played the game by their own rules and were not above using bribery, political corruption, and vicious price wars to win regardless of the human or social cost.

"Cut-throat" competition like this meant dizzying changes in prices, costs, and profits that added to the instability that was natural in a dynamic economy. The business cycle took unpredictable turns, and 14 of the 25 years after 1873 were years of recession. Trying to smooth the economic ups and downs into a more steady (and more profitable) pattern of growth, entrepreneurs tried several tactics to reduce competition and increase profits. They formed pools, making informal agreements to set prices. Larger companies built trusts that combined several related businesses to monopolize a product. Later, after trusts were made illegal, these "robber barons" constructed complex holding companies that owned controlling interests in the stocks of many corporations. Standard Oil managed to corner 90 percent of American oil production before 1880. Another trust, United States Steel, controlled 60 percent of all the steel and iron made in the nation when it was formed in 1901. Perhaps the most important and strongest holding company was the House of Morgan, named after its director J. P. Morgan, which had access to millions of dollars for financial investment. Morgan's financial power and expertise were such that in 1895 President Cleveland appealed to him to protect the financial standing of the American government, which he did, making a tidy profit as a result of the transaction.

The economic power of these industrial and financial combinations allowed them to dominate the American economy. Although these economic developments reduced the cost of living and made more and cheaper goods available to the public, it also created an enormously rich elite. One such family, the Vanderbilts, had a mansion that required a staff of 30 servants. Most Americans rented a home and furnished it for less than the cost of a half-dozen of the Vanderbilts' imported salad plates. To complaints that this huge gap between the wealthy and the rest of society was unjust, John D. Rockefeller replied, "they have but to master the knack of economy, thrift, and perseverance, and success is theirs."

THE GOSPEL OF WEALTH

Rockefeller was not being cynical; he was merely voicing the tenets of a philosophy that was widely accepted in his day. Based on the rock of the Protestant ethic, this gospel of wealth simply stated that the rich were rich because they were more righteous than their fellow men. Opportunity was all around—one Baptist minister insisted that America was covered with "acres of diamonds" and that by "right thinking and right living" the secrets of wealth would be revealed. An Episcopal bishop wrote "that in the long run, it is only to the man of morality that wealth comes" and, bluntly, that "Godliness is in league with riches." Andrew Carnegie, poor immigrant turned millionaire, was one of the foremost advocates of the "gospel of wealth." But he maintained that responsibility went with fortune, and that the rich man should act as society's steward to return surplus money for the cause of the improvement of humanity. Only stewardship justified the acquisition of wealth. Carnegie practiced what he preached, building libraries and hospitals and supporting colleges across the nation. He was, however, more the exception than the rule. Most wealthy families preferred the less self-sacrificing notion that since they made the money, it was theirs to spend as they chose. And they chose to spend it on themselves.

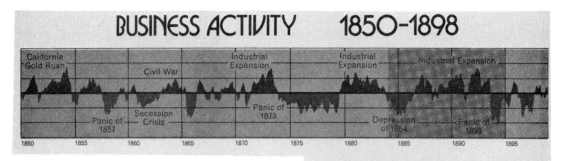

BUSINESS ACTIVITY   1850-1898

This chart shows the instability of the economic expansion the United States was undergoing during the industrial revolution. Overspeculation, especially in western lands and railroads, was the bane of sustained growth. The detail at right shows the peaks and valleys representing panics and depressions—the "steepness" of these peaks and valleys indicate the rapidity of economic fluctuation.

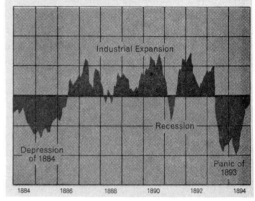

To people who required a more scientific explanation for the gap between rich and poor, apologists offered the natural law of "survival of the fittest" as adapted to fit the American social scene. The "fittest" were, of course, those entrepreneurs who had prospered in economic competition. Yale professor William Graham Sumner and English economist Herbert Spencer applied the biological theories of Darwin to social and economic questions and popularized Social Darwinism in the United States. Concluding that economic competition was society's evolutionary test, these scholars maintained that those who succeeded were America's "fittest" and that their "natural selection" benefited both the nation and the race. To tamper with this "natural" state of affairs, Sumner warned, was "the greatest folly of which a man can be capable." The poor had simply lost the race. Government and society must allow evolution to right any existing injustices. "Perhaps," sighed one Darwinian, "in four or five thousand years evolution may have carried man beyond this state of things."

If most Americans accepted these arguments and "this state of things" it was because they expected or hoped to succeed and become one of the "fittest." Such emphasis was placed on financial and social achievement that philosopher William James sarcastically announced the introduction of a new deity—"the bitch-goddess success." Handbooks on "How to Succeed" in all types of endeavors sold more copies than any other book except the Bible. Nearly as popular were the novels of Horatio Alger, whose young hero always managed to go from "rags to respectability" with a combination of "pluck and luck" in books with titles like *Struggling Upward.*

All of these comments on the justice, or at least the righteousness, of the capitalist system as it was operating in America encouraged Americans to believe that with the right combination of morality and hard work they too could become Rockefellers or Carnegies. Actually, upward mobility at the time was limited mainly to moderate property accumulation. Moving way up on the social scale was more difficult and far less common. Some Americans declined to accept the precepts of the gospel of wealth or of Social Darwinism. A California newspaperman named Henry George insisted that the "contrast between the House of Have and the House of Want" was unjust. He proposed a single tax on any increase in land value that was not a direct result of the owner's effort, thus returning to society what society as a whole was responsible for: the value of land. Another dissenter, Edward Bellamy, wrote a bestseller entitled *Looking Backward* about a socialist utopia of the future tempered by humanitarianism and world peace. Though both George and Bellamy attracted a devoted following in the eastern United States, they were not as well in touch with the national temper as was Alger. For Alger told a people obsessed by the pursuit of success what they wanted to hear—that they could all be rich.

GROWTH OF THE CITY: THE URBAN FRONTIER

Industrialization wrought even deeper changes than providing more goods more cheaply and elevating a new social and financial elite to the top of American society. It also changed the basic scene of American life from a rural setting to an urban one. This switch had been made possible by advanced agricultural technology, which in the 1870s and 1880s allowed farms to produce enough to release most of the population from the necessity of growing their own food. Urbanization was also greatly aided by the railroad, which supplied the expanding city with the enormous amount of food and goods that it required.

Economic opportunity was what drew people to the cities. Older centers like New York and Baltimore with capital and labor already plentiful and with good railroad connections quickly became huge manufacturing centers for growing businesses. Newer cities like Denver or Chicago grew up around western industries like mining or meat-packing that drew job-hungry Americans like a magnet. Chicago's development was typical of the process of urbanization throughout the country. When that city became an important rail center and marketplace in the 1870s, its population tripled in a decade. By the 1890s Chicago had become a major industrial town and the focus of many railroad networks, and its population had soared to over a million. One disgusted writer recorded that the making of money was Chicago's "genesis, its growth, its end and its object," and that everyone who came to the city came "for the common avowed object of making money."

The enormous influx of people that allowed cities like Seattle and Los Angeles to double their population and other cities like Denver and Dallas to quadruple theirs meant that growth was often haphazard and unplanned. New dwellings and industries mushroomed nearly overnight, faster than cities could take care of them. People in Philadelphia threw sink and slop water out onto gutters and sidewalks. Manufacturing wastes and sewer water were emptied into the Delaware River, where Philadelphia initially got much of its drinking water. Horse dung attracted

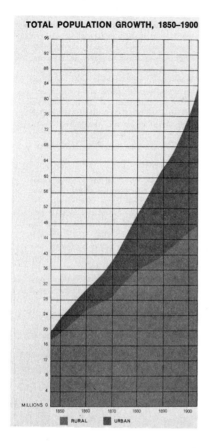

TOTAL POPULATION GROWTH, 1850–1900

MILLIONS

RURAL   URBAN

A high birth rate and massive immigration caused the American population to soar during this period. Urban population was increasing at a greater rate than rural population (from less than three million in 1840 to more than 36 million in 1910.)

swarms of flies to the city streets, especially in western towns where the horse remained the chief mode of transportation well into the twentieth century. Most streets consisted of dust or mud, depending on the weather. New Orleans had only 100 of its 500 miles of streets paved (with brick), and asphalt only came into use later with the introduction of the bicycle and automobile. There was little or no planning for open spaces. New York's Central Park, built by Frederick Law Olmsted in the 1850s, was a notable exception, but many cities used more land for cemeteries than for parks. Tenement dwellings sprang up to house workers in areas close to the factories, many of which had eight or more occupants crammed into one small apartment. The living room often served as the kitchen and even the bedroom for boarders, and the narrow alleys and streets served as recreation areas. One English visitor asserted that American cities were bland imitations of each other, differing "from one another only in that some of them are built more with brick than with wood, and others more with wood than brick."

Desperate city managers tried to ease some of these conditions and provide needed services to their residents. New York City created a board to deal with epidemics. From 1880 to the 1890s the number of public water works serving American cities increased five times. Various wonders were invented to improve city transportation: San Francisco's cable car, New York's elevated

As the pace of industrialization continued in Gilded Age America, the gap between deep poverty and great wealth widened. The living conditions of immigrant tenement dwellers and the great entrepreneurs in New York City reflects this development at the turn of the century. (Top: The Jacob A. Riis Collection, Museum of the City of New York.) (Bottom: The Vanderbilt mansion, 1908. Courtesy The Byron Collection, Museum of the City of New York.)

railroad, Richmond's trolley car, and Boston's subway. These developments enabled many of the urban well-to-do to leave the grim central city area for new suburbs in the countryside. Frequently, urban expansion would swallow these suburbs and new ones would spring up farther beyond the city limits. In this manner cities slowly began to spread across the countryside. The only alternative was building up; Chicago built the first skyscraper in 1884. Not until Olmsted's construction of the "White City" at the Chicago World's Exposition of 1893, with its paved streets, parks, electric lights, and immaculate buildings, did urban planning begin to catch on.

Great social changes as well as physical changes were taking place in the city. For those who had left rural communities and come to the city, life was transformed. They were thrown together with a conglomeration of people with diverse origins, interests, and occupations. Complained one transplanted farmer, "there is no sense of common earth, a common fortune and a common fate." Thrown together with so many people, there was little privacy. Yet the bewildering array of differences and everyone's tendency to mind his own concerns made life impersonal. "In the city there is no sense of neighborhood," observed one clergyman. "You may be separated from your next neighbor by only a few inches and yet for years never see his face or learn his name." The poor families of unskilled or out-of-work laborers crowded into inner-city slums. A social worker in New York wrote concerning one family: "The man, his wife, and three small children shivering in one room through the roof of which the pitiless winds of winter whistled. The room was almost barren of furniture; the parents slept on the floor, the elder children in boxes, and the baby was swung in an old shawl attached to the rafters." Prostitution, crime, drunkenness, and gambling were widespread. The very pace of city life, with its constant change and emphasis on competition broke down the traditional social institutions of religion and family and made for anxious, insecure, and lonely living.

The churches were the first to recognize that these problems "threatened our Christian civilization." Religion wilted in the city as many workingmen left the church. When asked why he didn't attend services, a laborer said "the rich folks build their churches for themselves and they keep them for themselves, and I ain't never going to interfere with that arrangement." Sundays were usually a worker's only holiday, and many felt that the church was indifferent to their concerns. Aroused ministers and laymen alike urged their congregations to begin to meet the problems of poverty, crime, disease, and loss of personal worth that were massed in the city.

SOCIAL GOSPEL

The issues of social, economic, and political reform were quite prickly for American Catholics and Protestants in the late nineteenth century as church leaders had long warned against state intervention in society and the economy. Many religious leaders did not attribute poverty to systemic social injustice; instead, they saw the plight of workers caused by their own lack of thrift and moral resoluteness. Conservative Catholics and Protestants argued that through virtue, personal initiative, and self-reliance, the impoverished would eventually attain upward mobility. In the meantime, the plight of the poor could be eased through charitable works sponsored by churches, the community, and voluntary service by individuals rather than through welfare legislation hammered out by the government.

During the 1880s and 1890s, liberal Catholics and Protestants developed the social gospel movement to reform the inequities of American industrial society. Protestant and Catholic social gospelers questioned the traditional Christian emphasis on *personal* piety and *individual* salvation while advocating a community approach to the problems arising from rapid industrialism and urbanization. Catholic and Protestant progressives lamented that "the things of God" in the United States were being "crowded out" by the pursuit of money and lavish personal expenditure. They asserted that Christian tradition had always emphasized man's social nature and that it drew tight moral barriers against social and economic conditions which demean human dignity.

Protestant social gospelers professed that Christianity was obligated to condemn poor wage levels, inhuman living and working conditions, materialism, and narrow individualism. Contending that men and women were pressed by a moral obligation to help others, liberal Protestants argued that social reform was as indispensable as prayer to Christian life. Protestant social gospel advocates such as Lyman Abbott, Washington Gladden, and Walter Rauschenbusch urged Christians to perform good works by meeting the ethical demands of their religion and preparing not just themselves as individuals, but the entire human community, for salvation.

Gladden, a Congregationalist minister and journalist, witnessed the suppression of two coal strikes in the Ohio River Valley in 1884 and 1885. Stunned by the brutal treatment of the miners, he denounced *laissez-faire* capitalism as "antisocial and anti-Christian." Arguing that social salvation is as vital as the salvation of individuals, Gladden called for the unification of economics and ethics in a democratic and humanitarian community. Gladden and other liberal Protestant urban ministers began to preach "social salvation." In his 1886 social gospel manifesto, *Applied Christianity: Moral Aspects to Social Questions,* Gladden proclaimed: "The doctrine which bases all the relations of employer and employed upon self-interest is a doctrine of the pit; it has been bringing hell to earth in large installments for a good many years." Gladden urged Christain clergymen to become mediators in the often violent confrontation between labor and capital.

Rauschenbusch, another leading figure of the Protestant social gospel, began his Baptist ministerial career in the notorious Hell's Kitchen district, a sprawling slum on Manhattan's Lower East Side. Life was so desperate there, he later recalled, that "one could hear human virtue cracking and crushing all around." Like Gladden and other liberal Protestants, Rauschenbusch called for a new society structured on ethical principles and communal fellowship. Rauschenbusch argued that "the force of the religious spirit should be bent toward asserting the supremacy of life over property." He asserted further that "it is unchristian to regard human life as a mere instrument for the production of wealth." In fact, Rauschenbusch believed that Christianity had more in common with socialism than capitalism. He merged the nineteenth-century tradition of evangelical reform and the twentieth century scientific approach to reform. Rauschenbusch called upon the government to legislate reforms for the poor and laboring class and appealed to American churches to offer material as well as spiritual care.

In 1896, another Protestant social gospel clergyman, Charles Sheldon, published a novel, *In His Steps: What Would Jesus Do?* The book became an instant best seller, depicting a fictional Protestant congregation whose members committed themselves to live in full compliance with

Christ's teachings for one year. They rejected materialism and dedicated themselves to the selfless service of others. Sheldon's book was a searing indictment of a society which embraced Judeo-Christian values but routinely worshipped at the temple of money.

American Catholic ideological opposition to social and economic reform also originated during the generation following the Civil War as working class Catholics became involved in political and labor movements. At first fearing that the church would be stigmatized by Catholic involvement in political agitation and labor unrest, American Catholic leaders urged their followers to renounce union membership and warned against participation in labor-management confrontations. However, throughout the 1870s and 1880s, large numbers of Catholic craftsmen and factory workers, including working women, joined the first moderately successful national labor union, the Noble and Holy Order of the Knights of Labor. Founded in 1869, the Knights called for the abolition of the "wage slavery" of capitalism and the creation of a socialist economy comprising small producer cooperatives. The union's leaders promoted the eight-hour day for industrial labor, health and safety regulations in factories, the abolition of child labor, equal pay for equal work for men and women, and a graduated income tax. The Knights allowed African Americans, women, and unskilled workers into the union and, in 1886, its peak year of success, the Knights boasted a membership of 703,000 workers, of which perhaps as many as two-thirds were Catholics.

Since management often met union activities with harsh reprisals, the Knights of Labor kept their affairs clandestine; newly-initiated Knights were required to swear oaths of secrecy. From 1879 to 1893, Terence V. Powderly, an Irish American Catholic machinist from Scranton, Pennsylvania, served as Grand Master Workman of the Knights. Although Powderly brought some of the union's activities into the open, notably by replacing the secret oath with a word of honor, many Catholic conservatives still intensely distrusted the Knights and unionization in general.

One of the leading figures in the Catholic social gospel tradition, Cardinal James Gibbons of Baltimore, rejected the conservative arguments against labor unionization. Sympathetic to the plight of miners in western Maryland, Gibbons argued that unions were the only protection workers had from "economic slavery" and "the oppression of the wealthy." Archbishop Gibbons discussed the grievances of labor in separate meetings with Powderly and President Grover Cleveland. In a petition to Rome in defense of the Knights of Labor, Gibbons insisted that the union provided workers with organizational protection from the "greed" and "avarice" of owners and monopolies. The cardinal feared that the Church would lose vast numbers of working-class Catholics if it appeared to be the adversary of labor. "To lose the heart of the people," Gibbons maintained, "would be a misfortune for which the friendship of the few rich and powerful would be no compensation." In 1888, after months of deliberation and indecision, Rome ruled that the Knights of Labor could be "tolerated" if the union would agree to minor revisions in its constitution. Specifically, church officials wanted removed "words which seem to savor of socialism and communism," insisting that the Knights' constitution must clarify that individuals have a natural right to land, but that they cannot acquire it through violence and by usurping the property of others. In September, Gibbons met with Powderly, who agreed to the constitutional amendments. In the wake of the Church's conditional acceptance of the union, *Catholic World* published an article urging workers to "Be Knights."

In 1891, Pope Leo XIII issued the encyclical *Rerum novarum* which bemoaned the deteriorating living and working conditions of urban dwellers. In this document, the pope contended that modern urban destitution was largely the result of unethical practices of industrial entrepreneurs who hoarded wealth and exploited workers. He denounced industrial capitalism for permitting the rich to lay "a yoke almost of slavery on the unnumbered masses of non-owning workers." Although the pontiff had grave reservations about industrial capitalism, he suggested that moderate structural reforms, such as living wages for workers, reasonable hours, safe working conditions, and the right to join labor associations, could make the capitalist system more humane and equitable while preventing a radical transformation of society. If employers refused to treat their workers with dignity and justice, Leo XIII affirmed the prerogative of the state to remedy exploitation. "When there is a question of defending the rights of individuals," he declared, "the poor and helpless have a claim to special consideration. The richer population have many ways of protecting themselves. Those who are poorly off have no resources of their own to fall back upon and must chiefly rely upon the assistance of the State." However, the pope argued that government did not possess broad, discretionary powers. He endorsed only enough state intervention to protect workers from the grossest maladies of urban-industrial society.

Catholic progressives saw the encyclical offering a new and dynamic version of Catholicism, reconciling the Church to the modern industrial world. Catholic social gospelers embraced the papal document to buttress their own criticisms of capitalism and their calls for social reform. Father Edward Brady, for example, saw *Rerum novarum* as a stern "rebuke" to Catholics who preached and practiced "a little too much of the passive, some might be disposed to call it the contemplative spirit of religion."

The social gospel awakened the nation's conscience which had been dormant since the abolitionist crusade had attained its goal of eradicating slavery at the end of the Civil War. The social gospel movement, as one historian has written, sought "to realize a solidarity that would turn America away from the worship of Mammon. Purifying society mattered more than personal piety." The social gospel of American Catholics and Protestants emphasized rational choice, social planning, and a communitarian ethos, replacing both the rugged individualism of the Gilded Age and the fatalistic Spencerian view of social development through natural selection and brutal competition. Catholic and Protestant social gospel ministers organized boys' clubs, recreational facilities, health clinics, and industrial training programs to ease the plight of the urban poor. In addition, social gospelers called for government arbitration to settle industrial discord and appealed to federal, state, and local government to legislate reform ranging from the eight-hour day, child labor laws, and antitrust legislation to factory safety codes and municipal laws regulating noise, smoke, and sanitation.

The American political system and labor movement did not become radicalized, in part, due to the Catholic and Protestant social gospel. The social gospel activists helped to attain moderate reforms within a free market capitalist and democratic society, thereby blunting the appeal of Marxism and thwarting efforts aimed at revolutionary unionism and the establishment of a workers' political party in the United States.

JANE ADDAMS

Born to a wealthy Cedarville, Illinois family in 1860, Jane Addams lived her early life in the shadow of her father and in uncertainty regarding what to do with her life. A spinal operation cut short a possible medical career and left Jane sterile and so an unlikely candidate for marriage. She acknowledged her life was "absolutely at sea." Then vague desires to serve the poor crystalized in a visit to a London "settlement house" devoted to that service.

In September 1889, Addams and a few female friends moved into a large rented house in one of the most impoverished areas of Chicago. Hull House gradually became a center of hope for the surrounding community. Child care, English instruction for immigrants, hot lunches, and parties could all be found there. More than a thousand people came through in a day. Addams and the volunteer staff also set up a community improvement association that lobbied for city parks, playgrounds, and paved streets. A consumer cooperative was established to work for lower prices and higher quality goods. Addams herself served on the Chicago Board of Education to press for practical education that would be more useful to the poor. For a time, she even walked behind a negligent garbage collector every morning to improve community cleanliness. Over the next thirty years, Hull House would serve as a model for hundreds of similar efforts all over the United States.

But the 1890s were a difficult decade for Addams. The depression that began in 1893 created misery that Hull House could barely dent, even in Chicago. The brutal smashing of the Pullman Strike of 1894 caused her to question the whole capitalist system, but socialism seemed too caught up in dogma. Addams tried to identify directly with those she served by taking a job baking bread. She found this "more logical than life warrants" and discovered that she could not bake and also help.

In the years that followed, reform efforts at Hull House broadened and deepened. Addams supported labor unionization, an end to child labor, and urban political reform. By 1910, with the publication of *Twenty Years at Hull House,* Addams had become nationally famous. She lent her voice to the Progressive Party in 1912 and to Woodrow Wilson in 1916 because of his peace platform and his (belated) support of women's suffrage. The approval of the Nineteenth Amendment giving women the right to vote was a celebrated victory. Although her strong efforts for world peace received a setback with America's refusal to join the League of Nations, the 1920s found Addams in the forefront of the antiwar movement. In 1931 she was rewarded with the Nobel Peace Prize. Her last years were clouded by the Depression, but before she died in 1935 Jane Addams saw hope in some of the programs of Franklin Roosevelt's New Deal.

By the turn of the century many churches were emphasizing that Christian charity must be applied to society and that Christians become active in social work and reform. But despite the efforts of Catholic and Protestant churches to meet urban problems, one group in particular continued to bear the brunt of inner-city life almost unaided: the immigrants.

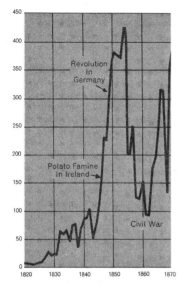

THE OLD IMMIGRATION TO THE UNITED STATES 1820–1870

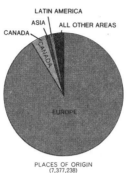

LATIN AMERICA
ASIA   ALL OTHER AREAS
CANADA

EUROPE

PLACES OF ORIGIN
(7,377,238)

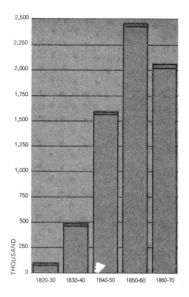

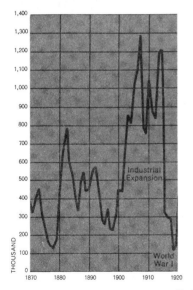

THE NEW IMMIGRATION TO THE UNITED STATES 1870–1920

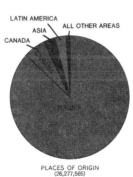

LATIN AMERICA
ASIA   ALL OTHER AREAS
CANADA

EUROPE

PLACES OF ORIGIN
(26,277,565)

Northern and Central Europe ▨
Britain, Ireland, Scandinavia, Belgium, Netherlands,
France, Switzerland, Germany, Poland, Finland,
Austria, Hungary, Czechoslovakia, Yugoslavia

Eastern and Southern Europe ▨
Russia and Baltic States, Romania, Italy,
Bulgaria, Turkey, Greece, Spain, Portugal

IMMIGRATION "SALAD BOWL"

The immigrants who came to the United States between 1820 and 1930 were part of the largest mass migration in history. During this period more than 62 million people left their homes to seek new lands and a better life. Over two-thirds came to America, the "land of opportunity." Unlike most nations that have been peopled by immigrants (like Australia or Argentina, which were made up of a few nationalities), the United States absorbed great blocs of many nationalities. Historians have divided them into two groups, the *old* and the *new* immigration. The old immigration originated chiefly in northern and western Europe, including Englishmen, Frenchmen, Germans, Netherlanders, and Scandinavians. It peaked in 1850 and never exceeded a half million a year until the 1880s. The new immigration came mainly from southern and eastern Europe, consisting of Italians, Greeks, Poles, Russians, and Slavs. It peaked between 1905 and 1910 with more than a half-million entering the country every year.

They came in such numbers because the United States had a reputation as the land of opportunity and equality. Wrote one immigrant, "no one can give orders to anybody here, one is as good as another, no one takes off his hat to another as you have to do in Germany." Even with the new entrepreneur elite, American society was far less stratified than its European counterpart. The spirit of equality seemed to be catching: a disgruntled Italian landlord wrote that "the men who come back from America walk through the streets as if they were our equals." Many immigrants writing home to their relatives represented the United States in glowing terms as the home of the common man and the hope of the oppressed. Nor was the nation's image of having a wealth of opportunity for the industrious belied. Immigrants did more of the nation's work than natives in proportion to their numbers. During the 1880s they were one-third of the work force and only 13 percent of the population. "By reason of this incoming, our almost limitless resources have been partially developed, forests leveled, railroads built, and canals dug . . . and the wilderness has been made to blossom," exulted the *North American Review* in 1892. The Treasury Department estimated that each immigrant was equivalent to $800 in new capital; Andrew Carnegie believed the figure was closer to $1500. There were other less tangible benefits. A national magazine observed that "when the foreigner came in, the native engineered the jobs. . . . The American in every walk and condition of life has been the boss ever since." Immigrants who had been in the country longer also moved up socially and economically as new groups came in. All this reinforced social mobility. It also encouraged businessmen to mechanize to take advantage of the cheap labor provided by the immigrants.

Of all these advantages and benefits, the only one directly useful to most immigrants was a job. Usually it was in the least skilled, most menial task available. Women worked in "sweat shops," textile mills or, if more fortunate, as domestic servants for the middle and upper class. Men labored deep underground in dangerous mines, drove spikes with railroad construction crews, and did monotonous factory work requiring little skill. "If you could see the conditions of the Norwegians in America at present, warned one immigrant, "you would certainly be frightened; illness and misery are so prevalent that many have died." Living conditions for these people were bad at best. They tended to collect in the big cities where, to preserve some sense of belonging and for self-protection, they clustered by nationality in

The pride and prosperity of an immigrant farmer in North Dakota are reflected in this photograph sent back to relatives in Norway. Large families were considered an excellent source of labor needed on midwestern farms at the turn of the century. This stern patriarch eventually fathered a total of 11 units of manpower. (Courtesy of the Solberg Family.)

neighborhoods. This tendency was a major factor in the process of urbanization—twice as many immigrants lived in big cities as did native Americans as a whole. The actual neighborhood in which most settled was generally a poor one because they could afford no better. An entire family often lived in a single room in a tenement that had to share one toilet and one water faucet. Garbage piled up in the streets and disease was rampant. "My people do not live in America," wrote a despairing Slavic immigrant, "they live under America." Culturally isolated from their surroundings by their language and customs, immigrants were under intense pressure to conform. Germans living in Milwaukee were astounded to discover that native Americans regarded them as "drunkards" because of their traditional beer parties on holidays. The natural desire to become accepted led many to conform to dominant American patterns, but others firmly refused to abandon their old heritage. Thorstein Veblen's biographer wrote that Veblen's mother was so insistent that he and his brothers learn the Norwegian culture and language that they were unaware that she even knew English until they were almost adults.

Thus the "melting pot" thesis that immigrants were molded into some sort of standard American is not accurate Those who came to America from abroad brought varieties of food, language, religions, festivals, books, dress, dances, literature, and theatre that have made American culture a colorfully rich and cosmopolitan one. Perhaps the process of assimilation is best described by one historian who refers to it as a "salad bowl," where "though the salad is an entity, the lettuce can still be distinguished from the chicory, the tomatoes from the cabbage."

RURAL REACTION

The effects of industrialization and urbanization were also reaching beyond city and factory into the rural areas of America. Inventions like the reaper and the combine harvester-thresher allowed greater acreage to be put into production, and the railroad made it possible for the farmer to get his crops to distant markets. The opening of the trans-Mississippi West brought immense new land areas under the plow, and new centers of wheat production in the Dakotas and corn production in Kansas developed. By 1880 the production of wheat was five times what it had been in 1860, and the corn crop doubled. A vast majority of farmers now concentrated on cash crops like wheat or cotton, and large commercial farms appeared. "Now the object of farming is not primarily to make a living, but it is to make money," declared the magazine *Cornell Countryman*. "To this end it is to be conducted on the same business basis as any other industry."

Unfortunately, the business of farming was not doing as well as many other businesses in the United States. Farmers were now competing in a world market where a surplus of foodstuffs caused a decline in agricultural prices that continued to fall until the early 1900s. Dealers acted accordingly and the farmer had no choice but to sell for the offered price or make no sale at all; he had no control over the price of his commodity. When buying machinery or other manufactured goods, he also had to pay the asking price or go without the item. So the farmer was in a very poor bargaining position. He could not determine the price of his produce or the price of things he needed to buy. As agricultural prices continued to decline, farmers were faced with an increasing gap between their income and the cost of the goods they needed to purchase. Nor did they have any voice in setting the freight rates they had to pay the railroads to send their produce to market. Railroads would often be engaged in competitive struggles that caused the rates to fluctuate wildly, further angering farmers who could see no connection between the rates and market conditions. High loan interest rates (10 percent, double the normal rate in those days, was not uncommon) also frustrated the farmers. Since most needed some sort of credit for buildings, fencing, or a water supply, they were frequently forced to mortgage their farms. By 1900 over one-third of all American farms were mortgaged. A bad year or a sharp drop in prices would mean disaster for a mortgaged farm. One sarcastic Nebraska farmer wrote that his state had three crops: "One is a crop of corn, one a crop of freight rates, and one a crop of interest."

Under these conditions it is not surprising that many farmers abandoned their fields for the more promising cities. On marginal New England land the exodus was startling. The New Hampshire commissioner of agriculture counted over 1,440 abandoned farms in 1890. Many midwestern rural counties found themselves losing people even though their state as a whole was gaining. In the South, where tenant farmers and sharecroppers were always in debt and controlled by local banks or businesses that even told them what to grow, fewer could leave. Of those that did stay on the farm throughout America, more and more swelled the ranks of the Grange.

The Grange (or the Patrons of Husbandry) had been formed as early as 1867 to bring farmers together to improve their lot. By 1874 hard times and low agricultural prices had boosted Granger membership to a million and a half discontented farmers. Targets of the organization were railroads with their high freight rates and monopolies and middlemen who, farmers believed, were squeezing the profits out of farming. To place themselves in a better bargaining position with businesses, Grangers formed consumer cooperatives. These associations hoped to shrink the "surplus profits of middlemen," which they believed diminished their own gains, yet they generally failed due to poor management, inadequate credit, and a lack of the cooperative spirit. Granger attempts to get state legislatures to set fair rates for storage and transportation of their produce were more successful. But most of the regulatory laws were weak enough that corporate lawyers could find ways around them, and the stronger ones were usually struck down by the courts. With the temporary return of better times in the 1880s Grange membership declined and the organization devoted itself more to social and educational objectives. Similarly, the Greenback movement to bring cheap paper money into circulation, with which farmers could pay off their debts, lost steam in the 1880s.

But the economic woes that had sparked the Grange and the Greenback movement continued to plague the farmer. He was also well aware, through magazine advertising and merchandise catalogs like Sears and Roebuck's, that he was not reaping the full benefits of new comforts. Rural life still required long hours in the fields and was without the attractions of theatre, professional sports, and other amusements available in the city. "One of the chief difficulties," said President Teddy Roosevelt, "is the failure of country life, as it exists at the present, to satisfy the higher social and intellectual aspirations of country people." Rural life had not really become worse; rather, country dwellers had come to expect better things.

EARLY STRUGGLES OF LABOR

Industrial workers, on the other hand, could complain that things had deteriorated. Working at monotonous jobs under dangerous factory conditions and living in slum tenements, they were both the backbone and the victim of industrialization and urbanization. After laboring sixty or more hours a week many workers still did not earn enough to support a family. Their children had to work as well. And many jobs were periodic; factories would push their production until their inventories piled up, then suddenly lay off many workers until business picked up. A few factory owners had a *noblesse oblige* sense of responsibility for their workers' well-being, but most insisted on hiring and firing on their own terms. Labor was a commodity and therefore working people became a commodity, a thing to be manipulated.

The obvious answer to this situation was labor unions, but it was an answer workers themselves were reluctant to adopt. First, joining a union could cost a laborer his job since many employers made membership grounds for dismissal, or worse. "I have always had one rule," an employer stated. "If a workman sticks up his head, hit it." A union organizer might also find himself blacklisted—no business in town would hire him. The very size and power of corporations and the surplus labor force made resistance futile in the eyes of many workers. Second, and perhaps the key to the American laborer's reluctance to join unions, was the fear of being labeled "working class." Nearly all working Americans expected to rise from their condition to new heights of success. They believed in the "gospel of wealth" and the American Dream. To be termed "labor" implied permanent occupation and status, a surrender of future hopes for success. These factors, including some government hostility to labor organizations, explain the fact that only five percent of the work force belonged to unions by the turn of the century. Even today only about 10 percent of all workers are organized. Those that did join union ranks in the last decades of the nineteenth century did so to preserve their humanity and sense of belonging in a system that threatened to destroy both. They continued to accept profit and property because they were "waiting for the break." In the meantime, unions served to improve working conditions and raise pay levels.

As early as the 1860s trade unions were developing among skilled workers, such as glass blowers and railway engineers. Ironworkers established the National Labor Union in 1866, and within six years it had a membership of 300,000. But the NLU could not dominate any trade and its goals were somewhat diffuse and idealistic. Founder William Sylvis hoped that by pooling their capital, workers could own their own factories, market their own product, and thereby collect their own profits. "By cooperation," he prophesied, we will become a nation of employers—the employers of our own labor." His hopes were short-lived. The NLU fell apart in the business panic of 1873. Another group called the Knights of Labor attempted to build a stronger base. The Knights called upon all workers to join their organization, including blacks and women. Seeking to return to self-employed units in small businesses, the union declared itself "at war" with the industrial system. "There is no reason," maintained one leading Knight, "why labor cannot, through cooperation, own and operate mines, factories, and railroads." Through education, cooperation, and political action the union hoped to "abolish the wage system." Strikes were a last resort because the Knights hoped to gain public support, which was usually alienated by the tactic. Ironically, their successful strike against a railroad was what boosted their membership to 700,000 in 1885. But a year later when a demonstration for the eight-hour day in Chicago turned into a bloody riot in Haymarket Square during which seven policemen were killed, public opinion turned against the Knights. Though they were not responsible for the riot, they had sponsored the demonstration. Shortly thereafter a major strike against the same railroad defeated in 1885 (whose management had broken the agreement) was crushed. By 1900 the Knights had disappeared from the national scene.

Even as this organization floundered another rose to the surface. The American Federation of Labor was a trade union of craftsmen (carpenters, printers, brewers, and others) who had a better bargaining position than unskilled workers who could easily be replaced. Its goals were simple and basic: "the best possible conditions obtainable for the workers," explained one AFL leader. That included the now typical demands of recognition of the union as the employees' bargaining agent, better conditions, shorter hours, and higher wages. Union President Samuel Gompers, a former cigarmaker, said that "the trade unions are the business organizations of the wage earners. . . ." The AFL was politically cautious and did not officially endorse a presidential candidate until 1908. Its chief weapon was the strike, but the union had no quarrels with the capitalistic system itself. "Labor unions are *for* the workingman but against no one," insisted an AFL leader. "There is no necessary hostility between labor and capital."

THE WORKING CLASS: TWO EXPERIENCES

Samuel Gompers

Born in 1850 in London, England, Samuel was working full time at age 10 as a cigarmaker. His family moved to New York when he was 13 and continued the trade. Shortly after the move he married and became involved in the trade union. Rising swiftly, he rebuilt it after the Panic of 1873 and an unsuccessful strike.

The Cigarmakers' Union became a craft union model. Gompers had developed a strong unity, stopped "wildcat" (unauthorized) strikes, built up a strike fund and avoided the temptation to commit the union to reform crusades or political causes. Discouraged at the failures of the Knights of Labor, to which his trade union belonged, Gompers withdrew to form the American Federation of Labor with other craft unions in 1886. He quickly became president of the new AFL and remained in that position (except for one year) until his death. At first, his only staff member was his son.

He dedicated his life to the union and fought for its acceptance. It campaigned for shorter hours, better wages, and better working conditions. When asked what his union's ultimate aim was, he simply replied, "More!" Gompers branded the socialists in the AFL "unrealistic." At one meeting he thundered, "Economically you are unsound; socially you are wrong; industrially you are an impossibility."

The AFL grew during World War I and Gompers's prestige rose. But inflation and unsuccessful strikes in the early 1920s cut union membership by 25 percent. Urged to organize unskilled workers, Gompers refused. It may have been his greatest error. He died in 1924, the union's fate still uncertain.

Eugene Debs

Debs was born to a working family in Terre Haute, Indiana in 1855. He started working on the railroads at 14 and showed such a genius for organization that he helped form a railroad fireman's union at 20. After a brief stint as a state legislator that left him disillusioned with both Democrats and Republicans, he returned to the railroad. By 1893 he had become president of the American Railway Union.

That year a panic struck the financial world and depression set in. The Pullman Palace Car Co., a major employer in the area with a "model" company town, reduced wages by 25 percent but kept rent and store prices the same. Pleas for reductions were refused. Workers struck the company. The ARU, with Debs at the head, staged a boycott of the trains in support. Over 2000 Federal troops arrived to get the mail and the trains moving. Riots followed, and the court ordered the ARU back to work. Debs and the union defied the order. He was thrown in jail and 14,000 strikebreakers were brought in. The strike and the union collapsed.

The experience radicalized Debs. "In the gleam of every bayonet and the flash of every rifle, the class struggle was revealed," he wrote. In 1901 Debs led in the formation of the Socialist Party. He kept the group together with his talents as a speaker and organizer. He opposed revolution, calling instead upon American workers to see that justice could only come when they ran the factories.

He ran as the party's presidential candidate in the elections of 1904, 1908, 1912, and 1920. In 1920 he campaigned from prison, where Wilson had sentenced him for opposing American entry into World War One. Debs lost, but polled a million votes. He died in 1926.

MOTHER JONES

Mary Harris Jones (1830–1930) was one of the most charismatic leaders in the history of American labor. Born into a Catholic family in Cork, Ireland, Jones immigrated as a child with her father to the United States. In 1867, after her husband and four children perished in a yellow fever epidemic in Memphis, Jones moved to Chicago where she earned a meager income as a seamstress. Disturbed by the unequal distribution of wealth and political influence, Jones immersed herself in the struggle of workers for adequate wages and improved working conditions. She was initiated into the labor movement during the Baltimore and Ohio Railroad strike in 1877 and soon joined the Knights of Labor as an organizer, recruiting thousands of new members. Although she was a persistent crusader for the rights of American and European immigrant laborers, Jones, like most American labor leaders of her time, had no empathy for Chinese immigrant workers. Along with other American unionists, she entered into anti-Asian agitation which culminated in the passage of the Chinese Exclusion Act of 1882.

Attracted to pro-labor, pro-farmer politics, Jones participated in the Socialist Labor party in 1895 and attended the Populist party convention the following year. More significantly, Jones became active in the United Mine Workers of America, advocating the rights of miners from the coal fields of West Virginia to Arizona copper mines. Jones's relentless advocacy of workers earned her the sobriquet the "Mother of Labor." After 1900, the conditions of American child labor became a primary concern for Mother Jones. "The little mill child," she wrote, drawing an analogy to Christ, "is crucified between the two thieves of childhood: capital and ignorance." In 1903, Jones led a legion of textile mill children in a march from Kensington, Pennsylvania to the Oyster Bay, New York home of President Theodore Roosevelt. Although Roosevelt refused to meet Jones and the young marchers, the incident called national attention to the issue of child labor.

Jones helped organize the Industrial Workers of the World in 1905, but the IWW's revolutionary agenda of violence troubled her and she soon left the union. She saw herself as a teacher and social reformer, not as a revolutionary. She hoped to bring conservative industrialists, politicians, and clergymen to the cause of social reform by education and persuasive arguments. In 1903, at Laconia, Maryland, Jones confronted a Roman Catholic priest who had been urging striking workers to end their walkout and to pay obedience to their employers. The cleric promised the strikers that their good behavior would be rewarded richly in heaven. Jones chastised the priest for his "blind reverence" for the business interests and for his characterization of striking workers as "children of darkness." She proclaimed that the workers should not have to wait for the next life to receive their compensation.

While serving a brief sentence in a West Virginia jail for inciting labor agitation in 1913, Mother Jones wrote a letter to Senator William Borah of Idaho, who had recently called for a federal investigation into mining conditions in West Virginia. In her letter to the senator, Jones described West Virginia's miners as "persecuted slaves" whose pleas to the state for help had been met with "jails and bullets." She called herself a "military prisoner" who was receiving the same brutal treatment that her Irish grandparents had suffered at the hands of the British government ninety years earlier.

After her release, Mother Jones traveled to Colorado, where she employed fiery rhetoric to urge miners to strike for improved conditions: "Rise up and strike! If you are too cowardly to fight for your rights there are enough women in the country to come in and beat hell out of you. If it is slavery or strike, I say strike until the last one of you drop in your graves. Strike and stay with it as we did in West Virginia. We are going to stay here in southern Colorado until the banner of industrial freedom floats over every coal mine. We are going to stand together and never surrender."

Jones gave detailed testimony before the United States Commission on Industrial Relations on the difficulties facing American labor and appeared before the House Mines and Mining Committee to provide vivid accounts of the 1914 massacre of sixty-six striking coal miners and other picketers by company-hired security forces at Ludlow, Colorado. Jones's accounts of working class struggles triggered federal investigations into factory and mining conditions. At the age of ninety, Mother Jones joined striking workers on a picket line. She died on November 30, 1930.

IF YOU DON'T COME IN SUNDAY DON'T COME IN MONDAY.

THE MANAGEMENT

With few exceptions, management was totally unwilling to recognize the legitimate demands of the working class in the last decades of the nineteenth century. Such intrasigence from the business interests often led to violent confrontations between striking workers and federal troops called in to "restore order." (Top: Courtesy of the I.L.G.W.U.) (Bottom: Culver Pictures.)

Despite trade union emphasis upon gaining community sympathy and employer cooperation, strikes that ended in violence did occur. Typically, this happened when strikers tried to block strikebreakers from operating the struck facility or when extremist groups incited riots (as at Haymarket). The riots of 1877 against numerous railroad companies was one of the few instances where wage cuts, job cuts, and poor working conditions were themselves enough to cause spontaneous strikes and violence. An attempt by 300 private police hired to reopen the Carnegie steel mill at Homestead, Pennsylvania, was met by armed workers and a brief battle ensued, but the strike was eventually broken by 8000 National Guard troops. The Pullman Company provoked a huge strike by railway workers in 1894, tying up all railroads west of Chicago, when it refused to discuss wage cuts and fired union leaders. Once again the federal government, siding with management, intervened with troops to keep the trains and mails running. Such experiences convinced unions that violence alienated the public, "justified" harsh reaction, and won few strikes. Despite government hostility and management stubbornness, AFL and other trade unions continued their struggle for recognition and the right to organize.

In short, the union movement remained politically and economically conservative. It never adopted the belief of philosopher Karl Marx that only by controlling the means of production could the working class enjoy the just rewards of its labor. Only the Industrial Workers of the World (IWW) insisted on a radical program of change along these socialist lines, and it remained a struggling minority on the labor scene. Socialism itself, which has been a standard response to capitalism and industrialization in nearly every other nation, never became a strong movement in the United States. One reason for this was that the fluidity of the social structure weakened class lines. Workers sometimes managed to accumulate enough money to own their own homes, or to enable their children to finish high school and become skilled laborers. People who hope to move up in society, and with reason for believing they can, do not develop much class identification. Since most workers could vote before they became unionized, they often decided political questions on the basis of their party affiliation rather than along economic or class lines. Socialism was also considered an "alien" philosophy associated with immigrants, and therefore aroused ethnic antagonisms that cut across class lines.

But the chief reason why socialism failed in the United States was that for most Americans capitalism worked sufficiently well. Real wages kept ahead of prices and Americans gained a relatively high standard of living. The Mosely Commission, made up of various English labor representatives, reported in the early 1900s that the average American workingman was "better educated, better housed, better clothed and more energetic than his British counterpart." One socialist summed it up well. He observed that "Americanism" consisted of "ideas like democracy, liberty, opportunity, to all of which the American adheres rationalistically much as a socialist does to his socialism: because it does him good, because it gives him work, because, so he thinks, it guarantees him happiness. America has therefore served as a substitute for socialism."

A FAILURE IN GOVERNMENT

Government in the United States may not have been faced with serious threats of a socialist takeover, but it was confronted by the twin challenges of growth and change. Industrialization and urbanization were creating stresses and strains on a political system designed and built to govern a more slow-paced, rural society.

Nowhere was this more evident than in the cities. Rapid and haphazard growth had rendered most city administrations incapable of providing such necessary services as water, power, or garbage removal, much less of easing the shock of rural and foreign newcomers. Political bosses like William Tweed in New York City emerged to cope with this chaotic change and growth. By appealing to the need for order, the clannish solidarity of immigrant ethnic groups, and cultivating every faction in the city, the bosses built a political machine to support their rule. Hardheaded men of little education, no social background, and accustomed to violence, they acted as "godfathers" especially to their poorer constituents. In return for votes they found people jobs, distributed food baskets at Christmas and Thanksgiving, and dignified social occasions. This lent a personal touch in an impersonal city. But it also created a climate for corruption in which the political machine dealt out jobs, contracts, administrative offices, and franchises to perpetuate its own power. City government under the bosses was not particularly efficient, although this upset few people since the cities were widely considered ungovernable. Independent and powerful, the boss was a force to be reckoned with at the state and even the national level.

At those levels politics seemed to be rather bland. There was very little observable difference between the domestic policies of the Democratic and Republican parties. Actually, both were made up of numerous factions that were constantly shifting position and angling for influence. Neither major party had an integrated political program. Congress worked at a leisurely pace because little was expected of it, and because leaders felt that tackling tough issues like high tariffs, the money supply or regulating business would destroy party unity. Laws that were passed were usually vague or advisory. Local governments interpreted them and enforced them or ignored them practically as they chose. Government bureaucracies were either inefficient or undermanned (in the name of economy) or both. Presidents confined themselves to suggesting measures for Congressional consideration, presiding over their party, and setting a proper moral example for the nation.

There were, however, some efforts at reform. The Pendleton Act of 1883 was the result of national shock over the assassination of President James A. Garfield by a crazed and frustrated office seeker. The act created a civil service commission that would offer government jobs on the basis of merit rather than connections. This was an important step in federal reform, but at first few jobs were brought under this act. Court frustration of state attempts to regulate the more outrageous acts of the railroads resulted in the passage of the Interstate Commerce Act of 1887. A commission was set up to make sure freight rates were "fair and reasonable." But the courts were the arbiter of what was "fair," and in fifteen out of sixteen cases decided in favor of the railroads. In a parallel situation, the Sherman Antitrust Act was passed by Congress in 1890 after state attempts at regulation had been voided by the courts. This act made illegal all trusts and other combinations "in restraint of trade." But its bold language was so vague that the monopolies simply reorganized and avoided prosecution. In short, attempts at reform in the late nineteenth century were ineffective.

To make matters worse, nearly all levels of state and national government were rife with corruption. Republican Vice-President Hamilton Fish accepted stock from a company that was seeking government subsidy in 1874. Democratic President-elect Grover Cleveland accepted responsibility for fathering an illegitimate child. During the campaign Republicans chanted "Ma, Ma, where's my Pa?" and after the victory exultant Democrats retorted "Gone to the White House, ha ha ha!" Though Cleveland's "sin" may have been more sensational, Fish's was more common. Business saw little wrong with influencing a legislator by giving him free railroad passes or cash "grants," especially if the business was located in the officeholder's constituency. A disgusted reformer remarked that "Standard Oil has done everything to the Pennsylvania legislature except refine it." Though each party tried to outdo the other in charging corruption, voters generally ignored it because it was expected. Politics as a calling was not highly regarded—saints entered the ministry and geniuses made a fortune in business. Government, despite a veneer of confidence

THE SUPREME COURT: A CONSERVATIVE FORCE

During the period from the end of the Civil War to the turn of the century, the Supreme Court tended to protect the social status quo and the economic doctrine of laissez faire.

Minor vs. Happensatt (1874)

The court declared that, although women were citizens, they did not thereby have the right to vote. This decision led to the long movement for women's suffrage.

Wabash, St. Louis & Pacific Railroad vs. Illinois (1886)

State efforts to regulate railroad rates for interstate carriers were declared unconstitutional. This led to the passage of the Interstate Commerce Act in 1887.

U.S. vs. E. C. Knight (1895)

By declaring manufacturing businesses exempt from the Sherman Antitrust Act of 1890 because manufacturing was different from "commerce," the court destroyed the effectiveness of the act.

In re Debs (1895)

Labor unions are defined as "conspiracies in restraint of trade" under the Sherman Antitrust Act and therefore can be regulated or broken up by the federal government. A major blow to union organization.

Maximum Freight Rate Case (1897)

The court declared that the Interstate Commerce Commission had no power to fix railroad rates. This badly damaged the work of the Commission.

Williams vs. Mississippi (1898)

Approval of state poll taxes, literacy tests, and residence requirements effectively deprived blacks of the right of vote.

Lochner vs. New York (1905)

The court forbade states from setting maximum working hours. Another setback for unions and laws limiting child labor.

and respectability, was neither willing nor able to handle the massive national problems resulting from the industrial revolution and the rush to the cities.

STRAIN ON THE FABRIC OF SOCIETY

That same veneer of confidence and respectability lay over all aspects of American society during the last three decades of the nineteenth century. Mark Twain called the period the "Gilded Age." But the bright gilt of multi-million dollar mansions, impressive figures of industrial production, and pronouncements of opportunity and success for all only covered deep and serious stress on

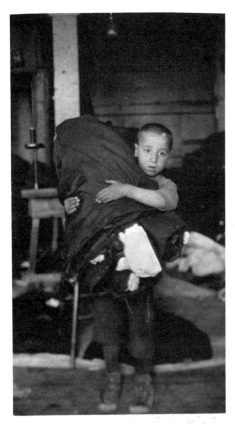

The working conditions that children labored under were no better and frequently worse than those of their fathers. The long hours and usually lower wages combined to deprive many urban youngsters of the childhood experiences that today are considered essential to normal maturation. Effective legislation governing child labor did not appear until 1916. (The Granger Collections.)

the fabric of American society. Henry Adams wrote that "society here . . . is shaking. Men die like flies under the strain."

These strains were evident in the changing roles of men, women, and children in society. There was a high demand for female labor in factories and in service industries. Though the female population rose only 28 percent in the 1880s, the number of women working outside the home rose 50 percent. As higher education opened its doors to more women, they also made their way into the professions. Restaurants, packaged foods, and store-bought clothing also affected the role of women in society. In short, women were gaining more independence. This was not without its price. Women joined the struggle for better working conditions and pay in the Women's Trade Union League, and they were still faced with the domestic routine at home in addition to outside work. Children also joined the ranks of the working class. By 1880 more than a million between the ages of 10 and 15 were employed outside the home and that figure went up by 75 percent in 10 years. At the same time American children were receiving a better education. All of this tended to loosen traditional family bonds, especially in the city where the family was not an economic unit as it had been in rural areas. The father had trouble exercising authority over a household where wife and even children might make the same wage as he, or replace him as family breadwinner if he were incapacitated. He might also find that children with a superior education

PRESENTS OF THE UNITED STATES

Administration	President	Party	Achievement
1865–1869	Andrew Johnson	Republican	Generosity towards the South angered his party. Impeached but not convicted.
1869–1877	Ulysses S. Grant	Republican	A Civil War hero whose presidency was ruined by scandals inside his administration.
1877–1881	Rutherford B. Hayes	Republican	Won a corrupted election. Ended Reconstruction and began civil service reform.
1881	James A. Garfield	Republican	Assassinated after six months in office by job seeker, his death helped advance civil service reform.
1881–1885	Chester A. Arthur	Republican	A former machine politician, he ran an honest administration and promoted economy in government.
1885–1889	Grover Cleveland	Democrat	Honest and blunt, he fought land fraud, high tariffs, and overspending.
1889–1893	Benjamin Harrison	Republican	He approved a Congressional spending spree and an even higher tariff.
1893–1897	Grover Cleveland	Democrat	A supporter of the gold standard and anti-imperialism, he also used the army against striking railroad workers.

and command of the English language tended to be independently minded. Family traditions were becoming confused.

In fact, American society was generally disorganized—a society without a core. Politics and government seemed largely irrelevant to people and so they lacked national centers of authority and information to give order to the accelerating rate of change. Institutions were still oriented toward community life and old patterns. Even business, which was supposed to be leading the rest of society around by the nose, suffered from the chaos. The range and complexity of corporate affairs made the trusts unmanageable. Even many factories were not particularly well-organized before the turn of the century. Home offices were so swamped that company policy was often determined by local agents and officers acting on their own initiative. The shift from newly opened western areas to established urban centers as areas for economic growth and opportunity in the 1890s went largely unrecognized by business, resulting in a serious depression in 1893. Despite the trend toward centralization, haphazard growth and its resulting confusion still dominated the economy.

The village communities that had been characteristic of American society were changing and being absorbed. Though many people would continue to reside in them for decades, the community's ability to manage affairs within its own boundaries was dwindling. Some people still tried to understand the changing world in terms of the more settled and personal society based on village communities. They felt that something fundamental was happening to them—something that they had not asked for and did not want. They saw the dark side of the city, its corruption, crime, overcrowding, and dirt. Nativists regarded immigrants suspiciously as importers of "contaminating" morals and habits as well as dangerous philosophies like socialism and anarchism (which insisted that all forms of government are oppressive and should be overthrown). Monopolies were angrily attacked for making essential public services "the playthings of private profit." But what frightened people most of all was that these issues seemed to be beyond their control. Farmers were subject to changing freight rates, interest rates, and market prices all determined without their understanding or participation. The very existence of some cities depended upon industries owned by absentee managers, to whom appeals were made without success. Many workers not only depended upon their company for a job but for a home and goods supplied by company-owned towns. Helpless natives could only watch as immigrants who would work cheaper got jobs and "turned cities into decaying slums."

Many Americans saw monopolies and immigrants as the chief forces that were threatening the local community values and ways that they clung to. They began in the 1890s to strike out at these enemies in an effort to regain control of their lives and to preserve the society they knew.

SUGGESTIONS FOR ADDITIONAL READING

Blake McKelvey, *The Urbanization of America,* (1963). A study of the growing pangs of American cities during the period they came of age, 1860–1915.

Alexander B. Callow, Jr., *The Tweed Ring,* (1966). A study of the post-Civil War political machine that provided a model for later bosses in New York City.

Matthew Josephson, *The Robber Barons,* (1934). An indictment of the great Gilded Age entrepreneurs.

Jacob Riis, *How the Other Half Lives,* (1957 edition). A book written in 1890, attracting widespread public attention to the economic, social, and political problems arising out of slum conditions.

Richard D. Brown, *Modernization: The Transformation of American Life, 1600–1865,* (1976). A study of the profound social and economic changes that began to change the U.S. even before the Civil War.

H. Wayne Morgan, *From Hayes to McKinley: National Party Politics, 1877–1896,* (1969). An interesting and insightful examination of a period of politics many Americans have thought it best to forget.

Vincent P. DeSantos, *The Shaping of Modern America, 1877–1916,* (1973). A superb overview of the developments that forged 20th century American society.

Nathan Glazer & Daniel Moynihan, *Beyond the Melting Pot,* (1970). Originally controversial, this groundbreaking study updates the immigrant story.

© Charles E. Rotkin/CORBIS

CHAPTER SIX

PURSUING THE PROMISE: A CENTURY OF POLITICAL REFORM

1892
Populist or People's party is formed.

1901
Theodore Roosevelt becomes President; Progressivism becomes a national movement.

1912
Woodrow Wilson is elected President to complete the Progressive agenda.

1920
Conservatives make a comeback with the election of Warren G. Harding,

1929
New York Stock Market Crash leads to the Great Depression.

1932
Franklin D. Roosevelt is elected President on his promise to restore prosperity in a liberal "New Deal."

1952
Americans return to the center, electing World War II hero General Eisenhower.

1965
President Lyndon B. Johnson builds his "Great Society" programs—height of liberalism.

1972
President Richard M. Nixon is reelected; promises to return government to local levels through the "New Federalism."

1981
President Ronald Reagan tries to limit growth of the federal government's powers and return to conservative values.

1995
President Bill Clinton moves the Democrats to the center in response to the conservative resurgence, winning reelection in 1996.

Copyright of the Library of Congress

AMERICA'S REFORM TRADITION

The dictionary definition of reform is "to make better by removing faults and defects; correct." Its simplicity is deceptive. Just what it is in America that needs "correcting," what the "faults and defects" are, has always been a subject for argument. For example, all three of the candidates who ran for president in 1912 stoutly defended their own versions of reform. Despite their varied approaches, the idea of reform as the process of making America better—of securing the blessings of democracy, liberty, social justice, and (not incidentally) prosperity—has been the promise of American life.

Since the turn of the century this promise has played a dominant role in American politics. Whether the target was business monopolies, political corruption, social inequalities, economic dislocation, or more recently, the size and power of the government itself, reformers lashed out to destroy them in the name of the American people. Most often they sought to create some order out of the chaos wrought by industrialization, urbanization, and by current technological change. The politics of reform embraced short-lived third parties as well as Democrats and Republicans. In the movements' ranks stood farmers, preachers, factory workers, business officials, educated professionals as well as the poor, and great numbers of middle-class people—a cross-section of

Although the Populists generally restricted their activities to forming
cooperatives and political action within the system, there were occasions when
their sense of outrage compelled them to violate the law. Here Kansas Populists
occupy the state legislative chambers, disputing the results of the off-year
elections of 1890. (The Kansas State Historical Society, Topeka.)

America. The common sinew that these diverse reformers have shared since the turn of the century
is the conviction that a rich and complex industrial society cannot exist as a broad-based
democracy on a foundation of sheer individualism. One hundred years later, the belief in activist
government persists, despite periodic efforts to challenge that tradition.

THE PEOPLE'S PARTY

The first nationwide reform movement began on the farms and gathered momentum during the
1880s. Farm problems had not died with the passing of the Grange as a reformist effort. A brief
period of prosperity was quickly followed by declining prices, increasing debt, and loss of farms
to mortgage companies. Farmers began to join local organizations that eased their social isolation
and promoted agricultural interests. These groups united to form large unions in several southern
states, and by 1888 they in turn had combined to form the Southern Alliance. Black farmers, not
admitted to the white groups, formed their own Colored Farmer's National Alliance. Though
separated, the two groups managed to work together to achieve some objectives. Farmers in the
North were also banding together until by 1889 the Northern Alliance counted 400,000 members
in several states.

Alliance organizations in Kansas, Nebraska, and the Dakotas chose to take their grievances
into the political arena in the elections of 1890. Demanding government ownership of transportation and communication, a graduated income tax, abolition of national banks, and inflation
through the unlimited coinage of silver, they soon realized that neither the Democratic nor

Republican parties would accept them. So they organized independent parties and launched vigorous campaigns on their own. In Kansas, "Sockless" Jerry Simpson denounced the "bloodhounds" of wealth and Mary Elizabeth Lease suggested that farmers "raise less corn and more hell." Despite poor organization and a lack of money the Alliance farmers won a few resounding victories, and when Congress met in 1891 about 50 Congressmen were sympathetic to or supportive of its interests.

Conservative Democrats and Republicans alike were frightened by this new sound and fury. It did not quiet their fears to hear that Kansas Alliancemen, convinced that they had won control of the state house of representatives, marched on the chambers with rifles and tossed out the resisting Republicans. The courts decided the dispute in favor of the Republicans, but the farmers retained control of the senate.

Encouraged by their victories, the Northern Alliance was now determined to form a nationwide third party to represent the interests of all "plundered people" in America. The Southern Alliance, which had had only limited success in working through the Democratic party, agreed to join. On February 22, 1892, representatives of the two groups met in a convention in St. Louis and, with the support of the Knights of Labor and other reform groups, formed the People's or Populist party. "We meet," declared the populist platform, "in the midst of a nation brought to the verge of moral, political, and material ruin. Corruption dominates the ballot box, the Legislatures, the Congress, and touches even the ermine of the bench." The solution was to expand the powers of government "as rapidly and as far as the good sense of an intelligent people and the teachings of experience shall justify, to the end that oppression, injustice, and poverty shall eventually cease in the land." Populists called for the free coinage of silver (which was expected to raise farm prices and help debtors), government ownership of railroads and telephone and telegraph lines, and a graduated income tax to force the rich to pay more to support the government. They proposed political reforms such as direct election of Senators by voters (rather than appointment by state legislatures), a single term for the President, and the right of the people to propose and approve their own laws (initiative and referendum). Basically, the Populists sought to return government to its true calling as the representative of all citizens and not just special interests, and then give government tight control over the economy to exercise on the people's behalf.

Here lay the real radicalism of the new party: the demand that government act directly upon areas of the economy that had been the preserve of private corporations. This was a direct rejection of economic individualism, the very center of American capitalism. Populists justified their position by insisting that a system which gave the farmer less money while he grew more crops and kept a hungry worker unemployed was plainly unjust. "People," observed one orator, "do not ask to be tramps." But their programs were still regarded as too radical by many Americans. Conservatives, especially on the east coast, ridiculed "simplistic" Populist proposals and labeled the Populists "country hicks." The dying Knights of Labor were too weak to give the party the urban support it required to gain a strong base. Rising trade unions like the American Federation of Labor were more concerned with wages and hours than with government ownership and social problems. Lacking an urban following of any size, the Populists lost the election of 1892 to Democrat Grover Cleveland. But their presidential candidate, James Weaver, did manage to poll

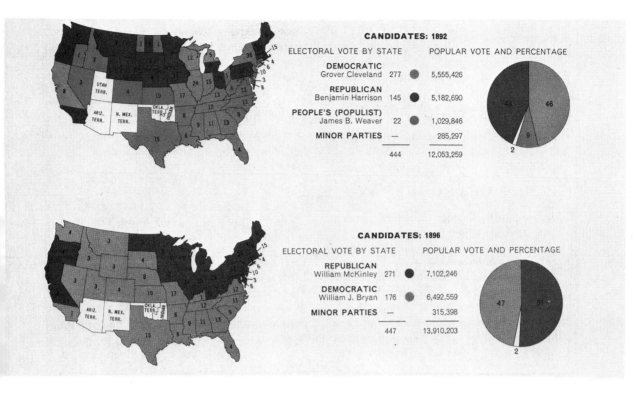

CANDIDATES: 1892

ELECTORAL VOTE BY STATE   POPULAR VOTE AND PERCENTAGE

DEMOCRATIC
Grover Cleveland   277   5,555,426

REPUBLICAN
Benjamin Harrison 145   5,182,690

PEOPLE'S (POPULIST)
James B. Weaver   22   1,029,846

MINOR PARTIES   —   285,297

444   12,053,259

CANDIDATES: 1896

ELECTORAL VOTE BY STATE   POPULAR VOTE AND PERCENTAGE

REPUBLICAN
William McKinley   271   7,102,246

DEMOCRATIC
William J. Bryan   176   6,492,559

MINOR PARTIES   —   315,398

447   13,910,203

a million popular votes. The party sent several senators and congressmen to Washington, and gained control of three state governments. Thus encouraged, the Populists began to plan for the election in 1894 and the presidential race two years later.

Cleveland aided their efforts by splitting his own party over a bill designed to protect Treasury gold reserves by preventing the purchase of silver for currency. When gold reserves continued to dwindle and hard times hit the country, an angry electorate repudiated the Democrats in 1894. Populist Jacob Coxey led a small army of unemployed and marched on Washington demanding work relief. After he was arrested for walking on the Capitol lawn, his followers dispersed. As the election of 1896 approached, the major issue became the currency question. Republicans endorsed the existing tight fiscal policy and nominated William McKinley for president. Dissident Democrats dumped Cleveland, chose the magnetic William Jennings Bryan, and drew up a program that gave the voters a choice. They called for tougher controls over trusts, a graduated income tax, and the free coinage of silver.

This presented the Populists with a dilemma. If they fielded their own candidate, they would split the vote on the silver issue so central to their program. After much debate most Populists decided to support Bryan in the hope that his victory would mean the adoption of the party program. This doomed Populism as a third party movement since most members were absorbed into the Democratic party. Bryan made a supreme effort, covering over 18,000 miles and making more than 600 speeches. But the Republicans conducted a highly organized campaign that dominated the press and spent 10 times more than the Democrats could afford. In the end McKinley won the election by carrying nearly all of the big states, although he only edged Bryan by 500,000 popular votes.

His victory marked the triumph of industrial over agricultural interests in the struggle for power in Washington. It also signaled the apex of conservative laissez-faire economic policy, which in plain English meant an unrestrained free market for the entrepreneurs. Nevertheless, the seeds of change planted by the Populists would soon begin to sprout all over the political landscape.

THE RISE OF PROGRESSIVISM

By striking out against the power of big business and its stranglehold on politics and the economy, the Populists seem to have changed the climate of resigned helplessness that had enveloped the nation. Americans were no longer willing to accept as the "price of progress" crime, poverty, squalid slums, political corruption, and dictatorial control of vital public services like the railroads by socially irresponsible businesses. Labor union agitation for better pay and shorter hours increased in the late 1890s and the Social Gospel that called for Christian aid to the impoverished and socially deprived became increasingly popular. The new philosophy of Pragmatism, popularized in the United States by John Dewey, maintained that people could and should use new techniques and ideas to deal with the problems of industrialized society. Contrary to the Social Darwinists, the Pragmatists believed that there was nothing "inevitable" about the course of evolution. Americans, they insisted, had both the right and the ability to create the type of society they desired. Professors studying the newly developing "social sciences" of economics, sociology, and psychology, maintained that social change could be guided by scientific methods to benefit all the people.

By the turn of the century this sense of optimism had combined with a determination to tame business's power, eliminate corruption, and promote social justice; the product was Progressive reformism. The Progressive movement dominated the American political scene for 15 years, yet it was never embodied in a single political party as Populism had been. Progressives came from all sections of the country, represented all classes, and were partisans of both major parties. The movement included such diverse people as William Jennings Bryan from the Bible Belt of the Midwest and urban atheist Clarence Darrow. Both Socialist Eugene Debs and conservative William Howard Taft embraced Progressive reforms. If the movement had a center it was in the cities among the large middle class, including white-collar workers and professionals such as teachers, lawyers, and newspapermen. Many Progressive leaders were young, well-educated, and from well-to-do families. Nevertheless, the Progressive reform movement has always defied the historians' efforts to categorize it. It remains one of the most diffuse reform movements in United States history.

Despite their diversity, Progressives did have certain characteristic attitudes and goals. Above all, they had an unshakable confidence in the common sense and morality of the American people. They believed that if Americans could regain control of their government they would have the ability and wisdom to make the necessary social and economic changes. So the first area of interest to the Progressives was political reform making the government responsive to the will of the people. To this end they adopted most of the Populist political program (direct election of senators, initiative, referendum, and recall). "Democracy" was the movement's guiding light and it colored all of the Progressive programs. Since the "unholy alliance" between special business interests and government violated the democratic ideal, it too became a primary target for reform. A common creed upon which nearly all Progressives agreed was that "big business" had too much political power and that this was the source of most corruption in government. Their solution was first to return government to "incorruptible" (fellow Progressive) representatives of the people and then invest a professional bureaucracy with the power to regulate the business activities that vitally affected the public interest. This uphill struggle against the "interests" took place at all levels of government: local, state, and federal. Another goal was to get the government to enact social legislation like abolition of child labor (it was not uncommon for 10-year-old children to work 12-hour days six days a week), unemployment insurance, more enlightened prison conditions, and slum clearance. Most of this activity took place in urban areas where reformers could better exert their influence. The common denominator of all of these efforts was to focus the power of government on problems involving the general welfare of the American people.

Actually, since all Americans did not share reform sentiments, Progressive programs were more for the people than of the people. Most Progressive leaders, and many of the rank and file, were Anglo-Saxon Protestants who regarded themselves as spokesmen for "the people" and guardians of the American heritage. Many were resentful of the businessmen who were replacing them in power. Like the Populist of the 1890s, there was a strong anti-immigrant sentiment running through Progressivism. Alarmed that immigrant cultures seemed to be "diluting" the Anglo-Saxon American heritage, the nativist movement aimed to dam the flood of immigration. One "liberal" reformer compared the newly arrived immigrants from southern and eastern Europe to "the oozing leak of a sewer pipe into the crystal waters of a well." Nor were most Progressives sympathetic to the plight of black Americans. In fact, when black southerners continued to vote for conservative candidates, Progressives helped white southern politicians who played on racial prejudice to win office and strip the blacks of their voting rights in the name of "reform." California Progressives were no less harsh on the Asian "intruders" in their states. Reformers also had a tendency to push legislation "for the good of the people" in spite of the people's wishes—when drinkers refused to abstain voluntarily from alcohol, Progressives passed Prohibition. Full of contradictions as it was, Progressivism was rising to the fore of American politics as the new century began.

ROOSEVELT, WILSON, AND PROGRESSIVISM

When the assassination of President McKinley in 1901 brought Theodore Roosevelt to the White House, Progressivism was already flourishing. It had made Robert M. LaFollette governor of Wisconsin, where he initiated a series of economic and political acts that made the state a "laboratory of democracy." Other states like California, South Dakota, and Iowa also elected Progressive governors. In cities like Detroit, New York, and St. Louis, local Progressive movements fought to eliminate the corrupt political machines of urban bosses, replacing them with

"Action" was central to Theodore Roosevelt's political life. He roared through his terms as President (1901–1909), providing national leadership for the Progressive movement. When asked in 1912 whether his health permitted him to campaign for the presidency on a third-party ticket, he bellowd: "I feel as strong as a Bull Moose!" (The Granger Collection.)

city managers and councils. Roosevelt himself had not been closely associated with the move-ment. As governor of New York he had shown only a mild inclination toward reform, perhaps because of the restraining influence of the party machine that had helped him win office.

But as President of the United States, Theodore Roosevelt came to personify the early Progressive movement. He was a young, well-educated man from an upper-class family who had a vigorous manner that made him a strong leader. Though he was ambitious and enjoyed the game of politics, he viewed issues in a moral light and regarded himself as "the steward of the public welfare." Roosevelt was well aware that the twentieth century had brought with it "many serious social problems" for which "the old laws, and the old customs . . . are no longer sufficient." He nevertheless believed that "the interest of the public is inextricably bound up in the welfare of our business." As President, Roosevelt therefore tried to tread the middle path. He distinguished

THEODORE ROOSEVELT

Theodore Roosevelt was born in 1858 to an old and prosperous New York family. He was a sickly boy, thin, badly nearsighted, and severely asthmatic. His family had him tutored privately at home until he was eighteen for fear of his health. But he outgrew his asthma and built his body with weightlifting until, by the time he entered Harvard, he became a skilled boxer. At Harvard he gave up plans to be a naturalist and turned to history and politics. In 1882 he was elected to the New York Assembly and made a reputation for himself as an independent reformer. That career ended when his young wife and his mother died within hours of each other. To relieve the depression he moved west to manage a ranch in the Dakota Territory. There he earned the respect of the cowboys by spending long days in the saddle and working as hard as anyone. He became an avid hunter and outdoorsman, reveling in the rugged life.

In 1886 Roosevelt returned to New York to run for mayor and pursue a childhood friend, Edith Carow. He lost the mayor's race but married Edith. Named the head of the Civil Service Commission as a political favor, he spent six hard years making the commission honest and nonpartisan over the protests of job-hungry fellow Republicans. In 1895 he returned to New York as president of the city police board. There Roosevelt personally visited gambling dens and brothels, eliminated much graft, modernized the force, improved the pay, and raised the morale of the department.

He resigned this post to become Assistant Secretary of the Navy in 1897, where he lobbied for a two-ocean fleet and an aggressive American foreign policy. On the eve of the Spanish-American war, he sent secret orders to the commander of the American Pacific Squadron to seize Manila Bay in the Philippines. Then he resigned to form and lead the First United States Volunteer Cavalry Regiment ("the Rough Riders"), a collection of wealthy New York polo players and friends from the West. Roosevelt used his VIP status to get his eager troops quickly over to Cuba, where he led a charge up Kettle Hill (not San Juan Hill—that was a reporter's error) and helped break the back of Spanish resistance on the island. He returned to New York a hero and won the 1898 race for governor. Once in office, he gained a reputation as a progressive reformer by raising corporate taxes, renovating tenements, and winning an eight hour day for state government workers. He managed this by giving in to the conservative Republican machine in minor matters and building public and bipartisan support for bigger (and, to the Republican conservatives, less palatable) measures.

But the leaders of the Republican machine in New York thought they had the answer. They joined with well-meaning friends of Roosevelt in the West to urge him to run in 1900 as William McKinley's vice president, thinking to "dead-end" him in a "useless" office. Roosevelt reluctantly accepted and McKinley won. But less than a year later McKinley was killed by an assassin. When New York's Republican boss heard the news he groaned, "Now that damned cowboy is President of the United States!"

---

between "bad" trusts which he tried to "bust," and "good" trusts which he left alone. At one point during the coal strike of 1902 Roosevelt reviled the "arrogant stupidity" of business leaders and later commented acidly, "Do they not realize they are putting a very heavy burden on us who stand against socialism, against anarchic disorder?"

This middle path of reform won Roosevelt some notable successes in his two terms as president. His campaigns against business monopolies and especially the suit brought against the enormous Northern Securities Company railroad combine earned him a reputation as a "trustbuster," though in fact he instituted fewer antitrust suits than his successor. The point is that he brought the issue of corporate abuses clearly before the public. Roosevelt also showed a much fairer attitude toward labor than his predecessors by refusing to use federal troops to break up a coal strike in 1902, forcing the mining companies to negotiate with the workers' union. The Interstate Commerce Commission was given new powers to regulate railroad practices by presidentially-backed legislation. Other bills protecting the public from business practices dangerous to its health, like the Pure Food and Drug Act and the Meat Inspection Act, were pushed by Roosevelt. He also supported conservation programs to bring the nation's resources under scientific management and wise use for the benefit of future generations of Americans. In addition, the trustbuster believed in the citizen-worker's right to the "time and energy to bear his share in the management of the community, to help in carrying the general load." A current observer sees this relationship between citizens and their government as an example of civil society:

> *If the government will pay more attention to communal values and civil society, it will more clearly perceive and more adequately protect the needs of individual persons.*

Certainly Roosevelt's most important contribution to the reform movement and American politics was to inaugurate a dynamic modern presidency that acted as the initiator of legislation, the forceful representative of the people, and the guardian of the public interest.

Progressive journalists were another group that played the role of guardian. Given the nickname of "muckrakers" by Roosevelt, who disliked their habit of always "raking up the muck" in American society, they conducted a crusade in newspapers, magazines, and books against illegal and immoral business practices. Articles like Lincoln Steffens's "Tweed Days in St. Louis" exposed corruption in city government while others probed the power of big business over United States senators. Ida Tarbell's landmark report on "The History of the Standard Oil Company" disclosed that corporation's social irresponsibility. Powerful novels told of squalid city living conditions, the impersonality of "the system" and of sickening conditions in the nation's food processing businesses. It was reported that Roosevelt did not eat sausage for a month after reading Upton Sinclair's *The Jungle,* which described the meat-packing plants of Chicago. These men and women alerted the public to dangers and issues vital to their well-being.

Americans used to the dynamic leadership of Theodore Roosevelt and the sensational articles of the "muckrakers" were less than enthused with the lackluster administration of Roosevelt's successor, William Howard Taft. Taft avoided the public and was such an inept politician that he managed to alienate the progressives in his party, though he did retain control of the party machinery. He also angered his mentor Roosevelt by firing Gifford Pinchot, Roosevelt's close friend and coworker, over a conservation dispute. Roosevelt then left the African bush where he had been hunting and returned to the United States. Seven months before the 1912 election, convinced that Taft had abandoned Progressive goals, he announced, "my hat is in the ring." Roosevelt's decision split the Republican party in two, the conservatives nominating Taft and the Progressives leaving the convention to form their own party and nominate

Roosevelt. Proclaiming that he felt as strong as a "Bull Moose" in spite of his age, Roosevelt hit the campaign trail sounding more Progressive than he ever had.

Roosevelt's long-brewing reformist views were galvanized by progressive intellectual Herbert Croly's influential *The Promise of American Life* (1909). Looking backward at the social wreckage of the Gilded Age, Croly wrote that a "morally and socially desirable distribution of wealth" must replace the "indiscriminate scramble for wealth." Although not a socialist, the writer emphasized the value of community, going as far toward accepting the welfare state as any progressive imbued with the pragmatism of John Dewey:

> *Every popular government should have, after deliberation, the power of taking any action which, in the opinion of a decisive majority of the people, is demanded by the public welfare.*

Now, during the political campaign of 1912, Roosevelt championed a fall reform program—government regulation to control business and government legislation to bring about social justice—what he called the New Nationalism. His remarks about laborers who work hard and play by the rules deserving a "more substantial equality of opportunity and reward" widened the gap between his Bullmoose followers and their more conservative Republican brethren.

The Democrats gleefully noted the Republican split and nominated their own candidate, Woodrow Wilson. From an upper middle-class family with a strong Protestant background, Wilson had served as president of Princeton College in 1910. Although an economic conservative, he had been a liberal governor of New Jersey and had fought for progressive programs. Wilson and Roosevelt soon dominated the 1912 campaign. In rebuttal to his opponent's New Nationalism, Wilson argued that only a return to competition through antitrust action would preserve economic democracy, whereas more government legislation would inhibit the self-reliant individual. He called his program the New Freedom. The voters, forced to choose between two methods of reaching the same goals, chose the New Freedom because it seemed less radical. This general moderation of the voters did not prevent Eugene Debs and the Socialist Party from capturing the votes of a million deeply dissatisfied Americans. But the Socialist appeal had hit its high-water mark without capturing the White House.

Even though Bullmooser Roosevelt lost the battle with Wilson over the issue of how to handle the large corporations or trusts, the new president soon veered toward Croly's idea of positive government. Borrowing from Roosevelt's New Nationalism, Wilson concentrated on regulating business through the new Federal Trade Commission. It had the power to issue corporations "cease and desist" orders rather than waiting for the courts to act. The Clayton Antitrust Act put specific teeth in the old Sherman Act of 1890 and prevented the law from being used against unions any longer. Wilson also drove through the Underwood-Simmons Tariff, which significantly lowered the tax on imports for the first time since the Civil War. The nation's finances were placed under a more flexible and safer system by the Federal Reserve Act of 1913. Congress passed the graduated income tax in 1913 reflecting the new assumption that higher income citizens should pay progressively steeper taxes than other Americans. Six years later,

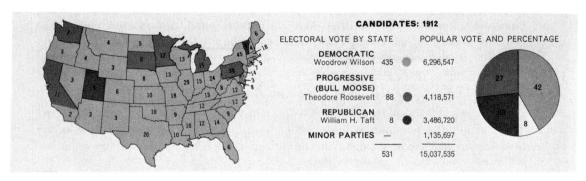

CANDIDATES: 1912

ELECTORAL VOTE BY STATE		POPULAR VOTE AND PERCENTAGE
DEMOCRATIC Woodrow Wilson	435	6,296,547
PROGRESSIVE (BULL MOOSE) Theodore Roosevelt	88	4,118,571
REPUBLICAN William H. Taft	8	3,486,720
MINOR PARTIES	—	1,135,697
	531	15,037,535

women gained the right to vote with the Nineteenth Amendment, the result of activist social reformers like Jane Addams.

Though Wilson was not particularly inclined toward further social reform, Congressional pressure and the necessity of winning Progressive support in the 1916 election persuaded him to take a more liberal position. Legislation was passed giving American seamen better living and working conditions, taking steps to eliminate the abuses of child labor, allowing workmen compensation for injuries on the job, providing low-interest loans to farmers and supporting an eight-hour workday. Yet even this legislation undergirded the conservative goal of class reconciliation. Progressive reformers realized that restoring a larger measure of economic power and social privileges to the masses of farmers and wage-earners would do much to alleviate class tensions increasingly exacerbated by business rule. These programs of "positive government" won Wilson reelection in 1916 when Roosevelt became absorbed by World War I and the Progressive Party collapsed.

By 1916 the nation's attention had turned from domestic reform to the struggle in Europe and the attempt to stay neutral. Progressivism had achieved all it was going to achieve at the national level. Although it had made the political system more responsive to the public and therefore more democratic—most particularly by enfranchising women—it had excluded blacks as part of its constituency. Fewer blacks could vote by the end of the Progressive period than in 1900. Nor did the reformers alter the domination of corporations over the nation's economy. Many businessmen, anxious to bring some sort of order to the system, even supported federal attempts to regulate their industries—then exercised a dominant influence over the very government commissions designed to control them. One cabinet member wrote that the FTC was "a counselor and a friend to the business world," not a club-wielding policeman. Labor improved its relations with management only very little. All in all, the Progressives concentrated more on improving the existing system by making it operate more efficiently than on changing the system itself. This pragmatic reform impulse may have been conservative in the sense of preserving democratic capitalism. At the same time, however, the deliberate hands-on approach of these middle-class reformers to social-economic problems represented a radical departure from their laissez-faire predecessors during the Gilded Age.

"NORMALCY" AND THE TWENTIES

The voluntary defection of Roosevelt's Bullmoose Progressives from the Republican Party in 1912 resulted in big business regaining control of the GOP. During the administrations of Harding, Coolidge, and Hoover, Republicans rejected the pre-war progressive reform impulse in favor of a return to policies which frankly acknowledged the primacy of big business. In the 1920 election campaign Warren G. Harding set the tone for the post-war period: "America's present need is not heroics, but healing; not nostrums, but normalcy . . . not surgery, but serenity." With the abrupt end of World War I, the bitter partisan debate over the League of Nations, and the Red Scare that swept the country in early 1920, the American people had had all of the excitement they wanted for awhile. Many considered their involvement in the war to have been a mistake and were tired of Wilson's "great crusade" rhetoric. They were also alarmed at the Communist revolution in Russia and what they saw as "radical stirrings" in the United States. Prosperity had shifted the nation's attention from reform to the business of making money. Harding's promise of "normalcy" was exactly what the public wanted to hear.

As president, Harding was not even master of his own administration. Three of his cabinet members were later convicted in the Teapot Dome Scandal of 1923 for taking bribes from oilmen who wanted access to federal oil reserves. Attracted to dishonest friends, poker, bootleg whiskey, and a mistress, Harding contributed to the decline of the power and prestige of the presidency although his warmth and good looks kept him popular. Under Harding, business was once again permitted to go its own way with only minimal federal interference and the government returned to the habit of using troops to end labor strikes.

When President Harding died unexpectedly, his vice president Calvin Coolidge took the oath of office. "Quiet Cal" cleaned up the administration and continued to follow the pro-business economic policy begun by Harding. Coolidge sought and succeeded in making his administration respectable and stable. This paid off in the 1924 election when the Republicans soundly beat both the Democrats and resurgent Progressives. America "kept cool with Coolidge," as the slogan said.

But the "cool" was only on the surface. Nativist groups fearful of immigrant "contamination" of Anglo-Saxon American culture had reduced the flow of immigration to a trickle through legislation by 1924. The Ku Klux Klan soared in membership in the South and Midwest, proclaiming its "one hundred percent American" opposition to blacks, Jews, Catholics, and nearly every other non-WASP group. More than 200 blacks were lynched between 1920 and 1925. American intellectuals disillusioned with America and American values were characterized as the "lost generation," and their attitudes were reflected in the works of Ernest Hemingway and F. Scott Fitzgerald. The "roaring twenties" flaunted traditional manners and morals as thousands of young people took up jazz, the Charleston, speakeasies, and necking parties. Prohibition was a failure and criminal gangs like Chicago's Capone mob terrorized American cities. Even though a majority of Americans clung to stability and refused to join the "roaring," society seemed to be restless, nervous, and vaguely dissatisfied.

Faith in America's future was symbolized by Herbert Hoover, president-elect in 1928. Hoover's "New Era" envisioned a marriage of convenience between the old values of individualism and private enterprise with the new "scientific" principles of industrial production. The

CANDIDATES: 1932

ELECTORAL VOTE BY STATE   POPULAR VOTE AND PERCENTAGE

DEMOCRATIC
Franklin D. Roosevelt   472   22,809,638

REPUBLICAN
Herbert C. Hoover   59   15,758,901

MINOR PARTIES   —   1,153,306

531   39,721,845

former Secretary of Commerce during the administrations of Harding and Coolidge was confident that the principles of voluntary cooperation practiced by rational and decent men were all that was needed to abolish poverty in America. As the presidential nominee remarked during the campaign in 1928: "We in America are nearer to the financial triumph over poverty than ever before in the history of our land. The poor house is vanishing from among us." Less than a year into his presidency Hoover would have the opportunity to test his political and economic faith.

What Hoover did not see was that the Republican policy of helping business had resulted in a situation where the rich could invest in growing industries but the poorer classes could not consume the mountain of goods produced. Easy credit only encouraged debt, which would be difficult to pay off in hard times. International trade declined in a surge of protectionism. Encouraged by surface prosperity, the stock market climbed to incredible heights as speculators traded and bought for quick profits. RCA shares soared from 85 to 420 points in one year. But on October 29, 1929, after several days of confused uncertainty, stockholders panicked and sold more than 16,000,000 shares at ruinous losses.

Wall Street's collapse sent deep shocks through the economy. Banks closely tied to the stock market through investment were shaken and those consumers who had bought on credit found themselves in trouble. The curtailment of credit reduced public purchases, and business began to decline. Since 39 percent of the nation's wealth was tied up in 10 percent of the country's families and these people tended to speculate or invest their funds, the Crash wiped out much of the national wealth in a few weeks.

Hoover first diagnosed the whole problem as one of confidence. The economy, he firmly declared, was "fundamentally sound" and would return to normal if people would not panic. To restore confidence he worked with businessmen to maintain current levels of employment and wages. But as demand weakened the businessmen simply could not hold the line. By the spring of 1930 more than 4,000,000 people were out of work and the situation continued to deteriorate.

In previous financial panics, the laboring masses had been forced to accept the hardships of unemployment as the result of the unalterable economic laws of Social Darwinism. Hoover's Secretary of the Treasury Andrew Mellon had advised that the economy be allowed to "bottom out" without any government interference:

The Depression fostered feelings of desperation that led to incidents of lawlessness. A Minneapolis newspaper in 1931 reported: "Several hundred men and women in an unemployed demonstration late today stormed a grocery and meat market in the Gateway district, smashed plate glass windows and helped themselves to bacon and ham, fruit and canned goods." (Top: United Press International.) (Bottom: Courtesy of Brown Brothers.)

FRANKLIN D. ROOSEVELT

Franklin Roosevelt was born in 1882 to a wealthy New York family with roots back to the early Dutch landowners of the colony. He grew up handsome, intelligent, and somewhat spoiled. As a young man he wanted to go to Annapolis, but his parents sent him to Harvard. After graduation he married distant cousin Eleanor over his mother's strong objections. Roosevelt quickly abandoned a planned law career for politics and was elected (largely on his personality) to the New York State Senate. There he turned on the state Democratic machine and earned the notice of Woodrow Wilson. Wilson may have regretted making Roosevelt Assistant Secretary of the Navy—Roosevelt pushed for a larger fleet and favored intervention in the First World War. A trip to the front after American entry into the conflict forever branded the brutality of war on his mind. In 1920, Roosevelt fought alongside James Cox for a Democratic victory in the presidential election. They lost, but his shrewd head for campaigning and his uncanny knack for remembering names and faces, together with seemingly boundless enthusiasm, made him a party leader.

Just a year later his world came crashing down. After a swim in frigid water he contracted polio and was nearly totally paralyzed. His mother wanted him to return home to a retired life as a country gentleman. But Eleanor and his aides encouraged him to fight back, and Roosevelt underwent years of rugged and agonizing exercises to regain some use of his limbs. This regimen, along with treatments in the mineral waters of Warm Springs, Georgia, won him the use of his upper body. By 1924, however, he was back in politics. He nominated Al Smith in the Democratic convention that year, and four years later as well. In 1928 the party asked him to run for the New York governorship.

At first he declined, feeling the election probably couldn't be won by a Democrat. Then he ran, and won. As governor, Roosevelt met the Depression with action. A public service commission was created, old age pensions were set up, an organization similar to the later Civilian Conservation Corps hired out of work young men, and the country's first state relief program was established. As the Depression deepened in 1932, Roosevelt made a bid for the Democratic nomination for president. He made speeches calling for action and pleading the cause of the "forgotten man." At the convention his managers made a deal with powerful publisher William Randolph Hearst to win the votes of delegates from California and Texas. This put him over the top. Roosevelt flew to the convention to accept the nomination, saying "I pledge you, I pledge myself, to a new deal for the American people."

Let the slump liquidate itself. Liquidate labor, liquidate stocks, liquidate the farmers. . . . People will work harder, live a more moral life. Values will be adjusted, and enterprising people will pick up the wrecks from less competent people.

Hoover rejected Mellon's advice. Indeed, the president launched a program to combat the ills of the depression that went further than any previous president to mobilize the federal government in an economic emergency. Reflecting his confidence in the "trickle down" theory, he proposed aid to the hard-pressed industries so that if financial health were revived at the top of the economic pyramid, its benefits would percolate down to the benefit of the working class through increased employment and consumer buying power.

Hoover began a program of limited federal intervention: an attempt to stabilize farm prices failed; the Reconstruction Finance Corporation could not lend enough money to banks and individuals to stem the tide; assistance to private welfare and charity organizations was inadequate; and federal work projects to relieve unemployment were too few.

By 1932, 85,000 businesses and 5000 banks had failed. In the same period national income and industrial production had dropped by half. Nearly one-fourth of the labor force was out of work. By 1932, 30 million destitute people sought public welfare, but the burden was beyond the means of insolvent local governments. Nevertheless, every possible stigma was attached to welfare aid. One community in Maine voted to bar all welfare recipients from the polls. Some hospitals refused to admit patients unless payment for services was guaranteed. Bread and soup lines lengthened in cities across the nation. "Rugged individualism" was not an adequate tool to dig out from under an economic disaster. Villages of shacks called "Hoovervilles" began to dot parks and dump yards. People, looking for a scapegoat, blamed it all on Hoover.

FDR DECLARES A "NEW DEAL"

The man chosen to lead the American people out of economic depression was no proletarian underdog himself. Franklin Delano Roosevelt was a member of the American aristocracy, tracing his roots back to colonial times when the Dutch controlled New York. As an only child he grew up in the lap of luxury, cutting his political teeth during the Progressive era and the 1920s. Contracting polio in 1921, he was paralyzed from the waist down, requiring sixteen pounds of steel leg braces and a wheelchair for the next twenty-five years of his life. This is the man who campaigned in 1932, assuring Americans that "nobody is going to starve."

In a vigorous campaign the physically handicapped Roosevelt expanded little on that promise beyond saying that the government would take action to relieve unemployment and low farm prices. He also capitalized on Hoover's use of tanks, troops, and gas to rout members of the Bonus Expeditionary Force, about 12,000 World War I veterans who had marched on Washington to demand early payment of a promised cash bonus for their service. Hoover warned that Roosevelt's program "would destroy the very foundation of our American system." But the electorate was not listening. Roosevelt won in a landslide that buried the Republicans under 12,000,000 popular votes. The nation responded to the warm, energetic Roosevelt with a confidence they had never given Hoover.

Like his predecessor Hoover, Roosevelt found solutions to the problems of the depression in short supply. Economic crises during the late-nineteenth century had been eased somewhat by the "safety-valve" represented by the farm and the West. However, since the turn of the century the American economy had become so industrialized that a massive return of the unemployed to the agricultural sector was no longer possible. Nor was orthodox economic theory espoused by the business interests for averting depression adequate, as Hoover's efforts prior to 1933 made clear. So, FDR sought new directions.

Unlike Hoover, the new president was no doctrinaire. He rejected the conventional limits on the power of the federal government preached by the Social Darwinists, arguing that the state should take whatever steps were necessary to safeguard the welfare of the people. Rather than

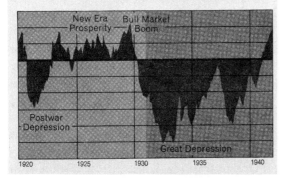

BUSINESS ACTIVITY 1920-1941

New Era Prosperity — Bull Market Boom

Postwar Depression

Great Depression

1920   1925   1930   1935   1940

The stock market crash of 1929 rippled out to strike the whole economy. Since most Americans were no longer self-employed, the collapse of corporate businesses and banks meant wholesale unemployment and loss of savings. Overexpansion of business and overspeculation in stocks led to the fall.

presenting a concrete plan for the restoration of the economy, he offered a point of view, never establishing clear-cut ideological guidelines. Borrowing the pragmatic principle from earlier Progressive reformers, Roosevelt declared: "the country needs bold, persistent experimentation." Indeed, his specific proposals were less important than his "style." On Inauguration Day Roosevelt told the American people that all they had to fear was "fear itself," and that they must regain their confidence and self-esteem. The President's fellow citizens responded to his inaugural speech with an avalanche of letters and telegrams expressing their enthusiasm for his encouraging words. One letter writer claimed that the speech was "the finest thing this side of heaven." Another correspondent declared that the President's message gave "the people, as well as myself, a new hold on life."

REMEMBERING THE "FORGOTTEN MAN"

What was different about Roosevelt's New Deal was his commitment to "balancing the human budget." No longer would Washington's actions be limited by business's resistance to government involvement. Instead, the economy was to be "managed." What emerged was a type of welfare state, containing a series of government programs designed to protect the "forgotten man" who had been overwhelmed by the ravages of industrial capitalism. Moreover, the President acted decisively. Immediately upon entering office, he declared a four-day banking holiday, the first gesture in his declaration of war against defeatism and despair. Admittedly, his attack may have seemed confusing and contradictory, nor did it end the depression. But it did check the decline and restore a sense of momentum for the American people. Reassuring his "friends" in one of a series of "fireside chats" broadcast nationally on the radio that "it is safer to put your money in a bank rather than under a mattress," he helped restore the nation's financial self-confidence. The country was on the move.

With the New Deal and the passage of the Wagner Act, the government shifted from its traditional hostility towards unions to protect the workers'right to organize and bargain collectively. (Courtesy of Library of Congress.)

Franklin Roosevelt, therefore, was at the heart of the New Deal—to a large extent he was the New Deal. Although others contributed ideas and proposals, it was Roosevelt who led and vitalized the program and held together the Democratic political coalition that made it possible. As a reformer who had worked for Woodrow Wilson's nomination, Roosevelt had been loyal to the progressive element in the Democratic party and had pushed through numerous reforms as governor of New York. He had always been impatient with ideologies and philosophies. "It is common sense to take a method and try it," he said. "If it fails admit it frankly and try another. But above all try something." As a reformist president, Roosevelt offered active, pragmatic leadership to solve the problems of the Depression.

Congress soon learned just how active Roosevelt would be. In the famous "Hundred Days" from March to June 1933, the House and Senate passed a record number of reform and relief measures that became the basis of the New Deal. First, the president stopped the run on banks that was destroying the nation's financial condition by closing all of them, shoring up the weak ones with loans, and then reopening them with assurances to the public that they were sound. People's confidence was restored—"Capitalism," wrote one observer, "was saved in eight days." Then Congress established the Civilian Conservation Corps, designed to help young men by giving them jobs planting trees, establishing parks, and building dams. Under the Federal Emergency Relief Act government relief money helped states support the unemployed, and later

Franklin Roosevelt used his charismatic leadership to bind together the diverse segments of the New Deal coalition and to win the confidence of the American people. Here in the first of his "fireside chats" during the banking crisis of 1933 President Roosevelt tells Americans that "it is safer to keep money in a reopened bank than under the mattress." (Courtesy of Brown Brothers.

programs of work relief were started, though this barely made a dent in the relief program. A Philadelphia social worker reported that "one woman said she borrowed 50 cents from a friend and bought stale bread for 3 cents per loaf, and that is all they had for eleven days except for one or two meals." Conditions on the farms were little better since most farmers were deep in debt because of falling prices. The Agricultural Adjustment Act (AAA) sought to raise prices by limiting production, and paid farmers for not growing crops. Critics protested that this policy encouraged the practice of slaughtering pigs and plowing under corn when people were starving. The Supreme Court later declared the measure unconstitutional. But other farm relief bills took the place of the AAA to help farmers keep their farms and give them a better return for their labor.

Perhaps the key measure in the early New Deal was the National Industrial Recovery Act (NIRA) passed in June 1933. Designed to help business and allow labor to share the expected benefits, the NIRA involved government-business cooperation in creating a planned economy. Part of the measure created an organization to fund public works projects like construction of roads and bridges. But the most important section dealt with establishing "codes of fair competition" that would govern production, and work standards. A high-keyed propaganda campaign was conducted to attract business cooperation and public support. Stylized blue eagles proclaiming "We Do Our Part" symbolized the crusade. Yet NIRA codes proved difficult to administer and nearly impossible to enforce. Labor, receiving new recognition, was enthusiastic, but business was only mildly favorable. Before it was finally struck down as unconstitutional by the Supreme Court, the NIRA had become a political burden and proved itself a failure.

Up to this point Roosevelt had tried to work with business and, with a few exceptions, within the bounds of political and economic tradition. Now, convinced that not enough was being done, Roosevelt directed the New Deal into more concentrated relief and recovery efforts that also included strong doses of reform.

Beginning in 1935, Congress passed several relief measures and social legislation to mitigate these conditions. The Works Progress Administration (WPA) sponsored thousands of

Dorothy Day and the Catholic Worker Movement

During the First World War, Dorothy Day wrote for the *Masses,* a leftist magazine that was suppressed by the Wilson administration. She supported birth control and was arrested in 1917 at the gates of the White House for participating in a protest for women's suffrage. Ten years later, after the birth of her daughter, Day converted to Roman Catholicism. She explained later that she was drawn to the Church "not for itself, because it was so often a scandal to me," but for the "Cross on which Christ was crucified." She lamented "the scandal of businesslike priests, of collective wealth, the lack of sense of responsibility for the poor, the worker, the Negro, the Mexican, the Filipino, and even the oppression of these, and the consenting to the oppression of them by our industrialist capitalist order—these made me feel often that priests were more like Cain than Abel. 'Am I my brother's keeper?' they seem to say in respect to the social order. There was plenty of charity but too little justice."

Despite her perception of the human frailities within the Catholic Church, Day remained celebratory of Catholic supernaturalism manifested in the mystical body of Christ. She extolled the men and women within the Church who hungered after justice, who were genuinely devoted to Christ's gospel of good news to the poor, "those who have put on Christ . . . those who have washed the feet of others." Day rejected the capitalist order and the culture of material acquisition. She spoke of human rights in explicitly inclusive terms, of giving prophetic witness to the living gospel by identifying with the victims of "the monstrous injustice of the class war [and] the race war." She strongly supported the Catholic Interracial Council of New York in its work in confronting social injustice affecting blacks, she picketed the German embassy to protest Nazi persecution of Jews, and helped organize the Committee of Catholics to Fight Anti-Semitism.

In 1935 Day opened a Catholic Worker House of Hospitality in New York City which allowed Catholics to commit themselves to evangelical poverty and providing the poor with material and spiritual care and to act as witnesses and agents of God's justice. By 1939, forty houses of hospitality, or communities of workers, and six Catholic Worker communal farms were operating in the United States. Throughout the Depression, Day and her fellow Catholic Workers set up soup kitchens on picket lines, offered strikers room and board at the Houses of Hospitality, and participated in sit-down strikes, including a notable 1935 strike against the Ford Motor Company in Flint, Michigan.

Catholic Workers emphasized a literal interpretation of the gospel commandment to love one's neighbor by maintaining an ongoing process of prayer, meditation, and specific social action. Day and her followers pursued community, rather than state responses, to poverty and hunger. As historian Aaron I. Abell said, they "preferred the picket line to the Wagner Act." As Day herself wrote in *House of Hospitality* (1939): "we are not denying the obligations of the State. But we do claim that we must never cease to emphasize personal responsibility. When our brother asks us for bread, we cannot say, 'Go be thou filled.' We cannot send him from agency to agency. We must care for him ourselves as much as possible." Day admitted that the Catholic Workers' radical vocation of serving the poor was antithetical to the prevailing ethos of "rugged individualism" in American society. "But," she added, "we are fools for Christ's sake. We are the little ones God has chosen to confound the wise . . . Surely the simple fact of feeding five thousand people a day, in all our houses [of hospitality] month after month for a number of years, is a most astounding proof that God loves our work."

Since Day and many of the commitments of the Catholic Workers was left of the political center, the movement operated under a cloud of ecclesiastical suspicion. In spite of her willingness to embrace political radicals and the substance of radicalism within the Catholic Worker movement, neither Day nor her cause was condemned by the Catholic Church. When Cardinal Francis Spellman of New York was asked why he would not censure Day, the cardinal reportedly replied, "She might be a saint." Day's work, which she chronicled in her 1952 autobiography *The Long Loneliness*, was vitally significant in maintaining the faith of countless Catholics who were either devastated by poverty or who were selflessly serving the poor, and, in so doing, witnessed the beauty of Catholicism's public dimension.

work relief projects such as the construction of libraries, highways, and parks, as well as hiring artists and other professionals who could not find work. By 1938 over three million Americans were employed by the WPA. A proposal by California's Dr. Francis Townsend to give all persons over sixty years of age $200 a month, and the "Share-Our-Wealth" plan of Senator Huey Long of Louisiana that advocated heavy taxes on the rich to give every family the necessities of life, sped the passage of the less radical Social Security Act in 1935. This act provided for old age pensions and insurance, plus unemployment insurance and support for public health programs. Although the measure was conservative compared to Townsend's or Long's plans, it was so successful that it is still the foundation of the government's social welfare program. In response to Long in particular, the administration passed higher corporate and estate taxes.

The area of labor relations saw the president and Congress actively promoting union organization and its goals. Child labor was abolished, minimum wages and maximum hours were set, and with the Wagner Act of 1935 workers were given the legal right to unionize and bargain collectively with management. With this encouragement labor began a massive organization drive that, despite violent confrontations with stubborn businesses, finally put industrial workers (miners, auto workers, steel workers, etc.) in a union—the Congress of Industrial Organizations (CIO). Labor was now in a position to bargain with business as an equal. When part of the Great Plains turned into a "Dust Bowl" after a long drought between 1934 and 1936, Congress passed New Deal conservation measures designed to halt erosion and improve farm techniques.

To support all of this legislation, President Roosevelt pasted together a patchwork coalition of farmers, intellectuals, workers, and minority groups, cemented the rural and urban factions of the Democratic party, and thereby forged a strong political alliance. He held it together largely by the force of his own warmth, vitality, and skill. Despite the bitter opposition of conservatives and radicals alike, this New Deal coalition won the election of 1936 and presented Roosevelt with a 28,000,000 vote mandate.

All barriers appeared to be overcome but one. Conservative judges on the Supreme Court had knocked down the NIRA and AAA, crippling major parts of Roosevelt's program. It seemed that they might block even more reforms passed by Congress. Early in 1937 Roosevelt introduced a bill that would give him the power to add six judges to the bench, thus "packing" the court in his favor. This ill-considered maneuver united New Deal opposition, split the Democratic ranks, and handed Roosevelt his first major defeat. No longer able to use the party as a willing tool, the president found his coalition crumbling away at the edges. The innovative stage of the New Deal was over.

Though the New Deal did not restore full prosperity (it took the Second World War to do that by demanding full production for the allied war effort) it had improved economic and social conditions from their low 1932 level. More important, it had restored Americans' confidence in their political, economic, and social system. Roosevelt, reminiscent of his trust-busting cousin three decades earlier, had stolen the thunder from the radicals by implementing moderate versions of their own proposals. To do this, he had given the federal government more power than it had ever wielded before. Washington agencies now supervised nearly every major social or economic activity in the nation. It had invaded the field of private enterprise with the TVA project. The "welfare state" had been inaugurated with the Social Security Act. Progressive and Populist trends toward government responsibility for the people's welfare and security had been largely realized by the New Deal. Indeed, some individual Progressives were influential in forming New Deal policies. Like Progressive reform, New Deal reform did not seek to change radically the American system—it sought to "better" it. By distributing the benefits of the capitalist system more broadly, Roosevelt's New Deal helped Americans weather a bleak depression and restored their confidence in gradual change within the system.

POST-WAR: TRUMAN AND EISENHOWER

When the nation turned to war again in 1941 the New Deal became a secondary concern. Even Roosevelt declared that winning the war must come first. After the president died in office on April 12, 1945, Harry S. Truman moved into the White House. With the end of the war the new president announced a progressive program that would extend the reforms of the New Deal. But a preoccupation with the Cold War and a conservative alliance between Northern Republicans and Southern Democrats frustrated his plans. A disapproving public coined the phrase, "To err is Truman," and returned a Republican Congress in the elections of 1946. Americans appeared to be turning toward conservatism as they had after the First World War. Despite being hampered by a splintered party, "give 'em hell Harry" beat the confident Republicans in a surprise upset in the 1948 presidential election.

Truman now sought to drive through his "Fair Deal," which included civil rights legislation, to create "a society which offers new opportunities for every man to enjoy his share of the good things of life." Congress, dominated by the conservative coalition, was indifferent at best. Public response seemed divided—one newspaper declared that the president's program "was the most frankly socialistic ever presented by a president of the United States."

How much was accomplished? First of all, Truman extended and codified New Deal measures already on the statute books. Social Security benefits and the minimum wage were raised and a federal housing program was farther expanded, all reflecting the progressive belief that a democratic society works best with a broad and thriving middle class. On the other hand, faced with a conservative Republican coalition in the Congress, other of Truman's proposals—like Medicare, federal aid to education and particularly civil rights measures designed to secure equal rights for African Americans—would be realized only in subsequent presidencies.

In 1952 popular World War II General Dwight D. Eisenhower won the presidential election, the first Republican in the White House since Herbert Hoover two decades earlier. And yet Ike and the moderate "modern Republicans" did not dismantle the pillars of the New Deal like the TVA and Social Security. Growth in the size of government slowed under Eisenhower budget cuts, but the momentum for activist government persisted despite the personal ambivalence Ike had for progressive reform. He signed the 1957 civil rights bill and used federal troops to enforce a Supreme Court order to integrate Central High in Little Rock, Arkansas. The President also secured the passage of the National Highway Act of 1956, creating the nation's huge interstate transportation network. But Eisenhower was more a reassuring, unifying national figure than a reformer.

While the Eisenhower years saw little reform originating from the legislative branch of government, the Supreme Court asserted itself as a pacesetter for social reform in America. Through the nation's history the Court had served as an arbiter of controversy. With Eisenhower's choice of former California Governor Earl Warren as Chief Justice in 1953, the judiciary assumed leadership in changing the social and political fabric of America. During the fourteen years of Warren's tenure, the Court came to be known as "the people's court" as it actively championed the cause of the common man in such controversial areas as civil and religious rights. The historic Brown decision in 1954, which overturned the *Plessy* decision of 1896 illustrates the point. This case launched a new era in race relations in America, offering opportunities for people long denied social and political equality. The assertion of minority rights reflected in the school desegregation mandate following 1954 was accompanied by the Court's protection of the First Amendment. In two important decisions in 1962 and 1963 the Justices insisted on preserving the doctrine of separation of church and state by voting against required prayer and Bible-reading in the public schools. Moreover, the rights of the poor were buttressed by the 1963 decision in *Gideon v. Wainwright* which declared that the government must provide legal counsel to penniless defendants in criminal cases. The *Escobedo* (1964) and *Miranda* (1966) decisions guaranteed a defendant's right to remain silent when accused of a crime. Although controversial, these landmark decisions by the Warren Court gave testimony to the nation's insistence of the basic tenet of equal justice under the law. While President Eisenhower may not have anticipated the revolutionary impact of his judicial appointments, his choice provided one of the enduring achievements of his presidency.

JFK AND LBJ

Unfortunately for the Republicans, Eisenhower's popularity did not rub off on their candidate for President in 1960, Richard M. Nixon. In the contest with Democratic nominee John F. Kennedy, Nixon labored under the difficulty of Kennedy's engaging personality and a Democratic majority among the nation's voters. The election was close, but Kennedy held his party together and emerged victorious. During the campaign, the young candidate struck the keynote of his presidency—to "get this country moving again." "The torch has been passed to a new generation of Americans," he exclaimed, who were about to face a "new frontier." "The New Frontier is here whether we seek it or not . . . uncharted areas of science and space, unsolved problems of peace and war, unconquered pockets of ignorance and prejudice, unanswered questions of poverty and surplus." Kennedy challenged Americans to explore this frontier and conquer it: "The energy, the faith, the devotion which we bring to this endeavor will light our country and all who serve it, and the glow from that fire can truly light the world."

The new president quickly created an administration of talent, including some of the most brilliant men in the world of business, law, and education. He proposed legislation for aid to education, medical care for the elderly, urban renewal, civil rights, a tax cut, and the space program. All Congress let through was the space appropriation—the old coalition of conservative Northern Republicans and Southern Democrats sidetracked the rest in committee. Kennedy seemed unable to move the legislation through Congress. The only major innovation his admini-

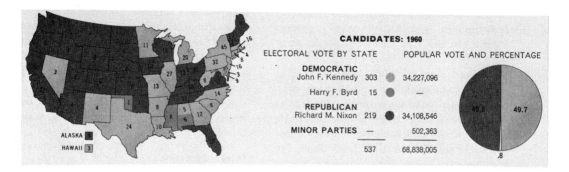

stration was able to produce was the Peace Corps, and that by executive decree. Nevertheless, Kennedy revitalized the office of the Presidency as the seat of national leadership. During his brief administration, Washington was transformed into a cultural and social as well as a political capital: poetry, painting, drama, chamber music, and a fresh sense of the possible enlivened the city. It was all cut short by Kennedy's assassination in Dallas on November 22, 1963. The nationwide sense of loss and the eulogies given to the fallen president at home and abroad testify to the hope many felt he had carried for a better future.

When a solemn Lyndon B. Johnson took the oath of office aboard Air Force One after the assassination, he inaugurated a great change in the national leadership. Johnson represented the rural Southwest as opposed to Kennedy's urban New England, projected an image of the common man, and could not match Kennedy's sophistication and charm. Under LBJ the White House took on a Texas flavor. Yet Johnson was a strong leader, a brilliant politician with firm ties to FDR's New Deal, which he had ardently supported. Above all a masterful manipulator of Congress, he liked to quote a passage from Isaiah as the key to his success: "Come, now, let us reason together."

In a climate of national remorse and by a combination of reasoning, cajoling, and arm twisting, Johnson got Congress moving on the stalled Kennedy program. The same Southern Congressmen and Senators who had blocked it had an emotional commitment to their fellow Southerner's success. LBJ assigned the civil rights bill top priority, and it was passed in February 1964. But the president was not content simply to follow Kennedy's program. During March he declared a "war on poverty" that resulted in the passage of the Economic Opportunity Act. This act created a multitude of new federal projects: the Job Corps, which like the earlier CCC provided work in conservation for young people but also trained school dropouts for technical trade positions; VISTA, a domestic equivalent of the Peace Corps; and "Head Start," an educational effort to give poor children a better chance to survive and learn in public schools. Success had its price, however. One newspaper columnist noted that Johnson "can make them do what he wants them to do, but he does not make them like it or him in the process."

The election of 1964 was only a brief interlude in Johnson's construction of a "Great Society." Republicans chose to give the American people "a choice, not an echo," and nominated the strongly conservative Barry Goldwater of Arizona. With Goldwater making statements such as the demand for "total victory" in the Cold War and a suggestion that the way to win in Vietnam was to drop "a low-yield atomic bomb on Chinese supply lines in North Vietnam," Johnson had

JOHN F. KENNEDY

John Fitzgerald Kennedy was born in 1917 to middle class, Irish-Catholic parents in Brookline, Massachusetts. Although his father later made a fortune in banking and investments, he was never accepted into the "old elite" of Massachusetts. "What do I have to do to be an American?" he once fumed to a friend. But the Kennedy family was close and less affected, their mother Rose instilling a fierce loyalty to one another while father Joseph built a tough competitive spirit. Joseph Sr. clearly had plans for eldest son Joseph Jr., who was near the top of his class at both Choate and Harvard in sports and academics, but Kennedy's future was less clear.

In Europe when the Second World War broke out, Kennedy returned to write an honors thesis, "Why England Slept," discussing the dangers of unpreparedness. It was published and sold well. After graduation Kennedy toyed with the idea of careers in journalism or business, but American entry into the war intervened. After initially being turned down because of a back injury suffered in his Harvard football days, Kennedy was accepted into the Navy. While in command of PT 109 on patrol in the Pacific in August, 1943, a Japanese destroyer came out of the fog and sliced his boat in two. Kennedy led his surviving eleven men to an island three miles away, towing one of them by a life jacket strap held in his teeth. After their rescue Kennedy got a medal for bravery ("It was involuntary," he later said dryly, "they sank my boat.") and was in the hospital for months with a ruined back. It never properly healed. While recovering he learned that his brother Joe had been killed during a special Air Force mission in Europe. When asked later if he made a career of politics to please his father and replace Joe, Kennedy said no. "But I never would have run for office if he had lived."

Kennedy returned to Massachusetts to run for a Congressional seat in 1946. He won in part on his family name, but a strong organization of personal supporters and plain hard work were crucial. His three term record in the House was mixed and impressed few fellow Democrats. In 1952 Kennedy chose to run for the Senate against popular Republican Henry Cabot Lodge. His younger brother Robert managed the campaign, which turned on personality in the absence of major differences on the issues. Kennedy won, attracting party notice for the first time. A year later, the playboy married wealthy socialite Jacqueline Bouvier.

His back getting worse, Kennedy interrupted his Senate tenure for back surgery. It nearly killed him, and he was not fully recovered for six months. Returning to the Senate, he hoped to be chosen by Democratic candidate Adlai Stevenson as a Vice Presidential running mate in the 1956 election. Stevenson chose another, but lost the campaign. By 1960 Kennedy felt confident enough to run for the Democratic nomination himself. He outran and outspent his rivals and was chosen by the convention on the first ballot. In a seesaw campaign against Republican Richard Nixon, managed again by brother Robert, Kennedy came out on top by less than one percent of the popular vote—the second youngest and the first Catholic president in United States history.

---

no difficulty labeling his opponent a "risky" choice for president. The country gave Johnson and the Democrats a landslide victory at the polls.

Johnson lost no time in pushing Congress to write the "Great Society" goals into law. He had astonishing success. The Eighty-ninth Congress proved to be the most productive since the New Deal: for aid to education, $1.3 billion; to fight poverty in the region of the Appalachian Mountains, $1.1 billion; for new housing, $7.5 billion; to clean up the nation's waterways and air, more than $3.7 billion; and $1.2 billion for urban development and the construction of "model

VISTA (Volunteers in Service to America) was in the tradition of President Kennedy's personal activism and an integral part of President Johnson's "War on Poverty." Members would serve the public in such varied capacities as workers in the urban ghettos, classroom teacher aides, and vocational training instructors. The ideals of social service would resurface in President Clinton's National Service program. (Ken Heyman.)

cities." The civil rights bill of 1965 removed serious obstacles to black voters. Economically the nation was experiencing unprecedented growth and prosperity. General Motors alone made more gross profit than the entire GNP of the Netherlands. As a result of federal spending, a tax cut, and business cooperation, Johnson could proudly say in 1965 that "We are in the midst of the greatest upward surge of economic well-being in the history of any nation."

Yet by 1967–68 the "Great Society" was in trouble. Despite Johnson's assurance that the nation could afford both the war on poverty and the escalating war in Vietnam—"guns and butter"—the attempt to do so was beginning to create an intolerable tax burden on many middle class Americans and resulting in serious inflation. Nor could the much publicized "war on poverty" show effective results—"the walls of the ghettos are not going to topple overnight," concluded one newspaper. A now cautious Congress refused to fund adequately the president's domestic programs. But the final and decisive blow was Vietnam. As American casualties mounted and no end to the war appeared in sight, public protest increased. Students, who had played a prominent role in domestic politics since the early civil rights movement in the 1950s, led massive demonstrations against the war on campuses across the nation. Under the pressure of events, President Johnson finally decided not to run for reelection.

THE SUPREME COURT—A LIBERAL FORCE

Under Chief Justice Earl Warren (1953–1969) the Supreme Court extended the rights of people accused of crimes and defended Constitutional freedoms. The Court also infuriated conservatives by banning prayer in public schools, extending abortion rights, and localizing obscenity standards.

Brown v. Topeka Board of Education (1954)

Segregation was declared unconstitutional in a unanimous decision that also ordered schools be integrated "with all deliberate speed."

Yates v. U.S. (1957)

Further protected political free speech by requiring proof of intent to commit violence before someone could be banned from speaking or arrested.

Mapp v. Ohio (1961)

Expanded protection of privacy by ruling that evidence illegally seized could not be used in court.

Gideon v. Wainright (1963)

Established the right of all defendants to a lawyer.

Wesberry v. Sanders (1966)

Ruled that Congressional districts must be equal in population—the "one man, one vote" principle.

Miranda v. Arizona (1966)

Suspects must be informed of their rights when arrested.

N. Y. Times v. U. S. (1971)

Reaffirmed the freedom of the press against censorship without a clear threat to national security. A more conservative court would, in the 1980s and '90s, redefine and restrict many of these rulings.

NIXON, WATERGATE, AND THE PRESS

Like Populism, Progressivism, the New Deal, and the New Frontier before it, the Great Society had sought to "better" the American system by removing its "faults and defects" That the system deserved saving was assumed from the beginning; other movements which dispute their assumption have never gained more than a small voice in American politics. Adhering to the progressive idea that the federal government is representative of the American people and guardian of the public interest, the Great Society followed its predecessors and sought their ends by granting the federal government a larger role in the economy and in dealing with social questions. Government spending also shifted more towards social programs while the percentage of the budget spent on

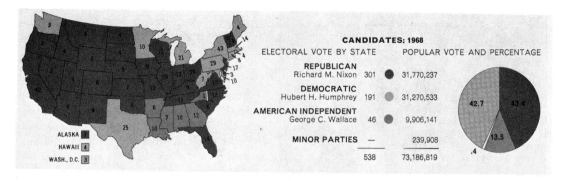

defense declined. Since the Great Society was Johnson's creation, it was expected that some of its programs could expire along with the term of their creator. But the trend toward a bigger, more involved national government that had been building since the turn of the century was expected to continue.

At first, this expectation appeared to be accurate. President Nixon, though a middle-of-the-road conservative, used the power of the federal government and especially that of the presidency itself to a level not matched since Franklin Roosevelt. Indeed, in his conduct of the war in Vietnam, the president demonstrated his willingness to resort to big government to accomplish his objectives. With the end of American involvement in Southeast Asia, however, Nixon was able to devote his second term of office to domestic affairs. He began to pursue his fiscally-conservative goals of government decentralization and an end to wage and price controls, and his campaign against the new "moral permissiveness." In his call for a return to the America that was "built not by government, but by people," Nixon appeared prepared to abandon "the condescending policies of paternalism" by cutting the funds for Great Society programs. The purpose, he maintained, was to balance the federal budget and inaugurate a "return to responsibility." The president's blueprint for reform, however, was torpedoed by both the complex and sinister events of Watergate and the "muckraking" of the scandal by the press.

Throughout his political career, Nixon had spoken about the need for moral standards and respect for law and order. And yet in their zeal to remain in office, the president and his men resorted to illegal means, thereby subverting the existing political system. With the news in 1973 that Nixon's Committee to Reelect the President (CREEP) had misused such government agencies as the FBI, CIA, IRS, and the Secret Service to discredit their enemies (CREEP even constructed an "enemies list" of those citizens who opposed the Nixon administration), Americans suffered a great loss of faith in their government. Media coverage also focused on other improprieties in the highest echelon of the government, including $10 million of taxpayers' money spent on personal conveniences for Nixon's estates in California and Florida, his attempts to stretch the limits of legality in his federal tax returns, and Vice-President Spiro Agnew's secret efforts at income tax evasion while governor of Maryland.

After the Washington Post's initial revelations about Watergate broadened into media exposes of pervasive corruption in Nixon's administration, his efforts to reform the government

President Nixon's campaign for re-election in 1972 was masterfully orchestrated by the Committee to Re-Elect the President (CREEP). His greatest political triumph was soon eclipsed, however, by the shadow of Watergate. (Courtesy of the White House.)

via his "New Federalism" were doomed to failure. Just as had been the case during the Progressive politics of Teddy Roosevelt, the muckraking tradition of the American press had played an important role in bringing about political reform. Ironically, although Nixon's reform program was thwarted by the tragedy of his excesses, journalistic vigilance had been instrumental in securing campaign finance reform and a reduction of the "imperial presidency's" powers. The unraveling of the Watergate conspiracy, one writer observed, "led to a searching critique of federal power and to a healthy distrust of the executive branch of government, of intelligence agencies, of vague appeals to national security. It stimulated a far-ranging discussion of political ethics, of basic moral and constitutional principles." The press had helped to restore Americans' faith in their government.

THE CARTER INTERLUDE

Public sentiment in the aftermath of the Watergate scandal reduced the Ford administration to a "caretaker" presidency, paving the way for a Democratic victory by Jimmy Carter in 1976. At a time when the ethics of the nation's highest officeholders were exposed to the American people, the Georgia peanut-farmer's campaign plea that "you can trust me" was reassuring. This born-again Christian vowed that he would "de-imperialize" the Oval Office in an effort to put distance between him and the regal trappings of the Nixon White House. Portraying himself as a "man of the people" who walked down Pennsylvania Avenue with his wife on Inauguration Day, Carter tapped a reservoir of support from citizens mindful of Franklin Roosevelt who rallied Americans around his reform program of the 1930s. Indeed, Carter's victory reflected the revival of the old New Deal coalition of ethnics, blacks and Hispanics, blue-collar workers, and the Old South.

Like most marriages of convenience, however, President Carter's did not last for long. After declaring a progressive agenda in accord with his party's reform tradition—including active enforcement of civil rights, revamping the income tax structure, and expanding welfare programs—the President found himself unable to mobilize his party or the nation behind these issues. To begin with, he failed to clarify the importance of his issues and to establish some priorities for dealing with them. Instead, choosing unwisely to campaign against the Washington Establishment, Carter lost crucial support by attacking "pork barrel" projects important to members of Congress. Although consistent with his campaign promise to cut federal spending, he needlessly alienated the legislative support necessary for his program's success. Not only was the president's own party not solidly behind him, but powerful lobbying of special-interest groups that prowled Capitol Hill led him to complain privately that the nation was becoming fragmented and ungovernable. Faced with these obstacles, there was a pressing need for a president who could twist arms, trade votes, and pressure congressmen to support his program. But Carter was neither an FDR nor an LBJ; his lack of leadership skills was joined by his lack of vision. One aide remarked: "Carter believes fifty things, but no one thing. He holds explicit, thorough positions on every issue under the sun, but he has no large view of relations between them." The result was a shift of power from the White House to Capitol Hill which the president was never able to overcome.

And yet his presidency was not without accomplishments. Carter correctly diagnosed the nation's deepening economic malaise as stemming from the spreading global energy crisis. To his credit, Carter recognized that an intelligent reform of energy policy must serve as the cornerstone for the nation's economic recovery. Accordingly, in a dramatic television appeal he implored his fellow Americans to join in an energy crusade that would be "the moral equivalent of war." He sought legislative action to improve energy conservation in an effort to lessen the nation's reliance on foreign oil. By October 1978, he had secured the removal of price controls on natural gas, special taxes on gas-guzzling automobiles, and tax credits for homeowners willing to engage in energy-saving innovations.

These reforms, praiseworthy though they were, were not enough. In 1979, the revolution in Iran and the downfall of its monarchy led to a new rise in oil costs and a resurgence in the inflation rate. Carter found himself in a "no-win" situation. A decline in government income precluded the continuation of his reform program. Concluding that New Deal solutions of the 1930s were no longer viable, the "outsider" from Georgia was now damned by liberal Democrats who charged that their president was actually a "closet Republican" who had betrayed their party. Instead of elaborating upon existing programs of welfare and relief, pragmatic Carter asked Americans to trim their sails by lowering their expectations of government and he proposed that federal spending be cut. Within one hundred days of his taking office many people thought that Carter had begun shifting to the right. Within a year disgruntled liberals believed that the president was

RONALD REAGAN

Born to a poor family in Tampico, Illinois, Ronald Reagan was raised by a shoe salesman father with a fondness for drink and a mother who loved the amateur theater. In both high school and college he was involved in sports and dramatic productions as well as student government. His college education was funded by jobs as a dishwasher and a lifeguard and by a partial scholarship. Shortly after graduation he became a sportscaster for radio station WHO in Des Moines. While on assignment in Southern California covering the spring training of the Chicago Cubs, Reagan was invited to do a screen test for Warner Brothers Studio. He looked good enough for the big moviemaker to offer him a contract.

Knute Rockne, All American (1940) was Reagan's most successful film, although he also won good reviews for his work in *King's Row* (1942). He married actress Jane Wyman in 1940, but the tensions of competing careers drove them to divorce eight years later. During the Second World War Reagan helped produce training films, having been denied combat duty because of his poor eyesight. Shortly after the war Reagan became president of the Screen Actor's Guild, and as a liberal Democrat campaigned for Harry S. Truman in the 1948 election. But by 1952 he had become more conservative and was backing Eisenhower for the White House. In the process of removing suspected communists from the Guild during the McCarthy "red scare," Reagan met a woman named Nancy Davis who complained of receiving unsolicited communist literature in the mail. They were married in 1952.

Two years later General Electric signed Reagan as the host of "General Electric Theater," a weekly TV drama. Reagan also made speeches to civic groups stressing the values of free enterprise. In 1962 he made the switch to "Death Valley Days." During Barry Goldwater's doomed race for the presidency in 1964, Reagan made a terrific speech on television for Goldwater condemning high taxes, wasteful government spending, a bloated bureaucracy, and the evils of a welfare state. The speech brought in a great deal of money and made Reagan a Republican star.

In 1966 Reagan was elected governor of California by a landslide vote. During his two term tenure, Governor Reagan slowed state spending and instituted some welfare reforms, but also raised taxes. He made a brief and somewhat unenthusiastic fling at the presidency in 1968 and then a real effort against Ford for the Republican nomination in 1976 which nearly unseated the President. By 1980, Reagan was the clear Republican favorite to face down Carter. Although his campaign had some early problems, Reagan's energy belied his 69 years and by May he had won 20 of 24 state primaries. He went on to a first ballot victory at the convention and one of the largest landslides in history against Carter in the election. His second-term victory was even greater, garnering the electoral votes of 49 out of 50 states.

---

the most conservative Democrat to sit in the White House since Grover Cleveland, charging that Carter was "a Democrat who often talks and thinks like a Republican."

By the end of Carter's term in office, prospects for the nation's economic well-being were bleak. Inflation had soared to 12.4 percent by 1980. By the end of the year, one dollar was worth only 15 cents in 1940 values. That is, on the average, it took one dollar to purchase what in 1940 cost 15 cents. The dollar had suffered fully half of this loss during the 1970s. With confidence in the dollar on the decline, the price of gold on the world money market skyrocketed. The prime lending rate reached an unprecedented 20 percent. An economic recession was in full swing by

1980, with the unemployment rate reaching 7.5 percent. As a result, Carter's searing attack on Republican policies in 1976, which he labeled the "misery index," came back to haunt him. Then he had invited Americans to blame the Republicans for current economic malaise; four years later they were inclined to place the nation's predicament at his doorstep.

REAGAN, BUSH, AND THE UNFINISHED REVOLUTION

The Republican presidential candidate in 1980 certainly provided the electorate with "a choice, not an echo." If that slogan was ill-fit for Barry Goldwater's candidacy in 1964, sixteen years later the voters indicated that they were disenchanted with the tired New Deal prescriptions for the economy. Previous administrations had favored the economic theories of John Maynard Keynes, the British economist, which called for stimulation of the economy at times of high unemployment and economic hard times, and for increases in government expenditures that would stimulate consumption and investment. Forty-three million Americans cast their votes for the man who vowed to reduce the size and cost of the federal government. Ronald Reagan's opponent, incumbent Jimmy Carter, garnered only 34 million votes; his electoral vote tally was even less than incumbent Herbert Hoover's in another decisive presidential race in 1932. How can Reagan's victory be explained?

The one-time Hollywood movie actor had already captured national attention as a fiscal conservative who served two terms as governor of California. Moreover, his presidential campaign strategy took advantage of important changes in electoral demography. Census data in 1980 indicated that the average voter was older and more conservative than in the 1960s. The large bloc of idealistic activists under age twenty-five during the 1960s had raised their voices in anger over racial violence and war; fifteen years later these same people were bidding on second homes or exchanging tips on winter vacations. In addition, there was a population shift from the more liberal "frostbelt" states of the Northeast and Midwest to the more conservative "sunbelt" of the South and Southwest. Middle-class Americans seemed to feel that their growing tax burden was being used to bankroll a spendthrift and ineffective bureaucracy during a period of deepening economic crisis. Reagan was able to capitalize on this public frustration and mold a powerful coalition of Americans whose conservative economic and social views echoed his own firm belief that government should "get off the backs of the American people."

Reagan chose "The New Beginning" to describe his policy for economic reform. He and his advisors advanced the notion of "supply-side" economics, which forthrightly preached the virtues of pro-business government practiced during the Republican era of the 1920s. Accordingly, large budget cuts were to be accompanied by environmental deregulation, and a massive tax reduction resulting from the Tax Act of 1981. Voters were promised that such steps would guarantee the end of inflation, stimulate higher employment, and increase investments and productivity. Reagan's economic reforms were also to be facilitated by the "New Federalism" proposed earlier by President Nixon, which suggested the shift of the increasing burden of welfare and relief from Washington D.C. to the state governments. This proposal was likewise consistent with the traditional conservative belief that the federal government had become too large and unwieldy, and that some of its functions could be administered more efficiently on a level of government

Regarded as a doctrinaire and relatively untested politician prior to his election in 1980, Ronald Reagan nonetheless stunned his opponents with a sweeping victory. During his first administration the president won grudging respect from administration critics. Seated Vice President George Bush contemplates his political future. (Courtesy of Mary Anne Fackelman, The White House.)

closer to the people. The architects of the "New Beginning" wished to dismantle all but the most basic elements of the New Deal and Great Society social programs in such a way that it would be politically and financially impractical to restore them.

Economic conservatives were not alone in rallying around Reagan's reform program. The Republican candidate's pronounced opposition to sexual permissiveness and pornography, drugs and abortion, busing, Affirmative Action, and the Equal Rights Amendment made him the darling of social conservatives who deplored the erosion of "traditional" American values. One segment of this "New Right" was the Moral Majority, an amalgam of religious fundamentalists whose several million followers contributed to Reagan's margin of victory over Carter in the presidential race. In short, the new president was seen by many as a moral crusader, given a mandate by the people to carry out their will.

How effective was the new president in the implementation of his goals? On the plus side, Reagan's expert use of the media created a rising tide of public enthusiasm that the Congress dared not ignore. For the first time in twenty-six years, the Republicans controlled the Senate, and by securing the support of "Old Right" southern Democratic congressmen nicknamed "Boll Weevils," the president was able to have the Congress do his bidding. By summer 1981 a wholesale slashing of the budget and a three-year tax cut (the largest in American history) had been achieved. The "Reagan Revolution" had imposed freezes on economic regulations and federal hiring, made large across-the-board cuts in social welfare programs, and even eliminated 37,000 jobs from the federal payroll. These efforts proved that the "citizen-politician" from California was no "bush-leaguer." Presidential popularity and old-fashioned politicking restored power to the Oval Office, absent since LBJ and his Great Society.

It remained to be seen how well the president would be able to sustain voter allegiance to his economic policies. "Supply-side" principles were not providing the steady improvement promised by Reagan. To make matters worse, his military budget called for a $1.6 trillion build-up over a five-year period. Political experts began to ask how taxes could be cut, defense costs increased, and the budget balanced. Faced with an incipient revolt from rank-and-file voters during his first term, President Reagan admonished voters in 1984 to "stay the course," pleading for more time to correct economic ills rooted in fifty years of liberal big-spending. The result was an unprecedented reelection victory for the president as he commanded the electoral votes of 49 states, eclipsing FDR's record 1936 electoral vote tally which included all but two states.

Reagan's domestic agenda was unchanged during his second term. The centerpiece of his tax policy was the Economic Recovery Tax Act of 1981, reducing the top levy on personal income tax from 50 percent to 28 percent. This law significantly altered the traditional assumption dating back to the Graduated Income Tax of 1913 that those receiving higher pay should contribute a progressively larger percentage of that income in taxes. Now there would be a major redistribution of income away from the poor and toward the rich. Tax relief benefited all taxpayers, but not equally, with the wealthy enjoying enormous windfalls, and by 1990 the richest 2.5 million Americans had scored a spectacular 75 percent income increase during the 1980s. They now had nearly as much income as the 100 million Americans who had the lowest incomes. As the poor became relatively poorer, the nation became more violent and less educated. More important, this new tax policy accelerated the shift in the larger debate over the role of government and federal spending. No longer was it a question of whether a social program should be expanded or trimmed, but whether it should be abandoned altogether.

Conservative Republicans were also committed to overturning *Roe v. Wade,* the 1973 Supreme Court decision regarding abortion, and the President insisted that prayer should be restored in the public schools. Ironically, implementation of these goals would have increased the government's role in the day-to-day lives of the people. President Reagan's social agenda was also conspicuous for what it ignored; despite his assurance that a "safety net" would prevent the "truly needy" from "falling through the cracks," far more families lived below the poverty line in 1988 than in 1980, including one in four children.

Yet nothing seemed to diminish Reagan's hold on American voters. Major industries like steel declined, no longer able to meet competition from abroad; labor suffered as well-paid positions in manufactures disappeared, forcing workers into low-income service jobs without benefits; farmers saw a brief prosperity end, and then endured a major crisis in which tens of thousands lost their farms. Despite such widespread misery, critics were unable to effectively advance their argument that this human suffering was a result of the social and economic policies of the Reagan administration. He was the teflon president so well liked that nothing messy stuck to him personally, neither bad decisions like trading arms for hostages with Iran nor scandals like those in the EPA and HUD.

It was no surprise, then, when his vice president and heir-apparent, George Bush, was nominated at the 1988 Republican convention. Although promising a "kinder, gentler America" in his race against the Democratic nominee, Massachusetts Governor Michael Dukakis, the Bush campaign was merciless. Brutal TV spots unfairly attacking Dukakis's judgment had a chilling effect on voters' perceptions of the Democratic candidate. During a televised debate between the two candidates, "political correctness" became a central issue. Facing a rising anti-government mood generated during the previous eight years, Dukakis valiantly insisted that the election hinged "not on ideology, but on competence," thereby disavowing his own and his party's progressive background. No longer was liberalism acknowledged as a legitimate force on the American political spectrum. Subsequently, it became a taboo word in the lexicon of the Democratic party. Liberalism seemed moribund. Moreover, Dukakis's campaign was marred by its own incompetence, including his rather cold and dull public image. As the Massachusetts governor grew drabber in the public eye, Bush and his running mate, conservative Indiana Senator Dan Quayle, promised to continue the policies of the Reagan-Bush administrations. Though Dukakis's loss was less devastating than those suffered by earlier Democratic candidates Carter (1980) and Mondale (1984), the perpetuity of the Reagan Revolution seemed guaranteed, as the Bush campaign overwhelmed its opponent in electoral votes by a ratio of 4 to 1.

When Ronald Reagan retired to his ranch near Santa Barbara, for many citizens it still seemed to be "morning in America," a phrase coined by the optimistic Reagan. Actually, George Bush inherited a series of problems rapidly becoming crises. The budget deficit had increased four times since 1980, resulting in a $1.5 trillion deficit by 1992. There was plenty of blame for the legislative gridlock after twelve years of Republicans in the White House and a Democratic controlled Congress. Yet few were willing to admit their culpability for the deepening economic chasm. Despite the GOP's constant patriotic breast-beating about America's greatness, the fact is that Americans' international purchasing power had plummeted to ninth among the nations of the world. Although the administration could boast of a record number of "self-made" millionaires and at least 50 billionaires as a result of tax policies during the 1980s, for many other citizens the American Dream was no longer within reach. For the first time since World War II the percentage of home-owning families declined. The younger generation of the 1980s began to face a bleaker standard of living than their elders had experienced. Moreover, Reagan-Bush housing policy exacerbated the looming problems of homelessness and poverty. If 500,000 subsidized private housing units were constructed annually under Presidents Ford and Carter, by 1990 the number had dropped to 25,000.

Other matters were treated with benign neglect during this period of Republican ascendancy; by 1990, 40 percent of Americans no longer had adequate medical care; the drug epidemic was not slowed by Reagan's simplistic anti-drug program ("Just say 'no'") nor by Bush's "taking out" of Noriega from Panama; as for the environment, sparse attention was given ecological concerns by the Reagan-Bush administrations. Furthermore, disregard for issues like race relations and the case involving the beating of black motorist Rodney King by police, resulted in the dramatic Los Angeles riots in 1992. President Bush's characterization of his administration as the "Age of the helping hand" hardly seemed appropriate to a growing number of Americans. As the president advanced the conservative idea of volunteerism, he highlighted his "one thousand points of light," suggesting that the private sector would replace and improve upon the services and supports formerly provided by the federal government. But the sentimental notion of "neighbor helping neighbor" was essentially a myth; in fact, volunteerism had never been able to meet the needs of poor Americans. Since the 1930s some form of public assistance has always been crucial to those in poverty.

The Reagan Revolution was losing its momentum. Twelve years of a GOP White House had raised questions about the nation's agenda but not changed its habits. Rather than matching their rhetoric about balancing the budget with action, the Republicans had presided over the largest budget deficit in history. Critics claimed Reaganomics was little more than the opportunity for the rich to become richer through generous tax breaks; "tax reform" had actually benefited the wealthiest five percent of Americans. President Bush was no more willing to face economic reality than his predecessor. Rather than confront the climbing deficit, he dared voters to "read my lips," promising "no new taxes." Soon after, however, Bush proceeded to implement the second largest tax increase since World War II to partly offset the now soaring deficit. Pro-business policies of deregulation led to Republican permissiveness toward mergers, anti-trust enforcement and speculative finance. The result was a tidal wave of fiscal mismanagement and scandal, including the saving and loan association bail-out, junk bonds, shaky real estate markets, and unprecedented numbers of bankruptcies. Several figures prominent in such financial illegalities received hefty fines and prison time for their crimes.

Blatant indifference to the gathering storm was not limited to the Republicans; the Democrats also bore complicity. No one blew the whistle on the bogus "tax reforms" of the 1980s, until their dire consequences became more obvious. Instead, both parties in the Congress participated in a frenzy of excessive and imprudent tax cutting without commensurate budget cutting, shattering the nation's fiscal stability. Countering the anti-tax mood engendered by the Reagan Revolution, politicians irresponsibly pandered to voters, while basic needs like road maintenance and environmental regulations went unmet. While taxes were cut, spending on entitlements like Medicare and Social Security were not. Indeed, Congress had provided automatic cost-of-living adjustments to these social services. By 1990, Medicare became the fastest growing area of the budget. When the spree was over, the permanent revenue base of the U.S. government had been slashed by nearly one-third! Little wonder that voters were confused. Reaganomics was losing its moral imperative, relabeled by its critics "smoke-and-mirrors" economics. Some Congressional Democrats and Republicans prominent in the previous decade's speculative disasters began to realize that the crucial task of the nineties would involve "cleanup." Indeed, representatives from both parties dared to suggest that in the interest of "fairness" those who reaped the greatest rewards during the eighties should bear a larger burden of taxation in restoring fiscal stability during the nineties.

CLINTON AND THE VITAL CENTER

The election of 1992 proved to be pivotal. While claiming their tent was large enough to accommodate diversity, the GOP convention at Houston was noteworthy for its exclusivity. Not only did the party platform deny the real concerns of the poor and people of color, but its stance toward women's issues and homosexuality was hostile. Continued party endorsement of the previous twelve years of Reaganomics suggested to many voters that the Republicans "just didn't get it." Reagan's former budget chief David Stockman lambasted leaders of his own party for failing to acknowledge their giant mistake in fiscal governance, charging that they "poisoned the political debate with a mindless stream of anti-tax venom while pretending that economic growth and spending cuts alone could cure the deficit." Even conservative political pundit George Will concluded that things got as bad as they did "only because Americans were not allowed to admit that they were bad at all."

Republican complacency with incumbent Bush was challenged by the Democratic nominee during the 1992 campaign. Sensing public skepticism with Reagan-Bush economic policy, Arkansas Governor William Jefferson Clinton campaigned on a platform of change. The youthful candidate reminded voters of Thomas Jefferson's assertion that in a democracy each generation must face up to its problems. Bill Clinton's idealism was evocative of the call for change uttered by two Democratic predecessors, Franklin D. Roosevelt and John F. Kennedy. Like their campaigns in 1932 and 1960, Clinton asked his fellow Americans for sacrifice in order to get their economic house in order. Deficit reduction was accompanied by plans for rebuilding the nation's infrastructure, a vague bureaucratic term referring to a system necessary to support a modern society such as roads and highways, sewage treatment plants, and communications.

The presidential race was complicated by the entry of a third candidate, Texas billionaire Ross Perot. As candidates Clinton and Perot blistered Bush's administration for its neglect of the deficit, citizens began to realize that the nation's economic future was truly at risk. Like Woodrow Wilson's victory in the three-way contest in 1912, Clinton emerged with only a plurality of the popular vote (43 percent), including 55 percent of the women's vote. Journalists speculated whether the support siphoned away from the Democratic column by Perot's candidacy deprived President Clinton of a genuine mandate for change. Some critics held out little hope for newcomer Clinton, noting that he was one of only four presidents since 1921—along with Coolidge, Carter and Reagan—who entered the Oval Office without Capitol Hill experience. In contrast, others were impressed by Clinton who, according to one scholar, came into office with a better grasp of economic issues "than any president in history."

The "man from Hope" began his inaugural festivities with a trip to Monticello, home of his namesake Thomas Jefferson. But the new beginning President Clinton wanted to make was almost immediately mired in problems. The "honeymoon" lasted only a few of the traditional 100 days. Early moves to satisfy long-exiled liberals, such as eliminating the military ban on gays, angered moderates. Washington "beltway" insiders questioned the new president's competence after several cabinet and Supreme Court nomination missteps. The administration's economic stimulus package died in a Democratic Congress, reviving fears of federal paralysis. Appearing to waffle on some important campaign commitments, the president's credibility and commitment were doubted. Just weeks into a four-year term, media pundits were calling the Clinton presidency a failure. Even a sympathetic columnist characterized the opening act as "six months of quiet success and loud failures."

Bill Clinton presented an ambitious program of change during his first year in the White House. Seated behind the President is Vice President Al Gore and Speaker of the House Tom Foley.

But the President was on a steep learning curve. Clinton moved to regain support from the vital center of American politics, dropping more radical proposals like a broad-based energy tax and compromising on the military's policy toward gays. The administration barely overcame cries of "tax and spend" from the united Republican opposition to win Congressional approval of its budget, ending "smoke and mirror" tactics and beginning to cut the deficit. Other bills that encouraged voter registration, established family leave policies, and created a national service program for youth emerged as law. Clinton won the fight to approve the North American Free Trade Agreement between Canada, Mexico, and the United States—an uphill struggle despite the bipartisan support of three ex-presidents and a strong majority of economists. In the fall of 1993, Clinton introduced his national health care plan, a measure one commentator declared was "the most far-reaching piece of legislation since FDR's New Deal." Vice President Al Gore unveiled his plan to "reinvent government," an ambitious five year effort to cut 200,000 government jobs, save $100 billion and make the federal behemoth more "user friendly."

Reflecting his party's own progressive roots, the president's plan accommodated the needs of "the forgotten middle class" whom Franklin Roosevelt had remembered sixty years earlier. In truth, the health care proposal *increased* user options, frightening Republicans who were fearful of a government program as popular as Social Security or the G.I. Bill decades earlier. Hence, the Republican strategy to attack and discredit big government worked, persuading voters that larger government meant a swollen bureaucracy infamous for its inefficiency. Anti-government sentiment mounting since the 1970s was reaching a crescendo.

The Republicans rallied in the 1994 congressional elections and carried out their "revolution," ousting the Democratic majority and electing a record number of conservatives. Under the leadership of powerful Speaker of the House Newt Gingrich, the Republican "Contract with America" became a radical manifesto to "end government as we know it." The conservatives of the 1990s waged war on the entire Progressive tradition dating back to Theodore Roosevelt and the turn of the century. In their initial euphoria, they were prepared to go far beyond Ronald Reagan in dismantling the government, arguing that less is better in every case. The Contract called for policies for a government regulatory system congenial to business, cuts in welfare and environmental regulations, and tax policies that primarily benefited the wealthy. Critics charged that this strategy signaled a return to "trickle-down" economic policy from the 1920s.

Clinton responded. Recognizing that the old New Deal coalition was no longer viable, the president was determined to redefine government, as Bryan had a century earlier. Campaigning for reelection in 1996, he declared that "the era of big government is over." At the same time, he added, "I believe the role of government is to help people make the most of their own lives." Clinton proved to be very adaptable, borrowing issues from the conservative agenda, eliciting complaints from Republicans that the president wasn't playing fair. Indeed, half-way through his second term, Clinton's most significant achievements were GOP priorities—deficit reduction, free trade, and welfare reform—just as Eisenhower legitimized such Democratic policies as social spending, civil rights, and containment during the 1950s.

While Clinton's 1996 return to the White House over his Republican opponent Bob Dole was remarkably easy, the Republicans continued their control of both houses of Congress. Yet they misread the temper of the country and the meaning of their own victory. Americans may mistrust government in the abstract, however they also support the federal government's commitment to health care for the elderly, environmental protection, expanded educational opportunity, and fighting crime. Just as laissez-faire economics failed to address the problems arising from a transitioning economy and society during the Gilded Age, neither the percolation theory of Herbert Hoover nor Ronald Reagan's supply-side economics was able to define such problems out of existence. When Republican leaders threatened to shut down the government in 1997 because President Clinton refused to further cut his priorities of education and environmental protection, the tactic backfired. The President's popularity in the polls soared to 64 percent, a paralyzing blow to the Republican Revolution.

THE ROAD TO MT. RUSHMORE

These voters expressed their relative satisfaction with the status quo by reelecting incumbents in 1996, keeping government divided. Citizens seemed to prefer a program of "risk aversion." Voters in the center of the political spectrum who had lost traditional party loyalties and were distrustful of the political system—were not very happy with either of the parties' prescriptions. Neither big, intrusive, government nor a small, "hands off" government seemed acceptable to the "Anxious Middle."

In this confusing scene, the pragmatic Clinton skillfully sought the political center of gravity. Historian Michael Beschloss credits Clinton with recognizing that presidential power was shrinking to 19th-century levels, when "presidential success depended on cooperating with, oftentimes yielding to, a powerful Congress." Indeed, the president began to transform the remnants of the New Deal Democratic party into a diverse and durable coalition capable of dominating American politics and advancing the progressive tradition into the 21st century. Despite the criticism of the old liberal Democrats, Clinton rejected both the big centralized bureaucracies long identified with the Democratic party and the virulent anti-government sentiments of many Republicans. He called for a new kind of public activism that was fiscally restrained, designed to help provide people with tools to solve their own problems and strengthen the middle class. "It is good for the progressive party to be fiscally responsible, effective on crime, moving people from welfare to work," insisted the president.

As the election year 2000 approached, voters anticipated an argument with two distinct points of view concerning a century-long debate over the role of government in people's lives. One view envisioned a society free from government; this perspective stresses individual initiative and a marketplace unhampered by unnecessary government regulation. The other vision of America's promise was voiced in the long progressive tradition, which asserted that the government can be used to expand individual choice and protect the community from the excesses of unfettered capitalism. These diverse philosophical points of view offered voters two clear directions for the nation in the 21st century.

Midway through President Clinton's second term that debate was derailed. He was wounded by revelations of a sexual liaison with a young White House intern. A private affair was transformed into a full-fledged political scandal when Mr. Clinton—under oath—first denied and then waffled in response to embarrassing questions from the opposition. The intense partisanship of House Republicans who saw themselves as moral guardians of the "Reagan revolution" led to the president's impeachment, the first time since Andrew Johnson suffered the same fate in 1867.

And yet, Clinton's historic humiliation proved to be a hollow victory for the conservative wing of the Republican party. His critics claimed his immoral private life rendered his impeachment more heinous than the minor political infractions of Andrew Johnson. Clinton's supporters replied that while Andrew Johnson had never been elected to high office, voters sent "the Comeback Kid" to the White House twice by wide margins. Indeed, polls revealed Americans' continued support for the president's policies regardless of personal indiscretions. In the midst of the 2000 presidential election, even conservative Republican politicians realized—however reluctantly—that voters would favor the incumbent party in the White House if they were satisfied with the country's direction. Despite President Clinton's declaration in 1996 that "the era of big government is over," the scaled-down, moderate policies advanced by his Democratic successor during the 2000 campaign clearly called for a more active role for government than did the Republican platform in that year.

A review of 20th-century presidential politics suggests that reformers like Theodore Roosevelt, Woodrow Wilson, Franklin Roosevelt, and Lyndon Johnson recognized the pragmatic

PRESIDENTS OF THE UNITED STATES

Administration	President	Party	Achievement
1897–1901	William McKinley	Republican	Led America to world power in Spanish-American war. Assassinated in second-term.
1901–1909	Theodore Roosevelt	Republican	First progressive and conservationist president. Expanded U.S. influence abroad.
1909–1913	William H. Taft	Republican	Continued business regulation, but his conservatism divided his party.
1913–1921	Woodrow Wilson	Democrat	Completed Progressive reforms but lost battle for American world role in League of Nations.
1921–1923	Warren G. Harding	Republican	Restored conservative leadership. Died as scandals emerged.
1923–1929	Calvin Coolidge	Republican	Pro-business, he benefited from national prosperity he did not create.
1929–1933	Herbert Hoover	Republican	Depression he did not cause but couldn't cure ruined his presidency.
1933–1945	Franklin D. Roosevelt	Democrat	Restored national confidence, helped end the Depression and led the country to victory in World War II.
1945–1953	Harry S. Truman	Democrat	Used containment in the Cold War and tried to lead a "Fair Deal" at home.
1953–1961	Dwight D. Eisenhower	Republican	Promoted less government at home; opened dialogue with the Soviets.
1961–1963	John F. Kennedy	Democrat	Supported civil rights and "New Frontier" reforms.
1963–1969	Lyndon B. Johnson	Democrat	Won many civil rights and liberal reforms but doomed by failure in Vietnam.
1969–1974	Richard Nixon	Republican	Pursued détente with China and the U.S.S.R.; forced to resign in Watergate scandal.
1974–1977	Gerald R. Ford	Republican	Tried unsuccessfully to whip inflation and continue a conservative domestic course.
1977–1981	Jimmy Carter	Democrat	Moved to the center, but discredited by inflation and Iranian hostage crisis.
1981–1989	Ronald Reagan	Republican	Tried to reverse big government trend at home and strengthen defenses abroad.
1989–1993	George Bush	Republican	Presided over the decline of the "Reagan Revolution."
1993–	Bill Clinton	Democrat	Brought moderate reforms, dominating the political center.

necessity of an activist government; they believed that government was a positive force, and sought to better the system by correcting its faults and defects. Earlier movements like Socialism and more current ones like the "New Left" which disputed this assumption that democratic capitalism was worth saving were not able to secure the allegiance of the American majority. Even the radical reform impulse behind the Republican Contract with America proved to be transient. From his unique pulpit, President Clinton took the opportunity to prove that the government can work effectively for the people. Pundits wondered whether the president's reputation would survive the damaging publicity about his private behavior. Would his efforts in building bipartisan coalitions allow William Jefferson Clinton to aspire to that tiny pantheon of American leaders, including his namesake Thomas Jefferson? One observer noted the allegations involving the private sex lives of both presidents were proven in 1999 by DNA evidence. It is ironic that although enshrined in the granite of Mt. Rushmore, even a prominent icon like the Sage of Monticello is subject to the scrutiny of his countrymen. Do recent revelations about Mr. Jefferson's private life two hundred years ago make his niche on the presidential monument in South Dakota's Black Hills less deserved?

SUGGESTIONS FOR ADDITIONAL READING

Richard Hofstadter, *The Age of Reform,* (1955). The classic account of the people involved in American political reform from the 1880s to the New Deal.

Norman Pollack, *The Populist Response to Industrial America,* (1962). A description of the Populist crusade against the dehumanizing side of industrialization.

Lincoln Steffens, *The Shame of the Cities,* (1904). An attack against the bosses whose corrupt political machines dominated the big cities.

Michael Harrington, *The Other America,* (1962). A study of how the "other half" lives; influenced the War on Poverty.

Otis L. Graham, Jr., *Toward a Planned Society; From Roosevelt to Nixon,* (1976). A study of the development of Federal and presidential power and the trend toward national planning interrupted by Nixon.

Michael Katz, *The Undeserving Poor: From the War on Poverty to the War on Welfare,* (1989). A penetrating study of the growing inequality during the 1980s.

David Stockman, *A Triumph of Politics: How the Reagan Revolution Failed,* (1987). The memoirs of President Reagan's Director of the Office of Management and Budget from 1981 to 1985.

E. J. Dionne, *They Only Look Dead,* (1995). An analysis of contemporary politics suggesting a revival of Progressivism.

Jeffrey Toobin, *A Vast Conspiracy; The Real story of the Sex Scandal That Nearly Brought Down a President.* (1999)

Bruce Davidson/Magnum

CHAPTER SEVEN

CHANGING VALUES IN TWENTIETH-CENTURY AMERICA

1913
Introduction of Henry Ford's assembly-line system.

1924
The National Origins Act established an immigrant quota system to maintain the existing ethnic balance.

1926
Bruce Barton's *The Man Nobody Knows* is published, providing religious sanction to contemporary business practices.

1935
The New Deal passes the Wagner Act, giving labor the right to organize and engage in collective bargaining.

1945
Benjamin Spock publishes his *Baby and Child Care,* which revolutionized child rearing.

1948
The Kinsey Report is published, a survey of American sexual habits.

1964
The Free Speech Movement erupts at Berkeley, signaling the rise of student activism during the sixties.

1972
The micro-processor chip makes possible the introduction of personal computers and their eventual use in thousands of consumer products.

1980
Jerry Falwell's Moral Majority and allied social conservatives contribute to Reagan's landslide victory.

1990
Vice President Quayle's "Murphy Brown" speech, condemning out of wedlock births, reignites the "culture war" over family values.

1995
Oklahoma City bombing of the federal building leads to national revulsion against extremism.

CHANGE: AMERICA'S HALLMARK

Never before had Americans faced a more bewildering pace of change than during the twentieth century. Although change had been a constant theme in the nation's past, the period following 1900 provided new tests of their capacity for adjustment. Never had indications of social instability seemed more threatening. The frontier had just been officially declared closed—and with it the end of the "safety valve" as a panacea for the untrammeled social problems arising during the nineteenth century. The plight of the farmer deepened as America made its transition from a rural to an urban society. The rise of the factory and the city had created a new urban labor class, complicated by the arrival of millions of immigrants seeking the employment opportunities of the new industrialism. The way industrialization and urbanization changed family life caused many of Americans' traditional values to be questioned. Finally, these economic and social forces also raised questions about the proper relationship between the government and the economy.

There was no consensus as to how these changes should be regarded. Surveying the social impact of 35 years of unrestrained industrialism shortly after the turn of the century, the historian Henry Adams complained: "The individual crawled as best he could . . . and found many values of life upset." Nine decades later, Adams's pessimism concerning change was countered by Bill Clinton who captured the Oval Office with his buoyant promise of change. It is clear that although many values and life styles changed rapidly during the 20th century, the nation's free enterprise system and republican form of government remained largely intact. This chapter seeks to examine how these developments challenged the basic assumptions and values of the American people, and how they responded to them.

BOOM AND BUST 1900–1929

Business and Labor

The rampant industrialization and urbanization of America since the Civil War had created great problems for the working class who provided the muscle power for the new industrial dynamo. During the Progressive era, efforts were made to establish the necessary balance between the prerogatives of the capitalist employers and the rights of the workers. The American people joined a crusade to check irresponsible power and protect the "common man." This crusading mood expanded to embrace the rest of the world, with the rise of the Great War in Europe after 1914. Both the reform movement at home and our jaunt into world affairs reinforced a sense of patriotism and unity among the people. This unity of purpose disappeared after 1919. According to one political pundit:

> *The people are tired, tired of noise, tired of politics, tired of inconvenience, tired of greatness, and longing for a place where the world is quiet and where all trouble seems dead leaves. . . .*

Americans' zeal for social justice and their concern for the common foe in the war were replaced by the pursuit of the "good life." Disillusionment with both the nation's recent liberal reforms and role in the Great War signaled a return to disengagement.

Rejection of these liberal political and social values marked a revival of the primacy of business. Beginning with the election of President Warren Harding in 1920, government more frankly represented the interests of big business. Whereas "progress" during the Progressive era had implied "social justice," now it was equated with "development," "growth," and "efficiency." Business values epitomized the age, reflected in *The Man Nobody Knows,* written by Bruce Barton, an advertising man who suggested that Jesus, rather than a carpenter in the building trades, was actually a first-rate businessman who "picked up twelve men from the bottom ranks of business and forged them into an organization that conquered the world." This reverence toward big business was echoed by President Coolidge who intoned: "The man who builds a factory builds a temple, and the man who works there worships there."

Actually, the apparent prosperity during the Coolidge presidency seemed to justify the neoconservatism of the era. The growth of American industry and the resultant prosperity reflected the increased mechanization and rationalization of corporate enterprise. The time and motion studies of Frederick W. Taylor and the assembly line first devised by Henry Ford earlier in the century were now implemented throughout American industry. As a result of these new production methods, the national income rose from $63.1 billion in 1922 to $87.8 billion in 1929. During the decade emphasis shifted from capital goods (coal, oil, timber, steel) to consumer goods, such as automobiles, radios, electric washing machines, and refrigerators. Almost half of all American families owned their own homes. Never before had so many enjoyed so much. The traditional American virtue of thrift was now rapidly being replaced by a spending spree. In this way the new consumer economy was changing basic social values.

Consumer satisfaction, however, did not extend to the laboring class that produced the goods. Gains made by labor during the Progressive period were nullified by the antilabor mood of the 1920s. The image of organized labor was tarnished by the political radicalism brewing in Europe since the turn of the century, culminating with the Bolshevik Revolution in Russia in 1917. Moreover, management attitudes toward labor unions were clearly unsympathetic. Henry Ford voiced his bias on the subject, vowing that "I'll never recognize any union."

He was not alone in that opinion. Enlightened employers tried to circumvent unions by providing benefits to the workers themselves. In 1914, for example, Ford established the five-dollar work day, an increase of about two dollars over prevailing wages. This corporate effort to treat the problems of the industrial labor class originated in the Gilded Age paternalism of Andrew Carnegie, who professed a concern for the well-being of his workers. In addition, the new business-school-trained managerial class recognized that to avoid costly strikes and to maintain consumer buying power, labor must be supported. Hence, corporate business began to embrace "welfare capitalism" during the 1920s, including accident, illness, and death benefits, pension plans, and even some profit-sharing and relief payments to laid-off employees. Labor unions responded with skepticism to this managerial solicitude, as workers' benefits lagged far behind corporate profits.

Labor had reason to be skeptical of management's motives. No longer did business interests pay lip service to the laissez-faire principles implicit in the Social Darwinism of the Gilded Age.

Now the government acted boldly as an advance agent for business. Not only were subsidies provided to the railroads, shipping and automobile interests, and the airlines, but the government also fostered the monopolization of American industry. During the 1920s the Justice Department stopped trust-busting, and in 1925 the Supreme Court encouraged competing firms to form "trade associations," which would share market data, standardize their technology, and reduce competition. In short, corporate consolidation and power ran unchecked. Although these business combinations spurred economic growth by eliminating waste and increasing efficiency in production, their larger profits were not reflected in correspondingly higher labor wages. The plight of these industrial wage-earners is explained partially by the competition provided by the immigrants.

Removing the Welcome Mat

By the turn of the century two-thirds of the nation's factory workers were immigrants (mostly European), welcomed by the efficiency-minded entrepreneurs who were hostile to the labor unions. There was a growing momentum among organized labor for policies favoring immigration restriction. As early as 1902 the AFL membership voted for a literacy test for incoming foreigners. Samuel Gompers expressed the prevailing view that "cheap labor, immigrant labor, takes our jobs and cuts our wages." In 1907 the Dillingham Commission was appointed by Congress to investigate the impact of immigration on American society. The result was a 47-volume report that confirmed all of the worst fears of the nativists, "proving" that foreigners were not compatible with American values. This report suggested that the foreigners brought with them ignorance and disease, provided competition on the labor market, and fomented political corruption and anarchy. The fear of social contamination was reinforced by *The Passing of the Great Race,* a book published in 1916, arguing that America's "Aryan civilization" was being threatened by inferior immigrants from Europe. After many presidential vetoes this vitriolic campaign resulted in the congressional enactment of the literacy test in 1917.

This test, however, did little to stem the influx of "inferior racial stock." Fueled by labor strikes and the Red Scare in 1919–1920 following the Great War, nativist fears were heightened. This anti-foreign, anti-Red sentiment was reflected in the Sacco-Vanzetti affair. In 1921 two poor Italian immigrants were convicted of murder during a postal robbery by a judge and jury who were prejudiced to some extent by the defendants' origins and political beliefs. The issue became a global cause celebre, and was regarded by many liberal critics as a "legal lynching." An objective review of the evidence a half-century later suggests that Sacco and Vanzetti were actually convicted (and subsequently electrocuted in 1927) for their philosophical beliefs, rather than for a murder which they probably did not commit.

By the time of the highly publicized Sacco-Vanzetti trial, the nativist bandwagon had gathered full steam. Congress passed a quota law limiting the annual number of newcomers entering the country from each nation to three percent of the persons from that nation living in the U.S. in 1910. When this law failed to still the nativist clamor, in 1924 Congress enacted the National Origins Act, whereby the quota was lowered to two percent of persons from any foreign

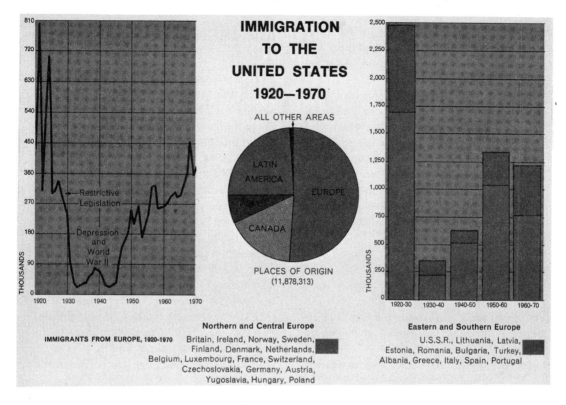

IMMIGRATION TO THE UNITED STATES 1920–1970

ALL OTHER AREAS

LATIN AMERICA

EUROPE

CANADA

PLACES OF ORIGIN
(11,878,313)

Restrictive Legislation

Depression and World War II

THOUSANDS

IMMIGRANTS FROM EUROPE, 1920-1970

Northern and Central Europe
Britain, Ireland, Norway, Sweden,
Finland, Denmark, Netherlands,
Belgium, Luxembourg, France, Switzerland,
Czechoslovakia, Germany, Austria,
Yugoslavia, Hungary, Poland

Eastern and Southern Europe
U.S.S.R., Lithuania, Latvia,
Estonia, Romania, Bulgaria, Turkey,
Albania, Greece, Italy, Spain, Portugal

This graph clearly shows the decline in immigration after the restrictive acts of the 1920s. The new policy called into question that promise of the Statue of Liberty to accept the world's "tired, poor and huddled masses."

country already present in 1890. By changing the base year from 1910 to 1890, the new immigrants from southern and eastern Europe were penalized most heavily. This quota system marked a dramatic change in America's immigration policy. It acknowledged that the nation's labor needs could now be satisfied with native workers, and that the new teeming urban population contained more than enough ethnic diversity. To Europe's "huddled masses" the out-stretched arms of the Statue of Liberty in New York Harbor had been lowered.

The City, the Car, and Consumerism

The United States passed through its urban revolution in the half-century following the Civil War. The devastating results of haphazard city growth and political bossism during the nineteenth-century Gilded Age were accompanied by the influx of both immigrants and rural folk seeking new economic opportunity. The social and political results of this rapid change were addressed during the Progressive era, as reformers cleaned up city government, replacing the corrupt political machines with a city-manager system. Galveston, Texas pioneered in the use of full-time trained professionals in city government in 1901, providing a model for other municipalities intent on eliminating partisan politics in city administration. By 1920, 51 percent of Americans

Ford revolutionized industry practice with assembly line mass production of his automobiles and high wages for his workers. (Courtesy of Brown Brothers.)

lived in urban areas, and in the following decade city planners had harnessed the flow of automobile traffic and water, designed parks and parkways, constructed playgrounds and bridges, and laid out streets and housing projects.

The rising city was accompanied by the birth of the horseless carriage. During the first decade of the twentieth century the car had been only a novelty, enjoyed by the rich or adventurous in racing competition (usually dominated by the Europeans) and in crosscountry endurance races. The basic hurdles had been the high cost of automobile manufacture and an inadequate road system. Both of these drawbacks were resolved by the 1920s. Luxury then became a necessity. Through the modern techniques of mass production, Ford lowered the cost of his Model T from $950 in 1909 to $280 in 1924. Car sales skyrocketed, so that in 1929 five million vehicles were sold, five times as many as in 1916. Moreover, auto traffic required a different road surface from the days of the horse and buggy. Responding to this muddy predicament, Congress enacted the Federal Highway Act in 1916; by 1921 387,000 miles of asphalt or concrete ribbon had been laid, a figure that almost doubled by 1929.

The impact of the automobile age was far-reaching. A wide array of new industries arose to serve a nation on wheels: garages and filling stations, the rubber, paint, and glass industries, trucking, car insurance, and tourism, to name a few. At the same time, this new mode of transportation helped sound the death knell for the electric streetcar in all but the largest cities,

HENRY FORD

Henry Ford was born in 1863 and raised on a farm in Greenfield township, Michigan. His distaste for farm life was accompanied by an intuitive understanding of machinery. As a teenager he migrated to Detroit to apprentice himself to a machine shop to learn about steam power and self-propelled gasoline engines. In 1897 he constructed a one-cylinder gasoline motor, and completed his first car, a light carriage powered by a two-cylinder engine, in 1896. The Ford Motor Company was begun in 1903, however disagreement with his backers led to his buying out their interests and becoming the major stockholder and president in 1906. Rejecting his partners' desire for a luxury automobile, Ford preferred to build a simple, inexpensive model. He was convinced that the future of the industry belonged to the quantity-produced small car. His impact on the auto industry resulted from his insistence that the automobile be affordable to the masses. In 1908 the Model T was born. The "Tin Lizzie" was a simple box on wheels powered by a light, durable, easily repaired engine. Through mass production, Ford was able to lower the cost of production. In his first year he sold 11,000 models at a price of about 800 dollars, and by 1914 he was producing 500,000 annually. Ten years later the Ford plant was turning out 9000 cars daily, or one every ten seconds, at a reduced price of $280. It is ironic that the country boy from an earlier, simpler America became the purveyor of such revolutionary change in the twentieth century. His affinity for the traditional virtues of agrarian America—self-reliance, hard work and thrift—helped to dictate his great success. Moreover, his modesty, idealism and kindness contributed to the legend of Henry Ford. By the twenties he became a folk hero, to be worshipped for his homespun simplicity and intense individualism. He almost won a senate seat in 1918, and a poll in 1923 indicated that he was the people's choice for president in 1924.

Such public adulation reinforced Ford's strongly judgmental qualities. He revealed a vain, harsh, and vindictive attitude toward ideals that clashed with his own narrow, provincial background. Although he found stiff competition from General Motors and Chrysler during the twenties, he refused to change his production of the Tin Lizzie until 1928, when the Model A rolled off the assembly-line, offered in four colors and 17 body styles. Despite the popularity of the Model A, never again would Ford capture more than twenty percent of the auto market. Moreover, the generosity of his offer of a five-dollar day in 1914 was tempered by an autocratic hold over his workers. He vowed that he would never deal with labor unions, and indeed, employed spies and bullies to enforce plant discipline. If a worker drove any car other than a Ford, he was tarred. His naive opposition to militarism and war led to his denunciation of World War I. In 1915 he chartered an ocean liner to carry peace delegates abroad to aid in negotiating an end to the European war. This naive gesture incurred the derision of the American press and the general public, which were largely pro-Allied. His aversion to the war also prompted his denunciation of "international bankers" and other Jews on Wall Street who, he believed, were responsible for drawing the nation into the conflict. When his anti-Semitic views headlined his own newspaper, *The Dearborn Independent,* personal lawsuits ensued, leading to public apologies and out-of-court settlements amounting to almost five million dollars.

Although Ford was a strong supporter of the isolationist movement during the thirties, once the United States entered the war in 1941, the Ford plant became heavily involved in national defense production. Two years after the war, Ford died of a massive cerebral hemorrhage. Despite his personal shortcomings attributed to his narrow provincialism, Ford was a giant in his time. During his lifetime he gave away 37 million dollars to various philanthropic causes. More importantly, he earned a niche in history for introducing the principle of moving mass production. His pioneering effort was spread around the world as a basic tenet for the organization of industrial activity, with far-reaching effects upon economic and social life.

and ended rural isolation. Country schools and churches were gradually phased out, as the consolidation of these institutions was made possible by the transportation revolution. Family life was inalterably changed as well, as youngsters were afforded a mobility and freedom their parents' generation had never known. Even the older folks enjoyed broader horizons as their new leisure time was spent on the Sunday afternoon drive or on summer vacations to distant places. Traffic jams and automobile accidents were additional features of the urban scene, and the noxious fumes and billboards posed new kinds of pollution for Americans, replacing the fly-breeding manure of an older, slower-paced society. The inner city began its long process of deterioration, leading to the later development of suburbia. These disadvantages were largely ignored by Americans, however, as they worshipped their cars as "part toy, part tool, and part symbol of American freedom, prosperity, and individualism."

Mass production of the automobile signaled the rise of mass consumption. In his *Theory of the Leisure Class* (1899), the social critic Thorstein Veblen had savagely attacked the industrial entrepreneurs for their "predatory wealth" and "conspicuous consumption." Within just a few years, however, the average American enjoyed a standard of living which, in some ways, approximated the conveniences enjoyed by the Gilded Age capitalists. Massive buying by the masses democratized the consumer market, symbolized by the rise of the chain store. By purchasing goods in volume, firms like A & P, J. C. Penney, Standard Oil, and Safeway were able to pass savings on to the consumer. Between 1910 and 1920 there was a noticeable rise in the discretionary income of the average family; this meant that Americans were beginning to be able to afford entertainment, silk stockings, visits to the beauty parlor, and enjoy such "durables" as their cars, radios, and other electrical appliances. This economic development was so far-reaching that it has been called a "consumer-durables revolution."

This economic change also marked a shift in consumer values. The older values of thrift and self-denial, inherited from seventeenth-century Puritanism and eighteenth-century Benjamin Franklin, were now replaced by new ones. After the Great War buying on credit became common, reinforced by new techniques of advertising and salesmanship to stimulate consumer demand. Installment-plan buying broadened the consumer market dramatically. "A dollar down, and a dollar forever" became the sales pitch of many merchants during the 1920s. "Buy today, pay tomorrow" seductively encouraged people to join the ranks of the best fed, best clothed, and best equipped society in history.

FREUD AND THE FLAPPER

The general restlessness accompanying these economic and social forces in twentieth-century America was also reflected in changing attitudes toward sex. The Victorian image of the woman, moral, dutiful, and domestic, underwent an alteration during the post-war years. Like the rest of society, women were eager to liberate themselves from the discredited idealism of the war years and pursue new opportunities on the job market which released them from their apron strings. She reappeared as the "flapper" with her bobbed hair, make-up, and cigarettes, ready for a party without chaperone. It was reported that a woman's dress in 1913 required 19-1/2 yards of fabric, whereas the short-skirted flapper needed a scant seven yards.

Popular culture during the 1920s focused on the erotic. Youth seized upon the theories of the celebrated Sigmund Freud, who caused a sensation during his first American lecture tour in 1909. His new approach in psychology stressed the emotional dangers of sexual repression, which was used to justify the freedom of youth from outmoded social mores. Freudian psychology, together with the handiwork of Ford, did much to liberate youth in its sex life, as backseat "necking" became a new ritual in the fast-paced society. "Flaming youth" in this age of jazz also indulged in the pleasures of black music, with its "passionate crooning and wailing of the saxophone." Youngsters now supplemented their sex education by reading in *True Confession* magazine such articles as "What I Told My Daughter the Night before Her Marriage." Moreover what was happening on the dance floor shocked many. Wrote one critic:

> *The music is sensuous, the embracing of partners—the female only half-dressed—is absolutely indecent; and the motions—they are such as may not be described, with any respect for propriety in a family newspaper.*

In truth, however, such images did not tell the whole story. Much of this rebellion was only a fad. One study indicated that during the post-war years only 25 percent of college coeds had engaged in premarital sex. As a result, the sexual revolution was in fact not more than a gradual and partial change, scarcely deserving the label "revolution." Indeed, although women gained the right to vote by 1920, anti-feminism remained strong.

Psychology was not a staunch friend of women. Freud himself had ambivalent attitudes toward the "fairer sex." Although he asserted that sex was natural for men and women, he also theorized that because of their gender, women were biologically inferior, fit only for motherhood and domesticity. The famed psychoanalyst's statement "anatomy is destiny" revealed the paradox in his antifeminist thought. In fact, despite the faddish flapper of the "roaring twenties," the middle class woman's traditional social role was more imperative than ever before, simply because she had more to do at home. Because of the gradual disappearance of domestic servants, the Department of Agriculture reported in 1929 that the average housewife put in 51 hours weekly at routine chores like cleaning and cooking. Some liberation!

THE REVOLT OF THE OLD ORDER

The cumulative effect of the rapid pace of change during the first two decades of the twentieth century was to confuse many Americans who concluded that the nation was going through a moral and social breakdown. Instead of devoting the Sabbath to the proper worship of God, for example, increasing numbers of Americans were enjoying their newly-discovered leisure time. Fun seemed to be replacing honest work. Scantily-clad women smoked, drank, and partied like their male counterparts. Blacks who had always known "their place" in earlier times, had migrated north to work in the expanded wartime industries, in the process threatening traditional attitudes about race. As a result, rural and small-town America—with its Protestant and political conservatism—rose up in revolt against these new forces. If "change" is a hallmark of the American character, the reverse side of that same coin has been the need to affirm the virtues of the nation's heritage.

The prototype flapper, symbol of the "flamiing youth" of the Twenties. (Courtesy of Culver Pictures, Inc.)

With the disillusionment following the Great War in 1919, there was an unmistakable yearning to renounce this present state of affairs, and revive the "strengths" of the past.

One effort to restore America's strength was the crusade to outlaw all beverages with more than 0.5 percent alcohol. This "noble experiment" stemmed from Progressive idealism prior to the Great War; social workers had promised that insane asylums and jails would be emptied, and husbands would be tending the home fires rather than frequenting saloons. The campaign for prohibition was furthered by the need for grain to aid the war effort after 1917. The Volstead Act was also seen as a means of maintaining control over the immigrants and other "wets" in the industrial cities of the North and the blacks in the South. In short, the hope was that prohibiting the consumption of alcohol would someday safeguard the morals of the people, including America's "flaming youth." This naive legislation became the Eighteenth Amendment in 1918. And it failed miserably. Americans' drinking traditions were simply too strong, and their government's tradition of weak centralized government prevented effective enforcement of the law. Instead, Americans got poisoned bootleg whiskey and organized crime, symbolized by Al Capone and the mobs during the roaring twenties. Moreover, it is ironic that Prohibition may have increased consumption, because it was taboo. Paradoxically, by the end of the 1920s the cocktail party had replaced the tea party in urban middle-class life, as tipplers slaked their thirst with

Partygoers celebrate the end of the "noble experiment" of Prohibition in 1933. (Courtesy of the Brown Brothers.)

"home-brew" or bathtub gin of unpredictable quality. Finally, the depression following the Stock Market Crash of 1929 created a dire need for new tax revenues, and this "noble experiment" was ended in 1933.

The efforts of Americans to rectify the ills of modern America were also seen in the revival of the post-Civil War Ku Klux Klan in 1915. The superpatriotism and intolerance generated by the War were easily adapted to the defense of white, Protestant America from the "invasion" by Catholics, Jews, "alien" immigrants, wartime dissenters, and blacks. "One hundred percent Americanism" became the slogan of these white supremacists. During the 1920s the "invisible empire" of the KKK became a powerful political force, especially in rural, small-town America. Campaigning behind white sheets and masks, perhaps as many as three million of these WASP (White, Anglo-Saxon, Protestant) crusaders spread fear and violence to those whose ethnic, religious, or racial origins were different from their own. By the mid-twenties they virtually controlled such diverse municipal and state governments as those in Denver and Dallas, Indiana and Oregon. Rejecting the heterogeneity of the modern melting pot, Klansmen wished to uphold "American decency" and other traditional values. Due to internal scandal and the common sense of most Americans, this vulgar caricature of American prejudice went into eclipse by 1926, and was practically dead by 1930. But the embers of this social movement remained, to be ignited in later years in response to new "threats" to traditional America.

The reaction of the rural, smalltown Bible Belt to the gains made by the liberal Protestant and secular values of the new urban society was also symbolized by the "monkey trial." Fear that the "old ways" were declining prompted religious fundamentalists to pass laws banning the teaching of "any theory that denies . . . Divine Creation" or, in other words, the teaching of evolution. It was contended that those who taught the latest scientific principles in the universities and high schools were contributing to the moral breakdown of youth in the Jazz Age. A popular young high school football coach and part-time biology teacher in Dayton, Tennessee named John Thomas Scopes agreed to serve as the defendant in a landmark test case in 1925. Sponsored by the American Civil Liberties Union (ACLU), the case challenged the constitutionality of the new anti-evolution law passed by the Tennessee legislature. The fundamentalists were now ready to do battle. It was unacceptable to them that the Darwinian hypothesis taught in the public schools implied that humans were the direct descendants of apes. William Jennings Bryan, three-time presidential candidate and ardent expert on the Bible, agreed to defend the law. Famed criminal attorney Clarence Darrow served as counsel for young Scopes. When the judge—a Methodist lay preacher—refused to allow testimony concerning the scientific validity of Darwin's theory the trial degenerated into a verbal duel between the fundamentalist Bryan and the agnostic Darrow. Although the attorney brutally attacked the simplistic reasoning behind Bryan's literal interpretation of the Scriptures, it did not take long to find Scopes guilty of violating the law. The significance of this first nationally-broadcast trial on radio was primarily to expose the intellectual narrowness and bigotry of the fundamentalists.

The need of many conservative Americans to vindicate their traditional values against the flux and change of modern society was seen not only in the monkey trial, but also in the "flight of the eagle." The solo flight of Charles A. Lindbergh across the Atlantic from New York to Paris in 1927 was welcomed by those fed up with the skepticism and loss of faith in this "New Era." "Lucky Lindy's" feat touched off a wave of hero worship unequaled since George Washington. The mood was a nostalgic one; one admirer commented that "Captain Lindbergh personifies the daring of youth. Daniel Boone, Davey Crockett and men of that type played a lone hand and made America. Lindbergh is their lineal descendant." Another common metaphor was to say that he had opened a new "frontier." To speak of the air as a frontier was to invoke an interpretation of American history deeply embedded in the nation's experience. Hence, by making Lindbergh a "pioneer," he became part of a long and vital tradition of individualism. By applauding the "lone Eagle" in this manner, the American public was expressing its belief that the source of America's strength lay in the past. Somehow America must look backward in time to regain its lost virtues.

There was, however, another interpretation of the flight of "The Spirit of St. Louis." Indeed, it was strange that the long-distance flight of an airplane should elicit an avalanche of praise for the solitary, unaided man. There was, after all, the irrefutable fact that the flight was a victory for the machine. Lindbergh was quick to acknowledge the importance of technology in his achievement; in Paris he told newsmen, "You fellows have not said enough about that wonderful motor." Even President Coolidge recognized this fact: "I am told that more than one hundred separate companies furnished materials, parts or services in its construction." In short, the flight was not the heroic lone success of a single daring individual; instead, it was the climax of the cooperative effort of technology. There were, therefore, two interpretations of Lindbergh's flight. The one saw America on the decline, and hence was backward-looking. The other said that America's greatness is still unfolding, and by utilizing the tools of a modern industrial society, progress would continue to be the nation's hallmark.

CRASH AND DEPRESSION

Americans had the luxury of focusing on such social phenomena because, for the growing middle class at least, the 1920s were a prosperous decade. Farmers in the nation's shrinking rural communities and seasonal unskilled manufacturing workers made virtually no gains, but they were either marginalized or promised that their benefits would eventually "trickle down." Optimism ruled.

The stock market crash of October 1929 overthrew optimism, and the Great Depression that followed thrust the nation into a social and economic chasm. By 1932, the Depression was having a devastating effect on millions of workers. The labor movement was almost extinct; AFL membership had dwindled from 4.1 million laborers in 1920 to 2.2 million, about six percent of the work force. Organizers of industrial unions were murdered, and the National Guard was called upon repeatedly to quell strikes by unruly workers. Many employers hired private armies armed with machine pistols, gas guns, and clubs to maintain "order" Although it was difficult to explain the social results of the crisis in terms of the irresponsibility of the working class, yet social workers during the 1930s reported that the jobless were suffering from feelings of guilt. Lamented one worker: "I haven't had a steady job in more than two years. Sometimes I feel like a murderer. What's wrong with me, that I can't protect my children?" For millions of Americans the depression experience was a searing ordeal. Massive unemployment was accompanied by human suffering on a large scale. People in the Land of Plenty actually starved, while farmers plowed under their crops and poured milk on the streets because of inadequate prices. The sense of social cohesion and respect for the institutions of authority—what one writer has labeled "the glue that holds societies together"—was rapidly disintegrating.

The election of Franklin Roosevelt in 1932 began to restore a sense of hope. Roosevelt promised to restore the nation's prosperity and to remember the needs of "the forgotten man" on the breadlines. He seemed to know what he was doing, to be in control of the situation. The Agricultural Adjustment Act reached out to farmers, the Taylor Grazing Act to ranchers, and the National Industrial Recovery Act [NIRA] to industrial workers. They were guaranteed the right to organize and bargain collectively with management. Later the Wagner Act, hailed as the Magna Carta of the modern labor movement, made permanent the gains tentatively made under the NIRA.

LEGACY OF THE GREAT DEPRESSION

Never did FDR enjoy the unqualified support of his fellow Americans. There were many— including those representing the traditional business interests—who felt great rancor toward "that man" who seemed guilty of sending the nation down the path of "creeping socialism." New Deal enemies charged that it had become a "dictatorship of do-gooders" intent on creating a "handout state" of "unlimited spending" through the various alphabet agencies composing the reform programs. These die-hard critics persisted in the belief that if all the "bureaucratic meddling" were replaced by the traditional economic principles of "laissez-faire," normalcy would return.

It is ironic that the patrician reformer was regarded as an agent for radical change. Like his predecessor Hoover, FDR believed throughout most of the 1930s that the budget must be balanced. Indeed, his reluctance to embrace the idea that a government program of deficit spending would provide a panacea to economic ills reflected the sentiments of the electorate. As late as 1939 a public opinion poll revealed that a majority of the people preferred reduced government expenditures in order to balance the budget. However, a dramatic nose-dive in the economy in August 1937 caused critics to begin speaking of "Roosevelt's depression." Faced with conflicting advice, FDR finally chose to implement the deficit-spending theories of the English economist, John Maynard Keynes. In short, since private investments in the economy were not forthcoming, they would be substituted for by government expenditures. In this way, employment would rise, stimulating consumer buying power.

What were the results of Keynesian "pump-priming" economics? The financial index showed steady improvement in 1939–1940. Moreover, war clouds on the European horizon stimulated a substantial increase in Allied military spending, benefiting American industry. Even more dramatically, America's wartime experience after the bombing of Pearl Harbor proved that government spending sparked economic growth. Upon American entry into the war, unemployment declined rapidly, and by 1945 the civilian work force had increased by 7 million, including millions of women.

Miners and factory workers flocked to the banner of the Democratic Party in 1936, providing a mainstay for the Roosevelt coalition. The gains of labor were reflected in part by the growth in union membership; the 3.6 million members in 1934 grew to 4.7 million in 1936, and 8.4 million in 1941. Never again could politicians ignore the labor vote, as a result of a power shift in the electorate's political preferences more dramatic than anytime since the Civil War. In addition, nonunion labor benefited from FDR's legislative program. Enactment of the Fair Labor Standards Act in 1938 put a "ceiling over hours and a floor under wages." Weekly hours were reduced to forty, benefiting 13 million workers, and the minimum wage was increased to forty cents per hour, affecting 750,000 workers. Never again would American workers endure the extreme abuse at the hands of capitalist management, as the norm had been in the six decades of untrammeled industrial capitalism prior to 1933.

But these benefits would be realized only gradually over the decade. Meanwhile, the impact of the Depression continued. In coal-mining areas hard hit by unemployment, for example, it was reported that ninety percent of the schoolchildren were suffering from malnutrition, leading to "drowsiness, lethargy, sleepiness, and mental retardation." In addition, with income falling, family life was altered. There were fewer births, and fewer divorces, and families were forced to spend more time together at home, instead of spending money on entertainment elsewhere. Nor did youth emerge unscathed by the depression ordeal. Adolescence during the 1930s tended to be a sobering experience. Children were imbued with a built-in need to achieve, and college students were intent on acquiring marketable skills. Getting a job was a top priority for that generation of Americans.

The drive for security thereby emerged as an important part of the Depression generation's values. Perhaps the most enduring aspect of the New Deal was the welfare state, guaranteeing at least a minimum standard of living for all of the people. It is true that the rejection of laissez-faire economics had a long history, tracing back at least as far as the Populist platform of 1892. But now the nation at large accepted the government as a permanent influence in the economy. Much of what came to be regarded as the legitimate function of government began with New Deal legislation. Laws creating controls on the stock market, subsidies for the farmers and insurance against old age and unemployment recognized the changes that had occurred in America after seventy-five years of industrial transformation. Indeed, in 1952 the first Republican president since Herbert Hoover announced:

Never again shall we allow a depression in the United States. As soon as we foresee the signs of any recession and depression, the full power of private industry, municipal, state, and federal government will be mobilized to see that that does not happen.

Eisenhower's pronouncement suggested that a revolution had occurred within twenty years. And yet, the question arises as to how revolutionary the New Deal was in fact. Against the backdrop of international politics during the 1930s, Roosevelt's actions were not very radical. With the global depression following the crash of the stock market, democracy did not appear to be the wave of the future. Instead, totalitarian governments were on the rise; fascism in Spain and Italy, nazism in Germany, the rise of militarist Japan, and of course, communism in the Soviet Union. Nor were many willing to predict the outcome of the tottering democracies still standing in western Europe after the mid-thirties. The situation at home and abroad after 1933 was so precarious that businessmen themselves fully expected FDR to take radical steps in altering the American economic system, including the nationalization of the banking system. Others proposed giving the president dictatorial powers, "knowing" that Congress itself was too impotent to save the capitalist system. However, Roosevelt's New Deal succeeded in salvaging in large part the system of private enterprise. A man no less than Raymond Moley—a former advisor who became FDR's severest critic—admitted that by closing the banks in 1933 with the Emergency Banking Relief Act, "capitalism was saved in eight days."

AWAKENING PAUL BUNYAN

Although the United States was never totally mobilized for war, World War II produced far greater government intervention in the nation's economic and social affairs than during World War I or the depression. As a result, the years 1941–1945 altered radically the country's self-image, restoring the self-confidence Americans had felt before the Crash. The years between Pearl Harbor and Hiroshima were a time of ferment leading to new values for the American people economically, socially, and in their technological outlook.

The most obvious change occurred on the economic front. The massive deficit-spending brought on by the demands of war resulted in a transfusion of cash into what had been an austere

Industrial expansion and the war opened up new opportunities for
employment to women. (Courtesy of Library of Congress.)

economy. By 1943 corporate profits were greater than in 1929. The government in Washington
was now pumping 300 million dollars daily into American wallets and purses. Not only did the
eight million unemployed in 1940 disappear, but the work force went from 45 million to 66
million in 1945, over five million of whom were women. The nucleus of a mass market was
thereby created, waiting to be unleashed at war's end.

Consumer spending during the war was seriously curtailed due to scarcities, patriotic
savings for the war effort, and anti-inflation controls imposed during wartime. With buying sprees
thus discouraged, the phenomenon of working-class affluence appeared. Bankrolls were thicken-
ing among blue-collar laborers; the Treasury Department estimated in 1943 that citizens' savings
totaled 70 billion dollars—what one observer labeled "liquid dynamite."

The social implications of these economic forces cannot be exaggerated. Traditional dis-
tinctions of social class and sex no longer commanded the deference Americans were accustomed
to in earlier times. Because of manpower needs in the war, for example, employment of women
tended to boost family income considerably, and stimulate a more egalitarian society. In 1940 the
percentage of women in the labor force was almost exactly what it had been in 1910. However,
by 1945 female labor was sought by employers who earlier would have laughed at their job
applications. For the first time in history, American women experienced occupational mobility,
taking employment with the railroads, shipbuilding, aircraft construction, and on the white-collar
job market as well. As a result, World War II provided a turning point for female Americans,

creating greater personal freedom, and laying the groundwork for the feminist movement which would blossom twenty-five years later.

As millions of women joined the work force, the war effort touched childrens' lives too. Employers seldom provided child-care for working mothers. Thousands of youngsters spent the nocturnal hours sitting in movie houses or loitering on the streets until their parents returned from their late work shifts. Housing was in especially short supply, leading to cramped living conditions; in some cases, kids had to wait until their parents left home to work the night shift before they could get into bed. Without proper supervision, juvenile delinquency soared. In San Diego, home of a major naval base and the aircraft industry, the arrest rate for young boys increased 55 percent in one year. The arrest rate for girls went up 355 percent. The stage was being set for momentous changes in family life in the post-war years.

The wartime use of technology also sowed seeds for great change in post-war America. The talents of people from many quarters of society—scientists, the military, economists, corporate executives, and public officials—had been pooled for a cooperative war effort. Their work contributed not only to allied victory in 1945, but also profoundly changed post-war America. Such innovative developments as radar, prefabricated housing, atomic power, frozen foods, diesel power, and the catalytic cracking of crude oil were crucial to military success and contributed to an abundant life in years of peace. Wrote one historian:

> *Certainly there took place during the war a cross-fertilization of thinking that was stimulating to all concerned. All in all, during the war American technology underwent a hothouse growth.*

In short, social forces had been brewing for virtually a half-century, stimulated by World War I, the depression, and World War II. At war's end, the cumulative momentum of these forces would now emerge in the light of a new day, to refashion an American society that few could have anticipated. The sleeping giant had awakened.

BRAVE NEW WORLD IS HERE 1945–1980s

When Johnny Came Marching Home

When the ticker-tape parades welcomed the boys home in 1945, the American people breathed a huge sigh of relief. No longer was it necessary to continue the personal sacrifices demanded by the war effort. Their idealism and discipline had brought victory against the Axis powers. Now that the war was over, the universal hope was for a return to such old values as tranquillity and security, revitalizing such basic institutions as the home and the family. For four long years, twelve million G.I.s had yearned for the day when they could resume normal lives. Domesticity seemed just as appealing to the women who had supported the war effort at home, living in crowded quarters (often with in-laws) and working in the war industries. They too looked forward to starting families and establishing their own household routines. What is more, because of their enforced savings through the war years, for the first time in history ordinary Americans possessed enough money to be able to afford their dreams.

The brave new world dangling before them promised the world's highest living standard, and they pursued it with a vengeance. America was now in the midst of what has been called "galloping capitalism"; in just a few years, the U.S. was producing half of the world's goods. The nation's Gross National Product (GNP) doubled, the budget of General Motors alone grew to the size of Poland's. In fact, the Detroit firm's annual income was greater than the combined revenues of New York, New Jersey, Pennsylvania, Ohio, Delaware, and the six New England states. Americans' discretionary spending power rose from $40 billion in 1940 to $100 billion in 1950, and $200 billion a decade later. American workers bore a decreasing resemblance to Europe's industrial proletariat; assembly-line workers (at least, those with working wives) could now afford expensive cars and stock investments. By the late 1940s the median family income had doubled to $6,000. Thrift had suddenly become outmoded, as Americans spent every cent they had, and then some.

After years of austerity caused by the depression and the war, Americans eagerly revived their spending spree of the 1920s. "Buy now, pay later" became a slogan of epidemic proportions. Prior to the war, extension of credit or installment buying had been infrequent, used primarily for such purchases as home buying. Now, however, short-term credit plans mushroomed across the country, offering credit cards for oil company chains, restaurants, and all-purpose spending such as American Express, Carte Blanche, and Visa. Living on credit and buying on margin became a way of life for millions of Americans. Life on the installment plan resulted in a 55 percent increase in the national consumer debt between 1952 and 1956, from $27.4 billion to $42.5 billion. Suddenly, consumer goods which had earlier been regarded as luxuries—if indeed they were even available—now came to be seen as necessities. The first automatic clothes washer appeared in 1946. Annual sales of electric dishwashers soon totaled 225,000, and garbage disposals sold at the rate of 750,000 per year. By 1970, half of all American families used credit cards, symbolic of their high living standard.

This rage of consumerism was stimulated by new trends in advertising. Sales techniques had become more sophisticated since Bruce Barton pioneered in the industry in the 1920s. Madison Avenue hucksters now invested fortunes in motivational research, in order to increase their efficiency in manipulating and exploiting the consumer. Indeed, during the 1950s ten billion dollars were spent annually for this purpose. Critics charged that by "creating" such wants among consumers, the advertising industry was "enslaving" the American people. Responding to conflicting ads for aspirin, Bufferin, etc., nonprescription drug sales increased seven times in the decade prior to 1957. Shoplifting also soared astronomically, as increasing numbers of Americans came to believe that there were certain goods they "had to have" regardless of cost. One observer noted that the three ideologues who had the greatest influence on American values were Marx, Freud, and Phineas T. Barnum, who once said, "A sucker is born every minute." Ironically while advertising had these negative results, it was argued that commercials stimulated the economy, and hence, supported the "American way." In this manner, advertising was equated with "Americanism." There can be no doubt that these economic and social forces were altering American values. As one critic of the 1950s observed: "Production, consumption, and profit have come to play the role that religion played in our grandfather's generation."

Nowhere was the surge of spending more evident than in the American love affair with the automobile. Wartime assembly-lines were converted to civilian production. Car registration soared from 25 million in 1945 to 40 million in 1950, as Americans spent 4.7 percent of their disposable income on cars. Auto sales increased exponentially; the 100 million vehicles built between 1893 and 1952 were matched by an additional 100 million manufactured by 1967. The peak year for automakers in Detroit came in 1955 when eight million new models rolled off the assembly-line. Revolutionary changes continued to accompany the car in American society; more cars meant more roadways, culminating with the Federal Highway Act of 1956, which allocated $32 billion for an immense interstate highway system. Ironically, while the intricate web of new roadways was hailed as a triumph of American technology and committed Americans to automobile transportation, it also worsened the plight of the inner city, and increased air pollution. Moreover, it created a conflict between "people-space" and "machine-space"; more than one-fourth of Los Angeles's 463 square miles came to be occupied by asphalt: streets, freeways, bridges, ramps, overpasses, gas stations, garages, and parking lots. The automobile also contributed to the growth of suburbia.

Life in the Suburbs

The American landscape was radically altered by "suburban sprawl." A pioneer in this development was William Levitt, who in 1949 built the first subdivision of homes on Long island, 17,500 of them, all exactly alike. Due to inadequate housing during the war, young married couples stood in line for four days to purchase one of his basic, four-room houses, which sold for less than $10,000, including everything from landscaping to kitchen appliances. Now the American Dream seemed within the grasp of ordinary Americans. Despite the monotonous standardization of this mass housing, ex-G.I.s and their wives who remembered military regimentation, quonset huts, and trailer camps were grateful to have their own nests.

And nests they were. After World War II the home became child centered. The age of first marrieds was plummeting, and family size was on the rise. One sociological study reported in the late 1940s that 55,000 married men reached 137,000 sexual climaxes weekly, resulting in an impregnated wife every seven seconds. The 37.5 million households in 1945 had increased to 53 million by 1960, largely the result of masses of subdivisions mushrooming across the nation. Moreover, with the end of the war-time economy, women's magazines like *Ladies Home Journal* began to promote the woman's role as a homemaker, gardener, den mother, chauffeur, etc. In 1954 *McCall's* coined the word "togetherness" to describe the new commitment to a close family centered around children, and one-family homes in suburbia with two-car garages (two-car families went from 28 percent of the population in 1960 to 50 percent in 1974). America was becoming the Land of the Young.

The high priest of this new child-centered suburban society was the renowned pediatrician Benjamin Spock, whose book *Baby and Child Care,* first published in 1945, revolutionized the philosophy of rearing children. Insecure as they faced the uncertainties of a rapidly-changing world, young parents nervously thumbed through Dr. Spock's handbook for advice on everything from breast-feeding to childhood diseases. In his chapter on "permissiveness," Spock counseled: "Doctors who used to conscientiously warn young parents against spoiling are now encouraging

"The American Dream" of owning a home was realized by many middle class Americans who moved into the suburbs in large numbers beginning in the 1950s. (J. R. Eyerman, Life Magazine © 1953, 1981, Time, Inc.)

them to meet their baby's needs, not only for food, but for comfort and loving." No longer would strict rules and nursing schedules be prescribed for infants; kids should not be told what to do. Guilt-ridden parents who had experienced the deprivation of the depression and the war were determined that their offspring should have opportunities denied them during their childhood. Consequently, a permissive spirit dominated the white, middle-class home during the post-war years. Pampered youth became a powerful bloc of consumers, spending billions of dollars for faddish fashions, dominating 43 percent of phonograph record sales, and 53 percent of movie admissions. Earlier values like thrift were casually discarded as American teenagers spent one-third of a billion dollars annually on toiletries. This permissiveness was also reflected in the schools. No longer were pupils expected to follow a fixed curriculum; instead, they chose electives, with "family living" enjoying much greater popularity than such earlier required courses as geometry, grammar, and foreign language. Even letter grades (A through F) were replaced in many schools by the less judgmental "satisfactory" and "unsatisfactory." This cult of the young spawned a generation of Americans by the mid-sixties numbering 20–30 million greater than demographic experts had anticipated.

These new Americans came to be called the "silent generation." Whereas generations of the thirties and forties had held to sturdy social values from their youth, their self-confidence or "inner-directedness" gave way after World War II to an anxious generation no longer sure of itself. Memories of the Depression, and fear of Communism and the atomic bomb ("better dead than red") contributed to this mood. Safety and security seemed to be the new norms. In his book *The Lonely Crowd* sociologist David Riesman now spoke of "other-directedness," whereby the driving need was to avoid "rocking the boat," and instead, to conform to the group. Eager for the approval of others, young people were as sedate and conservative in their values as their parents. One observer wrote that the "dedication of bourgeois America to personal security" had produced "a generation with strongly middle-aged values." By 1955 twenty percent of all college students majored in business, emulating their parents' desire for the job, the home, and the station wagon filled with kids. One poll in 1950 revealed that three of youth's greatest heroes were Joe DiMaggio, Doris Day, and Roy Rogers.

Moreover, the politics of youth were characterized by complacency. Political liberalism on the campus was tired and dull. Controversy was passé. One professor complained:

> *A dominant characteristic of students in the current generation is that they are gloriously contented both in regard to their present day-to-day activity and their outlook for the future. Few of them are worried—about their health, their prospective careers, their family relations, the state of national or international society or the likelihood of their enjoying secure and happy lives.*

Distrust of ideas and fear of controversy were reflected in President Eisenhower's definition of an intellectual: "a man who takes more words than is necessary to say more than he knows." Indeed, in 1952 the Republicans took the low road in Ike's campaign by subtly portraying the bald-pated Democratic candidate Adlai Stevenson as an "egghead" and his university-bred advisors as "longhairs" or "highbrows." Clearly, there was something "un-American" about intellectualism. Even the "beatniks" of the 1950s who asserted their antimaterialism and rejection of "square" conformists were not very threatening; they were poets and minstrels, but the "beats" broke no windows, planted no bombs, and never really threatened the establishment. In the meantime, the "silent generation" was sowing its oats by staging panty raids in college dormitories and other contests to see how many students could be stuffed into a telephone booth or in a VW bug. The mood was carefree and innocent.

Don't Shoot! We're Your Children!

By the 1960s the mood of post-war youth had changed. The values of that decade's college generation had been influenced from their earliest childhood by the permissive interpretation of Dr. Spock's child-raising philosophy. The pediatrician's rejection of traditional methods for rearing children was reinforced by other social and economic forces that had far-reaching effects on the young. This generation of youth had grown up in the lap of affluence unprecedented in modern America. Yet material possessions and opportunities were no guarantee of happiness. Since WWII it had slowly become apparent that the nuclear family—that bastion of authority and togetherness—was not perfectly equipped to deal with oftentimes conflicting social forces. Divorce began to skyrocket as early as the 1950s, and single-parent homes with working mothers became common. No longer did young people automatically defer to their parents' values, as it became more apparent that their "wisdom" was not unlimited.

Their growing awareness that all was not well was reinforced by serious social and political ills by the 1960s. The civil rights movement and the emerging war in Vietnam also fueled the flaunting of authority during the decade. The pace of student radicalism was set as early as 1964 when the Free Speech Movement erupted at the Berkeley campus of the University of California. Protests occurred when university officials tried to place a ban on political discussion on campus. No longer were students willing to be part of the "silent generation." Many college-age people especially were outraged by the injustices suffered by the minorities, and gave their unreserved enthusiasm for the civil disobedience of social activists like Dr. Martin Luther King, Jr. The campus became an important breeding ground for discontent as professors dared to examine festering social issues in America. Disenchantment with the system was further felt as a result of the assassinations of Dr. King, the Kennedy brothers, and Malcolm X, all youthful icons of the sixties. By the end of the decade, the anti-authoritarian mood was exacerbated by the undeclared war in Southeast Asia.

Rejection of the established social values also stemmed from a sexual revolution, originating with the research of an Indiana sociologist. Americans' general innocence about sex was dramatically changed by Professor Alfred C. Kinsey's interviews of thousands of people covering their sexual behavior. Kinsey's study covered the whole sexual spectrum—masturbation, nocturnal emissions, petting, intercourse before and after marriage, adultery, frequency of ejaculations, oral and anal sex, relations with animals, and other exotic (or erotic) pleasures. In so doing, Kinsey's work challenged those American institutions traditionally responsible for defining values and behaviour. It suggested that the church's teaching about sexual behavior no longer provided the only valid values about what is acceptable or "normal." Recognition of this diversity in sexual conduct contributed to a lessening respect for the institutions of authority. One college

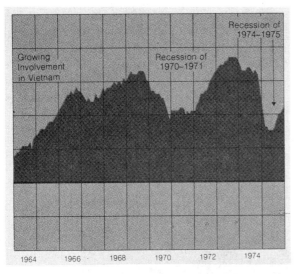

BUSINESS ACTIVITY
1941-1975

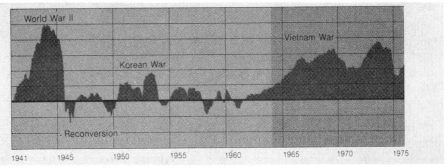

Post World War II Americans enjoyed the greatest prosperity over an extended time in the nation's history. This was accompanied by a shift to a services-oriented economy. Since 1975, "Stagflation" has plagued the market and the country experienced its worst recession between 1980 and 1983.

coed defiantly brandished a pin that read: "If it feels good, I'll do it." Intercourse did feel good, and young people flocked to the new freedom, liberated by The Pill, the diaphragm, and other birth control methods.

This spirit of permissiveness and dissent among young people was also the result of television and other media. After the war the "tube" invaded suburbia; by 1961, 55 million sets were in operation, acting as a surrogate parent and substitute babysitter for millions of youngsters. It has been estimated that by age sixteen, the typical American youth had spent 15,000 hours watching TV, more time than was spent with teachers and parents combined. TV offered a bill of fare that was much more explicit about sex and violence than radio had ever been. The toppling of old values could be traced back to the 1950s with the "beatniks" and actors like James Dean who starred in *Rebel without a Cause*. By the 1960s youth had acquired other cult heroes, like John Lennon of the Beatles who boasted: "We're more popular

Television has a vast impact on American life that is still being probed. By the 1980s, children were spending more time watching "the tube" than in interaction with parents and teachers combined.

than Jesus now." Another rock star named Janis Joplin asserted that "what I mean to kids is that they can be themselves and win"—shortly before she killed herself with whiskey and other drugs.

The general opposition of youth to authority reached a crescendo by the late sixties with the expanding war in Vietnam. All other issues of social concern were now subordinated to it, as a symbol of all that was wrong with America. Nightly TV news broadcasts drove home vividly the brute power exercised by the U.S. in the jungles of Southeast Asia, even engaging in ecocide. Reports concerning the use of Agent Orange to defoliate the Vietnamese countryside, thereby depriving the natives of food, enraged Americans especially when it was revealed that this chemical warfare damaged the human nervous system. Students began to take the law into their own hands by refusing to report for the draft, burning their draft cards, and even protesting violently in the streets against the war and war-related research projects. Youthful dissenters now refused to accept the politics of compromise stemming from their parents' political creed. Instead, because racial prejudice and nuclear war were evil, then evil must be opposed. This unrest reached new heights in the spring of 1970 when President Nixon expanded the war by ordering U.S. forces into neighboring Cambodia. An antiwar protest erupted at Ohio's Kent State University, resulting in the death of four demonstrating students at the hands of National Guardsmen who responded to the chanting with gunfire. The word of the tragedy spread quickly, resulting five days later with a peace march of 100,000 people on Washington, D.C.

Alienation from society was not just a political phenomenon, but was cultural as well. Youthful extremists concluded that the foundations of society were so corrupt that mere political reform was inadequate. The antidote to this sad state of affairs was to reject the "straight" society in its entirety. One radical leader admonished his followers to "trust no one over 30." In the place of conventional attitudes, hippies, anti-war protestors and other dissenters sought to implement the "counterculture" which was expected to humanize the existing society. Charles Reich in his book *The Greening of America* spoke of the youth rebellion, suggesting that materialism and imperialism would be replaced by a new consciousness of human values. By the mid-seventies, however, the war in Vietnam ended, and the subsequent economic recession spelled the end of the counterculture. Young people seemed to return to more conventional goals like finding a job, getting married, and working within the system. College enrollments were again burgeoning in such fields as the sciences, business, and computers. By the 1980s former radicals prominent in the protest movement like Jerry Rubin and Tom Hayden were carving out comfortable careers in the stock market or establishment politics. As one historian noted, the romantic, self-indulgent path of the "flower children" of the 1960s proved to be not the road to the future, but an historic blind alley.

Retrenchment and Reassessment

By the 1980s it was obvious that neither the counterculture of the 1970s nor LBJ's Great Society offered adequate solutions to society's ills. The big spending of the liberals had failed to bring the peace that Americans yearned for. The nation's education system was indicted in 1983 by a blue-ribbon commission appointed by President Reagan for failing to meet the basic needs of American youth. Nor had school busing succeeded in bringing about racial integration. The expensive social programs of the sixties had not solved the wide array of problems besieging society; the divorce rate now soared to half of all marriages. The impact on the family was even greater as millions of women entered the job market as sole providers for their offspring. Economically, the system was in the doldrums as well. By 1974 stagflation had set in, bringing the dual problems of inflation and a generally stagnant economy, requiring that President Nixon institute wage and price controls during peacetime for the first time. No longer were there enough jobs, even for college graduates.

Exhausted by the idealism and sacrifice required by the Great Society and the war in Vietnam, voters responded with a conservative mandate to rectify those social ills by placing curbs on school busing, taxes, abortion, homosexual rights, and by seeking to restore prayer in the schools. Reminiscent of the Revolt of the Old Order in the 1920s, President Reagan spoke repeatedly about restoring America's former greatness from the excesses that had afflicted the nation in recent decades. While encouraging prayer in the public schools, however, the President remained oblivious to his own education commission's strongly-worded recommendation that only through a huge allocation of the nation's resources can American education be restored to its former prominence. Reagan's simple nostrums for the nation's ills caused many to wonder about the president's blueprint for the future.

Indeed, despite Reagan's well-intentioned wishes, there was growing evidence that America's traditional role as the leading industrial, manufacturing, and producing economy in the world was no longer assured. In fact, many economists became convinced that the United States' position as industrial leader was already over. Statistics were marshalled to show a continuing drop in the industrial work force and a rise (topping 70 percent of the labor force) in service employment. Teachers, programmers, consultants, secretaries, salespeople, and professionals now outnumbered factory workers. What one economist has called the "knowledge sector"—that area of the economy devoted to developing and distributing new ideas—produced more than one-third of the gross national product.

Why the drop in manufacturing and heavy industry? One reason may be traced to the burden of obsolete plants and equipment that cripple competition with more modern facilities overseas. Another factor is the rising costs of labor in the United States as compared with other nations having a lower standard of living. "The general rule is that if it can be made abroad," affirms one expert, "it can be made cheaper," even without loss of quality. Both of these developments were brought out by the actions of large, multinational corporations based in America. These huge companies build most of their new production facilities abroad because they find fewer governmental restrictions, lower construction costs, an abundance of workers willing to labor for lower wages, and a generally more positive attitude toward industrial growth.

Significantly, most of the skilled personnel needed to operate these facilities are brought over from the United States. It is American professional and managerial talent along with American technical skill that continues to be in high demand. The nation's most vital resource may very well be trained, creative individuals. Drawing upon inherited national wealth and individual and technological innovation, the United States may well find that its most profitable export is ideas—concepts in economics, science, social development, and life-style that are the products of concentrated research and development. America could realize a new role as an "arsenal of experimentation."

It was obvious that the eighties were a time when the American people attempted to reduce their fiscal commitment to social programs at home, as they sought a clearer prescription for their needs as the twenty-first century drew near. Perhaps the greatest influence in that lesson entailed the broad revolutionary changes touching their lives. Hopefully, as personal lives were altered by the impact of the technetronic revolution, that awareness would be reflected in a new government policy which would enable the United States to regain its prominent role in the global economy.

CULTURE WAR AND ITS CONSEQUENCES

Religion has helped shape American values since the colonial period. Evangelical Christianity, for example, figured prominently in influencing opinion concerning 19th century abolitionism and prohibition during the early twentieth century. This evangelical force was manifested by a social conservatism during the 1920s; it surfaced again during the 1970s and 1980s, fueled by the powerful medium of television. Recognizing its marketing potential, televangelists attacked the "secular humanism" of modern culture. Confronted by the forces for change in this modern post-industrial, post-Cold War society, many "born-again" Christians reject the view that truth is relative, moral values are situational, and ethical judgments are tentative. Airing their evangelistic certitudes soothingly via their televised ministries, these church leaders have influenced the social values of countless Americans.

Their social conservatism was transmuted into political activism. Followers of Reverend Jerry Falwell's Moral Majority denounced the gay rights movement on the grounds that homosexuality is sinful. Pat Robertson's TV parishioners opposed the Equal Rights Amendment and the feminist movement. Evangelicals favor re-introducing prayer and the teaching of "creationism" in the public schools to counter the "theory" of evolution. These zealots ascribe America's moral decay to a political system no longer sensitive to "family values." Reminiscent of the "revolt of the Old Order" during the 1920s, President Reagan appealed to millions of Americans with his oft-repeated theme about restoring America's greatness from the excesses that had afflicted the nation in recent decades. He deplored the purported wave of humanism and hedonism: "I think there is a hunger in this land for a spiritual revival, a return to a belief in moral absolutes." The President proclaimed 1983 the "Year of the Bible." Campaigning for re-election in 1984, Reagan garnered the support of 80 percent of white, born-again Christians. Little wonder, then, that attitudes and values of the 1980s were reflected in volatile debates over such public policy issues as AIDS and the treatment of gay people.

The rapid growth of the AIDS epidemic during the 1980s served as a personal litmus test for Americans' attitudes toward gays. Caused by a slow-acting virus for which there is no cure and which is invariably fatal, the disease is spread through contaminated semen, vaginal fluids, and blood. The virus can be disseminated, usually through anal intercourse or shared hypodermic needles. Persons infected with HIV (human immunodeficiency virus) can remain asymptomatic for eight years or more, unaware that they are contagious. Ignoring this epidemic led to stunning consequences. Ten years after the first AIDS victim was reported in the United States, the mortality rate for 1991 alone reached 106,000. The number of HIV-positive carriers surpassed one million, including notable celebrities like former basketball superstar Earvin "Magic" Johnson. By the early 1990s, a new case was being reported every twelve minutes. Americans were slow to agree on a solution to the looming crisis; they were confused by the moral and financial implications that the disease posed for society. Reluctance to confront the epidemic squarely also stemmed from people's embarrassment to discuss sexual practices long considered taboo in society. Hence, it took several years for AIDS to enter the public consciousness.

The Reagan-Bush years were marked by minimal attention to the epidemic. When in 1986 United States Surgeon General C. Everett Koop called for AIDS education "at the earliest grade possible," he incurred the wrath of conservatives who complained that Koop's approach would encourage young people to have illicit sex. Perhaps the centerpiece of the social policy accompanying the Reagan Revolution was the emphasis on "family values," so much so that this slogan characterized George Bush's pursuit of re-election in 1992. In that campaign Vice-President Dan Quayle lashed out at a TV sitcom called "Murphy Brown," charging that by choosing to have a baby out of wedlock, its journalist namesake and the "cultural elite" (i.e., the media) bear complicity in the nation's moral decay. The Vice President's assessment of the nation's moral malaise was joined by Republican presidential primary candidate and journalist Patrick Buchanan. At the Republican national convention in Dallas in 1992 he delivered a scathing rebuke to "those who would destroy America," declaring that "we must take back our country."

My friends, this election is about more than who gets what. It is about who we are. It is about what we believe and what we stand for as Americans. There is a religious war going on in this country for the soul of America.

The notion of a culture war—simmering at least since the early 1980s—now became part of the mainstream political debate. Americans' longtime consensus about the basic goodness of their government was replaced by a shrill antigovernment rhetoric and hyperbole, supported by the powerful Republican Right. The conservative media (especially talk radio) issued an endless tirade of invective and mockery. In tiny sound-bites the message became a profound indictment of government itself, accompanied by popular impatience with genuine political argument; in the process public confidence in its government was being undermined. Buchanan's 1992 speech was echoed by other mainstream politicians who engaged in tactics of accusation and annihilation. An aide to Speaker of the House Newt Gingrich suggested that real problems do not play well with the electorate: "Important issues can be of limited value." For example, in his assessment of the virtues of big versus small government, House Majority Leader Dick Armey demonstrated this tendency to distort history beyond recognition:

Behind our New Deals and New Frontiers and Great Societies you will find, with a difference only in power and nerve, the same sort of person who gave the world its Five Year Plans and Great Leaps Forward—the Soviet and Chinese counterparts.

The temerity to equate Presidents Roosevelt, Kennedy, and Johnson with Stalin and Mao is noteworthy. For Armey, preserving freedom meant having government do as little as possible, simply because for him it is inherently inefficient and oppressive. The cumulative effect of such antigovernment hostility found a receptive audience in the "Anxious Middle," a large bloc of citizens extremely dissatisfied with the status quo. Tens of millions of Americans continued to experience the downward mobility that began in the 1970s. This sense of betrayal by the government was explained by Clinton's Secretary of Labor Reich: "All the old bargains, it seems, have been breached. The economic bargain was that if you worked hard and your company prospered, you would share the fruits of success." No wonder the middle felt anxious; the old assurances were gone.

In some cases this frustration with and disaffection from the federal government found extreme expression. Terrorist hate groups, some committed to white supremacy, and all to the overthrow of the system by any means necessary, fueled the fastest-growing grassroots movement in American history. Confronted with an avalanche of antigovernment venom, thousands of primarily white males joined hundreds of Militia units. During the 1990s major catalysts were the FBI's ill-fated siege at Ruby Ridge, Idaho, the Brady gun control bill, and

The conflagration at Waco aroused antigovernment passions that led to the growth of the extremist militia movement. © Reuters NewMedia Inc./CORBIS

the FBI's attack on the Branch Davidian compound at Waco, Texas in 1993. Militia retaliation against the government has led to numerous attempts on the lives of public servants, including a plot to kidnap and hang a Montana judge. Like members of the Ku Klu Klan in the 1960s, militia members view themselves not as part of a hate group, but rather as patriots trying to preserve a way of life under attack. Most are drawn to the movement by their anger over issues like gun control, environmental regulations, and the general intrusiveness of the federal government.

It was the Waco assault that seemed to validate militia anger. Prior to the April 19, 1993 incident, law enforcement at all levels dismissed these paramilitary groups as "overgrown boys playing with weapons." The destruction at Waco became for some militants "the ideological equivalent of Pearl Harbor." Oklahoma City bomber Timothy McVeigh reportedly visited the Branch Davidian compound in Waco, and he used April 19 for both his phony birthdate and the issuance date on his fake driver's license. Two years later to the day, the government building in Oklahoma was bombed, killing 168 innocent victims. One observer wrote that the assault was only a warning shot: "That hatred was not, and is not, limited to the few people who bombed the Murrah Building. Millions of Americans share it; thousands arm themselves in militias to express it; and there are an undetermined number who would act upon it."

The Oklahoma City bombing resulted in widespread calls for a return to civility. But civility requires some basic agreement and mutual respect, both increasingly frayed in political combat. Rather than honestly confront tougher issues, it was easier for politicians to repeat simplistic shibboleths like big versus small government, abortion and gay rights, or which politician is more corrupt. Yet free speech involves not only combat; it also provides the arena where citizens can engage in a common search for solutions. Politics is not simply about the struggle for power and defeat of one's adversaries. As one keen observer put it: "A society in which people listen seriously to those with whom they fundamentally disagree—an attentive society—is the proper setting for freedom." Indeed, critics claimed that the media can advance the cause of democracy by drawing citizens into genuine debate. Voicing confidence in the American people, the writer Christopher Lasch suggests that "the lost art of argument" must be revived. Expressing support for the voters' capacity for intellectual discernment, he noted:

> *If we insist on argument as the essence of education, we will defend democracy not as the most efficient but as the most educational form of government, one that extends the circle of debate as widely as possible and thus forces all citizens to articulate their views, to put their views at risk, and to cultivate the virtues of eloquence, clarity of thought and expression, and sound judgment.*

Do the American people possess the knowledge necessary for a healthy democracy? Recent studies report the "dumbing down" of the nation's educational institutions. Approximately 20,000 schoolchildren questioned about American history in fifty states revealed abysmal ignorance. For example, more than 50 percent of all high school seniors are completely unaware of the Cold War. Such reports are ominous in light of current strong antigovernment sentiment. Americans, more than other people, must study their history because they have no other way of knowing themselves. Unlike other countries whose homogeneous populations have common ancestry and language, the United States is a nation of immigrants. The study of history becomes the balance wheel to counter this increasing unawareness of the nation's past. By examining the ongoing story of America, we learn that the pursuit of the principles of liberty and equality must be accorded to all Americans. Ignorance of this American narrative can lead well-intentioned citizens in dangerous directions with explosive consequences.

There were signs in the late '90s that Americans were tiring of these tactics of accusation and annihilation. Recent evidence suggests that the antigovernment violence and terrorism of the 1990s are subsiding, as voters enjoy an economy rebounding beyond expectation, a dramatic lowering of the crime rate, and unprecedented gains by minorities; these signposts of progress help explain a "return to civility."

SUGGESTIONS FOR ADDITIONAL READING

Frederick L. Allen, *Only Yesterday,* (1931). An entertaining and often insightful account of the twenties.

William Manchester, *The Glory and the Dream: A Narrative History of America 1932–1972,* (1973). A superb chronicle of American social and political history through four crucial decades.

William E. Leuchtenburg, *A Troubled Feast: American Society Since 1945,* (1979). A survey of the oftentimes conflicting forces in modern America.

Theodore K. Rabb and Robert I. Rotberg, *The Family in History; Interdisciplinary Essays,* (1973). A study of family life in America.

David Halberstam, *The Fifties* (1993). A provocative review of a transitional decade for America.

Aldous Huxley, *Brave New World Revisited,* (1958). A reevaluation of his original study *Brave New World* published in 1932, which predicted the scope and dimension of change in a democratic society.

Alvin Toffler, *Future Shock,* (1971). A study of change in the post-industrial era.

Theodore Roszak, *The Making of a Counter Culture,* (1969). A study of youth culture of the 1960s.

Garry Wills, *Reagan's America,* (1987). A critical assessment of the Reagan era.

Randy Shilts, *And The Band Played On. Politics, People, and the AIDS Epidemic,* (1987). A shocking indictment of the nation's response to AIDS.

The National Archives.

CHAPTER EIGHT

AMERICA AND THE WORLD: THE EXERCISE OF POWER

1898
Spanish-American War makes the United States a recognized world power.

1917
President Woodrow Wilson breaks nonalignment to bring the U.S. into the First World War.

1920
America rejects a role in the League of Nations and returns to nonalignment.

1941
U.S. nonalignment is shattered at Pearl Harbor and America enters World War II.

1942
Creation of the War Production Board begins military-industrial complex that lasts through the Cold War.

1945
United States drops the first atomic bomb over Hiroshima to end World War II and usher in the Nuclear Age.

1947
President Truman declares that the United States will support "free peoples" against attack; Russia and America begin the "Cold War."

1965
America begins massive military intervention in Vietnam.

1972
President Nixon visits China and the Soviet Union, the height of detente.

1989
Eastern Europe breaks free of the Soviet orbit—the Cold War ends.

1991
President Bush suggests the emergence of a "new world order" after the Allied coalition's victory over Iraq in the Gulf War.

1999
The United States leads NATO forces to stop Serbian "ethnic cleansing" of Kosovo.

WHAT SHOULD BE AMERICA'S WORLD ROLE?

The Cold War is over, the risk of nuclear Armageddon has evaporated, the American military is being downsized. A third of the world's governments has moved towards democracy and free market economics since 1989. Unilateral U.S. action abroad seems increasingly to be limited to small-scale "safe" moves such as the seizure of Haiti in 1994.

Yet, according to one diplomat, "the status quo is everywhere under siege." United Nations peacekeeping efforts are stretching to the breaking point. The spread of nuclear weapons is bringing Iran and North Korea into the world's most exclusive "club." Trade disputes between the United States, Japan, and the European Community threaten to cripple already faltering economies. Government officials in Washington debate U.S. foreign policy: should we focus on "America first," or should we continue a vigorously internationalist role? Traditionally, these roles have both been a peculiar mixture of realism and idealism. What can our history tell us about these roles and these choices?

IMPERIALISM

After the Civil War Americans were focused on internal development. Settling the last of the western territories, industrialization and urbanization absorbed the energies of the country. Brief attempts by several administrations to consider overseas expansion or reigniting the pre-war passion for America's mission in the world flopped. Even the purchase of Alaska in 1867 drew a storm of criticism as a waste of money and energy.

By the 1880s, however, attitudes were beginning to change. The popular Darwinian concept of "survival of the fittest" was being extended to include nations and races, creating a vigorous international competition based entirely on economic and military power. This type of competition fed aggressive nationalism by making a country's power and colonial possessions the measure of its "fitness." All of Europe was engaging in the race for colonies and military power, and some Americans felt it was only realistic that America join them. Financiers and industrialists pragmatically argued that expansion was essential to the health of the American economy. Admiral Alfred Thayer Mahan's influential writings, which pointed out the necessity of a large navy to protect and secure markets abroad, helped convince Congress to appropriate funds for a modern fleet. At the same time in the heady spirit of nationalism that possessed the country, the new navy "showed the flag" overseas and gained influence in governmental circles as a symbol of national pride. This influence was shown during the 1891 dispute with Chile over a riot that killed two American sailors in Valparaiso, when one Washington diplomat noted that the Navy "practically made" policy regarding the affair. Other leaders revived the idea of America's mission, maintaining that the United States was obliged to bring Christianity and democracy to the "downtrodden pagans" of the world.

In this atmosphere, America joined the rest of Europe on the imperialist path. Pacific coaling stations to serve the growing navy were obtained, and Samoa and Hawaii were brought under American dominance. Washington boldly asserted its primacy in the Western Hemisphere by invoking the Monroe Doctrine against Britain in a dispute with Venezuela.

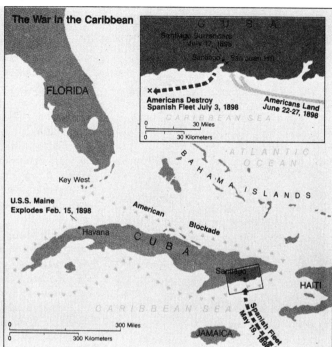

THE SPANISH-AMERICAN WAR

American strategy was to occupy Cuba and other Spanish possessions in the Caribbean, forcing Spain to surrender. The Philippines were a secondary target — the main objective of the war was supposed to be Cuban independence.

1898

Destruction of the Maine in Havana harbor infuriated the American public and led to war within two months (February).

Battle of Manila Bay destroyed the Spanish Pacific fleet and gave the United States control over the Philippine Islands (May).

Santiago besieged and doomed to fall after the battles of San Juan Hill and El Caney. The loss of this city meant the Spanish would lose Cuba (July).

Spanish Atlantic fleet destroyed at the naval battle of Santiago, and the city of Santiago surrendered two weeks later (July).

Treaty of Paris ended the one-sided conflict. The United States received the Philippines, Puerto Rico, and Guam from Spain. Cuba was granted independence (December).

1899

Filipino insurrection began in reaction to American annexation. The rebels sought independence. It took three years for American troops to end guerrilla warfare (February).

Then an indigenous Cuban revolt against Spanish rule brought that island to the forefront of American concern in 1896. The Cubans pictured their revolution as a desperate effort to overthrow repression. The American press picked up this theme and presented it to the public complete with notes of its disruptive effects on trade and investments and with sensational stories of atrocities designed to sell copy. But President McKinley, after trying to buy Cuba from Spain and offering to mediate the conflict without success, declared that "we want no wars of conquest" and refused to intervene. Shortly after his statement the mysterious sinking of the American cruiser *Maine* on February 15, 1898 in Havana Harbor sent a wave of war hysteria through the nation. Rather than defy the public and risk the breakup of his party, the President asked Congress to declare war on Spain, although Madrid had already acquiesced to most of the demands contained in an American ultimatum two days earlier.

The war lasted only 10 weeks; one American called it "a splendid little war." Once again the United States was poorly prepared. America had to resort to volunteers like Teddy Roosevelt's Rough Riders to augment the small number of regulars and make up an army to invade Cuba, Puerto Rico, and the Philippines. The biggest event was not the conquest of Cuba, whose independence Congress had already guaranteed, but the capture of the Philippines. Few in the government had anticipated this prize.

A great debate followed in Congress and the press over what to do with the Pacific islands. Many Americans had sincerely approved the Spanish-American War on the humanitarian grounds of helping the Cubans. They expected that the Philippines would be given their independence just as Cuba had, and felt that making the islands a colony without their consent would be a violation of basic American ideals. Some religious organizations, however, insisted that it would be better for the Philippines to be "governed, educated, and civilized" by the United States. Advocates of naval and commercial expansion argued that the Philippines were needed as a steppingstone to China and as a base to protect American commerce in the East.

Bowing again to public pressure and private business interests, McKinley sided with the imperialists and the Philippines were retained. The Filipinos resisted and American forces sent to pacify the islands used torture and concentration camps in a brutal effort to suppress the insurrection. An angry Mark Twain grimly proposed a new American flag "with the white stripes painted black and the stars replaced by a skull and crossbones." After the conflict, military influence shrank again, although the size of the armed forces themselves grew. Beyond outraging a minority of Americans, the Spanish-American War and its aftermath left only a faint imprint upon society at large.

But it made a major change in America's world role. The United States now had an overseas empire. "Our war in aid of Cuba has assumed undreamed of dimensions," marvelled one newspaper, "willy nilly we have entered upon our career as a world power." It was a career recognized by the powers of Europe and a course that would lead to a break with the traditional American policy of nonalignment in European affairs.

PANAMA CANAL

As Americans conquered the North American continent and established towns, cities, farms, and ranches in the far western states, the commercial and military need for a canal across Central America intensified. A French company had tried and failed to build through the Columbian province of Panama. The U.S. government was very interested in digging and operating the canal but Congress was debating whether it would flow across Panama or through Nicaragua. Philippe Bunau-Varilla, the French company's representative in the United States, was anxious to convince the Americans to select the Panamanian route so that they would purchase his company's equipment before it rusted in the jungles of Panama. In fear of Nicaraguan volcanoes, the Senate soon opted for the route through Panama. In January, 1903, Secretary of State John Hay signed an agreement which granted the concession to construct the Panama canal to the Americans, calling for the United States to pay Colombia $10 million and an annual rent of $250,000 in return for a ninety-nine-year lease on a six-mile-wide canal zone across the isthmus of Panama. President Roosevelt believed that the deal was generous. The Colombian Senate, however, rejected the treaty, wanting more money and greater control over the canal zone. Roosevelt was incensed. He berated the Bogota lawmakers as "greedy little anthropoids."

Meanwhile Bunau-Varilla, along with Panamanian investors in the French canal company, organized a revolt against Colombian rule so that an independent Panama could sign its own treaty. Roosevelt ordered an American warship to Panamanian waters to prevent Colombia from deploying troops to suppress the insurrection. On November 1, 1903, the Panamanian rebels declared their province to be an independent nation. Bunau-Varilla proclaimed himself Panama's foreign minister. The Hay–Bunau-Varilla Treaty of 1903 granted the United States a permanent lease on a ten-mile-wide canal zone on the same terms that had been promised to the Bogota government. When a group of Panamanian diplomats arrived in Washington, the Frenchman Bunau-Varilla explained the treaty terms to them. One diplomat fainted. Another, flushed with anger, punched Bunau Varilla in the nose. For years, Panamanian citizens attacked the Hay–Bunau-Varilla agreement as "the treaty no Panamanian signed."

The first great challenge in the American enterprise was the persistence of yellow fever which had decimated the French. U.S. Army Colonel Dr. William Gorgas supervised a massive project to drain marshes and swamps, and, in so doing, eradicated the yellow fever-bearing mosquito. The actual construction of the canal began in 1906, under the direction of the Army Corps of Engineers. In November, 1906, President Roosevelt toured the canal zone, inspecting the work and exclaiming: "This is one of the great works of the world."

Construction was completed in August 1914, just as Europe was plunging into World War I. New York City was brought 8,000 nautical miles closer to San Francisco. The Panama Canal was one of the great achievements in the history of American science and technology. Nevertheless, Roosevelt's imperialism was not without its critics. Roosevelt simply dismissed the criticism, proclaiming defiantly: "I have a mandate from civilization to take Panama." The President reasoned "If I had followed traditional conservative methods, I would have submitted a dignified state paper of probably two hundred pages to Congress and the debates on it would have been going on yet; but I took the Canal Zone and let Congress debate; and while the debate goes on, the Canal does also."

BREAKING WITH TRADITION

Theodore Roosevelt did more than anyone else to bring about this break. As Assistant Secretary of the Navy, Roosevelt had given the orders that launched Admiral Dewey's attack on Manila Bay. He had also led the charge up San Juan Hill that had broken Spanish resistance in Cuba. When the McKinley administration had proposed to the European powers that China not be carved up into "spheres of influence" as Africa had been, Roosevelt supported this "Open Door" Policy for trade. The United States had involved itself in European policies to protect its growing overseas commercial interests. And when McKinley was assassinated and Roosevelt became President, he went further still.

He used intrigue, U.S. gunboats, and engineering to win construction of an American-controlled Panama Canal. Determined to secure the Western Hemisphere for the United States under the Monroe Doctrine, Roosevelt proclaimed that America had "police powers" in Latin America to insure order and prevent European interference. In the Caribbean and Central America, United States warships and Marines became common sights. Later, President Taft would use the "Roosevelt corollary" to defend American investments in the area. This "dollar diplomacy" protected American economic interests, but the use of the Marines in the Dominican Republic and Nicaragua antagonized Latin Americans. Roosevelt's idea that the United States should "walk softly and carry a big stick" had influenced events but won no Latino friends.

Roosevelt believed it was time the United States play a role outside the Western Hemisphere. In 1905, the President offered to mediate the 1904–05 Russo-Japanese War "in the interests of peace" and to protect the "Open Door." Later that year, when Germany and France clashed over control of the North African state of Morocco, President Roosevelt offered to mediate the disagreement, again "in the interests of world peace." Washington was still careful to maintain its freedom of action by refusing to tie itself to any European nation or alliance, but Roosevelt had established that the United States had a global interest—an interest at least partially based on the knowledge that a major war would endanger American commerce. To make it clear that the United States was capable of looking out for its increasingly global interests, Roosevelt sent the best ships in the Navy on a world tour.

The United States was now a fall participant in world affairs, going beyond its old "America First" policies of nonalignment to embrace an internationalist role. The last prohibition—against taking sides in a European conflict—was also about to fall.

"OVER THERE"

Intense competition between imperialist countries aggravated by aggressive nationalism had divided Europe into two armed camps: the Entente (France, Britain, and Russia) and the Central Powers (Germany and Austria-Hungary). The assassination of the heir to the throne of Austria-Hungary in June of 1914 sparked a series of actions and reactions that snowballed into war in August. Americans were appalled by the conflict, but since its origins were purely European they felt detached from it. "Luckily we have the Atlantic between us and Europe," observed one newspaper with relief. "It is their war, not ours." President Woodrow Wilson immediately proclaimed American neutrality, and at first the government tried to act with impeccable impartiality. When President Wilson read a newspaper report alleging that the War Department was drawing up contingency plans for war with Germany, he angrily ordered that any officer who participated be removed from command and thrown out of Washington. Despite confident European predictions of a quick war, the conflict soon degenerated into a prolonged and bloody stalemate.

As both sides stepped up their war efforts hoping to break the stalemate, the United States found itself gradually being drawn into the dispute because of its trade. The Entente violated America's neutral rights by preventing all trade with German-held territory, but Britain was careful to conciliate Washington to avoid a break and to increase her ties to American businessmen by getting loans and buying huge quantities of supplies. The Central Powers also modified their originally strict submarine blockade of England, agreeing to observe the rules of sea warfare to conciliate President Wilson's strong stand on neutral rights. But Allied propaganda against German atrocities and incidents where German submarines sank ships with Americans on board (like the *Lusitania* in 1915) angered many of Wilson's constituents. Efforts by the President and by private American citizens to mediate the war failed because neither side would accept Wilson's formula of "peace without victory." His own alternatives were narrowing because of his idealistic stand on the right of Americans to travel anywhere they choose and the principle of "free ships make free goods."

In January of 1917 the Germans decided to make a final effort for victory by resuming unrestricted submarine warfare. The resulting indiscriminate sinkings and the interception of the Zimmermann note to Mexico (offering that country her former territories in the Southwest if she would go to war with America) were enough to persuade Congress to declare war on the Central Powers. America's break with the tradition of nonalignment was complete.

Although the nation followed Wilson into war, it was not unanimously popular. To promote national unity and mobilize enthusiasm for the war effort, a Committee on Public Information was created. It enlisted armies of artists, writers, and educators to flood the country with patriotic propaganda presenting the struggle as a "war to end war," "a war for democracy," and a battle for "honesty and decency" against "despotism." A draft system was instituted in conjunction with patriotic appeals to enlist. The government also set about smothering protest and dissent. Laws were passed against "false reports or false statements" that could hinder the war effort and later included any spoken or written attempt to bring "the form of government into contempt." Both the press and movies were censored, and all pacifist films were ordered burned. But all of this patriotism only made the abrupt end of the war and the failure to gain the nation's idealistic aims for a "just and lasting peace" more emotionally discouraging. Disillusionment set in and there was the suspicion that the whole effort had been wasted. This mood produced the "lost generation" of the 1920s, energetically seeking pleasure and deeper purpose yet pessimistic about finding it.

American participation in World War I also had economic side effects. It had been necessary to begin mobilizing all industrial resources as well as public sentiment to support the war effort. A War Industries Board established production priorities, fixed prices or controlled them by

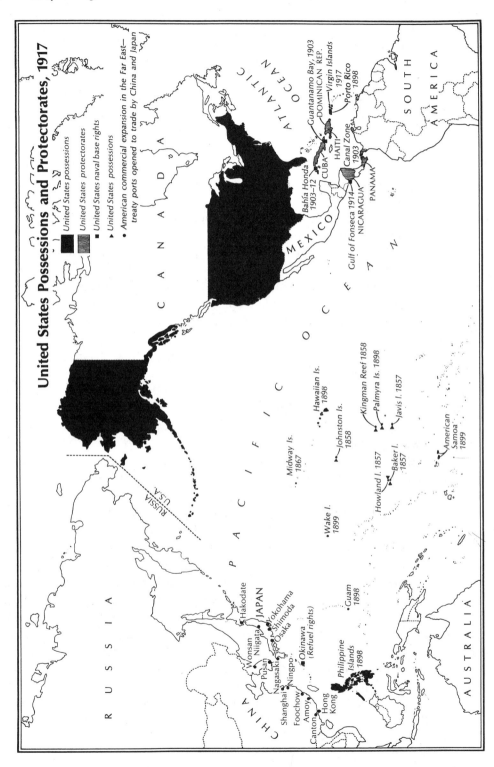

United States Possessions and Protectorates, 1917

■ United States possessions
▦ United States protectorates
■ United States naval base rights
▲ United States possessions
● American commercial expansion in the Far East—treaty ports opened to trade by China and Japan

WOODROW WILSON

Woodrow Wilson was born the son of a Presbyterian minister in Staunton, Virginia in 1856. His father's stern morality and vision were transmitted to Wilson early, and neither ever left him. Wilson was educated for the law, but it did not really interest him. Government did, and his doctoral thesis analyzed how the Congressional committee system fractured national politics and required the president to lead. For the next twenty-five years Wilson lived the life of an academic, teaching at Bryn Mawr, Wesleyan, and Princeton and building a reputation as a magnificent lecturer. Between 1902 and 1910 he served with distinction as President of Princeton, but he blew up a minor issue to major proportions, refused to compromise, and resigned from his post.

Wilson then turned to politics. The Democratic machine in New Jersey put him up for the governorship, seeing him as an economic conservative. Wilson, however, turned progressive on them. He won bipartisan support for a direct primary, a corrupt practices act, an employer's liability act, and regulation of state public utilities. By 1912 he was in a position to win the party's nomination for the presidency. It took forty-six ballots before the party decided he was their man. The Taft-Roosevelt division in the Republican ranks assured Wilson's victory.

Wilson drove through a host of progressive reform legislation, tackling issues like the tariff and national currency regulation that had frustrated many earlier efforts. But his greatest challenge came when World War One convulsed Europe in 1914.

The President declared American neutrality, insisting that "we must be impartial in thought as well as in action." Yet Wilson himself was a lifelong admirer of British civilization, and it became apparent early in the conflict that American power and resources could tip the scale of war. Those resources were available to the Allies because they had access to American ports and factories, while the Central Powers did not. Still, the British blockade angered Washington ("Each day that we meet," wrote one cabinet member, "we boil over somewhat at the foolish manner in which England acts") and it was not until the sinking of the *Lusitania* that public opinion was strongly aroused against Germany

Wilson fought for peace. "There is such a thing as a man being too proud to fight," he said in one speech. After two more U-boat strikes, the President secured a promise from the Germans to stop the sinkings. Twice, in January of 1915 and a year later, Wilson sought to mediate the war. He failed. "Everybody seems to want peace," he wrote, "but nobody is willing to concede enough to get it." Another effort in 1917 for "peace without victory" collapsed because both sides still thought they could win. In the end, the United States entered the conflict when the U-boat war resumed. Wilson clearly stated his principles: "Property rights can be vindicated by claims for damages when the war is over . . . but the fundamental rights of humanity cannot be. The loss of life is irreparable."

Wilson led the United States in a crusade "to end all wars." Victory brought celebration, but the real work lay ahead. The President traveled to Europe, the first American president to do so, in order to realize his vision of a world at peace. At Versailles he found the Allies less than cooperative. "President Wilson and his Fourteen Points bore me. Even God Almighty has only ten," the French leader snorted. But Wilson got his League of Nations in the Treaty of Versailles in the end. He then found he could not sell it to his fellow Americans, suffering a stroke when he carried his case to the people over the head of a resisting Senate. His wife ran the Oval Office for a time as he lay partially paralyzed. In 1920, the Senate, faced with Wilson's own stubborn refusal to permit any amendments to the treaty, voted it down. Woodrow Wilson died four years later in 1924.

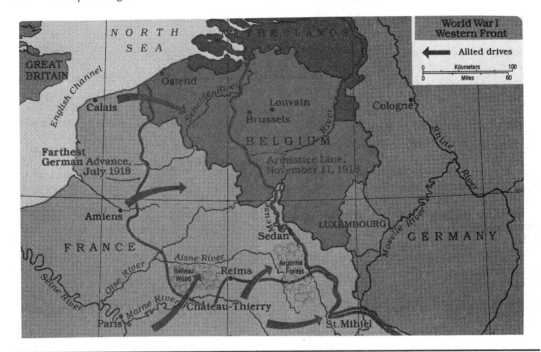

THE FIRST WORLD WAR

American strategy was heavily dependent upon Allied decisions. But in general it was to provide mountains of war supplies, help keep the sea lanes to Britain and France open, and ship as many men as possible to the western front.

1917

German submarines sink six American ships after the resumption of unrestricted submarine warfare, forcing Wilson to either give up his principles or go to war (February).

The United States declares war on the Central Powers (April).

The convoy system cuts Allied losses to the submarine after its adoption in the summer, reducing the U-boat menace.

1918

American Expeditionary Force under General Pershing helps stop a massive German offensive in battles at Chateau-Thierry and Belleau Wood (July).

American troops land in Russia at Archangel and Vladivostok to keep supplies from falling into German hands and to aid the counter-revolutionaries against the Bolshevik "Reds" (August).

The first independent operation of the AEF ends in victory for the Americans at St. Mihiel (September).

German defenses broken with American help in the Argonne Forest (September).

Armistice signed to end the fighting (November).

agreement, and taxed surplus profits, generally seeking to increase the efficiency of wartime production and supply. Industry generally benefited from this government coordination and scientific management (corporate profits rose to three times their pre-war level), and labor also profited from 20 percent higher "real wages" and better bargaining power.

President Wilson was determined that the war should be justified by nothing less than the creation of a new world order. Even as American money, supplies, and troops were turning the tide of the First World War and bringing about an Allied victory, Wilson declared his hope for "a universal dominion of right by such a concert of free peoples as shall bring peace and safety to all nations and make the world itself at last free." Mission had again come to the forefront of American policy.

Within months the President thought he had his "concert of free peoples" and the key to future peace with justice in the League of Nations, established at Versailles in 1918. But many Americans were surprised by the Versailles Treaty's harsh terms for the losers and territorial gains for the victors. The world, it appeared, had been made safe for the winners rather than "safe for democracy." Disillusioned by failure to achieve war aims, tired of crusading rhetoric and anxious to enjoy post-war prosperity, the American people sought "a return to normalcy" and political peace and quiet. Capitalizing on this national mood, Wilson's isolationist opponents determined to reject the collective security of the League for an "America first" policy. In the Senate they united with the Republican opposition to block United States membership in the League despite the President's strong effort to push the treaty through.

The consequences were profound. Rising political conservatism and the changing manners and morals of the emerging "Jazz Age" combined to bury the progressivism of Roosevelt and Wilson. The fading of progressive reform also led to a decline in the power of the presidency. More importantly, the United States largely withdrew from the post-war world, a world America had done a great deal to create. "America First" leaders who sought a return to nonalignment, though in harmony with American tradition, were at odds with the world role that America had created for itself over the preceding 20 years. By rejecting responsibility for the post-war world, the United States turned its back on the situation that the Treaty of Versailles had created, a situation that would eventually result in another war.

THE FAILURE OF NONALIGNMENT

Ironically, another war was precisely what American policy makers hoped to avoid by preserving their freedom of action. The 1920s and '30s saw a bitter backlash against American involvement in foreign wars. A Congressional committee chaired by Senator Gerald Nye found a pattern of war industry lobbying and huge profits that convinced many Americans that the nation had gone to war in 1917 to secure the profits of a few "merchants of death." People were shocked by personal memoirs detailing the horrors and stupidity of war like Remarque's *All Quiet on the Western Front.* A strong nationwide peace movement, sustained by the belief that financiers and munitions manufacturers had driven America into a wasteful First World War, cried "never again!" The movement demanded that the government promote peace but remain neutral.

In contrast to President Wilson, the leaders of Great Britain, France, and Italy had strictly practical ends in mind—the punishment of Germany, acquisition of new territories, and redrawing the boundaries of Europe to further their own power and security. It was these goals, not Wilson's idealistic ones, that shaped the Versailles peace treaty and disillusioned the American people. (U.S. Signal Corps, National Archives.)

Washington's foreign policy mirrored this sentiment. Beginning in 1921, Washington sponsored a series of naval disarmament conferences that temporarily eased the naval arms race between Britain, the United States, and Japan. America also began to participate in the humanitarian efforts of the League of Nations, although she still declined to join. The crowning achievement of the peace movement came when 64 nations signed the Kelloga-Briand Pact (1928) outlawing aggressive war, an event hailed by the American public as a "thing to rejoice over . . . it is superb, it is magnificent!"

Then the illusion was shattered. The Versailles peace had created international inequities that were especially rankling to Germany. Even Italy and Japan, who were among the victors, were dissatisfied with the second-class status accorded them. In 1931 the nation of the Rising Sun began a policy of expansion into Chinese Manchuria and later attacked China itself. Asia was engulfed in war. At the same time, Europe also faced the specter of invading armies. Adolf Hitler's rise to power in Germany in 1933 on the platform of prosperity, national pride, and national power was paralleled by the creation of other fascist (rightist dictatorship) governments in European nations dissatisfied with the status quo. Mussolini's Italy joined Hitler's Germany in a policy of rearmament and expansion, intervening to help Spanish fascists led by General Franco create a military dictatorship in Spain.

Initially, the American response merely acknowledged these threats to world peace by making diplomatic protests on the immorality of breaking treaties. To protect the nation from involvement, Congress passed a series of neutrality acts in the 1930s. One American policy maker flatly stated that the United States would not commit itself to "use its armed forces for the settlement of any dispute anywhere." America's refusal to trade with or aid any country at war sounded balanced, but actually hurt the weaker victims of aggression more. The Japanese continued to swallow China and began expanding into Southeast Asia shortly after the Germans absorbed Austria and Czechoslovakia in 1939. President Franklin Roosevelt's attempt to warn the nation that these aggressions were "creating a state of international anarchy and instability from which there is no escape through mere isolation or neutrality" fell on deaf ears. "America wants peace," pleaded one newspaper.

Peace, however, was fast disappearing. Britain and France finally declared war on Germany after Hitler invaded Poland in September of 1939. A shocked America watched the Nazis launch a blitzkrieg (lightning war) in Spring 1940 that conquered France and most of Europe within a year. The German air force showered Britain with bombs, and it appeared that Hitler was on the verge of winning the war. In the Far East, Japan joined Germany and Italy to form the Axis and put pressure on British and French holdings in Asia. Everywhere the Axis was triumphant.

Public opinion in the United States began to shift. Gradually, the President guided the nation away from neutrality in an effort to aid the battered Allies. He engineered a "destroyers for bases" deal with Britain that helped the Royal Navy resist the Nazi submarine menace. London received desperately needed war material on "loan," in the massive Lend-Lease program. American merchant ships were armed, and finally the navy began patrolling the Atlantic against German submarines. Washington placed strategic materials vital to the Japanese war economy on embargo to force Japan to halt her expansion. This measure forced Japan to reconsider her policy, but when faced with Washington's demand to withdraw from China in return for reopening trade, Tokyo secretly chose war rather than "humiliation" in the fall of 1941. Congress and the American people, however, were still deeply divided over whether to go to war. Acting as "the arsenal of democracy" was one thing, suffering the casualties of a world war was something else. Not until Japan struck with a surprise attack on Pearl Harbor on December 7, 1941, did the country unite behind a policy of total war.

Once again the nation mobilized. Steps had already been taken in some areas. The fall of France to Nazi armies in 1940 demonstrated that the less than half-million men in the armed forces would not be enough for national defense. Congress responded by creating the first peacetime draft. Ever since World War I the military's condition had been deteriorating, and measures were taken to bring its equipment and tactics up to modern standards. But it was in the area of industrial production that President Roosevelt, borrowing an idea from Wilson's War Industries Board, really exercised governmental powers of direction and control. Industrial production was the key to victory. As one British general observed, "God now marched with the biggest industries rather than the biggest battalions."

In January 1942, the President responded to the need for more and more efficient production by creating the War Production Board, which set goals for manufacturers and gave general direction to private industry. Wage and price controls were imposed. Scarce items like gasoline and meat were rationed. The government also loaned money for expansion to key war industries and in some cases even built the plants for them. All sorts of war-related scientific research were subsidized or entirely supported by the government. Some government agencies and the industrial management they were guiding developed such an identity of interest and outlook that for all intents and purposes they merged. This process forged in the heat of war a complex between business and governmental interests, both of which were directed toward satisfying military needs for weapons and supplies. The cooperation was a resounding success: the GNP doubled during the war years, and American industry produced an overwhelming quantity of high quality war material that enabled the Allied forces to totally defeat the Axis powers. American military leaders had their equipment, Washington had its victory, business had its profits, and the nation had a military-industrial complex.

Once again America's intervention proved decisive. Aided by Allied air power, American, British, French, and Russian armies finally forced Germany to surrender on May 8, 1945. At the same time American sea and air power had turned the tide against Japan in the Pacific. By August 1945, America had advanced to the home islands. President Harry Truman made the decision to drop two newly developed atomic bombs on Hiroshima and Nagasaki to avoid a costly invasion and bring a quick end to the war. Stunned by the desolation that the A-bombs created, Japan surrendered on September 2, 1945. World War II was over.

The Second World War brought about major changes in American social and political life. Many historians regard the war as a turning point in American race relations, a point where blacks were no longer willing to accept discrimination in housing, employment, and even in military service. They took the "war for democracy" seriously and identified their racial demands for reform with this ideal. Black organization of a march on Washington (canceled when Roosevelt met some of their demands) was a symbol of growing militancy. During this period the seeds of the civil rights protest movement of the 1950s and 60s were sown.

Politically, the war marked the end of New Deal reform. "I am not convinced," Roosevelt remarked, "that we can be realists about the war and planners for the future at this critical time." Since the President was the heart of New Deal reform, when the heart stopped the program died. Liberals helped to undermine their own cause and contribute to the conservative resurgence by not opposing the suppression of dissent or even the forced evacuation of Japanese Americans into "relocation camps." A combination of New Deal measures and war direction had given the federal government, and especially the presidency, enormous power and influence over everyday domestic matters as well as foreign policy. That role became an integral part of post-war American society because of public insistence that the government continue providing a social "safety net" and protection against another economic depression.

DOUGLAS MACARTHUR

Douglas MacArthur was born into a military family—his father had won the Medal of Honor in the controversial campaign against the Filipino freedom fighters at the turn of the century. MacArthur graduated at the top of his 1903 West Point class, and served as commander of the famous 42nd "Rainbow" Division in World War I. At the climactic battles that stopped the last German offensive in France, the division suffered 16,500 casualties and MacArthur won the Distinguished Service Cross. By the 1930s the general had become Army Chief of Staff. But his career was marred by the excessive use of force against the Bonus Army of veterans that had marched on Washington for relief during the Depression. MacArthur retired in 1937 and became head of the Philippine defense forces.

By 1941, the Pacific simmered with tension between Japan and the U.S. MacArthur was brought out of retirement in Manila to command Americans and Filipinos preparing to resist Japanese expansionism. Most leaders in Washington were confident that if war broke out the U.S. would quickly triumph. But the Japanese hadn't lost a war since 1598, and the attack on Pearl Harbor was quickly followed by a massive assault on the Philippines. MacArthur's small forces were driven back to a tiny, rocky island in Manila Bay—Corregidor. President Roosevelt felt he couldn't spare a commander of MacArthur's caliber, so he ordered the general to escape to Australia by PT boat and submarine. His command on Corregidor had to surrender. At least 7000 of them perished on the infamous "death march" to POW camps, and 40 percent of those who survived died in the camps in the months that followed.

When he arrived in Australia, MacArthur swore "I shall return." He and Admiral Nimitz developed the American strategy of "island hopping" that allowed U.S. forces to move toward the Japanese home islands without having to seize every piece of territory the enemy had swallowed in the early months of the war. MacArthur became Supreme Commander of Allied Forces in the Pacific. By 1944 he had retaken the Philippines and on September 2, 1945 he accepted the Japanese surrender on the deck of the battleship Missouri in Tokyo Bay. As occupation commander of Japan with almost total authority to reform Japanese society, MacArthur purged the civil service, abolished the secret police, ended press censorship, ordered land redistribution, wrote a democratic constitution and created a parliamentary government under the figurehead of the emperor. Many consider his work the foundation of modern Japan and credit him with making friends of former enemies.

Now seventy years old, MacArthur had intended to retire. But the North Korean invasion of South Korea put him once again at the center of war, and President Truman made him commander of U.S. and U.N. forces trying to resist this aggression. U.S. troops stopped the invaders at Pusan, and MacArthur launched a bold, risky invasion at Inchon to cut off North Korean forces. It worked, driving the communist forces out of South Korea and sending them fleeing to the Chinese border. Then MacArthur made a serious mistake. He told a concerned President Truman that the Chinese would never intervene, and continued to drive to reunite Korea under the U.N. But the Chinese did cross the border, sending MacArthur's forces into retreat. The angry general called for bombing Manchuria and blockading China. Truman, warned by the State Department and the worried Joint Chiefs that this could start a massive Asian land war, refused. But MacArthur wouldn't keep quiet, writing to the Republican leader in Congress that "there is no substitute for victory." The President fired MacArthur.

The general returned home to an adoring nation. On the steps of San Francisco's city hall he declared, "The only politics I have is contained in a single phrase known well by all of you—God bless America!" In 1952 he delivered the keynote address to the Republican Convention, but it had already determined to choose another famous (and less cantankerous) general as its presidential candidate: Dwight D. Eisenhower. MacArthur's popularity quickly faded. MacArthur retired, served as Chairman of Rand Corporation, and died in 1964 as another Asian conflict rose on the horizon—Vietnam.

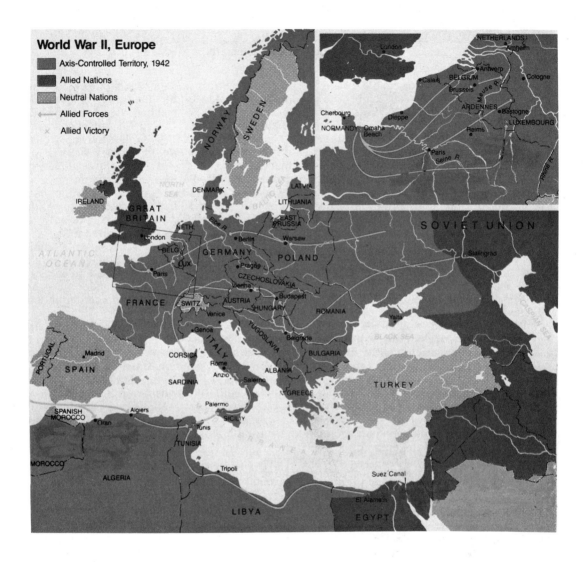

World War II, Europe

Axis-Controlled Territory, 1942

Allied Nations

Neutral Nations

Allied Forces

× Allied Victory

THE SECOND WORLD WAR

American strategy was to throw most of their weight against the Nazis as the more dangerous of the Axis powers and conduct a holding action against the Japanese. As soon as possible, a "second front" was to be opened against Germany in Europe to take the pressure off the Soviet Union, and Hitler's Reich would be squeezed to death. Eventually an "island hopping" strategy was worked out against Japan. Allied forces would bypass some Japanese strong points and seize strategic islands closer and closer to the home islands of the Rising Sun.

1941

Japanese attack Pearl Harbor, surprising and destroying much of the American Pacific fleet and forcing American entry into the Second World War (December).

1942

Fall of the Philippines is only one in a series of devastating advances by the Japanese, who seize most of the western Pacific (May).

Battle of Midway restores the naval balance of power in the Pacific as the Japanese suffer major losses fighting a smaller American force (June).

Invasion of North Africa, the first major Anglo-American offensive against the Nazis, eventually forces German troops from the area (November).

Battle for Guadalcanal turns against the Japanese as the first American offensive in the Pacific starts to show success (November).

Battle for Stalingrad turns against the Germans as the Russians counterattack, eventually capturing an entire Nazi army (November).

1943

Allies invade Italy and knock that Axis country out of the war, but continue to fight German forces there until war's end (September).

1944

D-Day, Normandy—the second front finally opens as Allied troops smash Nazi defenses on the coast and move inland (June).

Battle for Leyte Gulf wipes out the remnants of the Japanese fleet and secures the liberation of the Philippines (October).

Last German offensive fails at the Battle of the Bulge (December).

1945

Germans surrender after the fall of Berlin to the Soviets, who had pushed Nazi troops out of Eastern Europe and had met American forces pushing in from the west (May).

Fall of Okinawa cracks last-ditch Japanese resistance to put Allied forces within invasion reach of the home islands (June).

Atomic bombs dropped on Hiroshima and Nagasaki, causing over 250,000 casualties and forcing the Japanese to surrender (August).

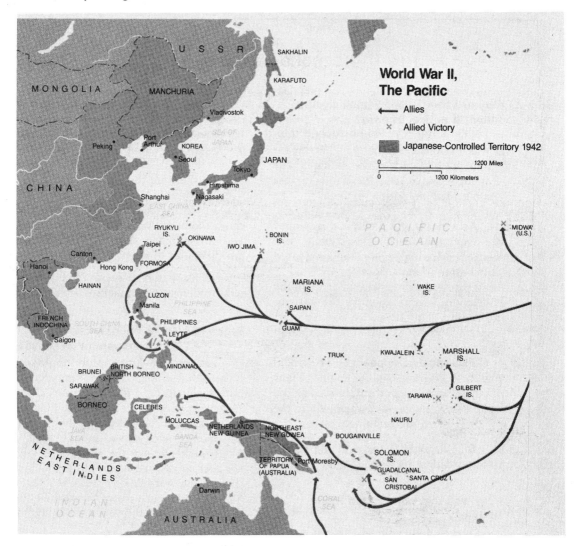

**World War II,
The Pacific**

← Allies

× Allied Victory

■ Japanese-Controlled Territory 1942

COLD WAR ORIGINS

Americans also expected that the Allied victory over the Axis would usher in an age of national security and world peace under American and United Nations guardianship. The United States was now ready, as it had not been after the First World War, to take responsibility for shaping the post-war world and for seeing that peace was maintained. Most Americans now felt that their nation's retreat from international leadership in the 20s and 30s had created a vacuum for fascists who had ignited a Second World War. "Never again" now had a new meaning. American plans for the post-war world continued the commitment to mission principles of democracy, opportunity and civil liberties.

An awesome product of the partnership between science and government was the mushroom cloud that appeared over Japan in August 1945. The development of atomic weaponry inaugurated a new age that required a heightened sense of human restraint and responsibility. The alternative remains nuclear holocaust. (United States Air Force.)

Unfortunately, Soviet priorities were different. Even during the war, the Soviets had been deeply suspicious of Anglo-American moves. Stalin had resented the decision not to open a "second front" to relieve the Soviet army until 1944. As the Axis threat that had cemented the alliance together receded, cracks began opening that endangered post-war harmony. All of the Allies wanted the restoration of world peace and security, but the Soviets viewed security in a somewhat different light. Russia had been invaded twice in a generation by the Germans through Poland, and Moscow was determined not only to destroy German power but also to retain dominance over eastern Europe. By early 1945 the Soviets had occupied much of eastern Europe in the process of pushing back the Nazis.

This "sphere of influence" approach was unacceptable to the United States without freely elected governments. However, the U.S. needed Russia to come into the war against Japan in order to prevent the Japanese from reinforcing their armies that would defend the home islands against an American invasion. The Yalta conference in February traded Moscow's promise to fight Japan for some Asian territorial gains. Washington did not insist on detailed resolutions of the growing disagreements over post-war Europe. FDR, however, was not overly concerned. He felt he could "handle" Stalin.

Stalin gave him reason to regret this. Since the Slavic states were traditionally cool if not hostile toward Russia, Stalin forced upon them communist governments friendly to Moscow. Only Yugoslavia, which had beaten the Germans on its own, was able to set up a communist regime that was nationalist in character and not subordinate to Moscow.

In the last of a series of wartime conferences, Churchill, Roosevelt, and Stalin met at Yalta to hammer out the shape of post-war Europe. Soon after, the Soviets violated the provision calling for free elections in Eastern Europe. Though it has been charged that FDR was hoodwinked by the wily Russian dictator, Churchill himself later recorded that "Our hopeful assumptions were soon to be falsified. Still, they were the only ones possible at the time." (Courtesy of Brown Brothers.)

When the war ended the Nazi threat, disagreements widened. Washington wanted to end Allied occupation of Germany and reunite the Russian occupied Eastern zone with the Anglo-American Western zone. Moscow was determined to strip its zone of resources and organize it into another puppet state. America demanded that Russia live up to its promises to permit free elections in Eastern Europe. The Soviet Union countered that since elections would not result in friendly governments to which they were entitled for security reasons, there would be no elections. Stalin, wrote the American ambassador to Russia, could not understand America's stand on a principle: "It is difficult for him to understand why we should want to interfere with Soviet policy . . . unless we have some ulterior motive." The Soviet government could not forget the American "occupation" of Vladivostok and Archangel in 1918, nor America's refusal to deal with Russia until 1933. The United States could not forget Moscow's suppression of pro-western groups in Poland—a direct violation of its promises. Neither side trusted the other, and neither side would yield. An "iron curtain," in Winston Churchill's words, slammed down between eastern and western Europe.

Washington now faced the problem of developing a new policy to deal with the emerging East-West struggle. Hope for peace through collective security in the United Nations now faded, since the U.S.S.R. could veto any U.N. move in the Security Council. United States policymakers realized they did not have the diplomatic power to "enforce" mission principles without resorting to war. And war, after the first flash of atomic fire over Hiroshima, now threatened death on a scale that could dwarf the millions of dead from World War II. So they adopted a policy of "long-term, patient but firm and vigilant containment of Russian expansive tendencies" that would support America's principles short of an armed conflict.

CONTAINMENT ABROAD AND AT HOME

Containment's first test was in Greece and Turkey. When the British warned Washington in 1947 that they could no longer help Greece fight off a communist revolt or counter Soviet threats against Turkish territory, President Truman announced that the United States would take over British responsibilities. "I believe it must be," he said, "the policy of the United States to support free peoples who are resisting attempted subjugation by armed minorities or by outside pressures."

This Truman Doctrine provided a model for the Marshall Plan, which was designed to revive the nations of western Europe and thereby prevent the ominous growth of the communist parties that were thriving as a result of post-war economic stagnation. When Russian-supported communists took over Czechoslovakia and the Soviets began a blockade of Berlin, America participated in the creation of the North Atlantic Treaty Organization (NATO) as a military alliance against communism in 1948. For the time being, the "Free World's" position in Europe appeared secure.

But the Cold War was not only transforming the U.S. role abroad. It was also making major changes in America. First, it meant that the emphasis on meeting military requirements for national defense that had dominated government during World War II would continue under the headings of "preparedness" and "deterrence." Despite America's historic suspicion of standing armies in peacetime, the large military establishment built during the conflict did not dissolve as it had after World War I. Not only was the draft continued, but military strategy played a dominant role in containing communism, thereby expanding the influence of the armed forces in Washington from its new headquarters in the Pentagon. This constituted a milestone in American attitudes toward the military.

Developments in Asia seemed to justify this larger role. Chinese communists, who had been fighting with the Nationalist government since the 1920s, gained the upper hand in the post-war devastation. In 1949, despite enormous American economic assistance, the decaying Chinese nationalist government fell to Mao Tse-tung's Red Army. Although the United States refused to recognize Mao's forces and continued to regard the nationalists now holed up on the island of Taiwan as the legitimate government, China went communist. The long and bitter debate over this event revealed that many Americans regarded any communist gain as the result of a global Soviet conspiracy for world domination. The next round occurred in Korea, which had been

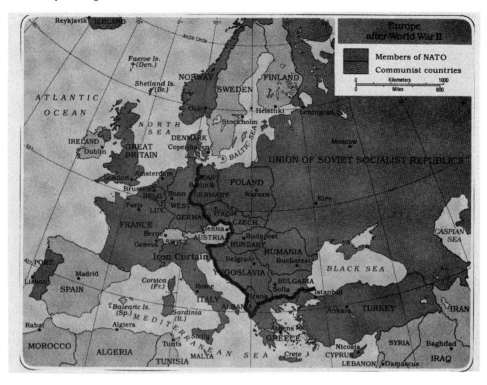

divided after Japan's defeat into a communist northern zone and a pro-western southern zone. Communist North Korea's invasion of South Korea in 1950 caused Washington to quickly extend the policy of containment to Asia. President Truman won United Nations approval for the movement of American forces into Korea to turn back the invasion. When the American effort triggered Chinese intervention and the "police action" became a frustrating stalemate, Washington adopted a "hard line." America opposed Communist China's membership in the United Nations, protected the Nationalist Chinese remnants on their Taiwanese sanctuary, and began containment against the Red Chinese.

The tensions and costs of the Cold War were creeping into the cracks of American society, causing new shifts and splits. Korea renewed fears of a "hot," possibly nuclear confrontation. Despite the fact that economic prosperity and technological advances gave Americans the highest standard of living in the world, people felt little security. A new, "silent generation" emerged. One magazine summed up the ambitions of the younger generation of the fifties by saying that they wanted "a good, secure job with a big firm, and with it, a kind of suburban idyll." Everyone seemed to be concerned with getting "well fixed," complained one writer. Young people were accused of being intellectually "stodgy," of "not speaking out for anything," for never "losing their heads," and for not expecting more out of life. "Youth today," declared one magazine in 1951, "has little cynicism because it never hoped for much." Even the "beatniks," who condemned the "rat race" of American life and dropped out of

THE KOREAN WAR

American strategy, closely tied to United Nations actions, was originally to push the invading North Koreans out of South Korea. But once this was accomplished, the decision was made to try to unify Korea by subduing the north.

1950

North Korea invades the south, expecting a quick victory and believing America would not intervene (June).

United Nations declares North Korea an aggressor and urges member nations to join together and repel the invasion. The United States contributes most of the troops to the U.N. force (June).

U.N. beachhead at Pusan holds despite North Korean attacks, and the North Korean invasion is stalled (September).

Successful landing at Inchon by U.N. forces under General MacArthur catches the invader in the rear, and North Korean troops begin a long retreat (September).

Chinese communist forces intervene and surprise the U.N. army, which had driven nearly to the North Korean-Chinese border. U.N. troops are forced to retreat (November).

1951

U.N. army launches counterattack that recovers most of South Korea and a deadlock occurs near the 38th parallel (January).

Peace talks begin, but fighting continues for two years (July).

1953

Armistice signed at Panmunjon ended the war and set up a demilitarized zone near the North Korean-South Korean border (July).

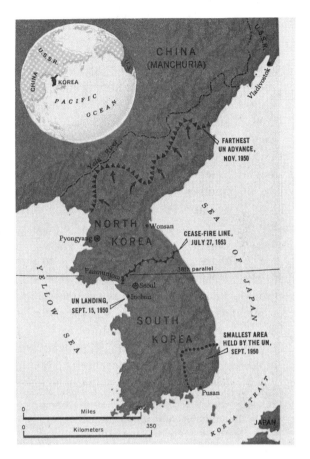

society to places like Greenwich Village in New York were accused of practicing "only another kind of conformism."

One reason for this attitude was that many Americans felt under attack by an insidious communist menace that threatened every aspect of the "American Way." Dissent, criticism, and even ordinary reformism were branded as disloyal or "un-American." The people accused of such activity faced more than social ostracism. Senator Joe McCarthy's angry campaign against those within government and education whom he considered to be "traitors" or "soft on communism" made it highly dangerous even to be "controversial." The Cold War tendency to paint everything in black and white—"Free World" vs. "Iron Curtain" slavery—encouraged the idea that all was well and good in American society. Political conservatism and defense of the status quo dominated the era. Right-wing groups such as the Minutemen militia flourished. This forced reform-minded leaders and the black civil rights movement to face even more determined opposition than they might otherwise have had.

The political scene was affected in other ways by the "crisis politics" of the Cold War. Every effort was made to build a "bipartisan" foreign policy so that America could stand united against foreign threats. The precedents set by Roosevelt during World War II, combined with the need to respond quickly to emerging crises anywhere in the world contributed to the further growth of presidential power and Congressional willingness to allow that growth. Another result of Soviet-American antagonism was the expansion of an intelligence community responsible for espionage abroad and surveillance of "un-American" groups at home. These agencies, including the Central Intelligence Agency (CIA) and the Federal Bureau of Investigation (FBI), employed 200,000 persons by the early 1960s. They operated in secrecy and had budgets practically invulnerable to Congressional scrutiny—an "invisible government" functioning largely outside public knowledge or control. The CIA became deeply involved in covert activities against governments regarded as pro-communist in Iran (1953), Guatemala (1954) and Indonesia (1958).

At the same time, the continued need for new weapons and more equipment made the war industries that had grown up during World War II a permanent feature of the American economy. Cooperation between business and government also continued, and soaring defense requirements gave the military and business common interests. Equipment needed by the military drew automatic support from industries seeking profitable contracts for themselves. Income from these contracts became the lifeblood of over one hundred corporations, just as the material produced became essential for the defense establishment. Eventually, this network became so influential that President Eisenhower felt compelled to warn the nation. He declared that the complex's

> *total influence—economic, political, even spiritual—is felt in every city, every state house, every office of the Federal Government. The potential for the disastrous rise of misplaced power exists and will exist. We must never let the weight of this combination endanger our liberties or democratic processes.*

Even the issue of civilian control of the U.S. military, long an American tradition, came up. During the 1950s civilians in the Department of Defense most frequently limited themselves to choosing policy alternatives presented by the Joint Chiefs of Staff. The case of General Douglas MacArthur became a symbol of military-civilian conflict. MacArthur rejected the concept of limited war in Korea and publicly insisted that "there is no substitute for victory." President Truman finally resolved the conflict by removing MacArthur from his command. But the General received a hero's welcome from New York to San Francisco. His solution of "victory" appealed to many Americans frustrated with fighting "brush-fire wars" and tired of maintaining a perpetual state of war readiness when no resolution appeared in sight. To many people, waging a continuous series of "police actions" and coping with crisis after crisis seemed like being caught up in an exhausting "perpetual war for perpetual peace."

THE PROBLEMS OF DIVERSITY

And the world was getting more complicated. By the mid-fifties the Cold War was beginning to assume a new shape. A "Third World" was emerging in Asia, Africa, and the Middle East, made up of former European colonies and native kingdoms. In these areas, nationalist revolutionaries coming to power were primarily concerned with independence, economic progress, and social reform. They tended to be Cold War neutrals, seeking aid for their struggling nations from any power willing to offer it with the fewest "strings" attached. Washington and Moscow competed for influence in the Third World as they had in Europe.

The United States tried to walk a fine line in Africa and the Middle East. Africa was ablaze with the fire of black nationalism, and America tried to insure that the blacks coming to power in former European colonies such as the Congo or in tottering monarchies were not communists. In the strategic Middle East revolution flared in the key nation of Egypt. The United States had hoped to woo the Arab nations of the area and secure oil supplies and trade routes there, but Arab nationalists distrusted America. Washington was an ally of Britain and France, nations with imperialist records in the Middle East. In addition, the United States supported the infant nation of Israel, which most Arabs hated as an intrusion into lands rightfully theirs. Even when America restrained Britain, France, and Israel in their assault on Egypt during the crisis over the Suez Canal in 1956, the Arabs refused to applaud. Instead, Soviet influence in the area seemed to grow along with the growth of militant Arab nationalism. The United States intervened in the late fifties to prevent "revolutionary takeovers" in Lebanon and Jordan under the new "Eisenhower Doctrine," an extension of Truman's commitment to halt the fall of governments favorable to America.

Developments like these in the Third World were breaking down the "bipolar" character of world relations (characterized by firm East-West divisions) and creating a situation where the superpowers had to respond to diverse demands, interests, and ideologies. They found that this diversity presented problems even in their own spheres of influence. The Soviet Union had to deal with Yugoslav independence, deteriorating relations with Red China, Polish unrest, and even a revolt in Hungary in 1956. It became clear that, if it ever had been, the communist bloc was no longer united. National differencesoutweighedcomradeship.TheUnitedStateshadfrustratingproblemswithitscontrary NATOally,France.Closertohome,WashingtonhadtocopewiththefalloutfromFidelCastro's overthrowoftherepressiveCubangovernmentin1959.Initially,Castrohadseemedfriendlyto America. But he quickly embraced communism and the Soviets, threatening to export revolution to the rest of Latin America. The United States tried to stop this "Castro contagion" by invading Cuba using anti-Castro Cuban exiles at the Bay of Pigs in 1961. The invasion was an embarrassing failure, but this did not end the confrontation. A year later, American U2 spy planes discovered that the Soviet Union had tried to sneak offensive missiles into Cuba. President Kennedy reacted firmly, demanding that the missiles be withdrawn and instituting a blockade of the island. As Soviet supply ships and submarines approached Cuba, the world seemed poised on the brink of nuclear war. But the Soviets backed down. Kennedy was cheered in America, and Premier Khrushchev was eventually ousted from the Kremlin leadership.

The Cuban Missile Crisis had two important consequences. The confrontation sobered both superpowers. Earlier talk of "peaceful coexistence" and competition short of direct clashes was renewed and bore fruit in the Nuclear Test Ban Treaty of 1963. This pact limited atomic weapons testing to underground sites. President Johnson and the new Moscow leadership held a series of low level talks to explore detente (a relaxation of tensions) further, but the Vietnam quagmire preoccupied Washington. Secondly, the events in Cuba and the situation in Latin America illustrated an awkward foreign policy problem for the United States. If Washington supported colonial or conservative regimes (as it had in China), it risked seeing them fall to more popular national revolutionaries. If it supported the revolutionaries (as it did initially in Cuba), it risked seeing them "go communist" (as Castro had). Cuba seemed to confirm an existing tendency in American foreign policy to prop up conservative regimes, who could be counted on to support containment, rather than chance "losing" another nation to the communists.

VIETNAM AND THE END OF CONTAINMENT

No example better illustrates this decision and its tragic consequences than the American commitment to Vietnam.

This commitment began under President Truman, in the shadow of the Korean War. The French had been fighting a colonial conflict in Indochina against a nationalist-communist coalition led by Ho Chi Minh since 1947. Seriously in need of American money and equipment, the French insisted that they, too, were fighting against the expansion of communism. Responding to China's aid to Ho's Vietminh, the United States began backing the French. By the time of the Eisenhower administration, Washington was underwriting 80 percent of the French war costs.

Nevertheless, the popular Vietminh inflicted a decisive defeat on French forces in 1954 at Dien Bien Phu. Desirous of a graceful exit, Paris turned the entire situation over to a convention of concerned nations at Geneva. The Geneva accords provided for the temporary separation of Vietnam into northern (controlled by the Vietminh) and southern (controlled by the French) zones pending a free election scheduled for 1956. The United States, though not a participant, assured the convention that it would not interfere with the settlement.

France promptly left the area, turning her zone over to a Vietnamese government favorable to the West. Washington hoped this regime might counter Ho's influence and keep at least part of Vietnam from becoming communist. Eisenhower's decision to aid the new regime in South Vietnam against insurgent Vietcong guerrillas reflected his outlook that "brush wars" were all part of the communist attempt to subvert the underdeveloped nations of the world. Vietnam, in particular, was felt to be the geopolitical key to Southeast Asia. According to the "domino" theory, if it fell to the communists so would the whole area. Eisenhower's administration supported the South Vietnamese government when it refused to hold the 1956 elections, which almost certainly would have resulted in a Vietminh victory. This action caused a renewal of the struggle for power in Southeast Asia in 1958 between the Vietminh and American-backed forces. The fighting spread outside Vietnam into neutral Laos and Cambodia with the Vietminh (renamed the Vietcong after Ho consolidated his communist state in North Vietnam) slowly gaining the upper hand.

By 1960 it was clear the South Vietnamese, divided and weakened by government corruption, were losing. Faced with the likelihood of South Vietnam's fall in 1962, President Kennedy extended the U.S. commitment by greatly increasing American aid and raising the number of military "advisors" there to nearly 16,000. Confronted by another crisis just a year later, Kennedy was in the process of deciding whether to limit America's role or to extend it even further when he was assassinated.

President Johnson had said in the 1964 election that American troops would not be sent to fight in Vietnam, but in 1965 he chose massive escalation of the war rather than see the Saigon regime collapse. By steadily increasing American air, naval, and land forces in Vietnam, Johnson expected North Vietnam and the Vietcong to have to give up the struggle because the cost would be too great. Yet despite the presence of a half million American servicemen and escalating spending of nearly 20 million dollars a day, the Vietcong and portions of the North Vietnamese Army were able to hold their own.

The war was no longer a distant guerrilla conflict on the edge of the country's attention. War costs were putting an enormous strain upon the economy. President Johnson chose to continue his expensive "war on poverty" while vastly increasing military spending for the Vietnam war without raising taxes. America could afford both "guns and butter," Johnson maintained. While the increased spending created more jobs and offered fatter defense contracts to many industries, it also caused a rampant inflation in prices and huge budget deficits. Inflation drove up the price of American goods, creating a balance of payments deficit for the first time in U.S. history. Neither an increase in taxes nor budget cuts, such as were made in the space program, seemed to be able to stem inflation.

Political and social reaction to the war was even more far-reaching in its consequences. As the 1950s faded into the 60s, the "silent generation" did a turnabout. Invigorated by the challenge of President Kennedy's Peace Corps and angered by conservative white opposition

Although the war was half a world away, it was brought home daily by the media to the American people. Televised newscasts and a free press depicting the inhumanity of war made a major contribution to the antiwar movement. (Donald McCullin/Magnum.)

THE VIETNAM WAR

American strategy was to defend South Vietnam and fight a war of attrition that would presumably convince the communists to negotiate. When it became clear that the North Vietnamese were prepared to take higher casualties than Americans were, the strategy changed. "Vietnamization" was designed to turn the fighting over to the South Vietnamese and end the American role, or at least limit it to air and naval support.

1961

Direct U.S. military aid is given to the South Vietnamese for the first time, although a civil war between the South Vietnamese government and Viet Cong guerrillas had been going on since 1958 (December).

1962

Strategic hamlet program is launched to provide security for villagers and begin social and economic reforms. It was supposed to take support away from the Vietcong, but the reforms were not carried out and the program failed (February).

1963

Kennedy increases U.S. "advisors" to over 16,000 by the end of the year, but the Viet Cong continue to gain support and control over many rural areas.

1964

U.S. naval destroyers fired upon by North Vietnamese PT boats under circumstances that are still not clear. In the Tonkin Gulf resolution Congress gave President Johnson permission to use military force in the area (August).

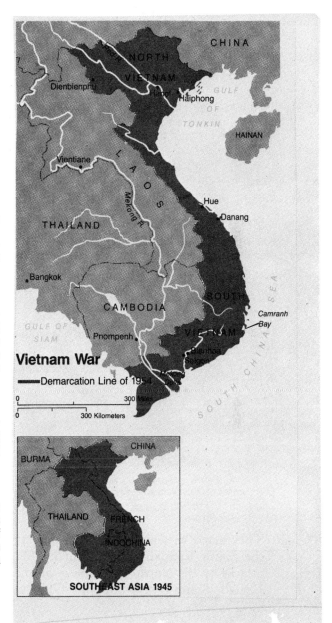

Vietnam War

Demarcation Line of 1954

SOUTHEAST ASIA 1945

1965

U.S. Air Force begins bombing of North Vietnam (February).

U.S. Army buildup begins, and American forces are committed to offensive combat (March).

American forces win a series of victories and lead the commanding U.S. general to say "The enemy's hopes are bankrupt."

1968

Communist Tet offensive hits nearly every major city in South Vietnam and destroys the Johnson administration's credibility. The Viet Cong suffer huge losses, and the North Vietnamese army carries the brunt of the war afterward (January).

1969

Peace talks open between the U.S. and the North Vietnamese in Paris (January).

Nixon administration begins withdrawals of U.S. forces under the policy of "Vietnamization" (July).

1970

U.S. troops invade Cambodia to destroy communist bases, turning the conflict into the Indochina War (April).

1971

South Vietnamese forces invade Laos with heavy American support but little success in destroying communist supply lines (February).

Major North Vietnamese invasion of the south is halted with extensive American air support (March).

Last U.S. ground forces leave South Vietnam, and Vietnamization is pronounced a "success" (August).

Massive bombing of Hanoi and Haiphong brings North Vietnamese back to the stalled peace talks (December).

1973

Peace agreement signed, ending the American role in the war but not bringing peace to Indochina (January).

1975

Powerful North Vietnamese invasion launched which leads to the fall of South Vietnam and Cambodia (April).

to the black civil rights movement, many young Americans joined the effort to aid impoverished foreigners abroad and persecuted minorities at home. There was a new idealism, sparked in general by the contradiction between the promise of American life and the reality of poverty, discrimination, and alienation. Impatient for the political system to act on these problems, students and other reformers turned to dramatic protests. Using tactics developed during the civil rights struggle, they initiated petitions, strikes, sit-ins, marches, and other demonstrations to dramatize their grievances. The Free Speech Movement at the University of California at Berkeley in 1964 quickly spread to other campuses as students demanded a larger voice in college rules and curriculum. But the key issue after 1965 quickly became the war in Vietnam.

Those against the war ("doves") staged their first big protest at the Pentagon in October of 1967. Americans who supported the war effort ("hawks"), however, cited reports from Saigon that the conflict was being won. But in early 1968 the "demoralized" Vietcong and North Vietnamese launched the massive Tet offensive, striking thirty provincial capitals in the South. Although this stroke ultimately failed, the Johnson administration suffered a major blow to its credibility. Casualties continued to mount, and television brought the ugly brutality of the struggle nightly into American living rooms.

That spring, President Johnson announced an end to the bombing, the beginning of peace negotiations in Paris and his own withdrawal from the 1968 presidential race. Richard Nixon, campaigning for "law and order" at home and "peace with honor" abroad, won the election.

The incoming Nixon administration, faced with spreading domestic polarization over the Vietnam War, adopted a policy of "Vietnamization." American casualties would be cut by withdrawal of combat troops while American air and naval power increased its support for a strengthened South Vietnamese Army. It was expected that a battered North Vietnam would agree to American proposals for "peace with honor" before the withdrawal of United States forces was complete. But despite an invasion of its Cambodian and Laotian sanctuaries in 1970 and 1971, and despite massive bombing of the North and even the mining of Haiphong harbor, Hanoi's forces hung on to their positions in the South.

The domestic scene exploded in May of 1970 after President Nixon, who had promised to wind down the war, widened it instead by invading neutral Cambodia. Hundreds of thousands of demonstrators took to the streets in protests scarred by mounting violence. Four students died at the hands of nervous National Guardsmen at Kent State, Ohio and two more students were shot in their dorms by police at Jackson State in Mississippi. Still the crisis deepened. By 1971 more than 30,000 draft resisters had fled to Canada. Polls showed the war was polarizing the country. In order to prevent tens of thousands of angry demonstrators from paralyzing Washington, D.C., the Nixon administration resorted to unlawful mass arrests and detention. The publication of the "Pentagon Papers" by the *New York Times* revealed that the government had been practicing concealment and deception upon its own people regarding the war since the 1960s.

In an effort to get the stalled peace talks going again and force a treaty that would release American prisoners of war, President Nixon ordered the massive bombing of North Vietnam in December 1972. By January, a peace agreement was reached. Called "peace with honor," it in fact simply allowed the American role in the war to end, released the American POWs, and left the fighting to the Vietnamese. In April of 1975, the North Vietnamese launched a powerful offensive which, in the absence of American action, crushed both South Vietnam and Cambodia. Over 140,000 refugees were evacuated by the United States, and the grim vise of poverty and oppression caused the flight of tens of thousands of others over the next eight years.

The postmortem was sobering. More than one and a half million Indochinese were dead, and a third of the forests of Vietnam had been destroyed by defoliation. Over six million tons of explosives had been dropped by American aircraft—nearly three times the tonnage showered on Japan and Germany during World War II. Almost 56,000 American servicemen had died in this longest of American wars, which had also cost the nation at least $150 billion. The inflationary wage-price spiral continued upward—even wage and price controls failed to stop it.

Yet the most profound consequences were difficult to quantify. Americans had not been so angrily divided since the Civil War, and the wounds were slow to heal. The armed forces themselves were severely demoralized, and veterans returned to nervous silence or outright hostility. Johnson's "Great Society" died in the mud of Vietnam, as Wilson's progressivism and Roosevelt's New Deal had died in the two world wars. Nixon squandered his political possibilities in winning a transient "peace with honor," and, in an attempt to plug "national security leaks" after the Pentagon Papers affair, began the illegal wiretaps and break-ins that led inexorably to Watergate. The powers of the executive branch of government were limited by an aroused Congress. Future presidents would find their ability to commit American military forces abroad restricted by the War Powers Act of 1973. Abuses committed by the FBI and the CIA in their zeal for national security resulted in their covert activities being restricted by Congress.

The Vietnam War also had a profound influence on American foreign policy. Washington had to adjust its decisions to the fact that most Americans sensed that the nation's commitments (375 major bases and one million overseas troops to protect 47 countries) overextended its power. As the Depression had ruined the credibility of the business community in the 1930s, so Vietnam damaged the prestige and power of the military in Washington. Few people now believed that a crisis in some corner of the world justified United States military intervention. The policy of containment suffered a mortal blow. Defense spending as a percentage of the nation's GNP declined, pressed by inflation and domestic spending. Successive governments would have to deal with a "Vietnam complex" that included a less trusting public, a more scrutinizing press, and a greater sense of the limits of American power.

DETENTE

The Vietnam conflict had pushed an older and deeper concern into the background—the fear of a nuclear war. This anxiety had begun in the early 1950s after both the United States and the Soviet Union had exploded massive hydrogen bombs and the word "fallout" began to creep into society's vocabulary. For awhile, civil defense flourished in an atmosphere filled with ads for $3000 "Mark I Kiddee Kokoon" shelters and even lead girdles. Fears turned ugly as some stocked their bunkers with weapons to fight off less provident neighbors on "H-Day." Then the anxiety seemed to recede as the danger of nuclear war became accepted, with physicists talking about mega-tonnage and Pentagon contingency planners calculating "megadeaths" (multiple millions of casualties).

But a series of crises in the 1960s renewed the terror of an atomic holocaust. American use of the U2 spy plane over the Soviet Union knocked President Eisenhower's hopes of reducing tensions aside. The Berlin Wall Crisis in 1961 and the Cuban Missile Crisis in 1962 made it clear that nuclear war could be initiated by stubbornness or miscalculation. While the Nuclear Test Ban Treaty of 1963 quieted alarm over the deadly dangers of fallout from atmospheric testing, on several occasions during the Vietnam War policymakers worried that American action against North Vietnam might trigger a Russian or a Chinese response.

President Nixon and special advisor for foreign affairs, Dr. Henry Kissinger, made plans to replace the policy of containment and lessen the danger of a confrontation. Acknowledging the necessity of opposing Soviet "adventures" outside their sphere of influence, Kissinger nevertheless saw that the United States could not hope to be a lone "free" pole in a no longer bipolar world. Instead, he sought to play "balance of power" politics. This would use American influence to maintain a complex but peaceful status quo while retaining more freedom of action, choosing which troublespots required a U.S. response.

Nixon and Kissinger saw that pursuing detente with Red China might allow the United States to use a three-cornered balance of power diplomacy with the two hostile communist giants. In May of 1972, President Nixon shocked the world by visiting China and opening the way for normal relations with that state for the first time since 1949. Shortly thereafter, Nixon became the first American president to visit the Soviet Union. There he signed a landmark Strategic Arms Limitation Treaty (SALT) that placed an upper limit on the numbers of American and Russian Intercontinental Ballistic Missiles (ICBMs). Nixon's and Soviet Premier Brezhnev's bear hug for the TV cameras in Moscow nearly obscured the fact that both nations still held tenaciously to their spheres of influence. The Kremlin had brutally crushed a liberal communist regime in Czechoslovakia in 1968, and the United States used the CIA to undermine and topple a legally elected communist government in Chile. Nevertheless, detente seemed to be producing a real relaxation of world tension, and there were great hopes for the future.

President Carter attempted to continue detente and reemphasize the American tradition of championing human rights. Carter improved America's post-Vietnam image in the Third World by promoting black majority rule in Southern Africa, backing the rights of Palestinian Arabs to a "homeland" in part of the territory held by Israel since the 1967 Arab-Israeli War, and securing the passage of the Panama Canal Treaty of 1977. His greatest success was at Camp David, Maryland in 1978, where by risky personal diplomacy he cajoled Israel and Egypt to make peace. Moreover, President Carter improved American relations with China and pursued detente with the Russians vigorously.

The Camp David Accords, signed by President Carter, Begin of Israel, and Sadat of Egypt, in 1978, were heralded as a breakthrough in the search for a wider peace. (Collection, Carter Presidential Materials Project, National Archives and Record Services.)

COLD WAR'S END

Moscow, however, seemed less interested. Soviet use of Cuban troops to back communist revolts in Angola and Ethiopia so strained Russian-American relations that the laboriously negotiated SALT II agreement was in danger of rejection by the United States Senate. Many Americans had already grown suspicious of the massive Soviet military buildup which had been underway since 1970. When the Kremlin aided the Marxist Sandinista revolt in Nicaragua and invaded Afghanistan in December of 1979, it not only killed the treaty, it buried detente. An angry Carter halted grain and high-technology sales to Russia, called for a boycott of the 1980 Olympics in Moscow, and issued the "Carter Doctrine." This statement promised that the United States would protect the Persian Gulf area from any outside interference, even by the use of force if necessary. American attention had already been focused on the area by the Iranian Revolution after Muslim fundamentalists had seized the American embassy there and held its staff hostage. The frustration over the hostage crisis and the failed military rescue attempt seemed to exemplify the frustration of the nation with the Carter presidency. He was badly beaten by Ronald Reagan in the 1980 election. As a final blow, the Iranians did not release the hostages until after Reagan's inauguration in January 1981.

President Reagan entered the White House determined to revive American military power and international prestige. Detente, he said, had to be a "two way street," and he believed that the Soviets had been enjoying most of the benefits of Western trade and international restraint without showing restraint themselves. Reagan returned to the harsh rhetoric of the Cold War, calling the Soviet Union an "evil empire" contemptuous of human rights. Soviet destruction of a Korean civilian airliner that had wandered into their airspace and the death of 267 innocent people dramatized this claim.

Reagan accelerated a military buildup begun in the Carter years, spending $1.5 trillion by 1986 to enlarge and modernize U.S. forces. Declaring that his administration would "fight fire with fire," the president backed Contra rebels in Nicaragua, mujahedin guerrillas in Afghanistan and opposition forces in Angola. He also challenged terrorists, cutting off "sponsor states" like Syria and Iran and ordering the bombing of some bases in Libya in 1986. Many of these efforts were successful, but there were failures: the collapse of the U.S. effort to stabilize Lebanon in 1984 and, most importantly, the Iran-Contra Affair. This effort by the Reagan administration to sell arms to Iran to win release of Western hostages in Lebanon while channeling the profits to the Contras in Nicaragua set off a scandal that rivaled Watergate.

Ironically, this "Cold Warrior" presided over the beginning of the end of the longstanding Soviet-American schism. The new Soviet leader, Mikhail Gorbachev, promised glasnost (openness), perestroika (restructuring the system), and reconciliation of East and West. The burden of maintaining a huge military establishment and far-flung client states from Cuba to Vietnam was breaking the Soviet economy. Afghanistan was abandoned. Negotiations to eliminate intermediate range nuclear forces in Europe (the INF Treaty) and cut thousands of strategic warheads (the START talks) began to bear fruit. The White House and the Kremlin began to work out compromises to end cold war confrontations in Cambodia, Angola, and Nicaragua. The United Nations Security Council began to become what its founders had envisioned: a forum to work for world peace.

But the real breakthrough came during the Bush presidency. Gorbachev's policies had raised expectations in the USSR and its satellites. By 1989 demands for reform reached a crescendo, and when Gorbachev renounced Soviet control every Eastern European state broke loose and rejected communism. Even the infamous Berlin Wall fell, and by 1990 Germany was reunited. NATO and the Warsaw Pact began to demilitarize their frontier. START I was signed, cutting each side's huge arsenal by 30 percent. Finally, after the failure of an "Old Guard" coup in Moscow, the Communist Party lost its hold on power. On Christmas day, 1991, the Soviet Union itself ceased to exist.

The end of the Cold War came with such rapidity that people were stunned. But journalists and historians immediately began to probe the smoldering ruins of the conflict's assumptions. Many believed that the conflict was unnecessarily deepened and extended by overestimating the threat from a Soviet Union battered by an anemic economy and drained by grasping client states. These critics contend that the price of emphasizing U.S. military readiness was neglected schools, decayed cities, disintegrated roads, and a mountainous debt that dragged down the economy. They also note how the struggle poisoned the climate for reform, from Joe McCarthy to Rush Limbaugh, by labeling strong proposals for change "un-American"—or worse. Other observers note that Pentagon spending laid the foundation for innovative aerospace, communications, and electronics industries by subsidizing research and development for guaranteed markets.

Declassified government reports show that the 1960 U2 overflight of the USSR was part of a regular program that sent American aircraft over Russian airspace to test defenses and spy—a program that led to captivity for U.S. airmen who may still be lost in the Siberian Gulag. On the other hand, KGB files now open to investigators show that the USSR planned and pushed the North Korean attack on South Korea, treated American POWs from the Korean and Vietnam war brutally, and sought to secretly improve its strategic position in Grenada, Nicaragua, and Cuba. When asked if the U.S. irresponsibly exaggerated the Soviet threat, prolonging the Cold War, former Reagan Secretary of Defense Caspar Weinberger snapped: "You should always use a worst-case analysis in this business. You can't afford to be wrong. In the end, we won the Cold War, and if we won by too much, if it was overkill, so be it."

A NEW WORLD ORDER?

At first, the collapse of communism seemed to augur a new "American Century." In 1989, seeking to bring dictator Manuel Noriega to heel, the Bush administration ordered the invasion of Panama. Success there was followed by the defeat of the Sandinistas in Nicaraguan elections and the end of the long Salvadoran civil war. Throughout the late '80s and early 1990s, nations from Brazil to Kampuchea (the former Cambodia) threw out repressive regimes and embarked on experiments in democratic capitalism. The U.S. military was recovering from years of post-Vietnam mediocrity and disorganization. More money was provided for basics like spare parts, realistic training exercises, and upgraded salaries and benefits. Investments were made in hi-tech weapons like the radar-foiling stealth warplanes, the Patriot anti-missile system, and "smart bombs" that could be guided to their targets by computer. The men and women who stuck with the military in the dog days after Vietnam were determined to build a force they and the nation could be proud of.

Then the Middle East blew up again, this time on the Persian Gulf. Iraq, left with a huge debt and a powerful army after the end of its eight-year conflict with Iran, invaded oil-rich Kuwait in August 1990. Freed from Cold War division, the U.S. and Russia joined in the United Nations Security Council call for Iraq's withdrawal and a total embargo against Baghdad. When this failed to move Iraq's dictator (Saddam Hussein), the UN threatened war. President Bush assembled an international coalition of European and even Arab forces to confront Iraqi aggression. But he had trouble convincing a skeptical American public that Kuwaiti oil and the Iraqi program to develop a nuclear weapon justified war until Saddam played into Allied hands with his brutal treatment of Kuwaitis and other captured foreigners. When Iraqi forces dug in instead of withdrawing, the Allied coalition, led by the U.S., launched an attack.

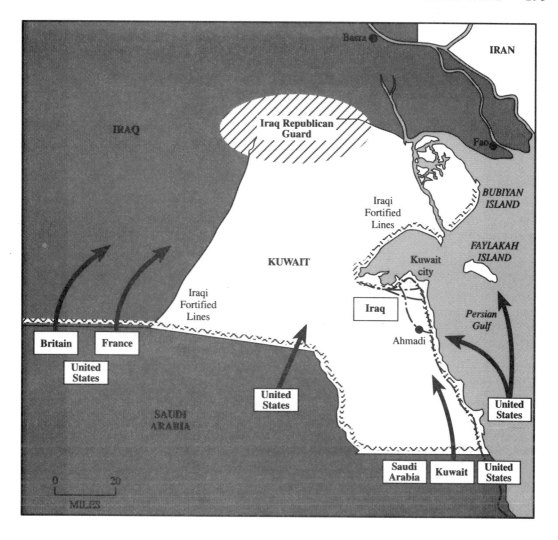

In the Gulf War, aided by a dictator who squandered his assets and played to American strengths, the military shone. The complex, expensive weapons worked, the sophisticated "Air-Land battle" tactics succeeded spectacularly, and the troops performed with solid professionalism. U.S. policy of restricting press coverage to escorted pools and censoring battlefield reports made the battlefield news upbeat. TV images of bombs going right through the windows of target buildings led some commentators to call the conflict the "Nintendo war." The problems—excessive casualties from "friendly fire" and difficulties getting intelligence quickly enough to keep up with the pace of the war—were shrugged off. Even those at home who protested that "war was no substitute for an energy policy" insisted that they supported U.S. troops. After a month of pounding from coalition air forces, Allied troops swept into Iraq and Kuwait, routing the enemy. Public confidence in the armed forces soared from a low 23 percent in 1977 to 78 percent after

THE GULF WAR

American strategy was to seize control of the air and batter Iraq's industry, infrastructure, and ground forces with "smart" weapons like cruise missiles. Then, using the "AirLand" battle techniques of coordinated, rapid moves, beat the elite Iraqi Guard units and cut off the rest of the Iraqi army in Kuwait.

1990

August 2—*Iraq seizes Kuwait* despite assurances of peace.

August 8—*President Bush begins the U.S. force buildup* of "Desert Shield" in Saudi Arabia.

August 30—*U.N. condemnation of Iraq* speeds construction of an international coalition to recover Kuwait; a total embargo isolates Baghdad.

1991

January 12—*U.S. Congress authorizes use of force.*

January 16—*"Desert Storm" begins* as U.S.-led air power launches massive attacks against Iraq after UN deadline passes.

January 19—*Iraqi scud missile strikes* against Tel Aviv fail to provoke an Israeli response, which Saddam had hoped would split the Allied coalition.

February 23—*Baghdad rejects U.S. ultimatum* to withdraw from Kuwait; Allied forces kick off ground assault.

February 26—*Allied units smash elite Republican Guard* forces as battered, nearly cut-off Iraqi troops try to flee Kuwait.

February 28—*Iraq accepts the loss of Kuwait* and U.N.-supervised destruction of its nuclear and chemical weapons programs in return for a ceasefire.

---

the Gulf War. It was not much of an exaggeration for President Bush to say that the men and women of Desert Storm "set out to confront an enemy abroad, and in the process they transformed a nation at home."

Triumph in the Gulf conflict led to the first substantive Middle East peace talks since the high hopes of Camp David had been dashed a decade earlier. President Bush hailed these developments as the birth of a "new world order." Taken from the Great Seal of the United States, this phrase was defined by the president as including "peaceful settlements of disputes, solidarity against aggression, reduced and controlled arsenals and just treatment of all peoples." In an ominous warning of things to come, however, the Bush effort to save Somalia from famine and restore civil order there came to grief. And, true to their historic pattern, the American people figured that with the Cold War finished and the Gulf War behind them, they could turn back to domestic concerns. Many were more concerned about the slumping economy and massive

NORMAN SCHWARZKOPF

When Schwarzkopf's father left the family for the front in the dark days of World War II, he brought out his West Point sword and presented it to seven-year-old Norman. Dreams of a military career were further fostered on trips to Iran and Saudi Arabia with his father in the 1940s. Graduated from West Point in the top ten percent of his class, he was invited to return and teach there. But Schwarzkopf wanted a combat command, and when the U.S. role in Vietnam escalated he volunteered to go.

Vietnam changed Schwarzkopf. His first tour in 1965 was what he had hoped it would be. As an advisor to the South Vietnamese Airborne, he worked hard and believed in the U.S. role. "I really felt that I was honestly helping people," Schwarzkopf recalled. But his second tour in 1970 as commander of a battalion was different. In one incident, one of his companies was hit by friendly fire. In another, a company wandered into a minefield and Schwarzkopf, in the process of saving one man, gave an order that killed three. He saw morale and effectiveness deteriorate. "I hated what Vietnam was doing to the United States, and I hated what it was doing to the army." When South Vietnam fell in 1975 he got quietly drunk.

But Schwarzkopf stayed with the army and helped to restore and renovate it in the '80s with a series of jobs at the Pentagon in planning and personnel. He was the deputy commander for the assault on Grenada in 1983, where both the effectiveness of the changes and the glitches were clear. Continued posts in operations and planning led to Schwarzkopf's 1988 appointment to Central Command, whose primary task was to plan for a war in the Middle East. The general and his staff believed the real danger was not from a possible Soviet move, but from a regional conflict that overspilled its boundaries. They focused on Iraq as the biggest threat.

In 1990 war gaming turned real when Iraq invaded Kuwait. Schwarzkopf was given overall command of a force that grew to almost 750,000 troops, hundreds of ships, and thousands of tanks and aircraft from over a dozen countries in the Allied coalition. Schwarzkopf handled the multinational sensibilities, the combined air, land, and sea operations, and the press with exceptional balance and skill that reminded older observers of Eisenhower in World War II. At times the Saudis seemed more concerned about the cultural effects of the American "invasion" than they did about the Iraqis. Schwarzkopf had to remind himself that he "had a lot of guys who could do the military planning, but I was the only one who could assure the Saudis that the Dallas Cowgirls were not going to come over and corrupt the kingdom. . . ." The general's first concern was that he might have to fight the Iraqis with the inadequate forces of Desert Shield. Once that fear had been relieved by Washington's decision to more than double the U.S. force, he was ready to set up the huge air and ground effort code-named Desert Storm. The final victory was stunning. The Iraqi aggression had been turned back at the cost of 155 Allied dead—"Almost miraculous," said the general, though "it will never be miraculous for the families of those people."

Schwarzkopf retired after his triumphal return to the U.S. Asked if he would classify himself as a hawk or a dove, he rejected both. "Maybe I would describe myself as owlish—that is, wise enough to understand that you want to do everything possible to avoid war—that once you're committed to war, [you're] then ferocious enough to do whatever is necessary to get it over as quickly as possible in victory."

"downsizing" (layoffs) by businesses across the country. President Bush, slow to grasp this mood shift, lost reelection in 1992 to Bill Clinton.

Clinton pledged to focus "like a laser beam" on the economy. But the world would not leave him alone: Saddam hung on in Baghdad, periodically caused alarms in Washington with one maneuver or another; North Korea was busy trying to develop nuclear weapons even as its people faced mass starvation; a truck bomb possibly set up by Iranian agents killed 19 American servicemen based in Saudi Arabia, and tensions with China over Taiwan brought an American aircraft carrier into the South China Sea. Even the Dayton Accord which promised peace among factions embroiled in the Bosnian civil war was hanging by a thread despite the deployment of thousands of NATO troops. The Clinton administration seemed to respond to these situations as they arose without any clear overall policy other than to encourage the development of free enterprise and democracy. The outline of any "new world order" remained hazy and ill-defined.

The President worked hard to expand U.S. trade with the North American Free Trade Agreement. But he even found his efforts to promote global economic growth stymied by protesters at the World Trade Organization meeting in Seattle in 1999. The demonstrators expressed resistance to the WTO's lack of consideration for labor, safety and environmental standards.

Multilateral action also seemed bogged down in Europe. There, an effort to defend Albanian Kosovars against Serbian ethnic cleansing with NATO military intervention brought mixed results. While the 1999 operation ejected the Serb army from Kosovo, the post-conflict peace featured vicious attacks by people of both ethnic groups on each other with the NATO peacekeepers caught in the middle. U.S. relations with both Russia and China deteriorated as both countries resisted what they labeled as American hegemony (dominance). The New World Order, widely anticipated at the end of the Cold War and hailed with the Gulf War victory, never materialized.

WAR AND PEACE IN THE TWENTY-FIRST CENTURY

As the twentieth century came to a close, three facts seemed certain to set the framework for American diplomacy.

The first was that the American people remained mostly disinterested in world affairs in the absence of war clouds such as those that gathered over Kosovo in 1999. Only when international issues affected the domestic scene, such as the war on drugs or the jobs vs. free trade debate, did the general public seem to show much interest. The decision to expand NATO into Poland, Hungary, and the Czech Republic to enhance European stability was a good example. President Clinton tried to whip up domestic support by reviving memories of the Marshall Plan to rebuild Europe in 1947, which stabilized the West, boosted U.S. markets, and led to an outpouring of transatlantic good will. But the national response was skeptical. What threatened Europe now that Russia was weak? Why couldn't the Europeans handle their own problems? How much would it cost? While public apathy gave the president a certain freedom in setting foreign policy, it also made getting the necessary backing for any policy—especially one involving spending in the new era of balancing budgets—very difficult.

The second fact is the continuing global tug-of-war between people's instinct to hang on to their traditions and an increasingly interdependent world economy that is challenging those traditions. One observer has referred to this struggle as "tribalism vs. McWorld." Tribalism has not been merely Croat vs. Serb in Bosnia, Catholic vs. Protestant in Northern Ireland, or Hutu vs. Tutsi in Rwanda—religions and ethnic groups at odds. It has also been the resistance of peoples to the tides of change, especially economic change. As the Muslim fundamentalist Taliban seized power in Afghanistan in a crusade against the "corruption" of westernization, the Iranian people overwhelmingly chose a President more open to social liberalization of the fundamentalist regime in Teheran. Even in Europe, the effort to create a common currency (the Euro) has created a backlash in countries like France and Britain where people believe the forces of the free market threaten their political and economic traditions. This struggle has been one of the primary forces making the world a messy place at the close of the century.

The United States has responded to the struggle mostly by siding with McWorld. The Clinton administration's efforts to expand free trade are a major force in creating global economic interdependence. The North American Free Trade Agreement, signed in 1994, linked Canada, Mexico, and the U.S. Agreements in the 1990s to build a more powerful World Trade Organization and a more unified European Union have spawned similar regional efforts in Africa, Asia, and the Pacific Rim. Toyotas are built in America, Pepsi and Coke fight for the soft drink trade in Africa, and McDonald's serves Big Macs in Moscow and Beijing. Secretary of State Madeline Albright has described U.S. policy as bringing as many nations as possible into a system of the rule of law, free trade, and peaceful behavior.

But Washington has still had to respond to the upheavals of tribalism. The military, while still prepared to fight a Gulf-War-style conflict, is shifting its emphasis to smaller scale actions: evacuating American citizens from trouble spots, peacekeeping, fighting terrorism and guerrillas. Fortunately, this trend has coincided with the need to reduce spending under tight budgets. The multi-billion dollar effort to build a workable antimissile defense system has come under fire in the face of crying domestic needs in health, education, and decaying cities. Tens of thousands in the military have been "laid off" in the 1990s and bases at home and abroad have closed. The armed forces are making an effort to improve military intelligence through satellites, unmanned aircraft, and remote sensors that can be linked by computer to eliminate the "fog of war." But the absence of a serious threat or a clear, overall policy has made the role of the American military perhaps the most ill-defined in its long history.

The third fact is the continuing tension in the United States between idealistically promoting human rights abroad and pragmatically pursuing the country's national interests. This tension has been with the country for most of the century, but its nature has changed with the end of the Cold War. For the generation fighting first fascism and then communism, the choice was often between aiding or opposing brutal dictators like the recently overthrown President Mobutu of Zaire (now The Congo) who were on "our side" of the fight. Often,

America sided with the dictators. In the 1990s the choice has been whether to promote human rights or further our economic interests. The clearest case is China, whose repressive communist government also represents the largest market for investment and sales in Asia. Does the United States pursue "business as usual" or restrict trade with China, knowing that other countries with fewer scruples will step in to take advantage? What if China terminates the civil rights of the people of Hong Kong? Can America afford to keep U.S. troops in Bosnia and Kosovo long enough for these devastated areas, boiling with ethnic hatred, to rebuild and achieve a semblance of peace?

The challenge to twenty-first century American diplomacy will be much the same as it was in the twentieth: to protect national interests while continuing to stand for its core values of freedom in an unpredictably dangerous world.

SUGGESTIONS FOR ADDITIONAL READING

William Appleton Williams, *The Tragedy of American Diplomacy,* (1959). An indictment of United States foreign policy for its tendency toward imperialism.

Daniel M. Smith, *The Great Departure: The United States and World War One,* (1965). A study that interprets American participation in the Great War as the result of Wilson's mix of pragmatism and idealism.

George Kennan, *The Realities of American Foreign Policy,* (1966). An analysis of American foreign policy, arguing that the United States should exercise greater restraint and respect in its dealings with other nations.

David Halberstam, *The Best and the Brightest,* (1972). An incisive account of the failure of the architects of America's Vietnam involvement to understand the conflict, highlighting how the bureaucracy tends to suppress data critical of accepted policy.

Robert L. Beisner, *From the Old Diplomacy to the New,* (1975). The shift from the narrow, more defensive 19th century policy to 20th century internationalism.

John E. Wilte, *From Isolation to War: 1931 to 1941,* (1968). The path to Pearl Harbor.

Walter LaFeber, *America, Russia and the Cold War 1945–1980,* (1981). A "big picture" account of the conflict that finds enough blame for both sides to share.

Samuel Eliot Morison, Frederick Merk, and Frank Freidel, *Dissent in Three American Wars,* (1970). An insightful study of the nature and extent of modern American antiwar protest.

George E. Kennan, *The Nuclear Delusion,* (1976). A survey of Soviet-American relations and the fallacy of the nuclear arms race.

Thomas C. Reeves, *The Life and Times of Joe McCarthy,* (1982). An examination of the profound impact of one man on the 1950s American psyche.

Courtesy of Declan Haun from Black Star.

CHAPTER NINE

WE SHALL OVERCOME: THE CRUSADE FOR HUMAN RIGHTS IN AMERICA

1882

Chinese immigration to the United States forbidden by Congress; not lifted until 1943.

1895

Booker T. Washington gives his "Atlanta Compromise" speech, encouraging a gradual approach to black civil rights.

1919

Nineteenth Amendment gives women the right to vote.

1942

Over 70,000 American citizens of Japanese ancestry forcibly evicted from their homes and interned in "relocation camps."

1954

Brown v. the Topeka Board of Education: The Supreme Court declares separation of the races unconstitutional; black civil rights movement accelerates.

1955

Four million Mexican immigrants deported without legal due process, including many American citizens of Mexican descent.

1966

Stokely Carmichael states that black people must look to themselves for improvement, beginning the Black Power movement.

1967

Cesar Chavez and the United Farm Workers begin a nationwide grape boycott to win recognition and better working conditions.

1973

American Indian Movement occupies Wounded Knee to force government action on Indian problems.

1982

Equal Rights Amendment (ERA) defeated by the state legislatures.

1992

The acquittal of L.A. police officers in the brutal beating of black motorist Rodney King results in the South Central Los Angeles riots.

". . . WITH LIBERTY AND JUSTICE FOR ALL"?

Although many Americans would agree that the ideal of equality contained in the Pledge of Allegiance has not been fully realized, they are generally unaware of the pervasive legacy of discrimination in modern times. Despite evidence of lessening prejudice in recent years, it has been argued that racial, ethnic, and sexist discrimination continues to be a harsh reality for many people in American society.

Such attitudes have persisted in the United States, supported not only for economic reasons but by less tangible psychological motives as well. An examination of American history suggests that society has always required that the various minorities keep their "place." Only in this way could uncertainty and fear of them be contained. Thus the history of each "oppressed" group in the American experience has been one of having its position in society defined and, in the process, its rights circumscribed. This process has borne two major results: first, the impact of discrimination has had a profound psychological effect on its victims; second, the official sanction given the exercise of discrimination has simply confirmed and reinforced prejudice.

Adequate attention has only recently been given to the role played by racial minorities and women in America's historical experience. Such an oversight is particularly unfortunate because it cripples our understanding of the nation's development. This is especially troubling in an age that has witnessed such a growing demand for human rights by peoples around the globe.

The drive for human rights has been a major feature of American history during the last century. The goal of its participants may have been the same, but the underlying philosophy propelling the movement and the means employed to secure those rights have shifted through the years. A strategy of accommodation, and working within "the system" was gradually replaced by protest and other extra-Establishment methods such as revolutionary rhetoric and riots. In the process significant successes during the past thirty years of the human rights crusade have moderated the movement as large numbers of America's under-class were mainstreamed. Some glimpses of America's underside can aid us in comprehending the energetic drive of minorities toward full citizenship in the United States.

Although many groups have rallied to this modern crusade, historically African Americans have been in the vanguard of the movement. To a very large extent, it has been their efforts and experiences that have provided a blueprint of inspiration and change for other groups who more recently have seen themselves as the victims of institutional oppression in American life.

FREEDOM AFTER SLAVERY

The process of excluding black men from the rights of American citizenship persisted after the Civil War despite the fact that they had helped fight for the Union. Even passage of the Fourteenth and Fifteenth amendments to the Constitution, which were designed to safeguard those rights, failed to do so. Indeed, during the last three decades of the nineteenth century the Supreme Court handed down a series of decisions that rendered these amendments meaningless. The due process and equal protection clauses of the Fourteenth Amendment were interpreted by the Court very narrowly. The Justices argued that the Federal government had no legal jurisdiction over civil rights violations by individuals or private organizations. Such legal loopholes allowed white supremacists to evade the spirit of the law.

The trend toward the segregation of the races climaxed in the 1896 Supreme Court case *Plessy v. Ferguson.* Stripped of its legal jargon, the conservative, states'-rights-minded Court stated that blacks and whites may be separated. In this way a system of segregation emerged in America, fully sanctioned by the highest court in the land. Furthermore, the legal subordination of African Americans was not simply a regional phenomenon; although Americans often looked disapprovingly upon the South for its Jim Crow laws, it should be noted that seven of the nine justices who decided the Plessy case were from the North. It is clear that the segregation laws that appeared by the early twentieth century enjoyed the approval of the entire nation. Indeed, it was during these same years that the facilities of the national government itself in Washington, D.C. were segregated. Finally, the full impact of the *Plessy* decision can be understood only if one realizes that the "separate-but-equal" doctrine contained in the 1896 case would remain the official law of the land until 1954, when it was overturned by the landmark case *Brown v. the Topeka Board of Education.*

Thus, the contest between the forces of equality and racial inferiority that had been raging for more than a century following the American Revolution was finally resolved. By the opening years of the twentieth century America was unequivocally a white man's country. This reality was recognized by Booker T. Washington, African-America's most prominent spokesman at the turn of the century, when he gave his famous "Atlanta Compromise" address. Aware of the diminishing options open to his race, Washington counseled patience and vocational training to his black brothers until white people were willing to accept them as fellow Americans.

The lawmakers and justices of the courts were not alone in reducing African Americans to second-class citizens. During the first decades of the twentieth century spokesmen from other influential areas of American life contributed to the tightening ring of control that defined and circumscribed the black man's freedom. Journalists were quick to stereotype black behavior in the most degrading terms. A literature appeared that portrayed the ex-slave as a bumbling child like Sambo.

These vicious distortions were mirrored in the scientific community's dehumanization of Africans. In 1906, for example, a well-known zoological society in New York City proudly announced a new exhibit that demonstrated the theory that the black man was much closer to anthropoids than to the Caucasian on the evolutionary scale of Charles Darwin. Hundreds of thousands of curious sightseers flocked to see a five-foot African "pygmy" named Ota Benga together in the same cage with an orangutan. Organized protests by local black clergymen to free the African failed, eliciting the bland reply that this was a "purely ethnological exhibit." This shocking ignorance of Africa and its people was echoed in 1909 by President William Howard Taft, a learned man and later Chief Justice of the United States, when he stated that Africa had no history at all ". . . except that which we trace to the apes."

Even historians were partners in this conspiracy against African Americans. Concerning the topic of slavery, for example, two prize-winning American historians wrote in 1930: "As for Sambo, whose wrongs moved the abolitionists to wrath and tears, there is some reason to believe that he suffered less than any other class in the South from its 'peculiar institution.'" When a second edition of this widely read volume appeared 20 years later, these comments on the slave remained virtually intact.

During the course of many decades, the black American gradually found his place in a nation governed by white men. In spite of some efforts to guarantee his political character and humanity after the Civil War, he was effectively stripped of that protection and, instead, found himself the target of stereotypes and misunderstanding of great magnitude. The negative image that emerged was that of the "nigger," and stamped on that image was the phrase "Made in America."

EARLY STIRRINGS TOWARD EQUALITY

By the twentieth century, Jim Crow legislation had been enacted throughout the South, reinforcing the economic deprivation and political disenfranchisement of African Americans. Booker T. Washington's "Atlanta Compromise" address in 1895 recognized this and called for a new partnership that could bring progress for both blacks and whites. But Washington's gradual approach to the racial problem was not welcomed by all. Over a period of a few years some blacks and their white allies began to advocate more militant methods to gain equality. Calling themselves the Niagara Movement, in 1909 they met to create the National Association for the Advancement of Colored People (NAACP). Although most of the officers of the organization were white, its guiding spirit was W. E. B. DuBois, a black man who stridently demanded an equal place for his people in American life. To him, nothing less was acceptable. Challenging Washington's role as a spokesman for black people, DuBois claimed that the Alabama educator's approach "has tended to make the whites, North and South, shift the burden of the Negro problem to the Negro's shoulders . . . when in fact the burden belongs to the nation. . . ." The NAACP, with its black-white liberal alliance, became the most influential organization designed to serve black interests. It later continued its work primarily through lawsuits in the federal courts. But progress, both economic and political, was painfully slow. Actually, during the early twentieth century lynching became an even more widespread means of controlling or intimidating blacks.

The violence and bloodshed perpetrated against blacks aroused a powerful force after World War I that anticipated the Black Power Movement of the 1960s. It is estimated that as many as a half-million black people became followers of Marcus Garvey, the charismatic founder of the Universal Negro Improvement Association. Rejecting the politics of compromise and cooperation with whites that characterized the NAACP, Garvey instilled pride in his followers, insisting that "we of the UNIA do not want to become white." Though Garvey was later convicted and imprisoned on charges of fraud, his movement planted the seed of black nationalism that would surface again in the form of black power four decades later.

In the meantime, black people did make significant gains in their crusade for human equality. As Washington's philosophy of accommodation declined, it was replaced by the more aggressive, mass-action strategy of the NAACP. Moreover, the progressive trend reflected by Franklin Delano Roosevelt's New Deal created a greater sympathy for the oppressed and poverty-stricken. The insistence of the Congress of Industrial Organizations (CIO) upon the equal treatment of white and black workers also contributed to the realization of black rights. Finally, in June 1941, President Roosevelt issued an executive order that led to the formation of the Fair Employment Practices

Commission. This order prohibited discrimination in government employment and defense industries on the basis of race, creed, color, or national origin, and thereby paved the way to new economic opportunities for African Americans and other nonwhites in many of the most important sectors of the economy. President Harry Truman continued Roosevelt's use of the office to further the cause of civil rights, including his leadership in integrating the armed forces in 1949.

"I HAVE A DREAM"

The post-war years proved to be momentous ones for the cause of civil rights. Perhaps the greatest blow to inequality came in 1954, when the United States Supreme Court handed down its desegregation order in the case of *Brown v. the Topeka Board of Education.* The Court ruled that the "separate but equal" clause of the Plessy decision of 1896 was contradictory because "separate educational facilities are inherently unequal." The *Brown* decision rendered unconstitutional the elaborate system of segregation that had enjoyed the official approval of the land for more than a half century. This decision was all-important in stirring the national conscience. Now, with the law on their side, blacks began a more active pursuit of their rights.

The symbol of this new mood first appeared in December 1955 when Mrs. Rosa Parks of Montgomery, Alabama, refused to surrender her seat on a municipal bus to a white man. Her arrest by local authorities led to a massive black protest and boycott of white businesses, catapulting the Reverend Martin Luther King, Jr. into national prominence. Better than any other black leader, the Rev. King articulated the feelings and hopes of his people. Through his philosophy of nonviolence, derived from the tenet of Christian love and the technique used successfully by Mahatma Ghandi in India's struggle for independence, African Americans across the nation were inspired to emulate the Montgomery protest.

Direct, nonviolent mass action achieved significant results. Beginning in 1960, an estimated 70,000 blacks and whites participated in more than 800 "sit-ins" followed by economic boycotts by whole black communities that forced the advocates of segregation to capitulate. The "Freedom Rides" in 1961 also confirmed the importance of nonviolent mass action, aided by the coverage of these news events by television and other media. The spectacle of thousands of black people willing to endure beatings, attacks by dogs, police clubs and high-pressure hoses, imprisonment, and even death conveyed a sober impression of black determination to the American nation.

On their television screens, Americans were able to witness these confrontations at Little Rock, Montgomery, Birmingham, and elsewhere, and the national reaction that followed played no small role in civil rights action taken at the highest levels of government. Both John F. Kennedy and Lyndon Johnson gave strong backing to the civil rights movement. The 1963 March on Washington by more than 200,000 persons helped to produce the Civil Rights Act of 1964 in which the federal government insisted that public facilities are for all people. Johnson also played the key role in securing the passage of the Voting Rights Acts of 1964 and 1965. These laws forbade discrimination in public accommodations, education, voter registration, and employment. African Americans could now enter the electoral process throughout the South.

But with the public accommodations and voting rights battles in the Congress over, how complete had the victory been? Certainly some dents in the wall of segregation had been made,

The willingness of thousands of black Americans to engage in this kind of nonviolent resistance to white supremacy in the South during the early 1960s was important in their quest for human equality. (Courtesy of Charles Moore from Black Star.)

yet discrimination persisted and resistance to change was still very strong. The dream eloquently voiced by the Rev. King before the March-on-Washington crowd was not as easily within the grasp of black people (nor their idealistic white supporters) as had been assumed. Despite their legal gains, they were learning that true integration into American life was not as easily attained as they had hoped. Indeed, the belief that the awakening of the American conscience, coupled with the increasing militancy of the civil rights movement after the 1954 decision, would result in equality was beginning to sour.

By the mid-sixties it was apparent to many African Americans that racism had scarcely lessened. Nor had white resistance disappeared. Nonwhites were not being welcomed into the mainstream of American society. As late as 1967, for example, only 4.3 percent of the South's black children were in desegregated school systems. Increasingly, blacks were beginning to realize that it would be necessary to step up their fight for equality. Rather than rely on the good intentions of their white allies, optimism gave way to mounting pessimism, bitterness, and rage. More than a decade had passed since the shackles of segregation were officially lifted in 1954, and the patience and moderation of the Rev. King gave way to a more strident cry of "Freedom Now!"

MARTIN LUTHER KING, JR.

Although Martin Luther King, Jr. was born in the best black neighborhood in Atlanta, Georgia in 1929, he experienced as a child the full force of "Jim Crow" segregation. In one incident, a bus driver forced King to give up his seat and swore at him during a long ride back from a high school debate. "I don't think that I have ever been so deeply angry in my life," King said later.

His father, the Reverend King, hoped he would continue the family tradition and become a Baptist minister. At first King resisted, considering law or medicine. But he finally decided that he could make a contribution to his people as a minister, and after his ordination he went to an integrated seminary in Pennsylvania. There he was exposed to the life of Mahatma Gandhi, whose spiritual leadership "electrified" him and whose doctrine of change through nonviolence interested him. After seminary he continued on to earn a doctoral degree and then turned to the Dexter Avenue Baptist Church in Montgomery, Alabama.

On Thursday, December 1, 1955, seamstress Rosa Parks refused to give up her bus seat to a white person and was arrested. Black leaders decided on a boycott against the bus company, and elected King their spokesman. Every pressure the white community could use was brought to bear to stop the boycott. King was arrested and tried and his home was bombed. But he held the people to the principle of nonviolence. "If we are arrested every day, if we are exploited every day, if we are trampled over every day, don't let anyone pull you so low as to hate them," King preached. Just over a year later, the bus company integrated their line.

Success made King a national figure. Along with other black religious leaders, King formed the Southern Christian Leadership Conference to end segregation and secure the right of blacks to vote. The Student Nonviolent Coordinating Committee organized sit-in demonstrations and "freedom rides" to integrate public facilities and transportation. After failures in Albany, Georgia, King chose "the most segregated city in America," Birmingham, Alabama as a target. Peaceful demonstrations there were met with brutal force—high-pressure water hoses, police dogs, electric cattle prods, and mass arrests were all employed by the city officials. The media coverage of these events in 1963, especially the TV news features, shocked the nation and won widespread support for the black civil rights movement. The August "March on Washington" marked the height of King's popularity, and by the next year the nation had its first significant Civil Rights Act and King had the Nobel Peace Prize.

But when King tried to expand the movement to the North, problems resulted. Blacks in the northern ghettos wanted jobs and decent housing, not integration. Frustrated, angry blacks rejected his leadership in Chicago and New York. "Jobs are harder and costlier to create than voting rolls," he conceded. When he rushed to Los Angeles in 1965 to try to help stop the rioting in Watts, many blacks had not even heard of him. The SNCC rejected nonviolence in 1966 for "black power" over King's objections and predictions of a white backlash. He hoped to turn the movement away from "self destruction" by a Poor People's March on Washington in the summer of 1968 that would call for an "economic bill of rights." But that April, called to Memphis, Tennessee to help support striking black garbage workers, King was assassinated by a white racist.

"FREEDOM NOW!"

A major shift in the mood of the black civil rights movement occurred during the mid-sixties. For several years the Student Nonviolent Coordinating Committee (SNCC) had played a major part in the civil rights struggle. After suffering many insults and risking their lives in their campaign to increase voter registration among Southern blacks, SNCC leaders gradually became convinced that prominent black spokesmen like the Rev. King were willing to compromise with their white allies too much. They concluded that the recently enacted laws were not being enforced vigorously and that the white establishment could not be depended upon to treat the black man fairly. By 1965, SNCC had ceased to operate within the traditional white liberal framework of integration. Since the American political system had not delivered on its promises, SNCC leader Stokely Carmichael stated in 1966 that his people must begin to think in terms of "Black Power" and to seek their strength from within their own ranks rather than to rely upon whites. Symbolically, the assassination of the Rev. King in 1968 ended the liberal, integration phase of the struggle for black human rights.

Perhaps the shift from the civil rights movement to Black Power was inevitable. Despite the seeming progress in "race relations" since 1954 , the gap between the earning power of blacks and whites actually increased by the mid-sixties. Although the old system of legal segregation was gone, the more subtle techniques that had been used for so long in the North were adopted across the nation to keep blacks "in their place." Moreover, increasing educational opportunities did not necessarily provide equal employment opportunities. The integration movement had little success in breaking through these barriers because it had to compromise with the white power structure—difficult to do even with the help of white liberals. Agonizingly slow progress frustrated many African Americans, particularly those in the ghettos of the North whose quickly rising expectations were not being satisfied. This led to the militant black reaction of the mid-sixties.

These people saw "Black Power" as the answer. The groups that arose during this period claiming to speak for black people had varying definitions of "Black Power." One principle they all agreed on was the rejection of Rev. King's doctrine of nonviolence. Malcolm X, one of the most prominent spokesmen for the Black Muslims (or Nation of Islam) advised his followers that "if someone puts a hand on you, send him to the cemetery." Stokely Carmichael, who had labored in the vineyards of integration earlier, now insisted that integration was merely "a subterfuge for the maintenance of white supremacy." The head of the radicalized SNCC announced that "the days of free head-whippings are over. Black people should and must fight back." Even the representatives of the church came to embrace violence as a just weapon to be used against racism. One clergyman told a worldwide conference of churchmen: "When a society does not permit restructuring power that produces justice through economic and political maneuvers, the church ought not to shy away from aiding and abetting the development of the only other weapon available—the power of violence." Such pronouncements were brazen calls to terror in the eyes of some Americans, but they electrified large sections of the black community and assured the Black Power movement a national audience.

The looting and burning that accompanied the riots in the ghettos during the 1960s was partly the result of the gap between black expectations based on liberal promises and the failure of the government to deliver on those promises. Although the rioters comprised only a tiny fraction of the ghetto population, one commentator stated that the majority of the neighborhood's inhabitants sympathized with those on the streets. As a black girl said after the riot in Watts, "Every time I looked out my window and saw another fire, I felt new joy." (Burt Blinn/Magnum.)

The reaction to this new trend was mixed. Many white Americans felt that the movement was attempting too much and expecting changes too fast. Yet the more heady doctrines of Black Power maintained that greater changes could and must come, and this sparked the anger of blacks—especially those in the northern ghettos. During the mid-sixties there were more than a dozen large riots in America's major cities, including Newark, Detroit, and the Watts section of Los Angeles. These tragedies usually began because of a minor incident (in one case, an arrest for a traffic violation), revealing the explosive conditions that awaited a small spark. Thousands of persons were injured and millions of dollars in property damage occurred as rioters vented their anger and frustrations upon a system that seemed insensitive to their needs.

BLACK NATIONALISM

Since the decline of the intoxicating idealism that characterized the March on Washington in 1963, many blacks concluded that if they were not welcome in white society then they should pursue a course of separatism. Numerous factors help explain the rise of black nationalism that occurred in the late sixties. As the white man became identified as the enemy of black interests, doctrines were formulated that stressed self-help, racial pride, and the unity of interests of nonwhite people around the world. One important development in black nationalism was the appearance of the Black Panther Party in 1966, formed by two militants named Huey P. Newton and Bobby Seale in Oakland, California. A year later they were joined by the powerful theoretician and ex-convict Eldridge Cleaver. Deeply influenced by such writers and activists as Malcolm X, Frantz Fanon, Karl Marx, Lenin, Mao Tse-tung, Ho Chi Minh, and Che Guevara, the Panthers declared their intention to liberate the "black colony" from the rule of the "white mother country" (i.e., black people from white-dominated America). Within three years, Panther membership had grown to an estimated 5000, in 30 chapters across the country.

Another major contribution to the dogma of black nationalism is contained in the writings of Stokely Carmichael. Drawing an analogy between the black communities in the United States and the African colonies under European rule, Carmichael points out that just as the white imperialist powers extracted the wealth of Africa for their own gain, so has the labor of the black ghettos been exploited for the profit of white America. By banding together and exercising their collective economic and political power over their own communities, Carmichael suggests that black people would be following a time-honored principle used by other ethnic groups in American history. The slogan "Black is beautiful" symbolized the hopes of black leaders that self-sufficiency was a realistic goal. Numerous "Black Studies" programs were now offered at colleges and universities across the nation, aimed at creating an appreciation for a cultural tradition that had suffered from long years of neglect.

Soon after the Nixon administration took office, it indicated its support for the more peaceful processes of change advocated by the black nationalists. The resounding support the nation gave to President Nixon's call for "law and order" made clear that the urban violence associated by many people with the Black Power doctrine would no longer be tolerated. Even the most radical of the blacks realized by 1970 that the temper of America was increasingly hostile to both an aggressive integration movement and the guerrilla militancy associated with groups like the Black Panthers. The Panther organization itself was largely broken up by arrest and imprisonment and in several cases its adherents were killed in shoot-outs with the police. Some of its leaders, like Stokely Carmichael, chose to exile themselves.

Thus with the onset of the seventies the black crusade for human rights and humane treatment entered a new phase in its long struggle. The Nixon administration made clear its opposition to busing and many welfare programs, while condemning permissiveness and praising the work ethic. The President's solution to the black dilemma centered on the notion of black capitalism, a concept put forth by the black nationalists and welcomed by a diverse collection of people who shared some of the President's sentiments. Whereas the integrationists of the sixties demanded confrontation with a seemingly inflexible government and society, the separatists offered Americans social peace. The prospective harmony involved a price: black nationalists were demanding white support for their plans.

Not all African Americans rallied to the banner of separatism, however. Many still believed that equality was possible within white society, and cited evidence of progress in the struggle for integration. As early as 1973 two white writers in *Commentary* magazine argued that:

> *A remarkable development has taken place in America over the last dozen years: for the first time in the history of the republic, truly large and growing numbers of American blacks have been moving into the middle class, so that by now these numbers could reasonably be said to add up to a majority of black Americans—a slender majority, but a majority nevertheless.*

WEIGHING THE EVIDENCE

The years between the bicentennial of 1976 and the early 1980s witnessed undeniable advances for many black Americans. Affirmative Action programs played a measurable role in upgrading their economic and occupational status.

By 1980 a black middle class was emerging, and ten years later, 40 percent of African Americans were newly middle-class or upwardly mobile working class. For young, college-educated two-earner married couples, income differentials between blacks and whites were negligible. The *New York Times* reported in 1990 that almost as many black workers between ages of 25 and 44 were college graduates as high school dropouts. Just 20 years earlier, there were five times as many black high school dropouts as college graduates in the labor force. Certainly, one important explanation for such impressive economic gains is Affirmative Action. Vigorous government enforcement of civil rights laws since Lyndon Johnson launched his Great Society reforms helped to create educational and vocational progress. Indeed, as two leading states—California and Texas—reversed their commitment to Affirmative Action in 1997, President Clinton reminded the American people that the program "has given us a whole new generation of professionals in fields that used to be exclusive clubs. "

These economic gains of African Americans were accompanied by progress in the political arena. Rev. Jesse Jackson's ability to mobilize the black vote resulted in 5.5 million new voters in the South. From 1970 to 1990 the number of black southern elected officials rose from less than 100 to 7,500, including 338 mayors. By 1992 the Congress included 38 African American representatives. Even that traditional bastion of white males—the U.S. Senate—was breached by the election of Carol Mosely Braun from Chicago's inner city. The appointment of conservative Clarence Thomas to the Supreme Court by President George Bush to replace Thurgood Marshall is another indicator of the established presence of African Americans in the political mainstream. In the 1996 congressional elections, black candidates received decisive white support in white majority districts. Clearly, the times were changing.

Yet these signposts of African American progress have not marked the arrival at The Promised Land. Although legal segregation is dead, replaced by an enormously successful black middle-class, injustice remains. Implementation of the conservative social and economic policies of the Reagan administration was accompanied by recession. This economic slowdown chipped away at social welfare funding, resulting in a deteriorating living standard for many African Americans. The gains made through Affirmative Action programs eroded, as the last hired became the first fired. If the black-white income gap was narrowing in 1970, by 1997 it had become a chasm. The black unemployment rate was double that of whites. Single women headed more than half of all black families, three times the white rate. A black family still earned only $63 for every $100 earned by white families, virtually the same disparity since 1961. "By 2000, 41 percent of black children remained trapped in poverty." As for advances in school integration, studies reveal that the rate of black-white segregation is approximately the same as in the early 1960s, before the civil rights laws were enacted.

The deepening crisis of economically-deprived African Americans in the 1980s and 1990s was noteworthy also for society's lack of concern for the plight of the poor. During both the 1930s and 1960s, a wave of public attention to the root problems of poverty was aroused via FDR's New Deal and LBJ's Great Society reform programs. There was no comparable support by middle-class Americans during the 1970s, 80s, and 90s for the amelioration of the conditions of poverty. When it was revealed that firearms are the leading cause of death among black males under the age of 35, few outside the black community seemed to care. One observer noted that Americans now suffered "compassion fatigue." Reflecting the attitudes of the middle-class white majority, the administrations of Ronald Reagan and George Bush treated African Americans with benign neglect and sometimes hostility.

African American frustration with the acceptance/rejection syndrome was reflected in two court trials in California during the 1990s, both involving black men. In 1992 pent-up tension in the inner city of Los Angeles exploded with rage when a jury from a white community acquitted four white Los Angeles policemen whose brutal beating of black motorist Rodney King had been videotaped. The ensuing lawlessness—including arson, looting, and violence—eclipsed in magnitude the riots in the Watts neighborhood of that city 27 years earlier. Such extreme urban unrest raised again the issue of justice in America. Despite the fact that two of the four police officers were ultimately found guilty of violating the offender's civil rights, the United States seemed almost two societies with little in common, one barely aware of the other's existence. Perception of the Rodney King incident was largely along racial lines. Three years later the acquittal of ex-football star and celebrity O. J. Simpson of double-murder charges elicited cheers of relief from a majority of African Americans, while two-thirds of whites who were polled believed

Simpson was guilty. The conclusion of the Kerner Commission Report following the Watts riots of 1965 now seemed even more applicable: "Our nation is moving toward two societies, one black, one white—separate and unequal."

The rising economic tide of the late '80s and mid '90s did not raise all boats. Although many African Americans were now enjoying the promise of the American middle class, those from the inner city were not. Affirmative Action programs did little for people of color from the underclass. For some the remedy lies in separatism. The Nation of Islam offers one alternative to black people. Leading the "Million Man March" on Washington, D.C. in 1996, Minister Farrahkan cautioned his listeners to beware of promises of white America, arguing that African Americans must solve their own problems. Other ideologues suggest that some school curricula should delete their Euro-centric perspective in favor of an Afro-centric point of view. This extreme version of multiculturalism even resorts to "race science" to support its view that sun people have more virtue and are less warlike than ice people, who have less melanin in their skin. Another gesture has been the demand for reparations from the federal government for generations of slavery. Following the lead of Japanese American World War II internment-camp survivors who received $20,000 each in 1988, African American groups in Detroit and Oakland during the 1990s began to demand commensurate financial compensation, ignoring the reality that the 80,000 Japanese American recipients were survivors of the camps. Distributing similar sums to 30 million blacks—none of whom experienced firsthand the institution of slavery—would total $3 trillion, a price tag American voters would not support.

Others in the African American community—perhaps the majority—reject that separatist agenda. The National Association for the Advancement of Colored People (NAACP) found disagreement among its ranks over continued liberal Great Society programs like school busing and Affirmative Action. Black school officials from Seattle to Washington D.C. have called for the end of busing and a return to community schooling, with equal financial support for both inner city and suburban schools. Says Howard University professor Ron Walter: "Many of the assumptions that undergirded the civil rights movement have been eroded. Clear lines have been erased."

THE NATIVE AMERICAN: A CENTURY SINCE WOUNDED KNEE

Near the turn of the 20th century, the lines were clearly drawn for Native Americans. They could move onto reservations, whose boundaries were drawn by the government in Washington, or they could fight. The dying gasp in the Indian quest for autonomy in the land of their forefathers occurred in December 1890. It was on the snow-covered prairie near Wounded Knee Creek in South Dakota that two regiments of United States cavalry opened fire on 350 defenseless men, women, and children, killing nearly 300 of them. After many decades of resistance to the white man's penetration of the western frontier, this massacre represents the final act in the centuries-long conquest of the original Americans. From the time that they were subjugated and placed on reservations as wards of the United States government, Native Americans have endured both the loss of their land and its natural resources to whites and the ravages of cultural destruction.

Out of a growing awareness of the government's historic maltreatment of the Indian, a campaign began during the 1920s to seek greater justice for Native Americans. Besides providing

The dramatic takeover of Wounded Knee by the American Indian Movement was meant to lend force to AIM's demand for full Indian self-government on the Pine Ridge reservation. © Bettmann/CORBIS

for more autonomy in tribal cultural matters, the Wheeler-Howard Act of 1934 sought to counter the depletion of native lands that occurred during the previous half-century. "The tribes' 138 million acres in 1887 had been reduced to 48 million acres by 1934 when this bill was introduced. Largely the brainchild of John Collier, the progressive-minded Commissioner of the Bureau of Indian Affairs (BIA), this law stipulated . . ." that Indian lands should revert back to the old tribal arrangement of communal ownership. Sale of land to non-Indians was drastically restricted. Provisions were made to restore former tribal lands to their original owners.

Despite the lofty vision of John Collier, repeated violations of agreements between Native Americans and the federal government persisted. One of the first acts of the Eisenhower presidency in 1953 was the Termination program, which proposed the total elimination of the reservation system. The government theorized that Indians were now ready to enter the American mainstream, and therefore the reservations were no longer necessary. Besides, the proposal would help lower the federal budget. Charges of "cultural homocide" quickly followed, implying that the government's action was really a disguised effort at a land grab by the timber, mining, and ranching interests. As a result of the public outcry, the program was rescinded in 1958. Through the 1960s, however, the Department of the Interior continued to lease large sections of reservation

The news media's exposé of the Broken Treaty Papers in 1972 prompted the radical American Indian Movement to take a dramatic step. AIM members seized the small community of Wounded Knee, South Dakota in March 1973, in order to broadcast their people's plight. The symbol of Indian despair dating back to the Indian massacre by government troops at Wounded Knee in 1890 was now transformed to one of Indian defiance. (Paul Conrad, © 1973, Los Angeles Times. Reprinted with permission.)

lands to giant corporations who tore up the earth, covered it with lumbering wastes, and polluted the waters with mining poisons. As late as 1972, Interior officials declared that no environmental impact statements under the terms of the National Environmental Policy Act of 1969 were required for "development" of reservation lands. Despite these years of exploitation, Native Americans were slower to recognize possibilities of militancy in pursuit of their rights than were their African and Latino counterparts. By the late 1960s, however, they were no longer willing to accede quietly to the authority of the BIA and had begun to act against these injustices.

Their new strident mood appeared first in 1969 when Indians from various tribes "captured" the abandoned federal prison on Alcatraz Island in San Francisco Bay. They announced that they wished to "liberate" the island from "white rule" and establish an Indian cultural center. They expressed their willingness to pay 24 dollars in glass beads and cloth for the island—the same price the Dutch had paid to Indians for Manhattan Island 300 years earlier.

Of greater significance to the rise of the "Red Power" movement was the "invasion" of the BIA headquarters in Washington, D.C. by young Indian radicals in 1972. They raided BIA files and found stacks of documents that, they claimed, support their contention that the federal government has not honestly faced its duty as guardian of Native Americans. These "Broken Treaties Papers" revealed that although the Department of Interior is responsible for protecting Indians, it has been directly involved in the conspiracy to rob them of their land and its natural resources. Despite the numerous government treaties made with these tribesmen, for example, the Broken Treaties Papers demonstrated that they still have not enjoyed justice in the courts. Although some Indians, both individuals and groups, have been awarded sums totaling millions of dollars in compensation for their losses, not all have been successful in their efforts to correct the violation of their treaties with the United States government. In many cases, reservation life has not improved, despite years of federal aid. The Broken Treaties Papers showed that for many decades the major portion of the funds allocated for the benefit of Indians has been wasted by the vast bureaucracy that administers the government's programs.

At the same time, these documents revealed that the conditions of urban Indians (those who left reservation life) were totally neglected by the government. A secret "Study of Urban Indian Problems" recommended that the BIA take a more active interest in Indians who moved to the cities. Although there may be as many as 300,000 urban Indians in the United States suffering from serious economic and social deprivation, this recommendation was rejected by President Nixon with the explanation that the needs of reservation dwellers were "sufficiently great that resources available to the BIA should not be dissipated elsewhere."

Perhaps the most dramatic symbol of the Indian's growing impatience with the federal government was the armed takeover of the village of Wounded Knee in January 1973. The radical, city-based American Indian Movement (AIM) assumed leadership in this act of defiance against the Indian's century-long benefactor. The leaders of the insurrection concluded that the takeover of the 1890 massacre site offered the most effective means of publicizing their plight, and they announced that they would persist in their insurrection until top government officials, including presidential aides, conferred directly with them. During the next four months Wounded Knee was under siege as the talks broke down repeatedly, interrupted by the exchange of thousands of rounds of gunfire, resulting in serious injuries on both sides. Although a ceasefire and peace were finally arranged, the issues that sparked the rebellion were never really resolved.

Thus, years of neglect had convinced Native Americans that the government was incapable of meeting their needs. During the seventies, they began to demand an end to the traditional policy of "white paternalism" and a greater voice in running their own affairs. In an important election early in 1974 voters at the Pine Ridge, South Dakota reservation reelected tribal president Dick Wilson over the more militant AIM challenger Russell Means, who led the insurrection at Wounded Knee. For years there was essentially a "cold war" between AIM and the more conservative tribal leaders on the reservations who felt that radical action raised more opposition than support. Not until the 1980s did the wounds between the two sides heal, and the Pine Ridge Souix were able to work together to maintain their culture and protect their lands.

But threats to the economic and political self-determination of Native Americans continued. Critics of government Indian policy charge that, historically, acquisition of the immense stores of natural resources on Indian lands has been the goal of white America. The saga of Indian land abuse is marked by the usofruct rationale of colonial times, the gross violation of Indian land treaties by the U.S. government throughout the nineteenth century, Eisenhower's "termination" experiment during the 1950s, and the statements by former President Reagan's controversial Secretary of the Interior. In 1983 Secretary James Watt advanced the opinion that the reservation system proved "the failure of socialism" more vividly than life in the Soviet Union. Critics charged that Watt's remarks represented "the greatest threat to Indian sovereignty and their God-given culture since smallpox." There was suspicion that Watt's real intention was to make available to private corporations the immense profits to be derived from the timber, mining, and oil and natural gas resources located on reservation lands.

Watt's pronouncements were especially ironic because, as a result of policies initiated by President Nixon in the early 1970s, American Indians were accorded more political and economic sovereignty, proving their success in their own capitalistic endeavors. Perhaps their greatest step toward economic self-sufficiency has been tribal gambling casinos across the nation, resulting in $6 billion in profits in 1995. By implementing the white man's free-enterprise strategies, the tribal council of the Fort Apache Indian Reservation in Arizona earns millions annually from their own land management policies and a highly successful ski resort. The Choctaw in Mississippi provide jobs not only for their own people but for 1,000 non-Indians who enter the reservation to work in factories making plastic utensils for McDonald's restaurants, electrical wiring assemblies for automobile plants, and greeting cards. Tribesmen of the Flathead Reservation boast of an unemployment rate below the rest of rural Montana by focusing on agriculture, tourism, and recreation jobs. As for the Nez Perce, their recent acquisition of 10,000 acres of land in Oregon lost to the federal government in 1877 has permitted them much greater autonomy. Creating a modern tribal economic infrastructure, they are rebuilding their famed Appaloosa horse herds, reintroducing the gray wolf to the Idaho wilds, and restoring the native salmon and steelhead habitats. A Harvard University professor explains these examples of tribal success:

Successful tribes are marked by what we call the "Nike strategy." They build their own institutions and their own bureaucracies, displace the federal government as primary decision maker on the reservation and then just do it themselves.

Not all Indians have benefitted from this bonanza. The 1990 census revealed that one-third of the Native American population lives below the poverty line. For every $100 earned by a U.S. family, a Native American household brings in $62. To complicate their plight, Native American tuberculosis rates are 900 percent higher than among whites, and lethal alcoholism 400 percent. Old safety-nets are collapsing; the $3.4 billion in government aid to Native Americans in 1991 was 40 percent less than twenty years earlier.

Faced with this paradox between Native American successes and poverty, in the 1990s there has been no unanimity regarding solutions. Internal dissension between or within tribes reflects a dispute in values. On the Navajo reservation, for example, two groups of tribesmen fought over cutting old-growth timber in the Chuska mountains. The loggers claimed 140 jobs were at stake, while the environmentalists cited federal law requiring protection for the endangered spotted owl. In New York members of the Seneca tribe are divided by the casino movement. On one side are "progressive" businessmen who see related profits from gas stations and convenience stores; on the other hand, the "traditionalists" argue that the paternalistic white system is morally corrupt, and that they must reject such lures offered by white society as casino gambling.

In any case, tribes are insisting on recovering lands wrongfully seized by the government and exercising sovereignty on their lands. Since the mid-1980s the traditionalist faction has spearheaded the fight to regain their sacred Black Hills in South Dakota from the federal government, including the site of Mt. Rushmore. Alaskan natives were encouraged by a federal appeals court ruling in 1997 that recognized their sovereign right to tax activities on or moving through their scattered lands and villages.

The drive for economic and political self-determination was accompanied by Indian determination to achieve a greater sense of cultural worth and ethnic pride. In the 1970s Indian studies programs had been added to college curricula across the nation, offering important lessons to all Americans. Long before Europeans touched the New World, societies existed there that were supported by sophisticated ideas in government, and dedicated to the concept of living in harmony with their fellow man and with nature. In 1947 former BIA Commissioner Collier wrote eloquently of what non-Indians can learn from the Native Americans:

"They had what the world has lost, they have it now; what the world has lost it must have again lest it die. Not many years are left . . . to recapture the lost ingredient—the ancient, lost reverence and passion for the earth and its web of life."

Perhaps of greatest concern is that Indians shall finally gain the position of respect and security they have long deserved as the original Americans.

STRANGERS IN THEIR OWN LAND

Respect and security remain a hope for Latino people of the American Southwest. During the nineteenth century the Mexican American first lost his ancestral lands to military conquest, and later to lawsuits and the rapacity of incoming settlers. After 1900, he found his fate tied to the economic development of the Southwestern states. The rise of agricultural technology coupled with the development of large reservoirs for irrigation purposes created heavy labor requirements. Irrigation farming led to a demand for cheap Mexican labor for work in cultivating, carting, packing, processing, and shipping. Workers were also needed in cotton production and on the railroads. It has been estimated that the number of Mexicans entering the United States between 1900 and 1920 in search of opportunity was equivalent to one-tenth of the entire population of

Mexico. Had it not been for this source of cheap labor, the economic development of the Southwest would not have occurred as rapidly and dramatically as it did.

The racial stereotypes that had developed during the late nineteenth century provided a convenient excuse to explain a division of labor in which the Mexicans were usually at the bottom. Although this source of labor enjoyed an initial welcome, the appearance of an increasing number of brown-skinned people with different customs and living habits heightened the racial fears of the new Anglo majority.

By the 1920s a deepening agricultural crisis culminating in the Great Depression of the 1930s made the Mexican's position in his ancestral lands much less secure. As the Dust Bowl migrants from the Midwest came westward seeking jobs, the amount of agricultural work available to the unskilled ethnic was drastically reduced. Gradually, newspapers and magazines began to devote more space to the presence and danger of the Hispanic element. Racial fears were now accompanied by charges of unfair economic competition. Patriotic societies and labor unions began to demand that the government must "close the back door" in an effort to restrict the continued immigration of Mexican nationals into the American Southwest. Besides preventing the influx of additional Mexicans, there was a move to "repatriate" those who were already residents of the United States. Between 1930 and 1934, for example, more than 64,000 Mexican aliens were forced to leave the United States without formal legal proceedings.

The coming of World War II, with its manpower emergencies, altered the economic situation once more and created again the need for Mexican labor. In 1942 the Bracero (contract labor) program was established. After the war, agricultural employers exerted their influence to continue the Bracero program. They argued that there were not enough domestic workers and that native Americans were generally unadaptable to the stoop labor needed in the fields.

Responding to the need for farm workers, Mexican immigration increased rapidly in the 1950s. This influx reached such proportions that a wave of anti-Mexican sentiment swept through the Southwest, leading to a repetition of the repatriation of the Depression era. "Operation Wetback" was designed to deport these aliens who had entered the country illegally; however only a small fraction of the almost four million immigrants deported during the mid-1950s received the right of a formal legal hearing. In the process, the civil rights of hundreds of thousands of American citizens were violated. The legacy of this emotionally charged government policy was to provoke greater distrust and alienation in the Mexican American toward "establishment" America.

THE HISPANICS

Like African Americans, Mexican Americans have continued to encounter serious obstacles in enjoying the benefits of the "American Dream." Although their presence in the United States predates American annexation of Mexican territory in 1848, attaining their constitutional rights has been a painfully slow process. From the Treaty of Guadalupe-Hidalgo through the 1930s, their role in the United States was almost completely apolitical. Aware of the ever-present forces of prejudice, the early pioneers of Mexican political organization were willing to accept the Anglo definition of the proper role for Mexicans in American politics. They realized that the two decades between World Wars I and II were not the time for controversy, especially since the Depression made them vulnerable to the charge of taking jobs away from unemployed whites. Their economic survival depended upon knowing the "place" white Americans had defined for them.

By the time of World War II, however, a policy of accommodation gave way to more aggressive political activity. The war not only created new opportunities in employment, education, and housing (still segregated), but as many as a half-million Mexicans served the United States in the armed forces and returned home determined to be full-fledged citizens of this country. Mexican Americans began to form organizations designed to advance their interests like the Community Service Organization (CSO). The CSO was based on the premise that American institutions were basically responsive to the needs of Mexican Americans. One important endeavor of the CSO was a vigorous voter registration campaign. Pressure was also placed on housing agencies, the Federal Employment Practices Commission, and the police to insure more just treatment of Mexican Americans. By the late 1950s, the CSO seemed to be losing its vitality, and some of its key leaders like Cesar Chavez resigned to pursue the quest for Mexican American rights in other ways.

The most important phase in the growing political self-consciousness of Mexican Americans came in the mid-sixties. Profiting from the example set by black militants, Mexican political activity was radicalized and the Chicanos (a derivative of the word "Mexicanos") emerged. By the mid-sixties, militant Reies Lopez Tijerina and his followers engaged in unsuccessful guerrilla warfare against the state of New Mexico, protesting the "illegal" seizure of Mexican lands in 1848. For the first time, Mexican American activists questioned not only the assumptions of their predecessors but some of the more basic premises of American society as well.

The Chicano movement challenged the widespread belief that Mexican Americans were thriving more than most other nonwhite minorities. Indeed, in income, occupational distribution, and housing, Mexicans are the nation's second-largest disadvantaged group (far outnumbering Native Americans and Puerto Ricans). Like many blacks, Chicanos saw themselves as an oppressed people—evidenced by their loss of communal and private property and the submergence of their culture by the white majority after the 1840s. When they were evicted from their own land, they were often forced to become migrant farm workers. Otherwise, they migrated to the city where their lack of education and unskilled labor made them particularly vulnerable to exploitation.

By the 1960s neither of these choices was acceptable to a large segment of the Mexican American population. Migratory farm workers responded to Cesar Chavez's efforts to organize them, and then used strikes and boycotts to gain recognition and better pay and working conditions from growers. Adopting Martin Luther King's doctrine of nonviolence, the union's strike and Chavez's promotion of a nationwide boycott of the grape industry in 1967 became the symbol of "La Causa" for all Hispanic Americans. By the early seventies, this movement or "cause" succeeded in convincing the great majority of the growers to sign contracts that would provide recognition of the farm workers' union and increase wages. Chavez's successes, however, were overshadowed by the heaviest influx of migrants—both legal and "undocumented"—in the entire American experience. Census Bureau statistics for 1990 indicate that one-fourth of the nation's

22.4 million Hispanics remained trapped in the poverty of hazardous migrant field work or central city barrios.

The complaint of the Chicano is based on cultural arguments just as much as economic ones. The Mexican community has decried the historic effort by the Anglo-dominated society to impose its values on the ethnic minority. Activists charged that this cultural oppression persists in many school systems attended by Mexican American children. Thus the Chicano recognized the urgent need to recreate his concept of self by building his pride in his history and culture. The idea of "La Raza" has played a key role in Chicano ideology, referring not so much to "race" as to a vague sense of ethnic identity. The American "melting pot" became a pressure cooker that tried to steam off their own culture and mold them into "standard" American. By the 1970s many Mexican Americans were no longer willing to submit to such cultural domination.

The results of the Chicano cultural revival have been mixed. Since textbooks on the secondary and college level traditionally ignored Mexican Americans as a minority group, "Chicano studies" were successfully established during the 1970s in the curricula of many schools. During the decade prior to 1980 the percentage of college-educated Hispanics had doubled to nine percent. At the same time, the continued poor showing of Hispanic school children—where the dropout rate was over thirty percent—prompted the creation of bilingual and bicultural education as a means of providing youngsters with a favorable self-image vital to successful learning. Government support for this program diminished after the Carter presidency. By 1981 there was a growing consensus that bilingual education constituted a high-minded ideal that does not work well. The election of Ronald Reagan signalled the rise of the more conservative belief that if these children are going to live and work in U.S. society, they will be better served by being taught from the beginning in English. A more global criticism suggested that bilingualism serves as a barrier to assimilation, possibly even leading toward separatist movements such as have been seen in countries like Canada and Belgium, where government efforts to promote official equality in two languages have led to increased social strife and, occasionally, bloodshed. Hence, by the 1980s Chicano activists found it necessary to adjust their strategies, recognizing that the liberalism of the seventies had been replaced by a more conservative mood a decade later.

Acknowledgement of these political realities dictated a change in the strategies of Chicano activists. The Brown Berets, a quasi-military youth organization with the radical rhetoric and style of the Cuban revolutionaries, entered a period of decline and disbanded by the mid-seventies. In the meantime, America's Spanish-speaking population was changing. In California, for example, the Chicano movement whose membership was Mexican American began to lose its edge, as hundreds of thousands of refugees from Central American countries began immigrating during the 1980s. A term referring to all Americans of Latin American ancestry—Latino—came into vogue. Today most Latinos scoff at the nostalgic notion of the 1970s Chicano movement that one day Aztlan, the Mexican's mythical Aztec homeland in the U.S. Southwest, will be returned to its "rightful" owners since the territory was "stolen" by the American government with the 1848 treaty of Guadalupe-Hidalgo.

The demise of the Chicano movement marked a new consciousness among Latinos. In some ways Latino society is characterized by the same affluence/poverty gap as other minority groups; indeed, their school dropout rate of 30 percent is twice that of African Americans, and yet its

CESAR CHAVEZ

Cesario Chavez was born in 1927 on a farm that had been homesteaded by his grandfather about 20 miles outside Yuma, Arizona. The Chavez family had done well, and had bought a small grocery store-garage to supplement their income. The children went to school, where Cesario's name was anglicized to Cesar and the speaking of Spanish was forbidden. The Great Depression broke the Chavez family—they lost the store and the farm to back taxes, and were forced to travel to California to find work as migrant workers in the fields of the central valley. There they joined others, often Mexican Americans or illegal Mexican immigrants, laboring hard for poor wages and facing discrimination in the nearby farming towns.

After a two year stint in the Navy, Chavez returned to California and married. He left migrant work for life in the barrio of San Jose (nicknamed "Sal Si Puedes," or "Get out if you can") where he met Father Donald McDonnell and Fred Ross. Father McDonnell imbedded in Chavez a strong sense of social justice, by using models like Saint Francis of Assisi and Mahatma Gandhi. Ross was a leader of the Community Service Organization, which organized Mexican Americans for voter registration and citizenship classes and aided them with welfare, business and mistreatment problems. Chavez was so successful in voting drives that in 1952 Ross hired him as a full time organizer. By 1960 he was named National Director of CSO, but he left that post when the board opposed a shift Chavez championed towards organizing farm labor. Previous attempts to organize farm labor had failed, and even the AFL-CIO had made little progress through its Agricultural Workers Organizing Committee (AWOC). But Chavez and his wife, despite the dangers of giving up a steady job and the responsibility of feeding eight children, decided to try it themselves.

They made their home in Delano, working in the fields by day and organizing house meetings at night. In 1962 delegates met in Fresno to form the National Farm Workers Association. Three years later the union included 1700 families. In that year Filipino workers, members of AWOC, struck grape growers in Delano. Despite misgivings, Chavez and the NFWA joined in. The press picked up "La Causa" during a 230 mile march led by Chavez from Delano to Sacramento, and on Easter Sunday in 1966 a mass was held on the steps of the Capitol building for 10,000 supporters. But the NFWA strike fund was low, and Chavez joined with the AWOC to form the United Farm Workers (UFW) to tap AFL-CIO strike funds that enabled "La Huelga" to continue. Appeals to ethnic pride and religious fervor united the Mexican American community, and by 1968 the growers of wine grapes capitulated to UFW terms. Table grape growers, however, remained stubborn. Chavez then organized a nationwide boycott that eventually became effective. Tendencies towards violence in the UFW were halted when Chavez went on a 25 day fast. "The strike is not worth the blood of a single farmworker or his child, or a single grower or his child," Chavez insisted. In early 1970 the growers broke and signed contracts with the UFW.

But "La Huelga" was not over. The Teamsters Union moved in and signed contracts with 200 lettuce growers despite the fact that the farm workers wanted the UFW to represent them. A weary Chavez now organized a lettuce boycott, but the battle widened when the table grape growers, their UFW contracts run out, signed with the Teamsters as well. The strike wore on—UFW members took home only $5 a week as strike pay—and there were some incidents of violence. In 1975 Governor Jerry Brown signed a law calling for elections in the fields so that workers could decide which union they wanted to represent them. "La Causa" won the right to represent many of California's farm workers when the voting took place two years later. Almost twenty years later, this quiet crusader for migrant farmworkers died without fully realizing his dream.

Caesar Chavez's efforts in building the N.F.W.A. have succeeded in giving Mexican
Americans in particular and migrant workers in general a rallying point and a voice in their
own lives. (George Ballis/Black Star.)

people seem more defined by hope than anger. By 1997 Hispanic households had a dramatic
increase of 5.8 percent in median income, the largest of any group. Efforts by the United Farm
Workers in 1997 to unionize with the AFL-CIO augured well for that labor sector. One Latino
writer points out that with more than one-third of California's population, "we are now more
concerned with renewing a society in decline than in preserving a minority movement." Earlier
reluctance to "Americanize" due to fear of loss of self-identity is giving way to the magnet of
assimilation. Indeed, the fastest growing sector of the Latino population is native-born, and
contrary to widely-held myth, virtually all native-born Latinos speak English.

Politically, relative quiet returned to the "barrios" (ghettos) as Latino organizations turned
away from open demonstrations in favor of working within the system for institutional change.

One leader stated that the nature of the struggle had changed, "shifting to areas that require day-to-day work like the building of a political party. There is less glitter, and less drama, but the indications are that it will be a much more substantial organization." By 2000, 29 percent of California's population was Spanish-speaking, and one-fourth of the Southwest's population was Latino. In New Mexico the percentage of Spanish speakers reached 40 percent, almost resulting in a demographic reconquista of lands lost by Mexico in 1846. Elections in the 1990s brought more than 4,000 Latino officeholders to California and resulted in the election of Latino congressmen. Still, the huge potential of the "sleeping giant"—a mobilized Latino vote—had just begun to be realized.

WHITE AMERICA AND THE "YELLOW PERIL"

In 1882, at a time when Mexican American immigration into the United States was just beginning to swell, Asian immigration was largely cut off. Economic bad times and the fear of being "overwhelmed" by numbers had caused Congress to stop Chinese immigration. As a result of the exclusion legislation, those Asians who chose to remain in the United States found little opportunity for success. They lived in ghettos called "Chinatowns" and their children often were required to attend segregated schools. Finally, in 1943, Congress decided to repeal the 60-year-old immigration legislation, hopeful that by doing so the morale of America's wartime ally in Asia might be boosted in the fight against Imperial Japan. In the meantime, however, the damage had been done, and their pattern of life had been established during the century since the first Chinese had responded to the call for labor on America's west coast in the 1840s.

Of course, both the Chinese and the Japanese who came to America later suffered from disadvantages that did not plague immigrants from Europe. The "ideal" newcomer was expected to be white, Anglo-Saxon, Protestant, and from a nation friendly to the United States. Neither "yellow" peoples could claim these traits. Instead, they were nonwhite, Asian, and non-Christian. In the case of Japan, that nation later engaged in all-out war with the United States. Moreover, the Japanese encountered adversity as a result of the previous Chinese experience. After 1885 thousands of Japanese men came to the continental United States from their homeland, often via Hawaii. Following on the heels of decades of harassment, acts of violence, and legal restrictions levied upon Chinese immigrants, it should be no surprise that the 22,000 Japanese who had come to America by 1900 were confronted with a variety of challenges.

The "Yellow Peril" had become such a specter that in 1906 the San Francisco school board ruled that Japanese American schoolchildren must attend special schools, although it was later revealed that only 93 children out of a school population of 25,000 were Japanese. The supporters of this school segregation order—including labor groups and patriotic organizations—advanced a variety of arguments to support their view. Like other minority groups, the Japanese were seen as different in their "values" from those of the white majority. One Congressman charged that there were no words in the Japanese language for such western concepts as "morality," "sin," "home," and "privacy." "The concept of 'commercial honor' is almost totally devoid in the Japanese mind," he added. Other concerns were also expressed. The sexual fears of the white majority were stimulated by a California politician who announced his determination to prevent

The need for Chinese laborers in the railroad construction crews and in the mines of the West did not last for very long. Soon they came to be seen as an alien and nonassimilable element. Undesirable socially and unwanted in the job market, the Chinese became the target of a series of immigration restriction laws enacted during the last decades of the nineteenth century. (Library of Congress.)

"matured Japs with their base minds [and] lascivious thoughts" from sitting in the classroom "next to the pure maids of California." To men of this mind, the exclusion of the Japanese was obviously necessary.

The uproar over the school order had international repercussions. The suggestion of inferiority elicited angry protests from Japan. To avoid the possibility of a break in United States-Japanese relations, President Theodore Roosevelt convinced the San Francisco school board to withdraw the segregation ruling if he would end further Japanese immigration. This he did through a series of diplomatic notes with the Tokyo government in 1907–1908, resulting in the so-called Gentleman's Agreement. This was made more concrete in 1924 when pressure from such groups as the American Legion, the Native Sons and Daughters of the Golden West, and the American Federation of Labor forced Congress to exclude the Japanese from migrating to American shores.

The insecurity of Japanese life in America hardened when the two nations went to war. The surprise attack by Imperial Japan upon Pearl Harbor had disastrous results for Japanese citizens of the United States. By the spring of 1942, 70,000 American citizens of Japanese ancestry, as well as some 40,000 aliens, were forcibly evacuated from their homes on the West Coast and interned in several "relocation centers" in the interior. No formal charges were made against these people, simply because no laws had been violated. Why did the extralegal action occur?

Economics is one factor that can not be ignored in explaining Japanese internment. For many years one of the few avenues of opportunity open to the Japanese immigrant had been in farming, especially in California. By 1941 the Japanese produced 42 percent of the state's truck crops. Their success had antagonized the caucasian vegetable growers and shippers, who sought the expropriation of their land. But a narrow economic interpretation does not adequately explain the government's action against these people.

It is difficult to avoid the conclusion that racism played an important role in the decision to evacuate the Japanese from the Pacific Coast. In Hawaii, for example, none of the Japanese population was evacuated, although the proportion of Japanese and the possibility of Japanese espionage there were greater than on the mainland. Relocation occurred despite the lack of any evidence of espionage or sabotage by the Japanese on the mainland. At the same time, individuals of German and Italian ancestry were not disturbed, although the governments of Germany and Italy were also at war with the United States. Moreover, internment was advised not only by the military, but by influential persons in civilian life as well. Liberals such as then California Attorney General Earl Warren supported the action, which was upheld by the Supreme Court.

The legacy of wartime evacuation and internment was deep. Established family patterns were disrupted and psychological studies show that feelings of hopelessness, personal insecurity, and inertia overcame many individuals who formerly had been an enterprising, energetic people. When the war ended, the internment camps had affected many of their inmates in a way similar to the reservations' effect on the American Indian. There were also economic consequences. In a poll taken in 1945, when asked if Japanese Americans should have the same opportunity for jobs as white people after the war, 61 percent of those polled replied negatively. Furthermore,

While Japanese Americans were summarily accused of disloyalty and shuttled off to "relocation camps" surrounded by barbed-wire enclosures and machine guns, many of their brothers and sons were defending their country in both theaters of the war. Their fighting units—comprising solely Japanese American soldiers—were among the most decorated units in United States military history. (The National Archives.)

many Japanese families were financially ruined by internment. Their property left behind on the West Coast was lost, sold, or confiscated. Fifty years later, only a fraction of the lawsuits initiated by Japanese Americans to recover a portion of their property losses had been satisfactorily resolved in the courts.

The pot of controversy was stirred anew in 1982 when Japanese Americans engaged in loud debate over the recommendations of a commission appointed by Congress two years earlier to study how this minority group was treated during World War II. This nine-member panel concluded that internment in 1942 represented a gross violation of the constitutionally-guaranteed rights of citizens and legal residents. The commission, whose recommendations were approved by Congress with the Civil Liberties Act of 1988, proposed that survivors of the detention camps be given an official apology and a payment of $20,000 in compensation. With 60,000 relocation survivors, this indemnity cost American taxpayers a total of $1.5 billion. Prior to the congressional vote on this issue the Japanese American community split, with one faction arguing that anyone denied justice in such a gross manner deserves such compensation. Others voiced the belief that money can never adequately compensate for the freedom lost by those behind barbed wire during the war. Indeed, these advocates feared that the financial gain would be overshadowed by the decline in good will enjoyed by Asian Americans in American society today. Moreover, argued opponents of the panel recommendation, logic dictates that other "victims" of injustice would then be entitled to compensation: Mexican Americans for their lands "stolen" in 1848, Indians for losing their lands through fraudulent treaties, and African Americans who have been subjected to discrimination past and present. Where does one draw the line?

Meanwhile the Asian American community became more diverse during the past quarter-century, echoing the experiences of other minorities, like the Hispanics. The arrival of large numbers of Pacific Islanders and political refugees from Southeast Asia altered Asian Americans' social status. The conventional image of the hard-working Chinese or Japanese immigrant was amended by other newcomers whose presence drove up the poverty rate, and among Samoan Americans, the rate of violent death is greater than in the African American community. Even Koreans—who earlier were perceived as indistinguishable from other Asians—have more recently had to fend off negative and stereotypical images that have been attached to them, perhaps because of the race riots in South Central Los Angeles during the early 1990s. Like other minority experiences, group solidarity among Asian Americans has lessened with their increased diversity in economic class and culture. These changing dynamics make the question of what it means to be an American an ongoing one.

THE NEW FEMINIST MOVEMENT

Another group in American society whose crusade for human rights began in the 1960s was women. By the early seventies the feminist movement had reached a high-water mark in its strident quest for equality. Although there is much about the modern women's liberation movement that is radical and new, at the same time it bears a strong similarity to its nineteenth-century counterpart. Both movements were propelled not by an increase in deprivation and suffering per se; they were, instead, revolutions of rising expectations by groups who found themselves deprived of status and frustrated in their hopes of being full participants in American society.

Actually, it was the accelerated pace of industrialization after the Civil War that gave momentum to the movement during the Gilded Age. The factory system provided many new employment opportunities for women during this period, as did new positions in service industries. Before the turn of the century, women outnumbered men in such fields as telephone work, nursing, and teaching. In the business world, the invention of the typewriter opened an additional

Not all persons in the early suffragette movement chose the moderate approach. Like the lady seated in the cockpit, after the turn of the century there were a growing number of women who rejected their exclusive role as "helpmate" in order to pursue a variety of interests outside the home. (Library of Congress.)

vocational frontier to women. The vast majority of these working women, however, received lower pay than men in the same jobs. Furthermore, most female wage earners still faced the same domestic chores when they returned home from work. Despite these continuing inequities, it can not be denied that these new economic forces led to profound social changes. As the result of the pioneering efforts of Margaret Sanger, for example, the availability of birth control information by the 1920s led to greater independence for the woman and a new image of her role in society. Not only did the size of the family begin to rapidly diminish, but an increasing number of women found other opportunities more attractive than marriage.

The focal point of the feminist movement during the late nineteenth and early twentieth centuries centered on such urgent issues as wages and working conditions of women and children, the right to birth control information, and living conditions in the urban slums. Spurned by the important trade union groups during the Gilded Age, including the American Federation of Labor, women found the attainment of these goals impossible. The result was the National Women's Trade Union League (NWTUL), founded in 1903, and dedicated to the advancement of the interests of working women within the trade union movement. Absorbed with these immediate economic and social concerns, leaders in the women's movement earlier had regarded the more obvious political issue of voting rights as secondary in importance. It gradually became apparent, however, that it was difficult to correct such inequities without the necessary political power. The NWTUL was instrumental in forging the alliance between upper and working class women that played an important role in gaining the right to vote (or suffrage) in 1919. But the right to vote

Susan B. Anthony

Susan B. Anthony was born to Quaker parents in Adams, Massachusetts in 1820. In her early thirties, Anthony left a career in teaching to dedicate herself to social reform. Her earliest interests were in the antislavery crusade and the temperance movement, a crusade to persuade individuals to moderate their consumption of alcohol. The exclusion of women in public affairs and the rigid limits on womens' role in the abolitionist movement convinced Anthony to champion women's rights, including the right to vote. In 1851, she joined the crusade for women's rights. Over the course of a half-century, Susan B. Anthony was one of the leading crusaders for social justice in the United States.

Anthony established a network of "political captains" to lobby the New York state legislature for laws to protect the rights of women. In 1860, Anthony and her captains celebrated the enactment of legislation in the Empire State which granted women the right to bring suit in court and to collect and spend their own wages, which previously could be controlled by fathers or husbands. That victory was prelude to more significant triumphs for the feminist movement during subsequent decades.

After the Civil War, Anthony delivered countless addresses, arguing that voting rights would invest working women with a voice in the nation's political life and would provide women the means to social justice. Along with other radical suffragists, Anthony opposed the Fifteenth Amendment to the Constitution which guaranteed the right to vote on the basis of race but was silent about gender. With its passage in 1869 (it was formally ratified the following year), Anthony and Elizabeth Cady Stanton founded the National Woman Suffrage Association (NWSA), an organization devoted to securing voting rights for women.

In the 1872 congressional election, Anthony cast a ballot and was arrested for voting illegally. At her trial Anthony proclaimed: "Here, in the first paragraph of the Declaration [of Independence], is the assertion of the natural right of all to the ballot; for how can 'the consent of the governed' be given, if the right to vote be denied?" Found guilty by a biased judge, Anthony refused to pay the $100 fine. Following the trial, public opinion of Anthony, which had been predominantly negative, softened. She began to enjoy the respect and praise of many newspaper reporters, political leaders, educators, and the general public.

During the early 1870s, Anthony served as editor of *The Revolution*, a newspaper dedicated to women's issues. As editor, she oversaw the publication of articles on an array of subjects, including women's wages and hours, sexual violence, and birth control. She was also active in the labor union movement. However, after Anthony tried to recruit women as strikebreakers in the printing trade, the male leaders of the National Labor Union expelled her from the union. Anthony then joined the Knights of Labor, which encouraged women to join its ranks and supported women's suffrage and equal pay for equal work, a radical concept in the nineteenth century.

In 1892, she became president of the National American Woman Suffrage Association, the successor organization to the NWSA. During her presidency in the 1890s, the suffrage movement expanded as large numbers of college-educated women entered the movement, distributing pamphlets, conducting public rallies, and lobbying state legislators. Anthony retired in 1900. She remained active in retirement; in 1904, at age eighty-four, she sailed to Germany to attend an international conference on women's rights and, the following year, crossed the nation by train to appear at a suffragist convention in Oregon.

In her twilight years, the venerable matriarch of women's rights celebrated liberalized divorce laws and voting rights for women in six western states. However, the great prize of a constitutional amendment guaranteeing women's voting rights remained as elusive as ever. Many men—and women—continued to oppose women's suffrage, arguing that the "delicacy" and morality of women would be corrupted if women entered the political sphere.

On her deathbed at the age of eighty-six in 1906, Susan B. Anthony measured a tiny space on one of her fingers and said, "I have been striving for over sixty years for a little bit of justice no bigger than that, and yet I must die without obtaining it. Oh, it seems so cruel." Fourteen years after her death, the Nineteenth Amendment was ratified, granting women the right to vote.

for women was seen by many of its supporters as a means, rather than as an end, concerned primarily not with women's rights but with a more general reform of American society.

The suffragists decided to adopt the tactic of expediency in gaining the right to vote. During much of its history, the feminist movement had been tainted by the "radical" label, which helps explain its relative lack of success during the nineteenth century. Feminist activists had marched in parades, participated in strikes, been arrested, and even murdered in their militant quest for equal rights. Not until the public was persuaded that the women's movement was "safe" middle-class, and middle-of-the-road could the feminists hope to achieve their goals. Accordingly, they made their appeal to the Progressive reformers: "Give us the vote to double your political power." A 1915 suffrage banner read:

Key leader for temperance, abolition of slavery and finally women's rights, Susan B. Anthony died just fourteen years before women's suffrage was finally won by the 19th Amendment. © CORBIS

For the safety of the nation
To Women give the vote
For the hand that rocks the cradle
Will never rock the boat.

The leaders who adopted this moderate tactic were confident that although it compromised their objectives to a degree, once suffrage was enacted women would surely support issues that affected them as an oppressed group in American society.

This strategy led to a short-range success, but was a long-range disaster. Although the Nineteenth Amendment was adopted in 1919 giving women the vote, it did not contribute tangibly to the growth of women's rights. The hoped-for bloc vote of female voters failed to materialize. The feminist movement had not been able to convince women of the large middle class that they were an oppressed group. Class, race, and ethnic factors rather than sex proved to be more significant in motivating voting behavior. In a fundamental sense the passage of the Nineteenth Amendment was a hollow victory. As one woman historian has written, "the political and legal gains of feminism amounted to tokenism. Economic advantage proved illusory as well, and consisted for most women of access to low-paid, low-status occupations. The winning of suffrage had failed to emancipate women.

Having gained the right to vote, the feminist movement assumed a low profile for the next 40 years. The morale of the movement received another staggering blow—the loss of any impact

Like other dissident political groups, the women's liberation movement has recognized
the need for publicizing their grievances. Through such eye-catching tactics as public
bra-burning and other forms of protest, they have succeeded in eliminating some forms of
sexist discrimination. (John Messina/Black Star.)

as a voting bloc—because during this lengthy period the issues that confronted the electorate were
generally oriented along economic lines and determined by class interests. With the possible
exception of prohibition, there were no prominent issues that enlisted the special support of
women or appeared to arouse their active opposition. In the meantime, statistics reveal that during
those interwar years American women lost ground in relation to their counterparts in other
industrial nations. Even today, most western European countries and Russia have a higher
percentage of women physicians than the United States. There are more women in the English
Parliament than in the halls of Congress. Though the number of working women in America is
higher than ever before, their occupational segregation is as great as it was in 1900. Moreover,
the gap in incomes between working men and women has widened steadily since World War II,
evidenced by studies during the 1990s.

New vigor did not return to the feminist movement until the 1960s when the college-age daughters born of the war generation grew up. Like their suffragette forerunners, they were generally white, middle class, and well educated. However, unlike their mothers who were raised during the Depression of the 1930s, these girls grew up in a society that was economically secure. Job security seemed an inadequate reward for their college training as they became aware of the pervasive discrimination that persisted on the economic front. It was their generation that had participated in the civil rights revolution of the sixties, although their own ideals and expectations continued to be thwarted by typing and other mundane tasks that they were frequently assigned. Their experiences led them to a closer examination of their own situation, and increasing numbers of young women in the late 1960s and 1970s concluded that they too had been victims of institutional oppression. As with other minority movements, women's studies began to appear on college class lists. Mounting impatience with continued second-class citizenship and economic handicaps surfaced. This, coupled with an awareness of the psychological damage that women have suffered as a result of their subordinate position in American society, caused them to act.

The organization of the contemporary movement comprises a variety of groups, including the National Organization of Women (NOW) and the National Women's Political Caucus (NWPC), in addition to various radical splinter groups. Generally speaking, the active membership of these groups is made up of the educated, white, and middle class. Leaders prominent in the movement include such diverse personalities as journalist and editor of *Ms.* magazine Gloria Steinem, and Betty Friedan, whose popular best seller *The Feminine Mystique* brought so much publicity to the movement. African American women have been almost totally absent from the women's liberation movement.

The experiences of the racial minorities impressed upon the women's liberation movement the need for organization and self-determination. Autonomy in their decision making and organization is a lesson the feminists borrowed from the Black Power movement. With men labeled as the "oppressor," militant members during the 1970s demanded that only females be allowed in women's liberation meetings, believing that male support should be permitted only in subordinate roles. By putting the "oppressor" in "his place," it was hoped that the woman's sense of human identity would be allowed to develop. These radical tactics were designed to lessen the self-denigration which, women's liberation advocates claimed, the male-dominated society imposed upon them. Once again, the analogy of the plight of women and blacks is noteworthy. A feminist pamphlet explained this parallel: "Women and blacks have been alienated from their own culture; they have no historical sense of themselves because study of their condition has been suppressed. . . . Both women and blacks are expected to perform our economic function as service workers. Thus members of both groups have been taught to be passive and to please white male masters in order to get what we want."

The agitation by "Women's Lib" resulted in some success. Sex discrimination in employment was finally prohibited by the Civil Rights Act of 1964. In *Roe v. Wade* (1972) the Supreme Court declared anti-abortion laws to be unconstitutional and maintained that the decision for abortion within the first three months of pregnancy was entirely up to the woman and her physician. Moreover, women began taking their seats in Congress in significant numbers. By

1973, the movement had established itself in more than 400 cities where it was accompanied by a spontaneous sprouting of women's groups in churches, businesses, and other organizations. Despite widespread predictions to the contrary, magazines devoted to the feminist persuasion continued to publish and gain in circulation.

As the struggle for women's rights entered the 1980s, the most dramatic issue proved to be the attempt to ratify the Equal Rights Amendment (ERA) in the state legislatures. The battle was bitter, with the anti-feminists arguing that the ERA would require women to serve in military combat, deprive them of protection in divorce cases, and end special safeguards for working women. When the votes at the statehouses were tallied in 1982, ERA proponents had failed to secure the assent of the thirty-eight states necessary for ratification. Similarly, the gains made by pro-abortion advocates during the early seventies were set back in 1977 when the Supreme Court ruled that the government was not obliged to pay for the abortions of the poor. The conservative swing in the public mood during the 1980s fueled the anti-abortion movement. Its advocates, many strongly religious, decried abortion as murder, pure and simple. They sought to limit abortion to cases involving rape or incest, and to require parental consent for minors.

The conservatism of the Reagan-Bush years helped push the women's movement to change its style. By the 1990s the more ideologically driven gender feminism—with its stress on nurturing femaleness—was effectively challenged by proponents of *equity* feminism. One writer argued that the movement needed to repackage itself as a movement for women, children, and families: "Lesbian rights, although basic in a democracy, will never energize the majority." The form and rhetoric of the radical movement were replaced by a more moderate attitude that sought practical solutions to women's issues. In the meantime, the achievements of the movement have been momentous; besides two Supreme Court Justices, a 1990 CNN poll revealed that 94 percent of American women believe the movement has helped them become more independent. During the 1950s women composed only 20 percent of college undergraduates, whereas in 1990 they represented 54 percent. Since the 1950s the number of female lawyers and judges rose 25 times, physicians 8 times, and the number of women in elected office had skyrocketed, including 47 congresswomen and 6 senators. In short, spokespersons for the women's movement acknowledged that some important gains had been made. But the struggle was far from over.

It is ironic that women's successes on the job market help explain the problems and promise of the future. For example, with 68 percent of women with children under age 18 in the work force, issues like maternity leave, child care, and abortion became topics of heated discussion. Central to the feminist perspective is that only after equality is applied in child-rearing, education, sex, and family can legal and economic equality for women be a reality. Only time would tell whether women would cease being prisoners of their gender.

TO BE AMERICAN

Certainly, the momentum of the human rights movement of the late 1960s and early 1970s had slowed, replaced by the sobering reminder of an overwhelming majority of American voters who supported the social policies of Presidents Nixon, Reagan, and Bush. This middle-income, middle-educated, and middle-aged political coalition demonstrated on numerous issues (busing, women's liberation, fair housing, and employment practices) that it no longer held strong sympathies for the demands of those who see themselves historically as victims of exploitation. This paralysis of social reform efforts poses a dilemma for the nation as it confronts the demands of the 21st century. Rejection of race-based Affirmative Action programs poses serious implications for a society still dedicated to the principles of freedom and equality. Do Americans still share the same values?

Today the erosion of commonly held values is decried by scholars and laypeople alike. During the 1830s, Alexis de Tocqueville, the perceptive French visitor to the United States, noted that American society was bound together by a common moral code and a deep regard for the rule of law. The churches, though of many denominations, promoted similar strands of Judeo-Christian ethics. By their vital social role in early America, these groups contributed to a widely accepted moral and cultural standard. By the 1980s, however, new forces began to question the presumed uniformity of American culture.

During the 1980s and 1990s a movement called "multiculturalism" challenged the nation's self-image. Its advocates reject the traditional unifying theme of consensus in explaining the American past. They dissociate themselves from the notion of a single shared experience, suggesting that the American Dream is actually a nightmare for those whose backgrounds do not match the traditional ideal—namely, a society dominated by white Protestant males. Hence, feminists and other "marginalized" people have attacked the conventional social and academic rules prescribed by white men. All persons, they argue, have a right to know about themselves: where they come from, who they are, and how they have participated in the American story. After all, everyone has been a player—including minorities and women—yet their roles were too often ignored by historians.

Disillusioned by consensus, some multiculturalists have chosen the avenue of isolation. Radical "red power" groups insist upon Native American tribal autonomy from the federal government; lesbian ideologues seek separation from the dominant (male) culture; and some inner-city African Americans demand parity for Ebonics or Black English with standard English in the school curriculum. Each of these groups wants recognition of its role in America. The traditional accent on individualism seems overshadowed by emphasis on group prerogatives. By the late 1990s, this tribalization of America by race and ethnicity was under attack.

Actually, critics question several of the assumptions of multiculturalism, noting that the concept is not new. American society has always been multiethnic, a fact pondered by nineteenth-century writers like Melville, Emerson, and de Tocqueville. Despite recent scholarly challenges to the "melting pot" metaphor to describe the making of America, assimilation has been a major theme. Many former immigrants who intended to remain apart from the mainstream culture eventually discovered that their loyalties shifted after a generation or two. One reluctant new-comer from Scandinavia finally realized that "to live at odds with the cultural life of the nation which has offered us hospitality shows neither wisdom nor gratitude."

Multiculturalism is not rejected entirely by its opponents. They recognize that people's understanding of their past is constantly changing, requiring frequent reassessment by historians. The feminist and civil rights revolutions, for example, have changed the way that Americans look at themselves. Today important scholarship is being generated concerning women, people of color, and diverse cultural backgrounds, persons whose roles and contributions were previously slighted by historians.

By the year 2000, the city of Los Angeles no longer had a racial or ethnic majority. As the entire nation continues its evolution into a multicultural society, there will be less effort by the nonwhite, nonwestern part of the population to assimilate into the traditional Anglo culture. Instead, some studies suggest that the white majority is beginning to recognize the need for reciprocity in the assimilation process. As the minority populations gain on the dwindling white majority, no single group will command the power to dictate solutions. Confrontation over public issues is likely to become the norm. Reaching agreement will require more cooperation than ever before.

Consensus gradually returned to the debate over American social policy by the late 1990s. A growing number of observers called for an end to the advantages afforded to people of color by Affirmative Action. With the unprecedented rise in median income and decline in poverty rates among all minorities during the mid-1990s, it became clear that the social dialogue must be broadened beyond race to include class. Data from the 1996 Census also suggested that although record numbers of Americans were enjoying prosperity, the bottom 20 percent got poorer. Even though the American economy evidenced its strongest surge in twenty years, this underclass seemed permanently entrenched in poverty. A rising tide still does not necessarily raise all boats.

In fact, Lyndon Johnson's original Affirmative Action policy did not include racial preferences, nor did Martin Luther King, Jr. or Robert Kennedy ever endorse that doctrine. Instead, LBJ's vision of a Great Society aimed "to ensure that members of all races had a fair chance to compete." A public policy debate in the late 1990s suggested that a return to LBJ's class-based program for social mobility would hasten racial integration, "but without the increased racial prejudice and hostility associated with racial preferences." By 2000 one poll revealed that Americans seemed eager to support affirmative action based on economic class.

Minority spokesmen echoed this need to redefine the dialogue on race and class. Perhaps multicultural diversity reached its zenith during the 1990s, replaced by a growing recognition of the need to find more common ground. African Americans, Latinos, and Asian Americans must put aside their group identity, said one black writer, arguing that "tolerant coexistence ultimately is not healthy. If we do not mutually pollinate our many cultures, mutual anger will decimate them." By late 1997 a former Chicano activist described in the *Los Angeles Times* the need to "inculcate some shared American values and customs necessary for a flourishing democracy." An African American writer suggested the nation has become so racially and ethnically complex that the race-based policies of the past were now obsolete:

"The time is approaching when Americans of all colors will have to give their racial banners decent burials and kiss even their hyphens goodbye." A Korean American professor predicted that if multiculturalism is to work in modern America, it will require mutual sharing and sacrifice: "It is simply not possible to live in a common social space without interacting. Despite all their differences, ethnic groups have to agree on basic social institutions, structures, laws, and means of communication and eventually produce a common culture." In other words, the price of a coherent unified national culture is sacrifice; accordingly, all ethnic and racial groups must "forego habits, practices and traditions, however hallowed, that promote clannishness, tribalism and callous injustice against the other to the utter disregard of the common good of a diversely constituted public."

Skeptics wonder whether diversity and commonality in America's social fabric are compatible. Even more menacing is racelessness, a kind of blending of the races where there is no longer any room for individual identity. But fears that mainstream assimilation requires giving up of one's own cultural roots are unfounded. One black writer explains that instead, one's own interests are not lost, but rather "subordinated to an overarching American culture." Another writer addresses this more subtle version of national identity, noting that it has two elements: while Americans based their personal identity in their ethnic or religious subculture, at the same time they join a more universal civic culture.

The City of Los Angeles provides a case in point. In the 1993 mayoral race a conservative business-oriented Republican defeated a Chinese American whose candidacy symbolized the new forces of multiculturalism. As voters made their choice, pundits wondered whether Mayor Richard Riordan could create a political climate where these competing ethnic and racial interests can achieve the consensus necessary to drive their municipal government. Four years later Riordan enjoyed reelection, this time against a prominent white liberal, suggesting that common urban coalitions are viable. In *The Rise of Selfishness in America* (1991), James Lincoln Collier writes:

> *What we must do, if we are to make any improvement in our visibly decaying society is, by means of our intelligence and imagination, understand that we are, whether we like it or not, members of a community, or rather sets of communities— neighborhoods surrounded by cities and towns, enclosed in counties and states and finally America. We must come to see that this America is our community, and that, as members of it, we are going to be damaged one way or another if we do not from time to time put the interests of the whole above our own concerns. A people who will not sacrifice for the common good cannot expect to have any common good.*

Achieving a sense of the commonweal at home, however, is not the only challenge. The end of the Cold War provides the United States with new opportunities to help establish a peaceful world order. One writer warns: "if 'tribalization' becomes the norm, it could bring about a country that is a federation of interest-based groups, aligned in only the loosest way. And fifty years down the line, the U.S. may well look like Yugoslavia." As ideological conflict is replaced by ethnic strife, the centrifugal forces of hatred unleashed in areas like the former Soviet Union and Yugoslavia augur poorly for world peace in the twenty-first century. In the meantime, the eyes of the world are fixed on America's noble experiment with multiculturalism, hopeful that social diversity can work.

For 200 years observers have been intrigued by the Frenchman Crevecoeur's celebrated question: "Who then is this new man, this American?" The motto E PLURIBUS UNUM is testimony to America's promise. The United States can demonstrate that the basic principle "from diversity comes unity" is still relevant. If this fundamental creed survives, the United States will become a microcosm of an increasingly interdependent world. America can still offer hope to all of its own citizens and to other countries, but only if it meets the challenge of multiculturalism.

SUGGESTIONS FOR ADDITIONAL READING

Betty Lee Sung, *Mountain of Gold,* (1967). A history of the Chinese in the United States since the gold rush days.

C. Van Woodward, *The Strange Career of Jim* Crow, (1974 edition). A study of the legal separation of the races at the turn of the twentieth century, tracing its repercussions to the 1970s.

Roger Daniels, *The Politics of Prejudice: The Anti-Japanese Movement in California,* (1962). A brief account of the anti-Japanese movement from its inception in the late nineteenth century to its first major triumph with the Immigration Act of 1924.

Carey McWilliams, *North From Mexico,* (1968). A history of the Spanish-speaking people of the United States.

Peter Skerry, *Mexican Americans: The Ambivalent Minority,* (1993). A controversial critique of the current Chicano movement.

Caroline Bird, *Born Female,* (1968). An indictment of the discrimination against women in the United States.

Sara M. Evans and Barbara J. Nelson, *Wage Justice: Comparable Worth and the Paradox of Technocratic Reform,* (1990). A study revealing that women must still cope with the "glass ceiling" on the job market.

David Shipler, *A Country of Strangers: Blacks and Whites in America,* (1997). Insists racism hasn't disappeared, it has just gone underground.

Stephen and Abigail Thernstrom, *America in Black and White,* (1997). Maintains the U.S. has gone a long way towards eliminating racism.

Orlando Patterson, *Rituals of Blood: Consequences of Slavery in Two American Centuries.* (1999).

Stone/Ernest Hass

CHAPTER TEN

ECO-CRISIS: THE ENVIRONMENTAL PROBLEM

1864
Man and Nature, written by George Perkins Marsh, becomes the first book on ecology and conservation in America.

1872
Yellowstone becomes the first national park.

1892
Sierra Club founded to preserve wilderness values.

1913
Conservationists and preservationists differ over the fate of Hetch-Hetchy, which is finally dammed.

1924
Teapot Dome scandal appears in the press; Secretary of the Interior is convicted of taking a $500,000 bribe.

1934–36
A long drought and overplanting turns much of the Great Plains into a Dust Bowl.

1962
Rachael Carson's *Silent Spring* issues the first warning of the dangers of toxic waste.

1964
Congress passes the Wilderness Act.

1970
Passage of the Environmental Protection Act creates an agency with the power and scope to enforce antipollution control measures.

1983
A scandal in the Environmental Protection Agency involving conspiracy to undermine environmental laws embarrasses the Reagan administration.

1992
Rio Conference on the Environment brings ecological issues to the forefront of international affairs.

1998
The U.S. signs the 1997 Kyoto global warming accord.

WHAT IS AT STAKE?

Nearly 74 million Americans live in urban areas that don't meet federal clean air standards. Georgia's endangered species list has grown in the last 20 years by 400 percent . The 1989 Exxon Valdez oil spill in Alaska killed at least 350,000 birds, while a 45 mile stretch of the Sacramento River in California will take at least 40 years to recover from a 1991 pesticide spill. Old growth forests in the Pacific Northwest, once covering 25 million acres, now cover about 4 million with 75 percent of that unprotected from further logging.

Environmental problems, an issue in the United States since the early 1890s, have become increasingly controversial. Concern for environmental health competes with concern for the economic costs of environmental protection and impatience with hordes of government rules and regulations. But for the country's first one hundred years there was no controversy because few believed environmental protection was necessary. The vast majority of Americans was convinced that the continent's abundant natural resources were there to be used, that development was progress. Wild lands were to be tamed, cultivated, and made productive. This "pioneer mentality" was the national attitude towards nature. No lands had to be conserved or preserved because there would always be enough resources for everyone.

THE BEGINNINGS OF APPRECIATION

There were only a few exceptions to this attitude. Some among the well-to-do classes that had leisure enough to read European literature were influenced by a late seventeenth and early eighteenth century philosophical movement called the Enlightenment. This movement was motivated by a strong desire to discover more about the workings of nature through careful observation and rational deductions. Science was reborn in Western society and made great advances. Benjamin Franklin was perhaps the best known American devotee of Enlightenment ideas and principles. Thomas Jefferson was another disciple. His *Notes on the State of Virginia,* published in 1785, recorded an appreciation for nature beyond its scientific descriptions of the land and its inhabitants. A view of the Potomac River rushing deep in the mountain gorge past Harpers Ferry, Virginia is a sight, Jefferson claimed, "worth a voyage across the Atlantic." Telling of a natural rock arch in western Virginia, the author exulted, "It is impossible for the emotions arising from the sublime to be felt beyond what they are here; so beautiful an arch, so elevated, so light, and springing as it were up to heaven!" Jefferson was also a believer in Deism, a religious movement springing out of the Enlightenment. Deism viewed wilderness benevolently, as God's creation and part of His beauty and majesty.

Romanticism, the late eighteenth century movement that reacted against the Enlightenment's emphasis upon reason and the power of rational investigation, went a step further. Romanticists preferred the solitude, awe, and mystery of the wilderness over "tame" nature. If wild country was God's creation, they argued, then it was a statement of His nature and the closer one was to wilderness the closer one would be to God. In land uncontaminated by the touch of people, the romanticist could escape "sinful" society and its works. Primitivism, an outgrowth of romanticism, even maintained that mankind's vigor, strength, and hardiness were the result of direct contact with wild nature. Thus in Europe at least, the American Indian became the "noble savage," imbued with the virtues of innocence and simplicity combined with animal power. Defoe's *The Life and Surprising Adventures of Robinson Crusoe,* an adventure novel about a castaway upon a desert island in the tropics published during this period, became enormously popular. The American author James Fenimore Cooper drew on the "noble savage" and other primitivist ideas to create the *Leatherstocking Tales*—the first stories casting the frontiersman as a hero.

The ideas of romanticism and primitivism reached America in the 1830s. Their New World counterpart was Transcendentalism, born in the villages of New England and raised by Ralph Waldo Emerson and Henry David Thoreau. Emerson was a dissatisfied Unitarian who had left the church to follow his own individualistic path to God. To him wild nature was "a symbol of the spirit," a reflector of "Truth." Behind it lay a higher spiritual world, and the individual having a "spark of the divine" within himself could discover that world and gain insights into its truths. "In the wilderness" Emerson wrote, "I find something more dear than in the streets or villages . . . in the woods we return to reason and faith." Like other Transcendentalists, he was repulsed by the rampant materialism of his day: "Things are in the saddle," he protested, "and ride mankind."

Emerson's disciple, Henry David Thoreau, took up this theme and offered his own solution. "I went to the woods," he explained in the preface to *Walden Pond,* a journal of his experiences in living alone, "because I wished to live deliberately. I wanted to live deep and suck out all the marrow of life, to live so sturdily and Spartan-like as to put to rout all that was not life. . . ." Out of this experience came Thoreau's belief that "the forests and wildernesses" furnish "the tonics and barks which brace mankind"—strength, inspiration, self-knowledge, and vigor. Thoreau was not quite a primitivist, however. His journey into the raw wilderness of northern Maine cured him of those tendencies. There he described the country as "more grim and wild" than he had expected, and he returned convinced that pure wildness was not the answer to mankind's ills. Instead, Thoreau conceived of an ideal blend between the influences of wilderness and civilization: people needed "to combine the hardiness of these savages with the intellectuals of the civilized man." The problem, he felt, was that civilization threatened to overwhelm the last vestiges of wilderness and with it the source of the "raw material of life." America needed wild country to offset the spiritual and physical weaknesses that infected civilized society. "In wildness," Thoreau insisted, "is the preservation of the World."

PROTECT WILDERNESS: A PRESERVATIONIST OUTLOOK

But Thoreau's words were not widely read in his day and he was even less well known than his colleague Emerson. Their ideas barely penetrated outside the borders of New England. Transcendentalist and romantic values would probably have remained intellectual curiosities if the United States had not been experiencing a cultural inferiority complex. American patriots seethed under the taunts of European (particularly British) critics who asked sneeringly if anyone had ever read an American book, viewed an American painting, or seen an American play. What Romantic values did was to provide Americans with a retort. They could point to the unmatched grandeur of the American wilds as a cultural asset and a source of national pride. "Nature was wrought

In "Kindred Spirits," one of the artists of the Hudson River school depicts wild country as a source of inspiration for the poet and painter standing on the rock outcropping. A culture-conscious America reacted positively to this stirring of appreciation for wilderness in the 1840s. (Painting by Asher B. Durand, Courtesy of the New York Public Library.)

with a bolder hand in America," proclaimed one pictorial volume, while another declared that America's vast wilderness wonders were "unsurpassed by any of the boasted scenery of other countries." Novelist Washington Irving felt that this asset was more than an esthetic one:

> *"We send our youth abroad to grow luxurious and effeminate in Europe; it appears to me, that a previous tour on the prairies would be more likely to produce that manliness, simplicity, and self-dependence most in unison with our political institutions."*

James Fenimore Cooper's frontier stories and the Hudson River school's landscape paintings also celebrated the asset of wilderness. The poet William Cullen Bryant urged America to "keep that earlier, wilder image bright."

That image was fast disappearing under the pioneer's onslaught. Strip mines and denuded forests could not qualify as cultural assets, and the "march of civilization" had already trampled many of the eastern natural wonders underfoot. The experience of watching 1400 buffalo massacred just for their tongues moved artist George Catlin to call in 1832 for a "nation's park, containing man and beast, in all the wild freshness of their nature's beauty." The idea was not entirely new. Thoreau had urged that some wild places be set aside, "for modesty and reverence's sake, or if only to suggest that earth has higher uses than we put her to."

But it was among a relatively small group of well-to-do Easterners who lived in the city and escaped to the wilderness for relaxation that the park idea began to take tangible shape. Besides being impressed by the romantic idea that America's scenic resources were her greatest national asset and should be preserved, they had seen many of the endangered areas first hand. One of these areas, Yosemite Valley, was declared a California state park in 1864 largely because of the influence of these traveling easterners. Six years later, responding to the rumor of fantastic "wonders," several others visited the Yellowstone area in Wyoming. They returned determined to preserve the unique geysers, hot springs, and canyons they had seen. A bill was brought before Congress in 1871 proposing the creation of a Yellowstone National Park. Supporters of the measure had to assure skeptical legislators that the country was too high and cold for cultivation and that its preservation would do "no harm to the material interests of the people." Yellowstone was presented as a valuable national scenic resource, but more as a "natural amusement park" than as a wilderness preserve. It didn't hurt the effort when the Northern Pacific Railroad, foreseeing mounds of tourist dollars, lobbied for the bill. Congress passed it in 1872—the nation had its first national park and preservation had won its first national victory.

WISE USE OF RESOURCES: THE CONSERVATIONIST IMPULSE

While these nationalists and romanticists were beginning to act on behalf of wilderness, another group entered the controversy. Pride in the grandeur of the American landscape or romantic love of nature's inspirational qualities were not the primary concern of these people. Instead, they feared that mismanagement and waste were destroying the nation's natural resources at an ominously accelerating rate. One of the first men to warn of the effects of this waste was George Perkins Marsh in his book *Man and Nature* (1864). Marsh pointed out that clear-cutting of the forests of northern New York was resulting in floods and erosion. America, he warned, was repeating the experience of ancient Greek and Roman Mediterranean cultures that had destroyed their land and fallen into decline as a result. "Let us be wise in time," he urged, "and profit by the errors of our older brethren." To safeguard the watershed that regulated stream flow and prevented disastrous runoffs, wilderness forest should be preserved "as far as possible, in its primitive condition." These areas could then be "a garden for the recreation of the lover of nature" as well as serving the practical function of a watershed. During the 1880s the Adirondack country in upstate New York, which Marsh had written about, became a popular recreational area for sportsmen. These people joined with those who agreed with Marsh's economic arguments and pressured the New York State legislature into preserving 715,000 acres of Adirondack forest.

It was these people who put forth economic arguments that carried the day. Without a constant water supply, these pragmatists feared for their profitable canals and farms and insisted that the cutting of the Adirondack forests "will seriously injure the internal commerce of the State." Nor was this sudden interest in the care of natural resources restricted to the state of New York. Carl Schurz, Secretary of the Interior during the Hayes administration, called for the creation of government owned and managed forest reserves. Such reserves were created a decade later, but there was no one to manage them. One-armed John W. Powell, head of the United States Geological Survey, warned that lack of water in the Southwest would make the traditional pattern of homestead settlement a disaster. He recommended that the government supervise development on a river basin scale, but he was ignored. Many small homesteaders and ranchers failed, and Arizona and New Mexico did not attract enough settlers to become states until 1912.

In fact, a "Great Raid" on the nation's natural resources was occurring. Spurred by the belief that resources were endless and unhindered by a laissez-faire government, it brought progress at a horrific cost in waste and destruction. Oil strikes often resulted in uncontrolled "gushers" that wasted thousands of barrels of "black gold" (the record was held by Spindletop, Texas—a gusher of 110,000 barrels a day for nine days). By 1920 over 80 percent of old growth forest was gone and over 25 million acres has been ruined by fire. The bison herds, once numbering an estimated 20 million, were down to a few hundred in 1880. Seal populations on the Pacific coast declined 97 percent, and the beaver was saved only because a change in hat fashions made it unprofitable to hunt.

PROGRESSIVE ENVIRONMENTALISM

But the passing of the frontier in 1890 brought the issue before the entire country. America's western frontier had been the symbol of abundance, growth, and progress for nearly 250 years. When it ended it also broke the myth of the land's inexhaustibility and even called into question the creed of perpetual progress. Articles appeared in newspapers and magazines across the country detailing stories of mismanagement and waste. Accustomed to abundance, Americans were afraid of scarcity. Frederick Jackson Turner's "frontier thesis" connected open western lands with the development of democracy and individual opportunity. Could the national character survive without a frontier? These questions created wider concern for environmental issues. The first forest reserves were set aside in 1891, and the Forest Management Act of 1897 opened them to careful use under government supervision. The Sierra Club was formed to save wild areas in 1892 after major campaigns to create Yosemite and Sequoia National Parks.

The 1890s raised other issues as well. Urban pollution and overcrowding, the poverty of the working masses, and the great power of the giant corporations created by industrialization were producing protests, strikes, and national unrest. The calls of reformers for government intervention helped make National Parks and Forests possible, and as the twentieth century opened a new movement dedicated to action on the nation's problems rose to power—Progressivism.

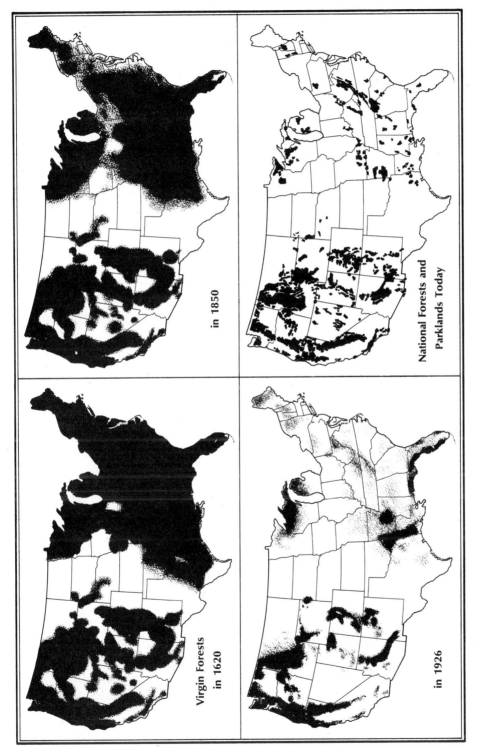

Virgin Forests
in 1620

in 1850

in 1926

National Forests and
Parklands Today

Before the American government imposed effective restrictions on logging activities, private companies had cleared vast areas of virgin forest in the United States. Even today, not all of the remaining stands of timber are adequately protected.

The Progressives began as a movement to clean up the cities and rescue state governments from control by development interests. At the national level, the movement was led by President Theodore Roosevelt (1901–09). Roosevelt was a hunter, an avid camper and naturalist, and enthusiastic about the emerging environmental movement. The president's spokesman for environmental issues was a European-trained forester named Gifford Pinchot.

Pinchot proposed to make conservation government policy and a household word. Conservation proposed, in his words, "the use of the natural resources for the greatest good of the greatest number for the longest time" under the careful supervision of the national government. Pinchot and other conservationists conceived of nature as a "farm" whose careful planning and management would yield "crops" like lumber year after year. To do this, areas of the national domain would, from time to time, be set aside and scientifically managed so that a continuous yield might be assured for future generations. In other words, efficiency in the public interest would replace private waste. Pinchot and the conservationists were not opposed to parks, but considered them something of a luxury.

Under Roosevelt's and Pinchot's leadership, Congress finally put the care of the national forests into the hands of a professional Forest Service. The Roosevelt administration more than tripled the acreage in the system. A Bureau of Reclamation was created to build water projects in the arid West and drain swamplands in the East. In 1906 the Antiquities Act created the National Monument system, designed to preserve areas of scientific and historic interest. The Grand Canyon was made a national monument, and five other new parks were set aside for the public to visit and enjoy. President Roosevelt also created the first National Wildlife Refuges to preserve endangered game animals. In 1908 he hosted a conference of state governors at the White House on the environment and insisted that conservation of resources was critical to national security.

In almost all of these endeavors conservationists and preservationists worked together to stop the worst excesses of the "Great Raid." The whole program angered many Westerners who felt that Federal forest reserves and parks and restrictions on water usage "locked up" raw materials, violating the "rights" of private enterprise. Pioneer attitudes were still strong in the West, where there was yet much unoccupied land and a wealth of untapped resources. Environmentalism was primarily an eastern-led movement.

Roosevelt's conservation and preservation efforts were nevertheless widely accepted as necessary and desirable. Conservation's doctrine of efficient use of natural resources was especially practical and utilitarian, matching most Americans' attitudes toward nature. After all, conservationists sought to insure continued growth and progress with less waste and more care. "The first duty of the human race," insisted Pinchot, "is to control the earth it lives upon."

CONSERVATION AND PRESERVATION CLASH

Preservationists who fought for the creation of Yellowstone National Park and worked with Pinchot and Roosevelt were nevertheless disappointed in conservation. "It is much to be regretted," wrote the preservationist-minded editor of *Century* magazine, "that the official leaders of

GIFFORD PINCHOT

Gifford Pinchot was born in 1865 to an old Pennsylvanian family made wealthy in commerce. He was graduated from Yale in 1889 with a desire to do graduate work in "silviculture," or forestry management. But at the time there was not a single school of forestry in the United States. Pinchot went to France and Germany to learn this science, old in Europe but new to America. Returning to the States, he was given a position on the 6000 acre estate of the Vanderbilts in North Carolina. There he began to turn the woodlands into a model of timber management and gained a reputation for skill, drive, and determination.

In 1896 Pinchot was asked to head the Forestry Commission, but it was a commission restricted to recommendations. Pinchot, over the objections of his friend Muir, sought to open the forest reserves to logging, mining, and grazing under government supervision. This succeeded in 1897, and the commission was upgraded to a division in the Department of Interior. But the Interior Department was focused on selling off most government land and was not interested in a service that would go out to the national forests and manage them. Pinchot worked to build up a small staff, dedicated to the principle of multiple resource use and trained in forest management. He drew them from the new Yale School of Forestry, endowed for $300,000 by his parents. In his spare time he advised New York Governor Theodore Roosevelt on the care of the Adirondack forest and the two became close friends.

When TR got into the White House, Pinchot became the President's advisor on conservation policy. By 1905, after a long bureaucratic struggle, the Division of Forestry was transferred to the Department of Agriculture and a National Forest Service was created. Pinchot and his foresters traveled throughout the west propagandizing for the principles of conservation, recognizing that unless the population understood and supported the policy that it was doomed to failure. Local rangers had full authority to decide local questions, and gradually public support grew. Roosevelt, advised by Pinchot, added nearly 100 million new acres to the National Forests, and called a White House Conference on Conservation that made the term a household word.

But after Roosevelt's departure, Pinchot's influence declined. Pinchot was a strong progressive, and Roosevelt's successor, William H. Taft, was more conservative. When an inspector in the Department of the Interior gave Pinchot information alleging a conflict of interest involving Secretary of the Interior Ballinger, Pinchot's fighting instincts were aroused. Ballinger had leased coal lands in Alaska to a mining syndicate that he had once represented as a lawyer. President Taft sided with Ballinger on a technicality and ordered Pinchot to drop the issue. The argument leaked to the press, Pinchot defended himself in a letter to his senator, and Taft fired him. When Roosevelt returned from an African safari, Pinchot complained that the progressive movement was suffering under Taft. "A sharp sword," said Pinchot of Roosevelt, had been "succeeded by a roll of paper, legal size [Taft]."

Pinchot supported TR in his Progressive party bid for the presidency in 1912. When that effort failed, Pinchot retired. He was rejected by the Republicans for the presidency in 1920 and turned to public service in Pennsylvania, although he was involved in the investigation of Secretary of Interior Albert Fall's alleged bribery in the Teapot Dome scandal. He served two terms as governor of Pennsylvania and offered to rally liberal Republican support for Franklin Roosevelt during the 1930s. Pinchot died in 1946.

Preservationist John Muir (fourth from right) often guided parties of influential men to his favorite haunts in the Sierras. On these trips, Muir hoped that his companions would be imbued with his enthusiasm for wilderness, and would join him in the preservation movement. Here he poses with President Theodore Roosevelt (sixth from right) on an excursion into Kings Canyon. (Courtesy The Bancroft Library, University of California, Berkeley.)

the conservation movement have never shown a cordial, much less an aggressive, interest in safeguarding our great scenery." To this cause the preservationists were dedicated, and they found a champion in John Muir.

Muir grew up in Wisconsin, but it was in California's Sierra Nevada that he developed a strong love for wilderness that inspired his writings and actions on its behalf. Muir adopted Emerson's and Thoreau's Transcendental views toward nature and wild country. Muir realized that the best way to insure the preservation of wilderness was to build public support for it by getting more people out into wild country where they could appreciate it. He became an avid writer of travel articles and an activist for wilderness. Along with scientists at the University of California, Berkeley, Muir established the Sierra Club to fight for preservationist values.

Increasingly, Muir's disciples and Pinchot's followers differed with each other over government policy toward the nation's remaining wilderness. Both groups fought private misuse of nature, but the preservationists were mainly interested in preserving wilderness from man while the conservationists wanted to use nature to serve man. Which "use" was really "wise"?

The two approaches clashed in 1906 when San Francisco, seeking to increase its water supply, asked the federal government for permission to dam the Hetch-Hetchy in the middle of Yosemite National Park. President Roosevelt, who had vacationed with Muir in the area and appreciated its beauty, hesitated. Government engineers told him that there was no other real alternative to Hetch-Hetchy as the site for construction. Pinchot and the conservationists sup-

JOHN MUIR

John Muir was eleven years old when his family moved from Scotland to the Wisconsin frontier to homestead a farm. Although the work was hard, Muir enjoyed the outdoors. He was a voracious reader, and his father had him commit all of the New Testament and much of the Old to memory. In 1860 Muir's mechanical genius won acclaim at the state fair, and he left the farm to spend two and a half years at the University of Wisconsin. While working at a bicycle shop, a file slipped in Muir's hand and pierced his eye. He spent a month in recovery before his sight returned, and this incident convinced him that he should go where his heart had long led — into the wilds of America.

Muir's first trip was a thousand mile walk to the Gulf coast, begun in 1867. He then made ambitious plans to go with an expedition that was searching for the source of the Amazon River, but a bout with malaria convinced him to opt for a cooler climate. Muir took ship for California. When he arrived he asked for directions to the nearest forest. It wasn't long before he crossed the central valley and hiked into the mountains that were to fascinate him for the rest of his life — the Sierra Nevada.

In his wilderness jaunts Muir traveled light. He usually took a knapsack, some tea, some bread, his journal, and occasionally a plant press. He loved the wild country, writing "going to the woods is going home." Redwood forests were "temples." "Civilized man chokes his soul," Muir felt, with the cares of the world. He urged Americans to "climb the mountains and get their good tidings. Nature's peace will flow into you as the sunshine into the trees. The winds will blow their freshness into you, and the storms their energy, while cares will drop off like autumn leaves."

After a decade in the Yosemite area where he was the first to identify the role glaciers played in the formation of that magnificent valley, Muir settled down on a ranch in Martinez and married. Disturbed by the poor care Yosemite was receiving from the State of California, Muir wrote an article for *Century* magazine calling for Yosemite to be made a national park. In 1890 that dream came true. The following year Congress created the National Forest Reserves, which Muir hoped would remain untouched as wilderness. This hope was dashed in 1897 when the reserves were opened up to government supervised exploitation and management. But the Sierra Club, which Muir had helped to form, led the fight to create new national parks and to keep some areas within the forest reserves wild.

Muir extended his travels to include Washington, Alaska, Arizona, and Oregon. He wrote so compellingly that his articles championing the cause of wilderness preservation were in high demand. In 1903 he led Theodore Roosevelt on a trip into the Yosemite area. The VIPs with the President had a hard time, but upon waking up with three inches of snow on his bedroll the President shouted, "This is the grandest day of my life!"

Muir's last battle was to save the Hetch-Hetchy valley in Yosemite National Park from being dammed as a reservoir for the city of San Francisco. Despite initial success, Muir and the preservationists eventually lost the fight. "They will see what I mean in time," Muir commented sadly. He died shortly after the dam bill was signed by President Wilson in 1913.

---

ported the plan, maintaining that the damage to the valley was "altogether unimportant compared with the benefits to be derived from its use as a reservoir." Reluctantly, Roosevelt agreed and sent the proposal to Congress for approval. A fierce battle developed between the conservationists and the preservationists led by John Muir. As far as the latter were concerned, the measure violated the whole national park concept as wilderness preserves from which the nation could draw enjoyment and inspiration. They were certain that once Yosemite was violated, it would be used as precedent for similar projects in still other parks. So the preservationists marshaled their forces. They appealed to the growing sentiment in America that the remaining wilderness was the nation's last frontier, the last places where people could go and experience what the pioneers had encountered. It was something central to the development of American institutions and the national character. They also made the issue one between God and materialism. Muir wrote angrily that "these temple destroyers, devotees of ravaging commercialism, seem to have a perfect contempt for nature, and instead of lifting their eyes to the God of the Mountains lift them to the almighty dollar."

Muir and the preservationists stirred up such a storm of public protest that the proposal to build the dam was stalled in Congress. But San Francisco was not to be so easily frustrated. Referring to the preservationist's position as "hogwash and mushy esthetics," it renewed lobbying efforts in Washington on behalf of the dam. Conservationists answered the preservation arguments over esthetics by maintaining that the lake behind the dam would be a beautiful area for public recreation. Congressional opinion began to shift. As one senator said, "I appreciate the importance of preserving beautiful natural features of landscape as much as anybody else," yet esthetics could not take precedence over "the urgent needs of great masses of human beings for the necessities of life." Congress finally passed the proposal in 1913. Hetch-Hetchy was dammed, but by their efforts to arouse public support the preservationists had transformed their cause into a national movement. Three years later, preservationists won creation of the National Park Service to protect America's great scenery.

ENVIRONMENTAL ENGINEERING AND A NEW LAND ETHIC

As twentieth century urbanization proceeded, middle class Americans turned increasingly to the out of doors as a source of recreation. Organizations like the Boy Scouts encouraged this as a way to maintain American frontier virtues in city boys. Fascinated by the exploits of Edgar Rice Burroughs's *Tarzan of the Apes* and Jack London's *Call of the Wild,* Americans even developed an interest in the old virtues of primitivism. The invention of the automobile made wild areas previously inaccessible more easily reached (and more easily overcrowded) by larger numbers of people. Conservationists also had some successes, such as regulating fisheries and promoting hydroelectric power projects.

Yet the rising levels of prosperity after World War I and the reassurance that America was not running out of resources so quickly after all dampened public enthusiasm for protecting the environment. Republican administrations filled regulatory agencies with permissive leaders and left environmentalism to the states. In 1924 Secretary of the Interior Albert Fall leased federal land reserves in Teapot Dome, Wyoming to a private oil company for a $500,000 bribe. Americans were light-headed with the progress and affluence of the 1920s.

The 1929 Crash and the resulting depression brought people back to reality. Unrestrained free enterprise had not brought the perpetual prosperity people had expected and ignoring conservation had extracted a price. Overgrazing and poor farming practices eroded millions of tons of topsoil, while careless management of federal lands had led to further waste and depletion.

THE TEAPOT DOME SCANDAL

The Teapot Dome scandal was one of the worst in American environmental history. One cabinet member eventually went to prison for his part in the affair, and so many leading Republicans were implicated that in 1924 party control of Congress and the White House were threatened.

Back in the Progressive era, a bipartisan policy had set aside oil lands (called "domes" because of the geologic formations that trapped the oil underground) as naval reserves to be tapped only in case war required it. As the 1920s began, however, conservative and Western Republicans claimed that rising national prosperity made the reserves obsolete. American oil companies, they claimed, could easily handle any anticipated crisis.

When former New Mexico Senator Albert B. Fall became Secretary of the Interior in 1921, the critics gained a sympathetic ear. Fall had been a land developer and a lawyer who had opposed Progressive conservation and was now in a position to change government policies. Fall convinced the Secretary of the Navy to turn the reserves over to Interior. In 1922 he secretly leased the Teapot Dome, Wyoming reserve and a California field to two big oil firms in return for $400,000 in gifts and "loans." But secrets are tough to keep in Washington, and when two Progressive senators discovered the lease they started a Senate investigation in 1923. The press played up the scandal, along with others that began to be uncovered.

The man who had given Fall the job at Interior, President Harding, died that year and was succeeded by Vice President Coolidge. Coolidge was an incorruptible New Englander who was determined to "clean house" in the administration. Fall had to resign. Fall's VIP friend, Attorney General Harry Daugherty, had winked at so many corrupt practices under Harding that he, too, was forced out in 1924. The Supreme Court invalidated the leases, one of the oil company CEOs was convicted of criminal contempt of court, and Fall was found guilty of bribery and sentenced to prison.

Conservationists had won the battle to save Teapot Dome, but they lost the war to continue Progressive policies and save the reserves. Pro-development Republicans continued to dominate the decade, and government agencies generally bowed to business appetites for greater production. Environmental initiatives were largely left to the states. The oil reserves, given so much importance in the press coverage, faded from public memory and were sold off after World War II.

President Franklin Roosevelt, elected to offer a "New Deal" to the American people, included a revived environmentalism in his reform program. A Civilian Conservation Corps was created to put men to work on roads, bridges, campgrounds, and reforestation. Measures to improve farming and grazing practices were passed by Congress. Another act protected fish and wildlife in an expanded system of preserves. Traditional programs of flood control and land reclamation were financed more generously. Yet the New Deal proposed to use recent technological and scientific advances to take conservation a step further.

This was the concept of environmental engineering. Developed by planner and engineer Benton MacKaye, it held that the environment could and should be totally controlled and managed in the best interests of society. This meant planning for city green areas, recreation, and parks as well as controlling logging, mining, and water needs. Part of environmental engineering was the concept of multipurpose development, the idea that a single area could be managed to perform

THE DUST BOWL

The Dust Bowl was the greatest ecological disaster of modern times. Covering almost 100 million acres of the plains states of Kansas, Oklahoma, Colorado, New Mexico, and Texas, it wiped out 32 million acres of the nation's productive farmland for almost a decade at a cost to the nation of over $400 million. And the tragedy of the Dust Bowl was that it was largely man-made.

Boom times during World War I led plains farmers to eye marginal lands that had been too far from water to be productive. Landowning railroads encouraged this by funded touring "scientific dry land farming" exhibits, promising bumper crops. Plowing would crack the tough prairie sod, break the soil up into fine, almost dust-like particles, and prepare it to soak up the anticipated rain. Drought-resistant wheat would be planted. When the rains came, tractors would turn over the soil, trapping the water and preventing it from evaporating.

By 1930 over five million new acres of wheat had been planted. A huge harvest rolled into the silos. What the farmers didn't know was that the Great Plains were subject to seasonal droughts. To make things worse, the land was being stripped of its natural cover, the tough prairie grass. The interlocking root system of the grass kept its grip on the topsoil, so even in the worst plains storms erosion was kept to a minimum. Now there would be no protection when the droughts returned and the windstorms blew in fury out of the Rockies and central Canada.

The first blow to the farmers came with the beginning of the Depression. Crashing prices broke farmers, who either abandoned their lands or were forced off by bankruptcy. Vast acres were left unplanted and subject to wind erosion. A drought set in. Dry wind storms began to whip over fields unsheltered by either grass or growing wheat in the spring of 1933. More than 300 million tons of topsoil just blew away. Some families endured, some went crazy, more than half of them simply left, packing up whatever they had left and heading along Route 66 for California where rumor said there were field jobs. John Steinbeck dramatized the human toll in *The Grapes of Wrath*.

Washington acted in 1935, passing the Soil Conservation Act championed by conservationist Hugh Bennett. Farmers would be trained to use soil conservation techniques like contour plowing, leaving the soil in clumps that weren't as subject to wind erosion, replanting bare areas in prairie sod, planting tree wind breaks and reducing grazing.

Slowly, rain, the new techniques, and replanting the grasslands began to make a difference. World War II helped land and wheat prices to recover, and wide use of the new conservation practices limited further damage. The Plains farms recovered—but the human toll was high. Conservationists today feel that reliance on the huge Oglala aquifer to water the plains crops at a rate greater than the rains can replenish will lead to another disaster when the aquifer dries up.

---

several functions. Environmental engineering's greatest achievement was the Tennessee Valley Authority (TVA), which was given wide powers to totally reconstruct and manage the valley's environment for the benefit of its people. Following a master plan and consulting with the valley's residents as the project developed, the TVA totally remodelled the entire valley as an economic and social unit. Roads, dams, power stations, housing, recreation parks, protecting local wildlife, and landscaping were all integrated. The project proved to be one of the most successful undertaken by the New Deal, and has only been exceeded in size or scope by NASA. By creating prosperity in a formerly depressed region, environmental engineering proved that with technology and science Americans now had the power to alter at will the face of their nation.

Like conservation before it, environmental engineering boldly assumed that people could change nature's order without really upsetting her balance. Aldo Leopold was one of the first Americans to challenge this assumption. Leopold began his career in the 1920s as a forester in New Mexico, where he also worked for the preservation of wilderness areas in the state. Like Muir and Thoreau, he believed that wild areas were essential to maintaining the quality of American life. He also agreed with historian Frederick Jackson Turner that the American character and experience had been formed by contact with the frontier. "Is it not a bit beside the point," Leopold wrote during the era of New Deal reform, "for us to be so solicitous about preserving American institutions without giving so much as a thought to preserving the environment which produced them and which may now be one of our effective means of keeping them alive?" Leopold was firmly in the preservationist tradition, and his protests helped to establish an official policy of preservation in the national forests. Private organizations like the Wilderness Society, founded by outdoor enthusiast Bob Marshall in 1935, also promoted preservation.

But it was not until Leopold began to study the new science of ecology (the interrelationship of all living organisms that share an environment) and visited Mexico's Sierra Madre wilderness that he realized that "land is an organism, that all my life I had seen only sick land." Drawing upon the ideas of Muir, Thoreau, and contemporary Albert Schweitzer, Leopold developed a "land ethic." "The land ethic," he explained, "changes the role of homo sapiens from conqueror of the land community to plain member and citizen of it." This was dramatized by the commonly accepted Darwinian theory of evolution, which maintained that mankind, like the rest of life, had evolved from a common origin. People should, therefore, extend their sense of ethics and decide environmental action "in terms of what is ethically and esthetically right, as well as what is economically expedient." "A thing is right," declared Leopold, "when it tends to preserve the integrity, stability, and beauty of the biotic community. It is wrong when it tends otherwise." Leopold now had three reasons for urging the preservation of wilderness: to study scientifically how the community of life operates; to remind people who "fancy that industry supports us, forgetting what supports industry" of the elemental man-land relationship; and simply to demonstrate respect for the biotic community of which people are a part.

THE IMPACT OF AFFLUENCE

Leopold, however, was ahead of his time. His contemporaries were more committed to full economic recovery than to environmental health. And in the 1940s, laboring under the incentives of wartime demands for huge quantities and varieties of resources, science appeared to offer an alternative to the "land ethic." Mountains of goods were turned out from increasingly efficient factories. Research and development produced man-made substitutes for scarce natural resources like rubber. "Wonder chemicals" like DDT appeared which promised greater agricultural yields by eliminating pests. Most awesome of all, the "Manhattan Project" expertise had produced an atomic bomb and promised a new age of cheap, clean nuclear energy. Technology appeared to have all of the answers, and many people came to believe that given enough money, experts, and time, any human or environmental problem could be solved.

This attitude produced public complacency towards resource and pollution problems in the 1950s. Rising demands for timber threatened forests in Olympic National Park. The growing hunger for energy led to proposals for hydroelectric dams in the Grand Canyon and in King's Canyon National Park. Serious air and water pollution problems spread beyond the old manufacturing centers in the Northeast and the Midwest. A mushrooming number of automobiles shrouded cities like Los Angeles in smog. Ignoring these problems or considering them the "price of progress," a rapidly increasing population expected to enjoy an ever-rising level of affluence.

Many Americans began looking for the "good life" in the southwestern "Sunbelt." Anticipating this region's growth, a blueprint emerged in Congress for the creation of an ambitious Colorado River Storage Project (CRSP). The billion-dollar project proposed a ten-dam, multipurpose complex to provide flood control, irrigation and hydroelectric power for the Southwest. There was, however, a problem. One of the dams was slated for Echo Park on the Green River, within Utah's Dinosaur National Monument. Preservationists rose in wrath against yet another threat to the aesthetic sanctity of the National Monuments and Parks. Three hundred organizations pooled their resources in a massive public relations campaign against the dam. An avalanche of mail descended on Congress, stacking up 80 to 1 against the Echo Park dam, and the legislators delayed a vote until after the 1954 elections. By the next year a new analysis of the dam revealed that evaporation and siltation rates made its value questionable. Faced with mounting opposition, proponents of CRSP finally yielded. They dropped the Echo Park dam and promised not to include in the project any other dam that would intrude on a national park or monument. The preservationists had avenged Hetch-Hetchy.

The 1960s brought a change of national mood. Although affluence continued to grow, deteriorating environmental conditions, especially in the cities, was leading to concern over the "quality of life." Possessing material prosperity, middle class Americans also wanted to enjoy healthy living conditions and natural beauty. Recreational vehicles (RVs) swarmed into the hinterland. New parks, like Redwoods National Park in California, were created by a responsive government. The Wilderness Act, introduced after the Echo Park fight in 1957, finally gave permanent protection to many remaining wild areas in the country after its passage in 1964. A Wild and Scenic Rivers Act, passed in 1968, complemented this system. President Lyndon Johnson, personally committed to both conservation and preservation, launched a "beautify America" campaign in the White House Conference on Conservation in 1965. Focusing on the cities, it instituted a cleanup campaign against litter and visual pollution across the country. The President's model cities and urban renewal programs promoted metropolitan reconstruction and a planned environment while promoting the preservation of historic structures like Sacramento's "Old Town."

The health issue was being dealt with simultaneously but more slowly. The fallout scare of the early 1950s was the first indication that technology could backfire, and the Nuclear Test Ban Treaty of 1963 was as much an environmental coup as a diplomatic one. Controversy broke out in 1962 with the publication of Rachael Carson's *Silent Spring,* which revealed the environmental impact of the indiscriminate use of pesticides like DDT on animal and human life. Some controls

DAVID BROWER

Born just two years before John Muir's death in 1914, David Brower would eventually inherit the old mountain man's mantle of wilderness spokesman. He began, however, as a painfully shy young man who developed his conversational style by verbally picturing his mountain hikes for his blind mother. Brower connected with the Sierra Club and became an accomplished rock climber, eventually pioneering ascent routes for thirty-three Sierra mountain peaks. As publicist for Yosemite's Curry Company, Brower frequently used the photos of his friend Ansel Adams to illustrate the promotions he wrote for the company. He would later regret encouraging people to mob Yosemite National Park, writing in 1945 after a visit to the Italian Alps that Europe had overdeveloped her mountains for recreationists and ruined her wilderness.

In 1949 Brower helped begin a series of conferences promoting preservation of the remaining American wilderness. "We have been playing," he wrote, "a game of strip poker with the American earth . . . all but guaranteeing that our children will lose as the game goes on." In 1950 Brower and the Sierra Club, at that time a California organization of only about 7000 members, led a national campaign against two dams planned for Dinosaur National Monument and won. Somewhat to his surprise, Brower found he could excel not only as a publicist but as a lobbyist and charismatic speaker as well. Later, when engineers claimed that hydroelectric dams proposed for the Grand Canyon would bring visitors nearer the rock walls, Brower asked sarcastically if we "should also flood the Sistine Chapel so that tourists can get nearer the ceiling." The dams were never built. As Executive Director of the Sierra Club, Brower designed a series of beautifully written and illustrated "coffee table" books that introduced many easy-chair Americans to wilderness and the values of wild country. These works, and hard-hitting full page ads in the nation's newspapers, boosted Club membership, helped pass the Wilderness Act in 1964, and preserved Redwoods National Park in 1968. Brower had become a nationally known environmentalist, nicknamed "the Archdruid" by an admiring biographer.

But Brower had left Club finances on the edge and had alienated powerful figures with his strident advocacy and individualist temperament. He was deposed as Club Director. But Brower wasn't finished—within a few months he had formed Friends of the Earth to tackle global environmental issues. By 1970, FOE membership had skyrocketed from 1000 to 16,000. He also worked hard to build the nation's largest environmental lobbying organization, the League of Conservation Voters, and another global environmental watchdog, the Earth Island Institute.

At 82, Brower came full circle when he was elected to the Sierra Club Board of Directors. Time has not dimmed his advocacy—"I was not always unreasonable," he quipped in his 1995 work *Let the Mountains Talk, Let the Rivers Run;* "and I'm sorry for that." Brower continues to hammer home his message: "We need a new ethic. Our current approach has led us to a brink. We do not inherit the earth from our ancestors, we borrow it from our children."

---

on the uses of herbicides and pesticides were gradually applied, but the wider and equally serious issue of toxic chemicals and wastes went untouched until the late 1970s. Initial moves were made to control water pollution in 1965 and air contamination in 1967, but neither of these efforts were sufficiently comprehensive or strict on polluters. Real progress in these areas awaited the onslaught of the "eco-movement" of the late 1960s and early 1970s.

THE ECO-MOVEMENT

A grassroots movement for environmental health appeared to blossom overnight when tens of thousands of people across the nation turned out for demonstrations on Earth Day, April 22, 1970. Actually, the movement had been slowly building since the mid '60s. One of its first successes had been the passage of the Endangered Species Act of 1966, the first time the government had extended protection to nongame animals. But events in the late 1960s had dramatized the need for strong action to halt severe environmental deterioration. The "death" of Lake Erie (prematurely announced), the heavily polluted Cuyahoga River catching fire, the clear rise in deaths during a particularly bad smog siege in Los Angeles, and the Santa Barbara oil spill all contributed to the evidence that swift action was needed. Scientists like Barry Commoner and Garret Hardin wrote alarming accounts of the nation's environmental plight. Although originating with the young, who were already protesting corporate and "establishment" misdeeds and even opting for a back-to-nature "counter-culture," it soon spread to the middle class as an extension of the concern in the early sixties over the quality of life.

For the first time, the federal government adopted stringent antipollution control measures. The Clean Air Act of 1970 set tough controls on auto emissions and Detroit began to invest in research and development on smaller, more lightweight and fuel-efficient cars. The Water Pollution Act of 1972 appropriated billions to clean up the nation's water supply. Most importantly, the Environmental Protection Agency was established to coordinate and enforce federal environmental laws, and to bring violators to court. Development schemes that would once have proceeded without questions, like the construction of a supersonic transport jet (SST), were stopped on the grounds that they could cause serious harm to the ecological balance. The ecocrisis seemed well on its way to resolution.

But conditions changed in the mid '70s. Economic stagnation, inflation, and higher taxes began to take the place of environmental cleanup as prime concerns of the American middle class. Anti-pollution control measures raised the costs of some products (like cars), placed an extra burden on investment-starved industry and even led to the shutdown of antiquated plants that could not afford to clean up their act. And another crisis intervened: the "energy crisis." Caused by America's increasing dependence on oil imports and the Organization of Petroleum Exporting Countries' (OPEC) decision to raise prices on foreign oil, the crisis was dramatized by long lines at gas stations and soaring petroleum bills. President Nixon hastily proclaimed "Project Independence," an effort to make the United States energy independent by increasing national dependence upon coal and nuclear energy. Environmentalists balked at the increase in air pollution and land damage that a heightened use of coal would bring. Despite opposition, a strip mining bill was passed under President Carter that required restoration of mined land. Questions were also raised about the safety of nuclear power; such questions increased in urgency with the serious accident at Three Mile Island in 1979. The energy crisis itself was moderated by the adoption under President Carter of a National Energy Policy that emphasized conservation and increasing energy costs, both of which led to a reduction in America's energy demands.

The process of strip-mining for coal leaves chemicals in the soil that make it extremely difficult to replant a mined area. (Courtesy of Grant Heilman.)

Industry has traditionally regarded America's rivers and lakes as the most convenient receptacle for its wastes. Surrounding the Cuyahoga River, for example, is a huge industrial complex that produces automobiles, rubber, paper, and steel. (Laurence Lowry/National Audubon Society.)

WHAT PRICE A CLEAN ENVIRONMENT?

But the problem of reconciling environmental cleanup with economic progress remained. The Carter administration and environmentalists fought a long battle in Congress over the Alaskan Land Bill with developers who thought that the creation of so many national parks, monuments, and wilderness areas in that "last frontier" would lock up vitally needed national resources. Other western states were already waging a "sagebrush rebellion" against the land policies of the federal government that were regarded as too complicated and protectionist. Many thought it was time for a change in Washington.

That change came with the inauguration of Ronald Reagan as president in 1981. The new administration determined to eliminate the Department of Energy, limit the regulative zeal of the Environmental Protection Agency and pursue more development-oriented policies within the Interior Department. The idea was to free private enterprise from "unnecessary" interference and encourage economic recovery from the worst recession since the end of the Second World War. Federal lands were to be opened up to more energy exploration and timbering or even sold off to private interests. Regulators were told to work with businesses cooperatively instead of using threats of fines or court action to stop questionable practices. As in the 1920s, demands for action on ecological issues were referred to the states. Environmental groups across the nation protested.

The environmental issue of the 1980s became the problem of toxic wastes. Belated government efforts to find and clean up hundreds of disposal sites left thousand of Americans wondering if their communities might suffer the fate of Times Beach, Missouri. (Geo. Houghton. EPA Angrolis Lab.)

President Reagan's outspoken Secretary of the Interior, James Watt, became a favorite target. Environmentalists accused Watt of leasing grazing, mineral, and timber rights at a loss to the government in order to encourage business development of those resources. Eventually, Watt was pressured to resign. Then a scandal broke in the Environmental Protection Agency, where key officials were accused of using toxic waste cleanup funds for partisan advantage and overlooking clearly illegal business activities. The head of the agency resigned, followed by others during a Congressional investigation. In the absence of Washington's leadership, states took the initiative. Oregon set up recycling in all communities over 4000 in population. Wisconsin set tough standards for emissions linked to acid rain. New England states adopted tough California regulations against smog. Public alarm over environmental problems led to large increases in the membership of eco-groups like the Sierra Club and Friends of the Earth.

It also led to the "greening" of the American lifestyle. Paper stamped "recycled," plastics labelled "biodegradable," and foods described as "organic" became big sellers. Producers found profits in health products. McDonald's, criticized for the quality of its fast food and the lavish use of paper and foam wrapping, changed its menu and its packaging. Environmental education moved down from college campuses to kindergartens. There were even "green" stock portfolios for sensitive investors.

Downtown Los Angeles. Despite the toughest laws in the nation regulating emissions, the smog problem in the Los Angeles basin is still very serious. (Fred Lyon/Rapho Guillumette.)

In the 1988 election, Vice President and Republican candidate George Bush campaigned for the "nature vote." Bush said he would be the "environmental president" and push for a new clean air act, claiming admiration for the leadership of fellow Republican Theodore Roosevelt. Bush's victory was regarded hopefully, and he fulfilled his promise in the Clean Air Act of 1991. But in other respects the Bush record was disappointing. Drastic cutbacks in protected wetlands were proposed. Loggers, miners, and ranchers continued to get cheap leases on federal lands. Over 70,000 acres of old-growth forest was being swept away annually, and the controversy over the endangered Spotted Owl led the administration to recommend an easing of the Endangered Species Act. As the economy turned sour, the Bush administration responded to critics by saying that human needs for jobs and resources had to take precedence over nature preservation. Many agreed. A "wise use movement" emerged among developers and other western interests who determined to organize a fight against "green policies" they insisted were crippling the economy and forbidding "reasonable" uses of federal lands. President Bush, running for reelection, attended the 1992 Rio Conference on the Environment. The conference saw the adoption of a climate treaty on greenhouse and ozone-destroying gasses and an agreement on biodiversity, while delegates committed themselves to "sustainable development" (economic growth that both limits waste and maintains the health of biological communities). But Bush

"Spaceship Earth" (NASA)

watered down key agreements on biodiversity and greenhouse gasses to protect the American economy.

His Democratic opponents, Arkansas Governor Bill Clinton and Tennessee Senator Al Gore, disagreed. Led by Gore, who had written a strong book on the need for greater action to stop pollution and promote preservation, the Democrats insisted Americans could have both a healthy economy and a healthy environment. Job retraining, an energy tax, and more emphasis on "green" technology would, in the long run, be more productive and profitable. However, the focus of the Clinton campaign was not the environment. On the wall of Clinton headquarters in Little Rock, Arkansas was the slogan "It's the economy, stupid," and the Democrats relentlessly pounded home their commitment to growth.

A MIDDLE WAY?

The Clinton administration began on a "green" note, signing the Rio Biodiversity Treaty, setting up a Council on Sustainable Development and promising to charge market prices for logging, grazing, and water on federal lands. But disarray in Democratic Party ranks, the huge budget deficits, and the reminder that it was still "the economy, stupid" in the eyes of the public brought the President around to a moderate approach. Compromise was the rule: working with the sugar industry to restore water flows and save the Florida Everglades; working with the timber industry to allow reduced but still sizable logging in old growth forests of the Pacific Northwest and the huge Tongass National Forest in Alaska; and signing the North American Free Trade Agreement with Mexico despite worrisome holes in environmental safeguards.

Environmentalists were not the only group disappointed with the President. In the midterm elections of 1994 Republicans won control of Congress for the first time in over 50 years, and their conservative leadership under Newt Gingrich was determined to destroy "big government." The Republicans slammed a host of major changes through Congress: government would have to pay businesses whose property development was limited by environmental rules; all new federal-backed projects would be subject to tough cost-benefit analysis; the EPA budget would be slashed by 25 percent; the Endangered Species Act would be eased to allow some species to become extinct if their preservation disrupted local economies; and the National Wildlife Refuges would be opened to "compatible" development. But the Republicans had misjudged public sentiment—people might not like big government, but they still feared the loss of environmental protection.

President Clinton vetoed the Republican measures. Emboldened by public support, presiding over a now booming economy, and heading for reelection in 1996, the President returned to his 1992 "green themes." He repeated his support of the Desert Protection Act, which created three new parks in California's Mojave Desert. By presidential order Clinton created the 1.7 million acre Grand Staircase-Escalante National Monument in Utah. After his reelection, the President went on to secure a 12 percent increase in environmental spending in his balanced budget deal with a chastened Republican Congress. And Clinton backed the EPA's effort to toughen air quality standards.

After his reelection, the President moved strongly toward Green initiatives. He banned new roads in 54 million acres of National Forests, directing the Forest Service to shift from logging and grazing to recreation uses and ecological management. Preservationists hailed the decision, which had the potential of ending most logging on public lands and doubling the nation's protected wilderness. Clinton also created three new National Monuments, including over a million acres on the north rim of the Grand Canyon. The EPA took the initiative to toughen air pollution control rules and ban the gasoline additive MBTE, a carcinogenic chemical that had seeped into water supplies across the country. After the Rio Summit of 1998, the President signed the Kyoto Accord to reduce greenhouse gasses worldwide.

More and more, however, the middle path seemed to be making progress. Local communities worried about urban sprawl passed bond measures to "buy out" farmers' option to sell to developers, saving 400,000 acres of cropland in 1996. Private nonprofit organizations like the Nature Conservancy wielded contributions to secure prime natural treasures like Santa Cruz Island off the California coast, managing them until the government could adopt them into the park system. Corporations offered to pay for the public relations advantage of being a sponsor of the National Parks, adding desperately needed funds for park maintenance and improvements. Developers and environmentalists both hailed a city of San Diego decision to protect critical natural habitat in some areas while allowing unrestricted development in others.

Tough choices remain. How should the National Wildlife Refuges balance hunting and wildlife conservation? Do we limit public access to a Grand Canyon besieged by 5000 cars a day in the summer? So far only about twelve species have recovered sufficiently to be taken off the endangered list. Should the act be revised, or should all endangered species be saved, regardless

THE BATTLE FOR HEADWATERS

The redwood forests of coastal Northern California and Southern Oregon once stretched over 2 million acres. Some of the giants have lived up to 2000 years, standing over 300 feet tall and 25 feet across at the base. Massive logging over the decades has reduced the forest to less than 80,000 acres. Battles to save the remnants have been going on since the formation of the Sierra Club in 1892 and the Save The Redwoods League in 1918. Almost half of the remaining acreage was preserved by the creation of Redwood National Park, now a United Nations World Heritage Site, in 1968.

In 1985 Houston millionaire Charles Hurwitz launched a hostile takeover of Pacific Lumber Company, one of the most environmentally responsible timber businesses in the Northwest. In order to pay off millions he owed in "junk bonds," Hurwitz tripled the rate of cutting in PL-owned forests, containing the last privately held stand of old growth redwoods on the planet. Environmentalists immediately challenged the logging, claiming it would endanger the coho salmon and a rare bird, the marbled murrelet. Passage of a "salvage logging rider" in 1995 by the Republican Congress led Hurwitz to apply to cut in the heart of the remaining Pacific Lumber redwoods, Headwaters Grove.

The 3000 acre grove contains the oldest and largest trees remaining. The "salvage" rule permitted Hurwitz to go in and cut at least 10 percent of volume of the huge trees, assuming (wrongly, in this case) that only dead, diseased, or pest-infested trees would be cut. Environmentalists turned out by the thousands to stop the cutting, demanding the federal government halt the project. Over a thousand people were arrested in demonstrations on the site and in San Francisco. The Clinton administration intervened, finally negotiating a deal with Hurwitz that would give the financier $380 million in cash or federal land in exchange for Headwaters and an additional 4000 surrounding acres. The battle appeared to be won.

But problems have developed since the 1995 deal. Environmentalists have protested that the arrangement still allows Hurwitz to log on the other 50,000 surrounding acres critical to stabilizing the Headwaters ecosystem and the endangered animals. Hurwitz has filed plans to heavily log all the stands not preserved by the deal. Protesters have set up "tree villages" in the redwoods to prevent further losses. The government is also suing Hurwitz for contributing to the collapse of a Houston savings and loan in 1988 that cost taxpayers $1.6 billion to bail out. For his part, Hurwitz has rejected the lands offered by the California state government as its part of the deal and has challenged the value of the oil and gas leases the federal government has offered to cover its portion of the $380 million.

By the end of 1997 both the state of California and the U.S. government had come up with the compensation. Finally, after some last-minute adjustments and just before the deal was about to expire, Hurwitz agreed to the government package, and Headwaters was saved. Debate continues regarding protection of the Headwaters watershed from upstream logging that could degrade the preserve.

---

of the costs? In the era of balanced budgets, how do we pay for the $4 billion dollar backlog of deferred maintenance in our National Parks? Should we continue to subsidize the logging industry (the government lost $234 million in 1996 on timber sales) or raise the fees and see both higher lumber prices and fewer jobs? And in the face of increased evidence of serious global warming that was already impacting world weather patterns, should the United States take the lead in reducing fossil fuel burning at the risk of crippling the nation's steady economic growth into the twenty-first century? The middle way offered potential solutions but promised continued argument as well.

SUGGESTIONS FOR ADDITIONAL READING

Aldo Leopold, *Sand County Almanac*, (1951). An intimate observation of the land and its inhabitants, with comments on proper man-land relationships.

John Muir, *Gentle Wilderness: The Sierra Nevada*, (1964). A vivid life-portrait by the author of his travels and reflections on the High Sierras.

Roderick Nash, *Wilderness and the American Mind*, (1982). A study of the American conception of wilderness, emphasizing the roots of contemporary wilderness attitudes and how they evolved.

Raymond Dasmann, *The Destruction of California*, (1965). A case study in California history of the ignorance of sound land management and values.

E. F. Schumacher, *Small Is Beautiful*, (1973). A challenging view of the problems of economic growth and some "human scale" alternatives.

Michael P. Cohen, *The History of the Sierra Club*, (1988). How people joined together in one of the nation's earliest environmental organizations have made a difference.

Al Gore, *Earth in the Balance*, (1992). A report card on how well, or poorly, the world is doing on environmental awareness.

Philip Shabecoff, A *Fierce Green Fire*, (1993). An overview of environmental history, with an emphasis on the latest trends and developments.

EPILOGUE

When the Carnegie Foundation published "A Nation At Risk" in 1983, detailing the abysmal performance of American students in all core subjects, the National Endowment for the Humanities set out to establish world class standards. Congress gave the task of creating history standards to the University of California's prestigious Center for History at UCLA. In 1994, under President Clinton's "Goals 2000" program, the standards were published—to a storm of criticism.

The former head of the NEH, who had started the study, condemned the standards as telling "just the sad and the bad" about America. Conservative critics said the program represented "PC [politically correct] history"—an effort to include everyone equally regardless of the weight of their contributions. They were, another hard-hitting reviewer said, "too critical of all things white and Western, and too uncritical of all things brown, black and other." Shot back one supporter, "Black children have been brainwashed since they started school in America to celebrate white heroes, concepts and values. What needs to happen now is a reverse brainwashing." Another defender of the UCLA program got personal: "These [critics] are academic fascists and liars."

How is it that after more than two hundred years of national life Americans are fighting over what United States history is about? And why is the disagreement so passionate?

One reason is that the United States was really the first "invented" nation. It was born not out of a long, shared heritage and history, but suddenly in the blood and fire of a revolution. In 1776 the thirteen American colonies had no common heroes, glories, or legends to unite them, only a common enemy. The Revolutionary generation built the nation around a shared set of values, first expressed in the Declaration of Independence and later the Constitution. "We, the People" would build a country based on "self evident" truths: equality, liberty, and opportunity. Near the end of this generation an effort was made to create a proud past to reinforce national pride and unity. Novelists, artists, poets, linguists, and historians all contributed: Noah Webster chronicled "an American language" in his dictionaries; Gilbert Stuart painted an impressive collection of Founding Fathers for posterity; James Fenimore Cooper preserved the frontier and the frontiersman in his novels; Henry Wadsworth Longfellow immortalized "The Midnight Ride of Paul Revere"; and Francis Scott Key wrote "The Star Spangled Banner." America's historical self-consciousness enshrined symbols like Plymouth Rock and the "stars and stripes," men like Daniel Boone and Thomas Jefferson, and places like the Alamo and Gettysburg. National pride was taught in the country's public schools, the crucible of a "melting pot" that was a conscious effort to "Americanize" immigrant children.

But this image was the creation of 19th century male Anglo-Americans, mostly of New England stock. Other groups weren't quite inside the picture frame. As early as 1751, Benjamin Franklin feared that "Pennsylvania, founded by the English . . . would become a colony of [German immigrants] who will shortly be so numerous as to germanize us, instead of us anglifying them." Indians (except, perhaps, for Pocahantas) were portrayed as savages; women were noble mothers, and African Americans were happy minstrels. There was barely notice for the Irish, much less the Chinese, who together built the first transcontinental railroad. Late in the 19th century, groups like the Oriental Exclusion League or the Ku Klux Klan zealously defended their narrow version of "Americanism." But, pushed out by famine, war, and persecution, millions of new immigrants pulled by relative freedom and opportunity continued to come to the United States in the twentieth century. Few of them had any connection to the traditional Anglo-American image. Migrant Mexican American farm workers, for instance, did not share in the landing at Plymouth Rock. They also have a different experience in mind when "American the Beautiful" sings of "amber waves of grain." Any fixed picture of the past could not last. It would have to be revised to include those who had been left out and updated to connect newcomers. "Unity," a champion of this multicultural approach wrote, "is the completed puzzle, diversity the pieces of the puzzle. Until we recognize every piece, we cannot have true unity."

But this has not been easy. And the main reason why Americans fight over history is because, as one writer said, "History is part of a society's attempt to structure a self-image and . . . a common identity." Rewriting history is one way of saying, "Americans are not like this, they are like that; the country doesn't stand for this, it stands for that." When the traditional image was challenged by the protest movements of the late 1960s, the inclusion of minority and women's studies made American history more whole. But the revisions also raised disturbing questions. Noting that the revered Thomas Jefferson decided to keep his black slaves long after he wrote that "all men are created equal" did more than add a fact to the nation's story. Americans have argued passionately about what the nation stands for since its birth. The Civil War was one such "argument." In 1995, on the 50th anniversary of America's World War II atomic attack on Hiroshima, the Smithsonian tried to set up a display that recognized the terrible death and destruction wrought by the bomb. The implicit message was that the United States had done something horrendous, and that use of the bomb was wrong. Veterans' groups exploded, insisting that use of the bomb had saved many of their lives and ended a war started by Japan. America, they believed, had not done anything wrong.

Obviously, history matters.

Ironically, foreigners have a valuable perspective. The large influx of immigrants in the last twenty years validated by their coming that the United States still symbolized freedom and opportunity. Before they were brutally crushed, Chinese students demanding democracy built a model of the Statue of Liberty in the center of Tienanmen Square. Recognizing that the practice of American principles needs improving doesn't mean that the principles themselves are worthless, or that no progress toward living them out has been made. The nation's motto, *E Pluribus Unum* (out of many, one) seems to be more an ongoing process than an accomplished fact. As Australian immigrant Robert Hughes wrote:

The social richness of America, so striking to the foreigner, comes from the diversity of its tribes. It's capacity for cohesion . . . comes from the willingness of those tribes not to elevate their cultural differences into impassable barriers . . . at the expense of their Americanness, which gives them a vast common ground.

The debate over United States history and the meaning of "Americanness" will go on. Yet this should not eclipse the richness of what the country already has. The hope for a national life more true to the country's principles depends in no small part on mutual restraint.

INDEX